A MODERN PRIEST

LOOKS AT HIS

OUTDATED

CHURCH

A MODERN PRIEST LOOKS AT HIS OUTDATED CHURCH

by *Father James Kavanaugh*

 TRIDENT PRESS NEW YORK 1967

To

Ora McManus, who gave me friendship and
courage; Gene Prakapas, who pushed me to
fight for justice; Red and Phil, who helped
me to be a man.

PREFACE AND DEDICATION

When I wrote the article "I Am a Priest, I Want to Marry" for *The Saturday Evening Post*,[1] I had no intention of writing a book. I had not the time or the need. When the letters came in response to my article, however, I knew that I must start again. The letters came in bundles, hundreds of them, from many continents, and I read each word with the hunger of a man who truly wanted to learn. There were as many from Protestants as from Catholics.[2] Children wrote, nuns and priests wrote, the feeble and tired hands of the aged wrote. It was a procession of warm hearts that passed before my eyes and opened to me as I had opened to them. Most of all, the wounded wrote. The story of my soul had opened the scars in their own. The letters were more eloquent than anything I could describe, since they were written in innocent blood. They told me of pains that far surpassed mine, and they begged me to speak for them so that all the world could hear.

Some of the letters scolded me as a spoiled son who wanted the best of both worlds. Some called me insincere, a "Judas," a "crybaby" who could not live with the promise he had made. Some told me that I had no right to happiness because life had offered them only grief and disillusionment. Some called me a "dangerous minority," a "deluded and lost soul," a "sentimental fool."

Most, however—ten to one, in fact—approved of what I said. One woman moved me to tears when she wrote: "If such as you walk away, who will stay to care for the sheep? Please don't go, stay and fight for justice!" Priests wrote and told me of the senseless struggle, the loves they had known and surrendered. Women wrote who loved priests and had lost them to the righteousness of law. Priests who had left and married wrote and asked that I understand the loneliness of exile from memories and friends. Protestants offered me shelter in their parish, bishops offered me work in their Episcopal diocese. Mormons offered love and family in a life of service in the Church.

Most of all, the suffering wrote, and begged me to write for them. The divorced and lonely, the couples with too many children, those fearful of sex, the spouses of alcoholics and homosexuals, those denied the sacraments, those whose marriage case was never solved, the sinner who could not be absolved—all of them wrote and filled my nights with suffering and shame. I, the unworthy priest, was asked to hear the misery of the Christian world without the power of Christ to make men walk.

I had always loved men as best I could, but now I was asked to love them even more. Names that had never known me told me of their love and concern. Letters poured in from hands that had never responded to an article before. These were not the letters of brief and cold comment, but the personal and touching stories of broken hearts. I had spoken to them and they had answered with the words that no one else had heard.

To these I dedicate my book, to those that have
suffered as I, and more. I thank them for trusting
me with their wounds, and promise that I will not
cease to seek a healing as long as God shall give me
breath. I well may lose my priesthood, though its
passing would not occur with lack of pain. I shall
not lose my faith, though the pressures of my superiors may well reduce it to the faith of a simple
man in search of an unknown God. There is one
hope that sustains me in the midst of bitter attack:
if a thousand men can understand my cry, then God
Himself will not dismiss me without mercy. I want
to speak for His children, for the lonely and the
lost, for the sons who find the faith that satisfied
their fathers too narrow to fill their present need. I
write not in bitterness, but in love, not in the
anger of demolition, but in the challenge of construction.

I need my Church, for without the strength of
Christ it gives I cannot live. I have known its comforts for almost forty years, and feel the right to
speak out as a son. Can I not be a son, your brother,
because I do not think as you, or speak as you?
Think before you answer, because I believe my
name is legion!

INTRODUCTION

Catholicism as a monolithic structure is disappearing.[1] Once the man who differed with the party line stole quietly away. Now he refuses to abandon his communion with God. From a timid rebellion has grown a courageous confrontation. This is not merely the roar of angry young men. It is the fruit of a tortuous, a studious examination of the foundations of faith. Faith has passed from the passive and complete acceptance of a body of truths to the honest search for total commitment.

The world has become man-centered, meaning-centered, and the individual measures the traditional truths in terms of personal value. He refuses to accept irrelevant sermons, a sterile liturgy, a passé and speculative theology which explores publicly dry and distant formulas, a law which does not explain its own origins. He demands a pastor who reaches him in honest dialogue. He will not be bullied by an authoritarian demand for the observance of parish boundaries, nor by moralizing which ignores the true and complex context of modern life.

The layman has witnessed a more humane eucharistic fast, a more open view of mixed marriages, a more understanding discussion of the birth-

control problem and of the dilemma of Catholic
education. He has recognized the human face of
the Church which has been forced to change its
expression or die. This has given him the courage
to hope and push for greater changes still.

This book is the account of a priest who has suffered in the leadership of a Church grown arrogant and
inhumane. It is the story of a suffering people witnessed in confession and private consultation. It is
the story of a suffering Church which often reflects
a dishonest theology far more than a divine im-
perative. This is a book born of the conviction that I
can still be a Catholic, that I can still search for
God and meaning in a Church which must exchange its authoritarian and regal robe for that of a
suffering servant. It is a book which hopes that the
world can begin to appreciate our Catholic sincerity and that we, the members, can face a future
life of freedom and joy within the Church.

This is not the speculation of a professional
theologian, although my education allows me to
wear that hat. It is the soul-searching plea of a
Christian for an evaluation of what is Christian, and
what is simply tired and imperious tradition. I want
to be a Christian, but I will not be terrorized
into believing that the present structure of the
Church is an adequate representation of the Christ
of Gospel and history. I merely tell you what
Christianity means to me and ask you to reflect and
discover if you share a part of my vision. If you do,
I want you to struggle with me to bring about its
fulfillment. If not, I ask you to tell me why, not
to curse me with fleeting words of fear.

I will not give up my faith. Nor will I accept the
travesty, born of another age, which caricatures the
Christian ideal. Catholicism offers so much that is
good and true that its faithful adherents cannot sit

by passively and watch it settle into structured idealism. It has so much to say, so much to offer, if only it can recognize the growing and positive drive for personalism in the world. A religion which expects men to march in identical step and to chant a univocal doctrine ceases to draw the atomic man to the holy God.

Vatican II is only a spark, a beginning—but it marks the future with a ray of hope. In the light of its encouragement I would like to describe my vision of the problem of an outdated Church and the direction in which we must move. I do not write for the professional, but for the sincere man, simple or sophisticated, whose living search for meaning moves the professional theologian from his comfortable perch and forces him to examine his presuppositions. I do not ask for a comfortable pew; far from it. I ask for honest dialogue, an open hierarchy, a Church which does not have all the answers or expect all men to walk in the wooden cadence of frozen categories. The recent *Declaration on Religious Freedom* leads me to believe that I do not hope in vain:

The declaration of this Vatican Council on the right of man to religious freedom has its foundation in the dignity of the person, whose exigencies have come to be more fully known to human reason through the centuries of experience. . . . It is one of the major tenets of Catholic doctrine that man's response to God in faith must be free . . . ! [2]

I write to tell the man who has been forced from the faith of his fathers: You can still believe and still be free. You can only believe to the degree that you are free. And so can I.

CONTENTS

A MODERN PRIEST

LOOKS AT HIS

OUTDATED

CHURCH

1. THE IDEAL BECOMES THE LAW

overview

Once, long ago, in a world of confusion and weariness, there exploded a new and exciting hope. A man appeared in Palestine and spoke in syllables that seemed to come from God. He was a Jew, steeped in the power and beauty of a religious heritage unparalleled in East or West. He was not locked in bigotry nor did he serve the interests of a single nation or a special race. His blood, indeed, was the sensitive and boiling blood of Abraham and David, the blood that would mark the Jewish peoples in ages yet to come. His vision, however, went past the boundaries of Palestine to encompass the world. His eyes looked to everyone who hurt, and his healing hand was extended to the weak and sinful woman, the outcast leper, the blind man who had worn out his friends and relatives with his wailing. Weary men heard him and felt a sudden surge of strength. The guilty listened to him, and began again to respect themselves as men. Fishermen followed him and so did the nobles who had discovered that wine and women did not satisfy each thirsting ache. Some men called him the "God-man," and even those skeptical of his stature marveled at the power of his words.

And this an accurate summary of Christ's life & teaching

In a sense he had nothing new to say when he insisted that every commandment must begin and end with love. Man had

1

learned of love before this God-man came to earth. The Egyptians had tried to love their wives, and Babylonians had been taught to treat each neighbor with dignity and respect. The Jews especially, nourished by the words of Isaias, Ezechiel, and Jeremias, had learned the responsibility of love, and for centuries had struggled to prevent the narrow and arrogant laws of men from smothering the underlying ideal of love. Yet man had not succeeded in loving his fellow man. For every just man there were a dozen pharisees who made a mockery of God by reducing Him to a set of rules imposed on the frightened and defenseless. Thus Jesus would speak of a new commandment, "that you love one another as I have loved you."

And so began the religion of love, to perfect and fulfill the other religions of love that proud men had reduced to the coldness of unyielding law. History had known noble ideals before, but time and fear had wrapped such ideals in the smothering moss of legal codes and tablets. Now Christ, in a manner beyond compare, offered to men a new and thrilling vision. Paul, sparked by such a vision, wrote in a *Letter to the Romans* that man had been "set free from the law" and would be able to live by the sweeping spirit of love.[1] He did not mean that there would be no religious law. He only meant that never again would a man in personal anguish have no recourse but the cold and universal rule that applied to all men. He could be a person because he could know a personal God Who refused to be bound by a single religious rite or the judgmental ruling of a high priest's tongue.

No longer could man reduce the vision of God to the dumb idols that only made permanent the pride and pettiness of man. No longer could man stuff God into the convenient pigeonholes built by men. Now no statue would contain His majesty. No law, or books of law, could prescribe the minute conditions of God's mercy and love. Even Christ, despite the unique possession of the Godhead that was his, could only appear in the simplicity of feet that struggled to walk and hands that tugged impatiently at a mother's breast.

Men could, indeed, call Christ God, even as I do, in simple and indefensible faith. Others might find their God in "Church" or "Abraham" or "personal honesty." But no longer could any man say that he had defined and comprehended God, nor that any other man was certainly without God's forgiving love. God has no name because He has no boundaries, and His love cannot be limited by the blindness or egotism of frightened men.

Yet, despite the efforts of Christ to end religious narrowness, and despite the warnings and reforms of history, I was once a frightened man who sought to contain and package God. I knew the boundaries of His love, the limits of His patience, the very color of His beard. I was, and always will be, a Catholic priest, but I cannot presently be the priest I was. I entered the priesthood with as open and generous a heart as my home and education would allow. I was determined to comfort the sick, to help the poor, to teach children the mysteries of life that I had only begun to live. I was flushed with ideals that promised me I could walk as Christ among the weak. At times I was able to offer His forgiveness, to calm the tragic widow, to encourage the alcoholic, to comfort the skinny adolescent who believed she would never get a date. I taught classes in high school and college, I preached with enthusiasm and preparation, and I knew the quiet and sustaining love the Catholic has for his priest.

Yet daily my anguish grew as I recognized the unholy limits that arrogant and unfounded laws had put on God. I could not walk as Christ because those that needed me most I could not help. The woman who came to me in confession was simply told that she could not practice birth control. There was no chance to tell me that her husband refused to sleep with her unless she took the pill. I did not have to hear of the endless nights when she lay with him, touched him, and felt him pull away. She tried to tell me of her fears that he would find another woman. She tried to describe the way her body ached for him, the memories of a marriage when she nestled warmly in his arms. She wept when she told me how four children under six years of age tore at her patience and how she could not survive without the comfort of her husband. I gave her my answer, I who had never known a baby's voice to interrupt my sleep. I told her that God was asking this noble sacrifice to test her love, that her generosity could never match His own.

It was senseless to talk to me because I had no ears. The pen of a lawgiver had taken them away. Here was a woman who wanted to love her husband, who did not dare to have another child, who gave of herself as I was never asked to do. She was married to a truck driver who was not interested in subtle arguments that told him how he could make love to his wife. He loved her as best he could and she found his love to be the very spark of her own. He loved his children with warmth and manliness, he supported them with the drudgery of daily work. He was giving of himself as much as he was able, and he refused to be intimidated by her scruples about the law of the Church. So she lay with him beneath the sheets in coldness and watched her marriage wither into death.

She came to me as she came to Christ. She came because she knew of nowhere else to go. She came without theology, without an answer for my stilted arguments, with the paralyzing fear that she well might lose the man that drove a truck and fathered her four little ones. And I gave her my theory and my law. I told her that birth control was selfish and unnatural. I told her what I had learned from my textbook and I offered her papal pronouncements to assuage her grief. Even as I told her, I knew that my words were in vain. I secretly hoped that she would return to her man and love him as a woman should, but I knew the guilt that would torture her if she ignored the finality of my words. She was caught in a trap, a careful brainwash that had dissolved her personal experience and left her as a conforming robot before the distant echoes of Roman law.

All she really wanted was to love her husband as Christ had told her she must. She had watched his patience with the children when they puttered with their food or dropped their spoons a thousand times. She had watched him return home from his weary hours on the road. She loved his quiet way, his soft voice, his attentive kindness during each pregnancy. She thought often of her deliveries and the gentle assurance he gave her in her moments of fear and pain. She had a permanent picture of the eyes that thanked her for every child. He was never much with words. He said it with his eyes and the stroke of his hands that soothed her as she lay with him in bed. Now she could love him no longer in the way that he needed to be loved.

The arguments I gave her did not honestly convince me, though long I mouthed them in loyalty, or fear, or misguided faith. She knew more of love than I could ever hope to know, and I, the other Christ, could only make her feel dirty and ashamed. The ideal of Christian love, that she longed to pursue, had been transformed by an angry law into an impossible life. Her marriage well could end, or freeze, or drive her husband to bitterness and neglect. She came to find the Christ who told her that God could never be contained in the chains of impersonal law, and I had ordered her to get in line or give up God.

Don't give me more learned arguments! I have read them all a thousand times.[2] Don't tell me that I must wait patiently for a Pope to appear on a balcony before I can send her home to her husband's bed! I have helped to produce this fearful and imprisoned child who comes helplessly to me. She is not strong enough to walk away as the more sophisticated do daily. She is a victim, a tragedy, a distortion, that I have helped to produce and perpetuate. She has not the intelligence or the courage to defend herself. So she will lose her husband in loyalty to a zealot's law, or ignore that law and join the millions of silent ones who come sheepishly to Mass because I have consigned them "to live in sin."

How did we ever produce the legalistic Church that Christ promised to take away? How did we pass from a gospel of freedom and love to a system that can tear husbands from wives in the name of justice? How did we manage to replace religion with the subtleties of a dead theology? Theology is meant to be a science that tells a man in every age how he can better love his God. It should take the treasures of the gospel and transform them into words and ideas that can tell a modern man how to live and love. Our theology, however, has become a scholar's game. It is a code of rules accumulated in the petty wars of religious bitterness. It is a tale of tired truths, which only serve to rob man of personal responsibility and reduce him to the listlessness of a frightened slave. Theology took away man's mind and left him memorized words. It took away his freedom and robbed him of the romance that should attend his search for God. It dared to enter bedrooms and to tell each man that he must love his wife as does every other man.

This is the theology I learned and transmitted in every confession I heard, every class I taught, every sermon I gave to the guilt-infected flock.[3] I could not preach to free people, I could not suggest, I could only command. I am forbidden to act differently! I must hear confessions as every other priest. I must tell the miserable that they cannot get a divorce—in the name of Christian love. It doesn't matter, the misery that marriage has brought, the bitterness, the vengeance, the distress to children. Obviously I know it all, for I am a Catholic priest. I can tell this woman that God has forbidden her to marry again, and I should know, because I have reduced God to the limits of the system I represent. She can tell me that her second marriage has brought her peace, that her husband has made her more kind and loving than she ever dreamed. He can plead as well, insisting that he loves her children as if they were his own. He can weep before my eyes, as he often does, and I am expected to tell him that this marriage has incurred the wrath of God.

It would be different if I had not studied the sources of such laws, if I did not know the naïve ignorance of the men who are obliged to enforce them. I know, too, the pain of many priests who reject such narrowness as I have described, and have not the tongue or the courage to fight back. Nor do

I have courage. I have only pain. But I refuse to be silent when the helpless sufferers, "the disregarded multitude of the bewildered, the simple and the voiceless" stand naked before the smug arrogance of Catholic law. What a comedy to watch a universal Church await a voice from Rome that will tell them how husbands may sleep with wives. Comedy indeed, if it were not so tragic.

The real tragedy is that Rome does not understand our need. We do not need a solution to the birth-control problem. We need freedom from a system that has taken over our lives.[4] We need freedom from a legalistic Church that has transformed the simplicity of a personal and Christian love into a world of fear and guilt. We do not know how to find God, we have never learned. We have only been taught to keep laws, to avoid sin, to fear hell, to carry a cross that we built ourselves.

I am aware of how the adolescent writhes with guilt when he masturbates. He has been taught by a medieval scholar that he has seriously offended God, that each furtive act in the silence of his room could cast him eternally to hell. I watch him lose all sense of a search for God and become obsessed with his private world of sin and madness. I watch him run to confession in the morning before class. I see him listless in school and I sense that he has known another night of the horror that I have helped to impose. I wonder why he does not hate me. I hide in his conscience on his dates and threaten him with hell if his hand slides curiously over his girl friend's breast. He runs to me to confess, to feel free, to know the warmth of God's forgiveness. Even as I offer him absolution, I well know that I have helped to make him a prisoner for life. I can remember the struggles of my own adolescence, the tense nights when a single memory from a normal day could leave me tortured with the sexual thoughts I had been taught to fear. I can remember my dread of sleep lest death might take me in the night to the court of the God Who sends masturbators to hell. I can remember asking forgiveness a dozen times before I settled into exhausted rest. I can remember the high-school dances when I feared to hold a girl too close lest God would call me in my lust.

No, we do not need a Pope to tell us that Catholics are permitted to use the pill. We need a God to tell us that we are free. We need a Church to deliver us from the legalism that has buried us in guilt and fear and taken away our God. We need a restored faith in ourselves, in the likeness of God that we bear in our bodies and our hearts. We want to learn to love and we have only learned a loyalty to ritual and rules. For years, we ate our fish on Fridays and learned nothing of love in this primitive denial. What kind of man could take such a law seriously? What kind of man could fear to violate this childish command? Yet millions of Catholics are such men, and were as devoted to an outmoded rule as any superstitious savage. How could God possibly care if we eat meat or fish? How could he be bothered with such trivia? And if a man thinks that God is thus concerned, it gives you some idea of that man's view of God.

Somehow, in the passage of kings and castles, we lost our vision of God. Really, it doesn't matter how, it only matters that we stand back and look at the rules and rites that have hidden from us our God. The scholars can tell me that He lurks beneath our codes and catechisms, but I will no longer play their game and join them in the search. I can only point to the people I have known as a priest, to the story of my own life, and let the scholars wrestle with their impressive texts. I watch the people at Mass as they read the prayers that do not reach them and struggle to be a community with unfamiliar songs and organized indifference. I listen with them to the sermons that mean less to the preacher than to his flock and watch them squirm at the irrelevance of his words. I watch them come to Mass and wonder why they come. And yet, with sadness I acknowledge that I know why. They come to fulfill a law, they come because they are afraid not to come with the fear that we nourished in them from youth. They come because we demand it, and they have been taught to respect our word as God's own tongue. They come and try each new gimmick that we force upon them to make the Mass more meaningful, and they leave with the same uninspired silence that has become so characteristic of the Catholic flock. They come to find what Christ promised, a community of love and concern, and we give them an auditorium filled with pointless gestures and monotonous words. They come as bodies without heads, faces without names or meaning, to fulfill the law, and they leave as headless and nameless as they came. They ask for God, for meaning, for the strength to give direction to another day, and we greet them with the emptiness of ritual and law.

And yet I cannot blame them for continuing to come. I cannot accuse them of a fear and guilt that I have not shared, a legalism that I have not known. Even as they have given up their search for personal ideals in their servitude before the law, I have permitted my priesthood to become the impersonal ritual and defense of the law that the Church expected. I, who had enough learning to fight, enough awareness to speak out, could only mouth the laws I had learned even as I feared to face the realities of my own life. I could call myself "poor" and continue to share each comfort of the upper middle class. I could bow in priestly "obedience" when I was in reality running from the responsibilities of personal thought. I could enforce laws which made no sense, preach devotions I didn't practice, ask sacrifices I couldn't make, and accept the praise of a people who were fooled by the externals of my life. And yet I kept the rules as they were written, even though they pushed me ever further into myself.

I kept the rule of celibacy in order to free myself to minister to men. I was to be a father to many spirits by denying the fatherhood and pleasures of the flesh. I would be free to care for the sick and lonely, to be available, when other men must chatter with their children or worry with their wife. I was always to be on call, to labor among the bewildered and the poor, to resist temptations to know of love myself. I guarded my thoughts, resisted the offers of love, avoided dangerous involvement, and undertook more projects to occupy my leisure time. Then one day I paused and discovered that I was not celibate at all.

I was a selfish and frightened man who had struggled to keep a senseless law. The celibacy that had promised to make me free, that had meant so much to monks and men of another cast, had only turned me in upon myself and hardened me to love.[5] I had never offered my celibacy to God, I had only kept a rule that shielded me from the involvement that could make of me a man. I had run from the companionship of women in perverted loyalty to a system and a law. I had refused to pause and think, to wonder if my single life had opened me to love. And when I knew, amid the fury of my work and pain, that I would be a better priest with children and a wife, I closed my eyes, turned traitor to my heart, and continued to accept the madness of the law.

Celibacy means misery to me and yet, for years, I was a silent coward, afraid to speak. I knew what a life without marriage had done to me and the hundred priests that revealed to me their heart. I knew our compensations and compromise, I know them now. Thousands of us grow ambitious and aloof, take expensive vacations we do not need, drink far more than we should, become pompous and arrogant, make a parish into a personal kingdom, tease women in the irresponsibility of our boyish charm, grow cold and cynical, make love in childish fantasy, carry noble crosses we build for ourselves, consider the indifference of our flock a personal affront. We are so righteous that we fail to understand weakness, so celibate that we make the sins of sex into the primary target of our religious concern. And yet few of us are celibates.

We are frightened men who keep a rule we do not really understand. We are the victims of a system that absorbed our youthful independence and molded us against our honest will. We have been taught to defend each facet of our faith, no matter our personal feeling, and such an education has made us masters at defending the folly of our legalistic lives. We are prisoners, jailed from the world of free and independent

thought, men without authentic choice. We accepted a way
of life we did not understand, and continue to embrace its
laws because we are robbed of courage to stand alone.

Thus we can pray in Latin when we can barely conjugate,
wear vestments that had meaning in another world, fill censers
with incense and sprinkle the people with water in archaic and
superstitious symbol. And we can be celibates as well, who
keep the rules and hope that God will help us in our dilemma
and our pain. We are afraid to leave the priesthood, afraid
even to alter it, although its legalism has smothered our love.
Since we are not even free to leave, it can't be freedom when
we stay. Legalism has made us into slaves.

If I were to leave the priesthood because celibacy makes no
sense and hides the very Christian love it once was meant to
serve, I would be a renegade, a traitor, a man without a home.[6]
I would still be a priest, but a wretched and lonely one, adrift
from family and from friends. If I were to marry, my parents
would be asked to ignore the wife I chose and to shun my children in the name of Christian love. And even though they
love me with a deep and filling love, they would not have the
freedom to ignore the rulings of the Church. In effect, they
would reject me, the son who made them proud and happy,
the son who wants to do it still. They would turn away and
offer all their misery to God. They would sneak to Church,
avoid the pastor, fear each conversation that could whisper of
their shame, and wonder where they failed in their labors for
my life. But they would reject me, because my arrogant Church
has torn away their choice.

And yet I am no celibate who freely gave to God. I am a
deluded legalist, who keeps the rules that pay homage to a
system and a cause. I am not a celibate because I play a game
that I was taught to play. I am a selfish bachelor, a pharisee
who speaks of love and only knows of law. I am a man of
sophisticated and expensive tastes, a man who never has to
get involved, a man more sinful than the ignorant children I
condemn, a man insulated from pain and personal concern.
My celibacy is an idol, an obsession, a navel-staring worship of

myself. I am a man who can ask for money and give to none, gather homage I have never earned, and cherish my body grown too celibate to love.

I see ambition substitute for love, a thirst for titles rob me of my heart.[7] I see my life of narrowness, lack of feeling, the growing inability to care. Celibacy is my shield from reality, my protection from people, the wall that bars me from concern. I am a soldier asked to guard an ancient fort, a sentry who paces with a gun upon a rock. I must not walk among the people lest I hear their anguished cry. I speak from a distance with words that only confuse. The ignorant do not answer me because I do not come too close, or I mouth arguments quite strange to them. And when they do not heed me, I turn my back in smugness and pray for mercy on their soul. I am not a celibate, transformed by service and by love; I am a frightened legalist who made a promise he cannot keep. I have become as helpless as the people whom I lead, as silent as the men who know not how to speak. I am as docile as the truck driver's wife whose contraception I condemned, as fearful as the adolescent who masturbates in guilt, as weary as the Mass-goer who wonders what the Mass means.

I cannot wait for Rome's decisions to change our legalistic ways. I am tired to death of tears I cannot wipe away, of wounds I can only reopen. I can no longer treat the innocent as bricks that feel no pain. I cannot treat men as faceless numbers. I cannot wait for bishops, too frightened and aloof to think, to discuss away our legalism in the comfort of their uninvolved concern. I cannot share their fear that an honest and less decisive Church will confuse and cripple men. I believe that God has touched man too deeply in creation to permit force and terror to make of him a son. Loyalty to law has made us slaves, and I will never more live as a system's serf.

There is no place for persons in our Church.[8] There is only room for groups that nod in blind assent. Each man is asked to accept the Church's stand on birth control, divorce, sex and sin, education and religious life, or if he has the courage to dissent, he is solemnly forbidden to act. I can make no decision in my work unless each syllable has been carefully formed by Rome. I am asked to reject the man who marries a second time, to condemn the single girl who cannot find marriage but knows a life of faithful sex and true, fulfilling love. I must turn from the homosexual or ask of him a promise I know he cannot give. I cannot stand back and help a man to question his ideals, to accept the decision that divorce alone will bring him one step closer to mature and Christian love. I cannot hear the Jewish boy who loves a Catholic girl but who cannot agree to all the smug conditions of my Church. I cannot speak honestly of the obsolete and desperate Catholic schools, of the horror of our convents, of the narrowness of parish life. I cannot experiment, question forms that have lost their meaning, stop hearing confessions that make no sense, unless I seek another way of life. I am not free to marry no matter how ably I might labor as a priest, no matter how selfish I have become without a wife. I am a Catholic, and Catholics must move as a body or cease to know the comforts of the Church. I must wait until each step is clear, and prudent hierarchs have written yet another law.

It is an arrogant Church that knows no way except the way of law. It is a smug Church that can keep a billion children waiting for its word. It is a proud Church that can hold its ears and ignore a million voices raised in pain. It is an un-Christian Church that can lose ideals in a multitude of laws. It is a desperate Church that has lost its confidence in men, an angry Church that can bristle and condemn. Yet it is my Church, and I will not walk away in silence and a wounded heart.

If I did not love her, I would not pause to write. If she could not hurt me, I would sneer and move away. But she has formed and fashioned me, nourished and forgiven me, applauded and laughed at me, and presently can break my heart. She can touch my hand, remind me of the priests that have known and loved me, whisper a word about my aging parents, recall the childhood we shared, and I feel sick and hopelessly afraid. I can kneel to her, hold her gently in my young and foolish arms, call her "mother" in hopes that I can be a son. But I cannot be silent when I see her love impoverished into law.

Long enough have I been a priest who forced the simple children against their will. Long enough have I enforced rules in and outside of the confessional which only led men farther from the love of God I sought to bring. I can no longer solve complex stories with the simplicity of law. I can no longer shake my holy fist before the naïve and bewildered soul. Too long have I been the loyal legalist who told children it was against their religion to swim or play basketball at the "Y." I refused the sacraments to the Catholic whose Protestant wife insisted on bringing the children to her Church, denied marriage to the Lutheran who would not raise his children in my faith, forbade non-Catholics to enjoy the dances at our schools, and preached orthodoxy with the fury of a man gone mad. Young men apologized to me when they dated non-Catholics and girls wept to me when I would not marry them to their agnostic fiancés in our Church.

The spirit of legalism, learned in my parochial school and molded in my seminary life, touched every phase of my priestly life. It infected my confessions, leaked through all of my classes, and bathed the whole of my pastoral work. The Church was always right, her critics were ignorant and seething with prejudice and hate. I fought the social workers who believed in birth control among the poor, and bragged about it over Scotch and steak. I condemned the hospitals which permitted abortion or sterilization, the doctors who suggested that mothers should have no more children, the professors who spoke of the intolerance of the Church. I did all of this in the name of law, a law which could ignore exception or discussion.

But now I have had enough. I can neither be silent nor a legalist any longer. I cannot accept this simplistic view of man and life. I can no longer force Catholics, blackmail Protestants, scorn Jews, or uphold Catholic ways which are ridiculous and obsolete. I can no longer deny the sacraments to anyone who asks for them. I can no longer hear confessions with an un-yielding eye held on the law, nor refuse burial to anyone who has requested such. I cannot live without mercy and personal love, nor cease to do the true work of a priest. I cannot be a mere judge and jailer, a ritualist and a mouther of tired words, a defender of a tradition which must reform or die. So I will protest with words that are written in the memory of the sense-less suffering I have known and seen, and this book is the account of that anguished protest.

Some men, despite the law, have become free in the midst of the system that reduced the rest of us to helpless pain. These men, however, are the noble exception who prove that there once lurked God beneath the law. They are the hope that man will survive the corruptions that made us prisoners even as it promised to make us free. They are the few men of courage who could walk alone without the gentle guidance of the Church. They had the wisdom to pick and choose, the joy to distinguish the rind from the fruit. The rest of us are not as gifted or as brave. We cannot stand alone without the Church that taught us to depend.

We know we need some law, as every family does, but we also know that the thickness of our legal code is proportionate to the absence of confidence and love. The man who must ever resort to the law to hold us is the man afraid of us, be-cause he is first afraid of himself. He does not trust man, nor believe in his nobility, nor sense the Creator's mark that rests on him. The fiercest confessor is the man who is nearest to sin. The most severe legalist is the man who is closest to sever-ing the law. He does not trust his own humanity and this is to admit a world's defeat. Only a loving father can give a child a goal and give him the freedom to pursue it. Only a genuine family can trust a child enough to make of him a man. Only a home can offer its children the chance to be wrong in order that they may know the joy of being right.

2. THE MAN WHO IS

A PRIEST

I was a legalist, born in a happy ghetto, and the history of my formation explains the leadership of my Church. Mine was not the ghetto of Boston or New York, where Catholics crowded together with beer and stick ball and elected Democrats as defenders of the faith. Mine was the ghetto of a lonely Catholic family in a neighborhood of ambitious WASPs.* Yet in essence it was the same—except that I had to travel farther to Church and school to know the security of my group. Once settled among people of my own kind, I knew the special joys that only a happy ghetto could give.

My parents had only dreamed of college, and went to work early to repay their own impoverished parents for the gift of life. They were intelligent, strong and disciplined, ambitious and afraid. The ghetto taught them to fear hell, to mistrust the rich and the products of state universities, to be in awe of the pastor, to be concerned with what others might think, and to live as if the present world really didn't count. I shared their fears, inherited their drive and ambition, admired their loyalty and sacrifice, adopted their anger and prejudice, knew the fierceness of their love and hopes, developed their capacity for hard work, and learned in their ghetto world of blacks and whites.

* White Anglo-Saxon Protestants.

16

We lived in a world without grays, as the Church carefully taught. It is the only world in which a ghetto can survive. I fought for my existence among ghettos equally as impervious and afraid: the Masons, who told us we were not Americans; the Jews, who spoke of persecution and secretly sought revenge; the WASPs, who laughed at the mounting laundry on our Monday lines and didn't believe their own blood was red; the Christian Reformed, who called starch and dour faces the mark of sanctity; and the Methodists, who got sin confused with bad posture and dirty fingernails.

We did not ignore our neighbors; we smiled and knew their names. We played football with their boys and teased their screaming girls, but we knew that they could never be as strong and pleasing to God as we. I learned in school that I was more proficient in the wisdom of the soul, that I must give a good example to those less fortunate than I. Above all, I knew that I could not date a Protestant or, especially, marry one.

The heroes of my world were the priests and sisters, more important than doctors or presidents, more wise than scholars or diplomats, more worthy of respect than police or even parents.[1] Their decisions were clear and final, and could invade each facet of my life. When I was caught kissing with seventh-grade passion, I was solemnly turned over to the priest. When I skipped school, I was sent to the enraged pastor. In my school, Lincoln's birthday was outranked by the pastor's own. I greeted the priest each time he passed, tipped my hat to him in winter, and opened doors for him all year long. I could not criticize his sermons, question his actions, nor even mention his name without charity or praise. If he drank and showed the effects, he obviously had a cold. If he snarled about sex or money, he was nervous and working too hard. I was not to talk back; I was to be grateful for criticism, and never to refuse the most impossible request.

I learned my religion without question and memorized each answer without complaint.[2] I knew the angels by name and size, and could prove the authority of the Church. Luther was a renegade who lost his faith, Calvin a troubled man who gave in to angry pride. I knew how fortunate I was to be a Catholic, how special in God's eyes I must be. God, however, began to look more like a Roman collar who heard confessions and said the Mass.

I never thought about attending the public school, steeped as it was in worldliness and sin. But the choice was never mine or my parents' to make. To attend a public school was to be cast among the wolves, to be disgraced within the ghetto as one too slow or stubborn to be taught. It was to study in a world where I could not learn of God or take the time to pray. I was lucky to be in a Catholic school, I learned, and often heard how generous were my parents and pastor to build me such a shrine.

I was proud of my school, and proud that I knew the comforts of my faith. Daily Mass was the first "class" of my day, and confession the last "exercise" on Friday afternoon. I gave up candy and movies during Lent, wore my scapular medal to bed as well as in the bath, said my rosary regularly, prayed at morning and at night, kept track of each sin of disobedience or unkind speech. I prayed for my vocation every day, and served at Mass from second grade.

I admired the priest with genuine respect. He was the biggest man in my life, and to please him was the secret target of my hopes. His approval made my day, his request for service was an honor, his visit to our home a triumph beyond all words. I watched my mother prepare his favorite food, my father lament the vastness of a priest's work, and the family grin with fondness and unaccustomed joy. I watched the attention each one gave his words, the majesty with which he spoke, the confidence with which he dispatched the unbelievers of the world. I saw the envy of the Catholic neighbors who watched him leave our home—and I knew that I would one day be a priest.

So, at fifteen years of age, when World War II was almost at an end, I left for the seminary. It was a hard decision to leave my home. It meant an end to freedom, a painful sacrifice of my chance to play quarterback, and a sad farewell to the first little dark-haired girl who tripped my heart. I will never forget the day we drove away from home. I felt I was leaving the world and in a peculiar way I was. I would return for vacations, spend the summer building houses or pumping gas, play golf with my brothers, or swim until our eyes were bloodshot and our appetites fierce. But I would never be the same again, since I had decided to be a priest. I was never to date, was to avoid movies, beaches, and mixed parties, and to attend Mass every day, meditate each morning of my life, and select a summer job which would not jeopardize my special call. I kept each rule as scrupulously as it was written and explained. My father told me I was too serious, my mother said that I had lost my personality and spark. There were explosions in the summer when the tension ran too high. There were frequent doubts about my choice, but I knew I had to be a priest. I had been "called," and I could not refuse the request that came from God. I was a hero in the ghetto when I returned home for vacation, armed with a black suit and tie, a bulky Latin missal.

I was exempted from the service by the importance of my work and felt cowardly and less a man when I talked to former classmates in the Army or Marines. But the pastor now invited me to his home, the sisters greeted me with new respect, and even my parents could not hide the special place they saved for me within their hearts. I was a seminarian, a chosen man, the pride of the parish, the future leader of our Church. And I was indescribably alone.

I, who once had been the center of every laughing group, the restless boy who could not wait for morning's light, was suddenly alone. I was in the world, but not of it; I was unique, untouchable, aloof, the special friend of God. And year by year, I learned to live alone. My parents could not reach me any more, my brothers could not share with me their dealings and their dates. I learned to fear the world, to hide from its social life, and gradually my solitary life was more the fruit of my warped psychology than of my devotion and sacrifice.

I even began to find vacations far too long and returned to the seminary with relief. Here every decision was made for me, and I was shielded from the fleeting pleasures of the world. I could not leave the grounds, see a girl, read a magazine, drive a car, escape the iron discipline that bound me in its arms. And when I faltered, the voices were always there to tell me I was different, unlike the rest of men: the hope of the world, the strength of the sinner, the lonely man who gave his life for all. I learned to see the world as sinister and dark, and I would be the feeble burst of life. I was called a man, a child of flesh and blood, a weak and sinful child like all of Adam's own—but I knew that I was set apart and chosen from the herd.

I was a seminarian and I cannot tell you what it meant. I cannot, with memory's help, tell you whether I was happy or sad, triumphant or troubled, longing to go on or afraid to give up. I only know that I returned to the seminary year by year and ceased to be a man. I was a prophet, a hero, a soldier, a trained mind, a judge, a reformer, a contradiction, an ascetic, another Christ, an island, a crusader, but not a man. I could never again be ordinary, doubtful, carnal, or confused. I do not know what drove me, whether God, or man's respect, idealism, personal choice, or fear of hell. I only know I struggled on and ended up a priest.

My education was difficult. I studied Latin and Greek, French and Hebrew, English, Philosophy, Speech, Theology, History, Science, and Math. I studied four years after college until I was declared ready to be a priest. My studies spoke seldom of doubts or opinions and most frequently of blacks and whites. In philosophy, for example, we could handle Berkeley, Hume, and Kant in a single week. John Locke was seen as patently confused and Nietzsche was an angry cynic with nothing of consequence to say. We memorized each thesis and definition and proved that "reason" could only lead an honest man to faith. We were the only honest men as we defended by "reason" all the moral teachings of the Church. Catholic opposition to divorce and birth control, to freedom of speech and thought, to mercy killing and adultery were all the obvious conclusions of a "reason" unclouded by passion and pride. It did not seem important that there were millions of "unreasonable" men. I still lived in a ghetto, a child's playground, where I could ignore anyone who refused to play according to my rules.[3]

It was an education without sympathy, a training without recourse. I heard what I was supposed to hear, and said what the administration expected me to say. Rebels were weeded out. Only the strong and legal-minded, or the naïve and passive, could last. Creativity was discouraged unless it pursued the accepted patterns which cautious minds approved. "Heresy" was a word which ended every argument, and "the Church teaches" was the narrow outline of every debate. I was not educated, I was formed. I was not encouraged to think, but trained to defend. I was not asked to reflect, but to memorize.

Even the final four years after college, the years set apart for the "advanced" study of theology, were no different. Only the devoted men who taught me made it possible to survive. I learned what I was expected to believe of heaven and hell, angels and men, even the mysterious God. The truths were laid out in cube form. The heretics who questioned Rome were peremptorily embalmed with a papal decree or conciliar attack. It was a peculiar kind of mathematics, but never a study of man and God. I studied the thousands of sins that had been gathered in the mire of a million confessions. I started with the presumptions that others demanded of me, and if I questioned them, I was asked to abandon the game.

Even the Scriptures were reduced to a defense of the Catholic Church. We read John to defend confession, Luke and Paul to forbid divorce. Even purgatory received its vague, unquestioned scriptural support. After a time I was able to see anything as proved from anything as long as my conclusions supported the Church. Then I could call myself a "theologian," a scholar, who could keep the mud from the sanctuary of the Church. I could no longer go nakedly to Scripture and walk in the wonder of its simple love.

It was also during these last four years that I was immersed in the 2400 laws or "canons" which control the Catholic

Church. The canons are the cryptic conclusions of scholars and religious lawyers long since dead—bastard laws, without apparent forebears, arranged side by side with the decrees of common sense. There are the rules for Christian burial in consecrated ground, the penalties for abortion and suicide, laws regulating the powers of the bishop, the duty of preaching, the sins whose forgiveness is reserved to the Pope. It is an archaic body of law, reeking of drawbridges and moats, which has long impeded the spontaneity of Catholic thought.[4] Canon law has always had the last word in the Church, and it can censor books or excommunicate men with the power of an atomic guillotine.[5] The nervous fingers of bishops can point to it when rebels threaten the complacency of the Church. I learned the laws and read the commentaries and was too frightened to wonder what had happened to the freedom that is Christ.

After such a training I was ready to labor as a priest. I had taken no courses in psychology or counseling. I knew nothing of man's true temptations nor the limits of his capacity to obey. I had never really lived, nor felt, nor hurt as other men. I was ready to enforce the law, and the narrowness of my training ensured the prospering of the Catholic world of black and white. I knew the laws and would teach them with vigor and unquestioned loyalty. I was still the same callow boy who had bowed to the pastor and kissed the confirming bishop's ring. Only my confidence and vocabulary had grown. I still had the ghetto mind, now fortified by formula and law. I was blind to the Church's weakness, I admired its strength. I could call a lack of feeling "courage," stubbornness "conviction," blindness "tradition," medieval prejudice "the unchanging law of Christ." I could explain away failure as success, any fault as evidence of strength, and injustice or cruelty as the modern expression of "God's will." And in such blind and narrow prejudice, I was desperately sincere.

So I took my place in the clergy as another Catholic priest. I would tell men how to love though I had never even kissed. I would chide the young lovers, warn the adolescent, threaten the husbands who used contraceptives, laud Catholic schools from the pinnacle of my ignorance, refuse sacraments to the lonely divorced, nag for money from the economically oppressed, demand sacrifices of the single I could not make myself, command Lutherans to raise their children Catholic, condemn Masonry for obsolete reasons, attack a world I only feared and never knew.

And in my new-found position of power I accepted the homage of the docile Catholic and ignored the hatred of those scorned and wounded by the Church. I did not question my leaders or my laws. I kept the first commandment of every bishop: "Thou shalt not rock the boat!"[6] Most boat-rockers are weeded out before ordination and only occasionally does a man of original and independent thought slip through. Soon enough are they silenced. The conservatives are the fabric that makes up the wardrobe of the Church. They are the young monsignors with the confident smiles and ambitious eyes. They are the bishops who have earned their purple by their uninvolved devotion to law. They are the men who can keep and make the rules because they have guarded their hearts from honest dialogue with men. They force the independent into line, talk more of money than of men, and equate progress with an absence of tension and unrest. From such a group there can never come a Bishop Pike, hardly a Monsignor Pike, and only until the word gets out can a Father Pike come. Yet herein are bred the leaders of the Catholic Church, who can debate the wisdom of the Friday fast when modern man is pondering the death of God.

I am no conservative, nor is my bishop apt to solicit my advice. Yet I have lived and worked as blindly as all the rest. I am a priest, and to be such is to be well guarded from the complexity that is truth. Not only has my education narrowed my mind into little cubes which reject or distort any information that is new, but my relationships with people are frequently insincere. People call me "Father" and they pay me no compliment. They stand aloof from me, they agree and grin, when deep within their hidden anger they would like to slap my face.

I am never "Jim," I am the patriarchal "Father," the man who sees but half of life and seldom hears the truth. People have been taught to fear me, to cater to me, to make few demands, to give me the benefit of the doubt. If I enter a room full of strangers, I am the center of attraction without ever knowing the struggles of ordinary men. Sweet ladies hand me coffee and cookies, men laugh heartily at my slightest joke. They clean up their stories, bore me with the memories of priests they have formerly known, nod seriously when I smother them with clichés. I can preach badly and make no effort to solve man's problem or reach his heart, and poor deluded fools will praise me for my words. Even the more intelligent are apt to excuse my meaningless words with pity for the abundance of my work. Yet I was not too busy to preach well—I was watching the late movie and sipping Scotch. If I told them this, they would call me "humble" in their stubborn refusal to see me as a man.

I am not "Jim"; I am a giant, the collected myth of the centuries, the arrogant and opinionated talking machine that beguiles and frightens men. They speak to me and seldom can I trust their words. They have been taught how they must speak to one as untouchable as I. They pamper me, baby me, caress me with the words that tell me I'm a "thing." They see my collar, my smug confidence, my centuries of angry tradition. They never see the fear that trembles within me, the doubt that lies buried in my heart. If they swear, they apologize. If they talk of sex, they garnish it with fig leaves and flowers.

I watch the gentle scrubwoman who cleans offices at night. Her husband drinks and rapes her once a month. She has seven children, each more delinquent than the next. She should have left her husband twenty years ago. She has stayed with him because "Father" told her it was best. She had the children because she couldn't practice birth control. She confesses minutely each secret thought of sex. She worries endlessly that God has cut her off. She comes to my office clutching her offering for a Mass and whispers her request. I take her money, throw a crumb of kindness to her fond, adoring eyes, and she kisses my priestly hand as she apologizes for taking up my time.

I am "Father," the man who never has to know the misery that is man. No question puzzles me, no moral dilemma puts me off. The man who talks back to me is proud, the sinner who quarrels with me is unrepentant and obstinate. I am always right, always deserving of respect. My faults are excused, my ignorance overlooked, my immaturity condoned. I sit in a restaurant and men who do not know me pay my bill. They send me drinks, slap my back, extoll my sacrifice, praise my school, quote my words. They do everything but treat me as a man.

They do not understand me, they do not even want to try. They do not know that I drink and lust like all the rest. They do not realize that the lewdest jokes are told me by priests. They smile at me with a smile I never earned. They respect my intellect when it has pondered nothing but the sports page for years. They give me their attention and acquiescence when they should argue with me, question me, strip off their shirts and show me their wounds. But they smile, and call me "Father," and treat me as a history's skeleton.

They do not react to me, they react to the illusion they have created in my place. When they tell me they love me, I cannot believe them. They love me for the forgiveness I give, forgiveness of sins that I have invented. They love me for the rituals I perform, the rituals I give meaning by my parroted words. They love me for the fear I calm, the fear I created by my terrifying vision of sin. They love me for the few sparks of humanity that my cassock cannot filter out. They love me with the love born of superstition and magic, the love I cannot earn or honestly deserve. And so they call me "Father" when I know I'm only "Jim."

I cannot trust their love because they do not speak their hate. They hold it in, swallow it, and smother it with that ever-present smile. If at times they would defy me, challenge my words, dissipate my certitude, mock my arrogance, question my infallibility, then I could know their love. If they could come to me as "Jim," a priest, and not to the impersonal "Father" who lives without freedom of decision and must treat every sin alike, then I could know when they loved me and when they only smiled because they were not free to hate.

I am a priest, a bully, a mouther of words, a man whose training forbids him to trust his heart. I cannot say, "Go in Peace," or "Much is forgiven because much you have loved." Rather, I must quote the law like a scheming coroner who runs a mortuary on the side. I see each sin in a paragraph and not immersed in the anguish of a searching soul. And after a dozen years of work among a smiling, docile people, I must pause and wonder who I am. I do not know if I am kind or beastly, open or narrow, strong or weak, faithful or comfortable, courageous or naïve, generous or selfish, because Catholics cannot react to me as a man.

Don't call me "Father." Call me "Jim," and make me know the reality that is life. Don't agree with the obsolete conclusions that I have memorized from musty books. Don't sit and listen to the pious irrelevance that I hand you in place of Christ. You have made me a witch doctor, a magician with secret potions and strange, esoteric words. Why can't I tell you of my fears and personal doubts? Why can't I share with you my weakness when you struggle with your own? Why can't I say, "Do what you think is best," rather than bully and frighten you with neat conclusions that neither you nor I have reached?

You have made me proud and arrogant with the docility of your smile. I do not have to search for new answers, for new approaches and insights, since you patiently accept the irrelevance I hand you from the past. You come to Mass and I bore you, but you bow and come again. You come to confession and I lecture you, but you thank me and promise to return. You don't need me, you only need an impersonal specter robed in black. You won't let me be myself, you permit me to be a tradition, a voice as dull and domineering as all the rest. What have you done to me? What have I become?

No man can take the unquestioned obedience you give and long remain a man. No wonder I think myself infallible when you treat me as the unerring custodian of truth. No wonder I have grown smug and arrogant, righteous and unfeeling, when you have not loved me enough to disagree. I am not a man, but only a seminarian grown to man's estate.

My God! What have I become? You asked me to minister with the weakness of my flesh, to serve the struggling sinner, and I have grown rigid and comfortable in the service of myself. I am not "another Christ," I am not even a man. I am only a prisoner, a synthetic paragon, a defender of the tired past.

O weak and wounded people, how often I long to comfort you with other words than law. How often I want to whisper that my God will understand. But I can only send you back to misery and to guilt and promise a misty happiness that follows after death. I know how you suffer and I grow bitter and angry in your pain. I am a doctor who offers leeches and blood-letting for your fever, because I fear to operate. I am an old lady who tells you how much fun I had in days forever lost. I am a statesman in his dotage who speaks of a world long since gone. I am obsolete, irrelevant, afraid.

O God, if I am to be a priest, first let me be a man! Do not let me hide behind my collar, my titles, my false front. Do not make me give answers I do not believe, nor mold men into impersonal and uncomplaining dolts. Let them know my doubts from my own lips, and let them tell me honestly of theirs. Let me not bind them with law and hell, nor frighten them with tales of unexpected death.

I know their struggles, their differences, the uneven patterns of their lives. It was You, God, Who made them different, and I who ask them all to be the same.[7] Let them know the romance of the search for You, the doubts and near despair that mark the path of honest men. Let me serve them in a personal way and not in the dispassionate sameness that has colored all my work. Let me root out conformity and offer faith, tear down compliance and build up love, eradicate guilt and produce unfailing hope. Let them see my manhood that they may pay homage to their own. Then I can be a priest and not the indentured slave of a system bound in upon itself.

One Sunday, while traveling, I stopped to assist at Mass in a neat suburban Church. I was distressed, fighting with simple fears that I knew I must resolve. I went to Church, not expecting a sudden solution, but hoping for a word that might provide the courage to live another day. I wanted someone to tell me that I was not all bad, that I was only human like the rest of men. The priest ascended the altar and I liked his young and gentle way. He seemed quiet, humble, a man. I fumbled with my own thoughts and waited for him to speak. He told me that the world was selfish, that the collections were down, that the people were not singing well at Mass. He whined of the sufferings of the friends we had in purgatory and shamed us that we had forgotten them so soon. He quoted Scripture to enforce his views on suffering after death, and bored me with the dullness of his words. Then he asked us all to stand and say the Creed.

I could not pray with him, I could only pity the ignorance he displayed. I wanted to stand up and shout, to lead a mob and tear the vestments from his back. I wanted to drag him from his pulpit and lead him to the world of men. I wanted him to walk among the lonely and the poor, to eat with them, to weep with them, to laugh and drink a beer with them. I wanted him to throw away his books and look at men, to look into the eyes of those who did not run from life. I wanted to tear off his collar and make him wear a tie, to send him to an anonymous job to buy his children bread. I wanted him to sweat over income tax, to experience the loneliness of the bewildered, the horror of living with a wife he did not love. I wanted him to bear another child when he could ill afford the three he had, to eat with infants, to lose a job, to make a friend, to be scorned and overlooked.

I wanted him to commit adultery, to masturbate in growing frustration, to fight with his wife, to drink too much, to think of suicide, and then to line up and confess his sins to an arrogant Catholic priest. Then I would lead him back to the pulpit, back to his vestments and lace, and I would listen to his words, and watch his human face. And maybe I would begin to see a man, and to respect him as a priest. Maybe then I could call him "Father" and mean it from my heart. But that Sunday I could only call him "boy" and ache and wonder when he and I could serve as Catholic priests—and still be men.

3. THE MAN WHO IS
A CATHOLIC

Some years ago, when I was a young curate, the Notre Dame football team came to Lansing, Michigan, to challenge the Spartans of Michigan State. The team chaplain visited our rectory the night before the game and announced that the squad would like to attend Mass at nine o'clock on the morning of the clash. He asked if I would help with communions and confessions for the fifty crusaders who came from South Bend to give glory to Erin and its God. I, a Notre Dame fan of considerable strength, was more than willing to be on hand. It was Paul Hornung's senior year and Aubrey Lewis, a great runner, was beginning to come to prominence.

After the Mass, the chaplain and I watched the players file to the front of the Church and kneel solemnly at the communion rail. They knelt as warriors, knights of Mary and the Church, the solemn heroes of Catholic education. They received a special blessing, a tiny medallion in their outstretched palms, and honored a relic of the true Cross. Their faces were drawn and serious, Hornung himself was flushed, as we passed by and brought them the protection of the heavenly patrons of an autumn afternoon. This was our secret weapon, the added strength unknown to television and the press. Unfortunately, however, the Spartans didn't get the word and Notre Dame went down to a decisive and inglorious defeat.

Years later, I took a trip to Lourdes in southern France. I
stood in the giant square in front of the Basilica and watched
the Catholics of the world await the special blessing of this
sacred shrine. I was jostled by the Italian ladies in their shawls,
distracted by Eastern Europeans who whispered their prayers
out loud. I watched the sick on their litters, the American
businessmen in their clean white shirts. I saw priests wrapped
in the cassocks of the world, excited Africans in their multi-
colored native garb. But most of all I saw the wrinkled faces,
speaking out the sincerity of their pain. They had come to ask
a favor, like the Moslem hordes at Mecca, and to know a
special contact with their God. They drank the water there,
which is noted for its miraculous effects. They bought the
plastic bottles to bring the water home. They bought rosaries
and medals by the basketful and had them blessed by the
pudgy hands of sweating priests. They covered the grounds like
locusts, bent on devouring each shred of special grace. They
kissed the feet of statues and groaned in mildewed shrines.
They confessed in every language and munched their mountain
cheese. Then, like a giant, contented herd, they went home to
bed. And so did I, as sick and confused by superstition as I had
been on that autumn day when the Spartans conquered Rome.

Not only was I sick and confused, I was deeply ashamed as
well. This was my Church and these were the Catholic men I
had helped to form, the statistics we added up when we counted
the catholicity of our Church. My mind was crowded with
thoughts that refused to let me sleep. I thought of a temple
court in Jerusalem when an angry Jesus cast the hucksters out.
I thought of a Moses who stormed down a mountain and made
powder of a golden calf. Then I thought of the frightened
Catholics who worried and prayed in every parish I had served.
I thought of the man who is a Catholic and I think of him
once again.

The Catholic man sees the world through a system which
forbids him to be himself. He can walk the city streets and
watch every face and every situation fall neatly into its proper

category. He has never really known the joy of search, the wonder of discovery, the exciting freedom of personal decision. The world is a stranger to him since he judges its citizens before he really knows and understands. He has been taught what to read, how to think, and whom to call his friend.

I watch the Catholic come to Mass and pity the formation that warped his mind and distorted his religious sense. He comes because he has been told to come by religious leaders who are as docile and listless as he. He reads the prayers wrapped in stilted phrases and makes the gestures totally foreign to his modern way of life. He lives in a world of jets and atomic bombs, and prays in a world of medieval magic. He is bored in the presence of his God. And yet he comes, because he has learned from his youth that hell is the home of those who miss Mass. He is too frightened to admit he is bored.

In his business his eye is tuned to efficiency and progress. He looks for shortcuts, for new ways to reach the public, for another service that will attract his fellow man. He has views on world peace, opinions on fiscal reform, thoughts on crime prevention, mental health, and transportation in megalopolis. But in religion he is a robot who can only recite the answers he has learned. He will accept the priestly decisions without protest, appear thoughtful when he hears a rehash of the truths he learned in school, and support the Church which has robbed him of his mind.

And his wife is as pitiful as he. She will live in guilt, raise her children in superstition and fear, and thank the Church for the delicate blueprint that prevents her growth. She will oppose abortion and sterilization without really knowing why. She will practice rhythm or abstinence to win martyrdom in her husband's bed. She will have another child when she neglects the handful that she has, and if she is finally abused enough to protest, she will be stilled by the gentle accents of the priest or be forced to walk away. I remember the mother who came to complain that I had taken away her husband by the papal rules I had enforced. He was sleeping with his secretary once or twice a week, because she, his wife, was too terrified to risk a pregnancy, and too brainwashed to practice birth control. She had returned to her parents' home with her four children, was taking tranquilizers every few hours, and lately had thought of suicide. Her doctor had sent her to me, suggesting that I might give her some secret permission to be a woman once again. She and I talked for an hour, reflecting on the mysterious ways of God. I told her of the holy women of the past, of Mary beneath the Cross, of the sainted martyrs of our parish Church. She grew calm, determined, guilty, courageous, ready to do God's will and bear her cross. She thanked me amid her tears, returned to her parents' home, and four months later joined another Church.

Indeed, she had sense enough to leave before she lost her mind. But can she live with the guilt and fear that we taught her from her earliest years? Can she feel a pain in her chest without wondering if God will suddenly welcome her to hell? Can she bear to pass a Church, or see a priest, or read a newspaper without feeling that she has done a crime? Will she ever love her husband without guilt? Will she lie awake when he is sound asleep? She didn't really leave her Church; we pushed her out, and such conversions do not lead to peace.

The man or woman who is a Catholic has lost his touch with life. He is afraid to read the books that others read, to see the movies that reflect our modern life. He is told that *Dear John*, a current movie, is harmful to his moral life, and he accepts this decision. I saw it, and found it more meaningful than *The Song of Bernadette*. It speaks eloquently of the simplicity of human love and reaches man where his sophistication meets his soul. It is more "religious" than most sermons heard in a Catholic Church, more meaningful than the trappings of the Mass. It is adult, worldly, true, poignant, painful, and sad—and forbidden to Catholics. The Catholic is not supposed to reflect on man and woman making love. He is not expected to explore the world in which he daily lives. He is asked to ignore it, to hide from it, to run from temptation, as if God were somewhere else than at the core of man's own soul.

The Church, like a frightened and angry parent, takes too

much credit for the help that it can offer man. Consequently, Catholics are treated as children and they continue to behave as such.[1] They confess their sexual affairs when they should pause and examine them. They call a loveless marriage virtue if it doesn't break the rules. They call a personal friendship sinful even if single adults grow mature enough to love within this close relationship. They offer solutions before they have examined the problem, give answers before they are informed enough to speak. They condemn family planning in India or Japan without awareness of the culture of the East. They do not reach decisions, they mimic the words that other men provide.

They made a saint of Franco without pausing to hear the other side. They supported the insanity of McCarthyism despite the protests of more balanced men. They approach every social question with a handful of principles that other minds have formed. They support Catholic education with arguments that have lost their force. If time tells them they were wrong, they refuse to apologize. The Catholic man is a little boy whose mommy tells him how to think. God is on his side and the power of God's Spirit rests within his Church. His defenses are made of steel, and he has given his arrogant solutions so often that he is convinced of them himself.

The Catholic man opposed evolution and he was wrong. He supported monarchy long after democracy had made the people free. He promoted racial prejudice until "pagans" showed him he was wrong. He fought mixed marriages and fights them still, although he enjoys the freedoms that pluralism has won. He asks for freedom of conscience and expects Protestants to raise their children in his faith. He condemned Stevenson and Rockefeller because they were divorced. He praised Kennedy because he was Catholic, and extolled Johnson because his daughter chose the Catholic Church. He takes credit for the athletes who go to Mass, selects a Catholic All American Team, and wonders how a Catholic football star could matriculate at Michigan State.

He still believes that the world will be Catholic before the judgment comes, that his faith is a mark of special love from God, that death will justify the valor of his choice. His priests are chosen men, while rabbis and ministers are ambitious, prejudiced, or misinformed. He sees his monks and nuns as proof of God's Shadow on the Church, and the Buddhist counterparts as deluded fanatics.[2] He is the man of the clear-eyed and simplistic look. No problem is complex, no position doubtful, no moral dilemma beyond the papal grasp. If the Pope will permit the pill, the Catholic attitude will simply be reversed. The Catholic will then defend the pill, make light of its physical effects, command its use as the holy will of God. Until it is approved, he will not move because he has learned to watch and wait. He has not the right to follow his own conscience, or the power to select the principles that give him help. He is a Catholic, a child, who demands that another make for him his choice.

He has nothing to learn from Lutherans, no wisdom to be gained from Jews, Masons are a mob of greedy and vengeful men who love to persecute the Church. Atheists are proud and selfish, agnostics educated beyond their brains. Scientists are suspect unless they join the Church, doctors are proud and dangerous unless they listen to the Pope. Thus, the Catholic man cannot truly know the meaning of dialogue, but only give arguments to defend the position he has inherited from his youth. His back is up before his mind begins to work, and he has his defenses well laid before his brother has had a chance to speak.

The Catholic man is an organized answering service whose first obligation is to protect his Church. He is not concerned with overpopulation, but only with guarding the Catholic position on the pill. He is not troubled about public education, but only about the growth of Catholic schools. He seldom spends time with programs of mental health or housing or city government, unless some Catholic value will ultimately thrive. Thus, in every social reform Catholic support has always been joined to the caboose. The Catholic did not support the Negro until the cause was popular and safe. He dared not rethink his views on Communism until our whole society suggested such a change. He did not battle for justice in the coal mines, or start a war on poverty, or strive for women's equal rights. He is a joiner, a sycophant, a man who marches to commemorate battles he has not fought. He cannot go out on a limb, he cannot risk his reputation, he cannot be a radical—he must bide his time and wait patiently for the priest.

And he waits still. The Catholic fears to be a pacifist until "Father" tells him that he may. His stand on Red China, or on Vietnam, will reflect the conservatism of his Church. He lives in a world without surprises, a world that resists experiment and change. He cannot take another look, for example, at homosexuality and wonder if the traditional moral position is realistic or sound. He will continue to condemn abortion even if the law approves it state by state. He will resist divorce until his extremism makes him the laughingstock of the world. He will close his eyes and stuff his ears and thank God he is shielded from the world.

He will come to "Father" and ask questions that do not require the answers of a priest. Parents will ask when teenagers should date, when evening curfew should come, when a boy should be allowed to drive a car. The young will ask how long an engagement should last, or wonder if they can attend a synagogue or wear a bikini on the beach. Workmen will ask if they can bowl in the Masonic temple, women will ask if they can trade in a drugstore that sells suggestive books, or if children can watch Walt Disney in a theater that showed The Doll and Jules and Jim, or swim at the YMCA.

The man who is a Catholic is a religious child who cannot make a moral decision without priestly support. This is especially true of anything that pertains to sex. The Catholic is obsessed with sex and the least deviation can leave him frantic until he finds a priest. He will hurry to confession to clear his eyes of miniskirts, to free his ears from dirty jokes. He will be guilty if his eyes rest on a rounded breast or gaze too longingly at swaying hips. Sex is the chief and single sin, man's fleshly battle with the world.

Sex is the target of the Catholic conscience, the preoccupation of the Catholic adolescent no matter what his age. It leers from billboards and hounds the Catholic on the beach or in his bed. I hear about it from the old men in rest homes who sometimes touch their withered flesh to test its life. I hear it from the children in their simple confessions when they whisper of the explorations held in some garage. It shouts at me from every confession, covers me with questions and detail. Each week I swim in hands and thighs, back seats and bedrooms, trembling lips and throbbing breasts. I hear the embarrassed voices of the weak and wonder if the Catholic thinks of anything but sex. And I know that its expressions cannot be so serious if its occurrence is as frequent as it seems.

Perhaps you are among the educated and independent and do not recognize the Catholic I describe. Perhaps you are a liberated Catholic, or your friends are, and you do not know the suffering of the millions bound by Rome. I know them, and I cannot forget their weariness and fear. I cannot leave them prisoners while I enjoy the freedom that my temperament and education can provide. Were I married, I could practice birth control without concern. Indulgences bore me and I have not tried to gather them for years. I do not pray to angels nor honor history's saints. I know nothing of heaven nor do I really fear the misery of hell. I do not run to confession, nor sprinkle holy water, nor seek from novenas what only time and effort give. I do not wait to hear each sentence from the Vatican before I act, nor do I fear the excommunications sent in solemn words. I will not accept the bishops' fears and arrogant commands as the unerring voice of God, nor permit ignorant pastors to transform their petulance into law.

But I am not the average Catholic man, who cannot escape the shackles and superstitions of his past. He cannot ignore the laws that have lost their meaning, or distinguish the mysteries from myth.[3] He is choked by sin, frightened by the fire of hell, and bound by the hierarchy which once was meant to serve. He is afraid to miss Mass no matter how barnacled it seems, afraid to marry again no matter how urgent his need, afraid to be himself, afraid to ask what he wants from the Church, afraid to stand alone. A collar can frighten him, a threat from the sanctuary can turn him back, a parent's tears can tear apart his soul. I am not such a Catholic, but I must fight for him, that together we can know the freedom that is God.

This very evening, even as I write, I remember the fortyish man who rang my office bell one summer night. He was tall and lean, athletic and well-dressed, the father of four children, and an usher in our church. His face was sad on this occasion as we settled down solemnly to talk. He told me he was leaving the Church and wanted me to know. He said it wasn't anything personal and that he had grown to consider me his friend. But he was tired of a Church that would not treat him as a man. He was tired of money drives and overcrowded schools, tired of living in a world that only spoke of varieties of sin, tired of empty confessions and rites grown meaningless and cold. He said he was taking his children from our school, where they studied law when he wanted them to learn of love. He wanted them to escape the fears that depressed his wife and him, to learn of God in words that told them they were loved, to grow in confidence and tolerance, to enjoy the world and treat it as a home.

I could not answer him; my defensive eloquence was gone. He was not a complainer, not a wild neurotic, not a proud and angry rebel in the crowd. He was the kind of man I hoped to serve, the kind of man I longed to be, a strong and loyal friend. He shook my hand and thanked me for the services I gave. I asked him why we failed, what he wanted from his Church. He said quietly that all he wanted was a home, a touch of wisdom to see him through the week, a word of mercy that made it all worthwhile, an understanding Church that reminded him of God. Tonight I know why we failed and what he wanted—and I'm sure the man who is a Catholic wants the same.

And I must speak for him because I hear his screams, they echo in my work and in my sleep! He says to me:

"You taught me in my infancy of God. You told me of His angels that followed me to school, His martyrs and His virgins who prayed with me at Mass. You filled my mind with stories that brightened my Christmas and made Lent a dramatic struggle in the company of Christ. You held me in the world of the soul, taught me to pray, introduced me to forgiveness and to sin. You brought the bishop to my Church in all his splendor, told me that my pastor was another Christ. You gathered nuns to teach me and fitted them with crosses that stared at me in school. You gave me a rosary and blessed it, enrolled me in my miraculous medal, and fed me with the sacred food to fill my emptiness. You brought me to holy hours, held relics before my eyes, stuffed my imagination with the saints' heroic deeds. You made religion the center of my life, gave me a reason for living, and promised me the peace that comes from God. You chided my weakness, threatened me with hell, urged me to love, and moved me to pray for the souls still suffering in purgatory's flames. I made the nine First Fridays many times, I honored the Sacred Heart, I said my three 'Hail Mary's' before I slept at night. I gave up movies and candy during Lent, I kept the Fridays, used my missal at Mass, guarded my thoughts, avoided occasions of sin, and honored my parents as best I could. All this you taught me and more. You made me a religious child, a bright and happy child—and when I became a man, you left me.

"You would not listen to the words about the world I tried often to speak to you. I tried to tell you that your promises were not enough, that your words and threats deserted me in the midst of other men. You told me to receive the sacraments, to come more often to Mass, to add a rosary to my daily prayers. I planned to tell you that your service was obsolete, but each time I came near, I feared to be honest. And so I remained a cripple and screamed silently for help. I tried to shake you, but you had formed me too deeply in the mysterious world of God. I tried to ignore you, but I knew not how. Your tales of hell had filtered through my soul. I tried to run from you, but I knew not where to go. And so I stay, a cripple, clinging to my youthful hope of discovering my God.

"This, then, is my dilemma, the dilemma of the man who is a Catholic: I cannot remain a religious child, but you will not let me be an adult. And so I remain a lonely, confused, angry, and abandoned creature, who will not accept an idol, and cannot find his God."

Parish Council

4. THE CATHOLIC PARISH

History offers no finer example of monarchy than the normal Catholic parish. It is a society without genuine channels of recourse, a structure fortified against effective complaint. The pastor can run "his" parish as he will as long as his financial records are reasonably sound. He can guard himself against distressing feedback by prudent control of his flock. If complaints do filter through to the bishop, they are returned to the pastor for "handling." The bishop is generally afraid to quarrel with pastors since removing them from their jobs is a troublesome process.[1] The pastor is the strong man of our system and has received the promotions that years of service and important "connections" can create. If he happens to be a monsignor, for whatever reason, and has some reputation for financial prowess, he is beyond the grasp of human hands.[2]

There are no supervisors to evaluate the pastor's work, no "spies" to inspect his sermons or the educational programs he provides. There is no court that can criticize his handling of the liturgy or his public relations. He can visit hospitals when he likes, knock on doors, or refuse to call on his parishioners. He can decide without consultation the hours of confession, the topics and length of his sermons, whether brides shall dress at home or at the Church, who shall be admitted or evicted

41

from the parish school, who shall use the parish gymnasium, whether there shall be alcohol at a parish dance, and for practical purposes, who can be buried from the Church. He can effectively oppose a new parish that will remove revenue from his own. He can decide who his advisers shall be or if he needs them at all. He can compose or edit the Sunday bulletin, determine how much to pay for a new Church and how soon the parishioners will pay it off. He can hire lay teachers or fire the coach. He can install a new public-address system or remove it and tell his assistant to shout without it. He can hire an organist or forbid music in the Church. He can snarl at people who leave Mass early and refuse to baptize babies whose parents were not married in Church. He can talk money until the people wonder if religion means anything but gold, and he can request an extra collection for any cause he wants. He can have an income that provides him with comforts that none of his people know. He can even ignore Vatican II in loyalty to Trent. There is hardly a parallel for this ecclesiastical phenomenon in all of democratic society, unless it be the bishop he represents. Both cases are simply a matter of frustration without representation.

This is not to say that every Catholic pastor is arrogant and despotic, rather that many are, and that no human being can handle such power. Power can make any man mad. When the man involved has no wife or family, no balanced perception of life's realities, when he functions without criticism or honest advisers, there are almost no limits to the level of his madness.

Historians trace the origins of pastoral authority back to the medieval struggles between the secular or diocesan priests and the monks or religious.[3] In those dark times, secular priests, often without education, were threatened by the growing popularity of the more sophisticated monks, who were not bound to any single parish. These monks could preach to the faithful and accept their offerings despite the protests of the parish priests, because lines of authority were confused. In order to survive, the parish and its pastor were made the legally pampered fortress of the Church. Canon law contains the history of this parochial defense in the decrees which decide where the flock shall pray, where the young shall marry and the old be buried, and especially where the people shall pay.[4] The defense of the parish has lasted to our own day, but with no corresponding protection for the monks. This is why, destined to earn financial support by their imagination, they run their tiny private schools and send us medals and statues through the mail. They are hardly to be blamed for bombarding us with the holy gimmicks when the Church has permitted the parish priest to become its chosen son, with his weekly revenue.

Nothing has changed in five centuries to alter the image of a medieval baron the pastor embodies. Canon law installs him in his parish with stiff dignity. His time off is guaranteed by precise legislation, his rights are those of a Jewish patriarch, and the only responsibility on which he is seriously checked— barring public scandal—is the financial solvency of his parish.

The Catholic pastor, of course, is more than a collection of such medieval laws and canonical protections, history having added a few colors to his coat without asking permission. In addition to his legal status, he is the accumulated compound of a fighter for the immigrants, a scholar to the ignorant, and the proud son of every family. Generations of children have learned never to question his decisions or advice. Young priests who serve under him soon learn how lasting must be their childhood.[5] The pastor is supreme—guarded by law, fortified by history, and defended by his people.

Here and there, indeed, there is some evidence of change. But the dozens of parishes that I have observed closely in the last two years indicate that most of the changes are token and without significance. Pastors are protesting Vatican II even as the people are waiting impatiently for Vatican III. The bishops may have learned at Vatican II that they share the authority of the Pope,[6] but the pastors have failed to learn that they share their power with the people. Catholic people are still dumb and patient sheep, who tip their hat to "Father" and refuse to challenge his arrogance, even as religion loses meaning in their life.

Pastors still urge tithing programs on their pitiful people, and the parish permits fund-raisers to preach the dishonest theology which demands a holy percent. The people fall for the propaganda in the glossy brochures and accept the method of financial contribution which made sense in a religiously ruled society. But a tithing campaign in a world of taxes and government support is a vicious and deceitful gimmick. It hides the needs of nervous pastors to build financial monuments and succeeds under the glib, smooth talk of professional advertisers. Parish after parish promises to tithe under the pressure of a pastor who, while asserting that tithing is the will of God, is not required to justify the costly Church or the obsolete school he builds.

So I watched the silent people tithed, schooled as they are in the docility of non-protest. I do not see the pastors tithed from their vast and unlisted incomes, nor the bishops. Only the people do—piling up money which will be used without their approval, too kind to suspect that often their money merely satisfies their pastor's need to build his kingdom or guarantees his rise toward priestly eminence. But bishops reward pastors whose buildings are expensive and quickly out of debt. Parish holdings are listed in the bishop's name, and faltering mortgages do not show up well on his coat of arms. So the pastor orders the ushers to pass out leaflets at all Masses, preaches each sermon in an important tithing campaign, plugs it as a new insight of modern theology, welcomes the professional fund-raisers from New York and Babylon, and another parish is successfully duped. The people question the fund-raisers in their homes, they express their disgust with them as they ride the bus to work. They wonder why the Church has adopted this impersonal policy in the last few years. But the pastor has spoken, and the gentle sheep will bleat and wag their tails in resigned agreement.

Catholic people do not count. Otherwise, they wouldn't be obliged to listen to the sick sermons they hear. It is a rare Catholic pastor who prepares his sermons; but then, there is no reward from the bishop's office for good preaching. Priests in general are among the poorest speakers in the world. The people continue to come because the fear of mortal sin pressures them, even though the greatest "sin" of all is the priest in his abominable preaching.[7] The dull phrases and stale ideas engraved since childhood, the archaic vocabulary born of Latin theology, the presentation of an idea without feeling or imagination, or what is worse, the presentation of a dull idea with feeling, the abuse of Scripture, the rehashing of personal obsessions—all of this is supposed to prepare the people for the banquet of Christ. Any other organization would go out of business, but the brainwash learned in childhood and the fear of death keeps the pews crowded and the parking lots full.

A decade ago we could, perhaps, endure the impoverished preaching in the Church. Then at least, the sermon was the only English island in a raging sea of Latin. Then, too, we were wrapped more carefully in our parochial ghetto. We were taught to carry home whatever little defective pearl was offered and to overlook the irrelevance that proved we had been to Mass. We did not then know that the sermon was to be the incisive word that Christ spoke to us at the common meal to interpret life to His brothers.[8] It was rather a defense of the system, a reminder of the details of the catechism forgotten since grade school, or commercial time to plug money or the sacraments, or to attack birth control and steady dating. The pastor was in charge and we accepted what he condescended to give.

And we do it still. We hear the long harangues on parish finances or listen to the dull letters explaining diocesan collections. We hear missionaries tell snake and lion stories to solicit more money. Last week I heard a pastor read all of the Mass intentions for the week even though they were listed in the bulletin. He then announced three meetings and gave the details of the next fiscal campaign. He bawled out the mothers for letting their daughters wear shorts and slacks downtown and told the adults that they were far too interested in pleasure and money. He proved this by stating that only one out of three envelopes had been used by contributors the previous week. Then he told us to say "Ay-men" and not "Ah-men" at communion time, and to place our hands on the table when we received. We were also to lean forward as long as we were not wearing low-cut gowns. After this "sermon" he returned to the altar and no one in the Church shook a fist or threw a brick. Ten years ago I would have admired the flock's restraint. Now I found myself lamenting their ignorance. They did not know what the sermon was supposed to mean. Luther had told them four hundred years ago about the importance and meaning of the sermon, but Luther has never sold too well in Catholic pamphlet racks.[9] The pastor had spoken and the patient adults and their squirming children listened.

But some did not listen. They had the good sense to remain away, or to seek out a pastor who makes an attempt to communicate. These are the people who cannot bear to hear words about God and man which only make them angry and bored. They cannot submit to a half hour of pious irrelevance that keeps them twitching in their seats. They do not ask much, and if they find a priest who preaches fairly well, he becomes a Fulton Sheen in present competition. They may even search in vain for such a priest, because there are no bonuses for preaching.

They walk away in ever greater numbers, but they do not walk away with uncomplicated ease. The aura of the Mass lingers in the memories carried from childhood, and they look in vain for substitutes. It is generally not the old who leave, since they are closer to eternity and have learned patience in the face of life's inanities. It is the young, because they demand more of life and still hope to find answers for the questions that will not be quiet. Thus far it seems that they are not missed, since the Churches are still full, the collections still fat. The pastors can continue to preach without preparation, and the people accept their religious "home" without right of protest.

It would be naïve simply to blame pastors or bishops for the lack of intelligent sermons, though such blame would not be totally without truth. I am blaming, rather, a parochial system that permits a pastor to run his parish without the reaction and suffrage of his flock. I am blaming a training program that does not insist on the importance of preaching in God's work. Years are spent in mastering theology which can be learned in months, and minutes are given to preaching which should have required hours. The Sunday sermon is the single most important avenue of communication that a priest has. No business can assemble all of its customers at once. Few leaders have fifteen precious and guarded minutes in which to address their people. But the priest does have this rare opportunity and he readies himself by jotting down a few notes during TV commercials or he "thinks it out" on his feet. He cannot preach because he does not have to, and the system which protects the pastor from the rage of his people is decadent and out of date.

Good preaching and an intelligible liturgy are necessary for the Church's survival in an age of discordant noises. The world in which we could simply remind man of his obligations and expect conformity is giving way to a world that wants relevance and communication. Once we could point to the mystery of the Mass and sacraments, and wait for man to come for his portion of grace. Now we know that there must be words to render the Mass and sacraments meaningful.[10] Man will not be satisfied with the silent forms that do not tell him of the mystery they contain, for this is to be satisfied with a silent Christ.

I hoped, for a time, that songs and English in the Mass would solve the problem of our bored and indifferent people. I thought that the obvious failure of our liturgical renewal was due to the resistance of the untouchable pastors. And yet, as the pastors have accepted the untrained laymen in the sanctuaries and scattered song sheets in the pews, I realize just how pitiable is our preaching. The liturgy is bad enough with its experimental confusion and its disorganized motion, which cannot compete with the meditative silence of the past. A liturgical reform, however, understandably takes time. But there is no excuse for our horrid preaching, and yet it does not seem to change. The bright young men with their new theology are as dull and pointless as their pastors; if anything, a trifle duller and less convincing.

Recently I made a survey of the sermons in thirty different parishes in five separate states, listening to an average of four sermons in each parish. The results of my study—however modest—are appalling. Only two of more than a hundred sermons I heard were worthy of an average audience. Money was mentioned with lengthy enthusiasm more than 40 percent of the time. In at least twelve of the parishes it is customary to read long excerpts from the bulletin. In at least ten of the parishes the public-address system is inadequate. Frequently I was scolded, even insulted, and most of the time I was talked down to. When the new laws came out on mixed marriages, lifting the censure of excommunication from those married outside the Church, I only heard that this did not mean that these invalidly married sinners were free from mortal sin. I heard nothing of the hope that this new legislation might contain, or the possibility of a more tolerant view of mixed marriage in the future. I was only told that the offenders were "living in sin" and could not be expected to be "buried from the Church."

But we hardly need private or public studies. We have simply to permit laymen to speak with unguarded honesty. Speak to them of the sermons they hear and ask them if they leave Church with a message that gives practical meaning to the realities of life. They will tell you of sermons which give evidence that "Father" has spent twice as much time with the Sunday paper as he has with sermon preparation.

Maybe every priest should not attempt to preach, certainly some should not. Priests without financial ability are quietly sent to parishes where they can do no harm. But wretched preachers, as long as they can raise money, are promoted to an even larger flock. Within the last few years, I served in a prominent parish—one with a number of sophisticated people —where the pastor spends every other Sunday lecturing his flock about their tardiness at Mass. The pastor is firmly founded in his parish, since he has efficiently handled an important administrative post in the diocese. His preaching, however, does injustice to fourth-graders. The tardiness of the parishioners could be helped if he gave shorter sermons and enlarged the parking lot. But no one can convince him that anything but selfishness keeps the people coming late.

For months he required the ushers to lock the Church doors once the Mass had begun, even though the Church was located downtown and served the visitors to the city. I admit that he is a neurotic but, after all, there is no avenue of recourse for the parishioners. He screams at the altar boys, barks at the communicants, insults the people regularly from the pulpit. To hear his sermon is to leave the Church a nervous wreck. I grant that he is a bit more colorful than the majority of poor preachers and impossible pastors, but thousands of Catholics can relate similar experiences. A man in any other profession would lose his job, but the Catholic pastor is beyond complaint.

If you want good sermons and intelligent religious leadership, you must demand it from us. Begin by cutting your contribution in half, or by paying for the value you receive. But do not act silently or without explanation. Tell us why you have ceased to pay. There is no other way to reach us in the present structure of the Church. The pastor is a man who does not have to listen until enough people refuse to pay.

Do anything but excuse us, or our irrelevance will grow, and the exodus of the faithful will increase. We can learn to preach, even though our seminary training did not teach us how. We learned to gather money without a course in economics, to run a parish school without a text in education or commerce. We will learn to communicate when the people demand it. We will throw away the tawny sermon books and the outlines in periodicals which have given us printed substitutes for thought. We will preach when we take the time to read and reflect and begin to discard the overworked platitudes that we haven't practiced in years.

Not only do the people have nothing to say about the pub-

lic relations and sermons in the average parish, but also they
are practically boycotted from the parish school. The present
policy is to build centralized schools to replace the individual
parish schools of the past. Each parish is assessed for a central
school or tithed to death to sustain its own. This policy continues even though there is serious question if they accomplish
anything except to perpetuate the ghetto and, in some cases,
to help the middle-class white keep their children from attending schools with Negroes. We will discuss the problem of
parochial schools in another chapter, but here we merely point
out that a parish can pour thousands of dollars into Catholic
education without the consent of the parishioners. A pastor,
sent to America as a missionary from Ireland, can and frequently does impose his rural views of education on an American parish. No matter that his intelligent parishioners teach
in public schools or lecture at state universities. They are
forced to hear the praises of an educational system which is
hard pressed to justify its existence. They may sincerely believe
that religious education comes largely, if not exclusively, from
the home, and yet they are "forced" to support the parochial
school of the local parish. For years we have complained
through our "official" episcopal spokesman that we have been
taxed to support schools we didn't use. No one seems to notice
that every Catholic parish is guilty of a similar violation.

  Nor do the people have anything to say about the liturgical
reforms that rock the parishes with clumsy force. A few years
back the people were required to recite prayers in gibberish
Latin which they didn't understand. Then they were told to
sing hymns, to listen to a variety of untrained laymen, and to
abandon ancient liturgy without anything comparable to take
its place. There was more than a grain of truth in the wisdom
of Father DePauw's insistence that the traditional Catholics
had been ignored.[11] It would seem more accurate to say that
the Catholic people have been "traditionally ignored" in every
major decision which affected their personal lives. They have
been forced, and still are, to adopt a series of liturgical symbols
that are meaningful only in the innocent lives of a group of

esoteric Church historians who call themselves "liturgists." To
reform the liturgy demands a knowledge of men. Simply to
permit the president of the altar society to carry the cruets to
the altar or to erect communion stations or Bible stands in the
sanctuary means little or nothing to the men I know. We need
a sense of community, and the latest dreams of the liturgical
in-group won't provide us with anything more than another
golden calf. The people, meanwhile, have nothing to say, and
they wait for the next "inane" suggestion from the desk of
some doting cardinal.

There will be a parish someday in which the people will
have an honest voice, and it had better be soon.[12] There will
be a parish which will have to concern itself with modern
novelties such as public relations and the art of communication.
In order to bring this about, both the collection and expendi-
ture of money will have to be in hands other than the pastor's,
because no man can sensibly handle his vast power without
the present abuse. It will be the people's parish and they will
support it willingly when they have a voice in its administration and the quality of its service! Parishes will have to be
much smaller so as to foster a sense of community somewhere
besides in the heads of all-knowing liturgists. No community
can exist without dialogue and a practical share in some obvious work, and no amount of liturgical reforms or prayer cards
will alter that fact.

The parish of the future will admit a married clergy. To
think otherwise is to be hopelessly ignorant. This will provide
the priests that are needed, something which no amount of
nagging or vocational "pitchmen" will accomplish. The priesthood is still attractive to a large number of young men, but it
will not continue so if the priest is not free to choose or to
sacrifice marriage. With an adequate number of priests, the
Church can go to people and not expect man to adapt his
needs to the worn-out structures of the Church. Some people
may well be satisfied with a large parish, since they derive a
sense of community in the impersonal Churches of the me-
tropolis. For most men, however, there can be no community

in a parish of five or ten thousand people. A subway station at the rush hour is as personal and intimate. The priest will have to know his people,[13] and this will be at least possible in a Church of five hundred souls. He can employ a layman to help him with the parish books and finances, and not depend on the obsolete commodity of volunteer help.

In such a parish he will not have to build a school, since his knowledge of his people and a couple of trained nuns could provide him with all the staff he needs. Nor will he wait until he is fifty or sixty to be a pastor. He could well be ready to accept a parish at ordination if his seminary education would abandon the "myth" of preparing "theologians" and begin to educate men of faith to preach, counsel, and think. He will not spend twenty or thirty years as the assistant to an omnipotent pastor, and lose his fire and ideals in the process. He will even have the freedom to make mistakes, and contact with a parish council will provide him with greater direction than any diocesan office could ever give. He will, of course, be paid a reasonable salary, and not be forced to rely on clever financial "angles" and mounds of "unreported income." This would put an end to the scandal of "Mass stipends" and seat collections, and a dozen other ecclesiastical games. He could even return the Christmas and Easter donations of the struggling pensioners which keep him from starvation in the Hiltons both here and abroad.

Nor will the priest of the future be strapped with the obsolete organizations that cripple the work of the priest in the parish. He will not need a St. Vincent de Paul Society to help the poor if he encourages his parishioners to investigate the channels of social welfare and to improve them. Nor will he spend his time with a Holy Name Society, which flounders around searching for some modern apostolate. He can abandon the Athletic Association when he permits the children of his flock to take advantage of the programs which satisfy the other children of the community. He can even disband the Altar Society, which spends each fall pleading for members and each spring wondering what in the world to do with them. He won't even need the Legion of Mary, whose archaic name is symbolic of its archaic program. It would, of course, mean an end to that historic cornerstone called bingo, unless it were salvaged to occupy our neglected senior citizens. He won't even have to build a convent, since the sisters can live in a neighborhood like everyone else and know the freedom that maturity and responsibility require.

The rescinding of the Friday law of abstinence permits us to hope that soon enough Sunday Mass will not be an obligation. Even now I question emphatically that missing Mass can bind under pain of "mortal sin." Mass will not have to "oblige" in a small community which cares about the people and teaches them to care about one another. Nor will there be a daily Mass in the Church to satisfy the sisters and the janitor. The priest will offer Mass in homes, or factories, or shopping centers, and its form will be brief and casual enough to admit restless children and holy enough to remind man of God. There will be no need of processions and gadgets to tell people they are a community. There will be a liturgy that flows from a genuine community, and not one that presumes or forces it. The freedom for variety and experiment will rest with local groups and not follow national directives in a nation which includes hundreds of levels. Boundaries will mean nothing next to the common experience which the community shares. The Mass can be as long or short as the community requires. It will be as brief and to the point as modern life, and yet provide the minutes of mystery and reverence that a profane man must have.[14]

It will, of course, be in the people's language, every syllable of it. It will consist of no more than readings from Scripture, an honest word from the priest, prayer, offering, and sacrifice. There will be time for simple ceremony, but none for enervating pomp. There will be time for the people to speak of their sick, their dying, their children, their joys, but none for collections or financial plugs or eloquent verbiage. The community will know each other's names and jobs and children, and will be taught through time and effort to communicate as friends. The people will not find it so hard to be friends, because the priest will be first their friend and only then their high priest.

Groups in the parish will be organized according to parochial needs. Non-Catholics will feel at home in this liturgy without the meaningless barnacles of tradition. The Mass will require no more explanation than a happy family, or a home-cooked meal, or a meaningful conversation. The parish will be a place of service which seeks to make God live among men and to help men discover God in mutual love. Long enough have we talked of community and offered only an auditorium. Song does not bring people together, be they Kiwanians or Catholics. We prove nothing when we pray aloud together; it is only when we live together or work together that common prayer means community.

We need such a parish, a home where man can belong. We need a religious family where a man can know the priest he speaks to, and can tell him of his fears and hopes. We hardly need theology classes for the occasional enthusiast; we need to practice religion. We don't need Catholic welfare programs or Catholic hospitals; we need only to recognize the aims that we have in common with all men. Then the vocabulary of Vatican II, such as "people of God" and "citizens of the kingdom," will not strike us as being as irrelevant as the language which it replaced. Too much of our renewed language is only another barrier to understanding, too many of our symbols speak to no one save the scholars who fashioned them. A parish will be a family only when it acts like one, not when we suggest parallels in complex analogies.

In such a parish we can find the peace and meaning that a ghetto world found in the comfort of its familiar surroundings. When the ghetto world grew, and the children climbed over its walls, there remained only an institution which offered us Mass and the sacraments, even though we called it a Church. Now we recognize how vast and impersonal it has become, and how quickly man runs to find his religious home in other communities that do not smother and swallow him. The lodge, the barbecue, group therapy, the beach, the golf course, the retirement village, the poker club will have to provide all the community that man needs until the parish truly becomes a family of friendship in God. One wonders how long we will have to wait.

5. THE LOSS OF

PERSONALISM

Deep in the heart of a modern city lives a man. He moves in a world of turnpikes and suburbs, owns a dozen suits with a pair of ties for each. Vietnam is as real to him as the taxes that cloud his every spring. Each new wrinkle on his face warns him of the young college graduate who is struggling to supplant him. Another child in his family can mean a new home. A high-school graduation can mean another college tuition. He watches the stock market, worries about retirement, and observes the bulging waistline that can bury him at fifty. He wonders what he has done with his life, wonders why he rushes so, and asks why he and his wife have grown apart. He was raised a Catholic. He seldom misses Mass and keeps Lent with honest concern. He receives communion once a month, has contributed to a half-dozen churches and their building funds. He takes a drink almost every day, about as often as he has indigestion and a nervous stomach. He frequently plans a program of daily exercise. His office is a daily rerun of Space Headquarters when an Agena rocket misfires. He rushes his lunch, fights the traffic on his way from work, and glances through a couple of newspapers. He has heard of the Good Shepherd, the land of many mansions, and the raging fires of hell. He has been told to be kind and forgiving, to control his thoughts, to pray for the dead. He is a Catholic, but his faith seems to miss him at the center of his life.

High in the mountains of Mexico I have often watched the simple Indians practice their faith. A roadside shrine decorates the highway, a burst of fireworks announces a wedding or a first communion. Here in the world of grass huts and corn tortillas, the war in Vietnam does not exist. There is no concern about styles or stock markets. A skinny burro, grazing by the highway, asks only slightly less of life than does his master. Each man seems to know his special task, and the very hardships of his life point to another world where the torrential rains cease and the shoulders do not ache under a load of wood. Juan lives here and is a practical Catholic. He has been taught some simple prayers and says them with great devotion. He attends Mass when there is a priest around to offer it, and finds it the most exciting pageant that a life without TV or transportation provides. The laws he follows are as uncomplicated as his life. He prays to the Madonna, feeds his children, and is kind to his wife. Occasionally he drinks too much. He may snicker at an obscene joke, or cast an unsavory glance at his blossoming daughter. He asks no more of life than its measure of meals and rest, a thatched roof to shield his family from showers, and children to support him when he can no longer stoop to plant the corn. He has heard of the Good Shepherd, the land of many mansions, and the raging fires of hell. He has been told to be kind and forgiving, to control his thoughts, to pray for the dead. He is a Catholic and his faith is as normal and natural as his sheep.

Juan did not choose his world of mountains and grazing goats, nor did the city man ask to live in the orbit of speed and ulcers. They are, indeed, brothers in Christ, locked in a life they cannot completely control. To each of them the Church has been commissioned by Christ to speak, but it cannot hope to reach them with an identical message and approach. Even a generation ago, a univocal system would not have been so difficult. Today it is impossible.

Once I could live in the religious world of Juan with only

slight nuances of distinction. It was the world of my parents and the ghetto I have already mentioned.

Our sincerity as Catholics was as much the result of nationalism as of simple and superstitious faith. To be Irish, or Polish, or Italian was to be Catholic, and the brogues and accents were as slow to disappear as the uncompromising fury of our faith. To have a priest of one's own nationality was more important than having a priest. To commemorate the customs and folkways of Europe was as religious as to observe the rubrics of the Mass. Parish suppers were more the mark of the Catholic community than the congregation that knelt each Sunday in the parish Church. And the courage that led us regularly to sacrifice and prayer was fed as much by antipathies born in Europe as by faith born of God. Behind our minority courage was a starving theology which supported closed minds and encouraged unrelenting law.

Even the Protestant world, with all its historic freedom, strangled under the grasp of an idealism which was as sure Rome was wrong as Catholics were that it was right. The political speeches of that day rang with the positive assurance that man would solve the social problem. Education, too, was sure of its goal and confident of its methods. The curriculum was settled and enshrined, and teachers seemed to know the courses and disciplinary devices that could mold a man. Even science, though its methods promised a never-ending search for truth, was pompous in its certitudes and arrogant in its facile promises. In such a world, the world of Juan and my parents, the world of my youth, my Church could easily survive. But in today's world, the world of the city man, little is certain, little—if anything—can be codified.

I did not choose my world. I merely live in it and struggle to remain a person in loyalty to the uniqueness handed me by God.[1] I cannot think as every other Catholic, nor can I have a conscience that accepts the charted program which suits another man. I do not require specific laws which bind my fingers and chain my feet. True, such laws may restrain me from striking my neighbor or stomping his children, but they also bar me from learning how to love. I need general directions, not detailed rules. I need confidence and motivation, not anxiety and orders. I have outgrown the mother who tells me when to eat, and when to sleep, and how to know a flower from a weed. I am a person, not a cardboard man, a man in search, and not a sheltered child. No church can change me, I must change myself. No code can regulate my soul, no creed can satisfy my thirst.

Creeds can only be offered, but I must take them to myself.[2] No one can tell me that I must embrace each shred of mystery, each symbol of the Trinity, each glory of Mary, each theory of death and judgment, each exaggerated dogma on the divinity of Christ, if I am to be a member of my Church. You can only explain to me your faith, reveal to me the tiny light you find in darkness, expose to me what gives you hope and warms your love, and know that God and I will do the rest. I am a person, free and struggling, living in light and darkness, walking the edge of love and hate, hope and despair, openness and narrowness, fear and courage. God is closer to me than my Church, closer than doctrine and ritual, closer than sacrament or saint. My Church can only be my servant, not my parent. It can only offer me truth, not cram it down my throat. It can only speak of God, not reduce Him to a cautious list of words.

Nor can a code contain His total will.[3] No woman can blueprint for a man each motion of his love, unless she wants a slave. She cannot direct his words, regulate his feelings, outline his duties, enforce his steps. She can only offer her love, reveal her feelings, suggest her hurts, whisper her fears, engage his attention, describe her needs, and hope that he will respond. A Church can do no more unless it plans to desecrate the persons it was commissioned to serve. It is no servant of Christ if it is satisfied with an ignorant people too docile to be persons. What does it gain if it wins compliance at the cost of personal love? Fear is not love, nor is listless silence.

Can I not kneel with my brothers if I do not share each facet of their faith? How will faith grow if I cannot compare the feebleness of mine with the strength of theirs? Can I not eat with my brothers at a common table unless I comply with laws that are as senseless to me as they are helpful to them? Are faith and love a single thing, a category, a catechism definition, the vision of a medieval mind? No man can tell me he believes, but only that he is poised between faith and doubt, certitude and despair. Faith is not a static thing, it is as dynamic and nebulous as life. No man possesses faith, or embraces it; he only grows a trifle farther from his unbelief. He can only struggle like the blind man in the Gospel and beg humbly, "Help thou my unbelief."

Faith is the jungle path that leads a man to see a glimmer of his God, not the well-marked superhighway that takes him from the earth. It is a beginning, a spark, not a clear and comprehensive summary of God. Must I believe as you do to have it? Must I say "I believe" to satisfy my Church when I can only say with honesty "I try"? Do you want a particular word from me, a meaningless assent? Then you forbid me to be a person in my life within my Church. Do I believe in the Trinity? I am not sure. I can say I do and tell you how long I tried to ponder it. I am not opposed to it, but it does not seem to reach me in my heart. God reaches me, so does Jesus, but I cannot keep their persons straight. Nor can I make an important friend of person number three. Do I believe in purgatory? I do not know. I only know that such a dogma does not cause me concern. Nor do indulgences, or angels, or devils, or special devotions to Mary and the saints.

I have a similar difficulty with morals and with law. I see couples remarry after divorce and I inwardly approve. Must I say that I don't to be a member of my Church? Again, you ask me to deny that I am a person, to ignore the experience that speaks to me of God. It is the same with birth control, or Sunday Mass, or sterilization, or mixed marriage: must I view them as every other Catholic to have a home within the Church? If so, I am asked to prostitute my person to enjoy the service of my Church. This I cannot do.

Man is more important than a system, and older than the

Church. The Church is for me and I cannot be silent when it ignores the personalism that Christ purchased with His blood. It has forgotten me and the other weak men. It counts me as one of its statistics and rejects me as a son. It demands I recite its dogmas and commands and that I accept its laws. It speaks to me in rites and symbols I barely understand. Its priests preach to me and I cannot answer back. Its ceremonies bore me and I cannot effect a change. I am forced to attend a Mass that has lost touch with the world in which I live. I sit and hear a sermon which makes me struggle to keep my faith. I listen to the ritual changes sent from Rome and I wonder if the men who made them have enough passion to sin, enough fire to hate, enough life to love.

I enter the confessional as a penitent and I am dispatched as a nameless face. My struggles do not matter, my agony counts for naught. I hear confessions as a priest and I am forbidden to understand. A bachelor tries to describe his first honest relationship with a woman and I shout at him of sex. I want to encourage him, to nourish his love, to strengthen his confidence, to praise him for the promiscuity he has abandoned, and I hear myself saying, "Marry her, or give it up." I hear his feeble protest and sense his fear. He tries to speak and I smother him with words. He grows angry and so do I. He came for love, for help, for Christ, and received a formula, an impersonal rebuff. I am forbidden to be a person in my Church, and the men who come to me for mercy and light are denied the same unique and Godlike right.

Voices spoke out long ago insisting that the Church was forbidding Catholics the chance to be persons in the Church. John Henry Newman (1801–1890), the great English scholar, recognized the Church's futility in forcing a system on man, refusing him the chance to search for a personal faith. Newman insisted that it was wrong to forbid a man the chance to seek within the framework of the Church when seeking was the very condition of true faith. The Church forbade a man to entertain doubts, and forbids it still, and attempted to enforce a body of propositions with an assemblage of logical supports that were logical only to the man who believed. Newman sensed our irrelevance when he said: "Logic makes but sorry rhetoric with the multitude; first shoot around corners, and you may not despair of converting by a syllogism. . . . To most men argument makes the point in hand only more doubtful and considerably less impressive."[4]

Newman understood—as did Max Scheler of Germany (d. 1929) and Maurice Blondel of France (d. 1949),[5] religious philosophers who criticized their Church—that religious experience is a personal communication between man and his God. God exists only when He becomes my God, and not merely when I can support Him with my arguments. Religion cannot be imposed from without. A nineteenth-century French scholar wrote that religious truth is: "A person who gives up his secret only to one who is deserving, not as something knowable from without."[6] Or, as Blondel, a layman, wrote at the turn of our century: "[Faith] is not a question of a theoretical adherence to a dogma which is external to us, but the practical insertion into our hearts and conduct of a lifegiving truth."[7] These were the voices of personalism, voices which recalled a Christianity long since dead. Such voices were called dangerous and their thoughts have not until recently come to life within my Church. They were largely lumped with a group called "Modernists," who were condemned by Pope Pius X at the turn of our century.

It is unfortunate that the Church condemned them in such a universal and defensive way. The Modernists understood the needs of modern man. They had seen religion grow stale and impersonal, and in the midst of their exaggerations they clung to an all-important truth: Religion had to find a response within the heart of man. It could not be imposed from without by fear, and long remain relevant. A religion of duty and obligation could only produce pharisees and children. It could make national boundaries more important than God and support the armies of France and Germany, which killed each other in the name of peace. The Church condemned the Modernists because they made God into a creature of man. But at least the Modernists recognized that the Christian Churches had turned God into a system of dogma without devotion, duty without warmth, and law without love. My Church had become a frightened old lady saying her rosary and dreaming of hell. My Church was impersonal and the Modernists were honest enough to admit it, honest enough to be condemned.[8]

Modernism, however, did not die, it only matured. It has clarified its position and demanded that religion be not a docile allegiance to a body of propositions, but an honest search for meaning and for truth. The Church has never given Modernists a chance, and even now, a half century after Pius X's condemnation of the Modernist "heresy," each new priest is asked to swear an oath against it. It is like asking Americans to deny their loyalty to a British King. But young priests swear the oath. Some laugh about it, but some are still too trapped even to laugh. They recite solemnly its mossy paragraphs and promise to preserve the Church from the sinister invasions of modern thought. The hierarchy should rather demand that each priest read the pages of the Modernists rather than condemn them in boyish ignorance. The Modernists were as alive as we are dead. They could distinguish a man from a clinging shadow and knew that religious faith was sick. The "God is dead" prophets are only the wordy children that the Modernists have spawned because no one took them seriously. They demanded that the Church permit a man to be a person, and fifty years later I must still demand.

There must be a place for persons in the Church, a place for differences, a place for variety of search.[9] Is there no place in the Church for the man who only begins to believe? Are there not presently, despite our condemnations and courageous front, as many kinds of Catholics within the Church itself as there are divisions of Protestants and Jews? I am closer to the faith of many ministers than to that of many fellow priests. I know rabbis who are more Christian than I, and unbelievers with whom I share a religious closeness I seldom find at home. Does this mean that I am not a Catholic? Or does it mean that I am beginning to be a person in my Church?

That I must be a person seems so simple and obvious it is difficult to determine how my Church has strayed. Somehow in the world of emperors and kings my Church became arrogant, and it perverted the authority handed it by Christ. It forgot the image of the Shepherd and mimicked all the panoply of kings. The king, surrounded with lords, was supreme. He could be benevolent or cruel, tolerant or calloused, but his decisions were absolute and beyond all recourse. It was a simple world, a decisive world, and it became the only world that could mold the Catholic Church. It taught the Pope to call himself a shepherd while men carried him on a throne. It gave the bishops rings to extend to docile lips, and filled our sanctuaries with incense and brocade. A modern man, removed from such traditions by time, painfully senses the discordant horror of this incredible display. His President wears a business suit, eats hot dogs, and shakes the people's hands. Modern man can play golf with his boss or share a beer with him in a backyard barbeque. He calls his doctor "Bill," and his banker "Bob," and drives on highways where deference is almost indecent. He is not unaware of the symbols of power and prestige, but he has learned that only the mightily insecure must support their office with pomp and silk. He wonders at a Pope who eats alone like an unfriendly mystic or retires to a summer castle to solve the birth-control problem for the world. Modern man wants to be a person and he cannot fathom this childish world of cabbages and kings.

It would be intolerable enough if our priests and bishops saw themselves as governors and corporation presidents, which they very often do. It makes me sad enough when I cannot see a shepherd but only a businessman, or I see only a shepherd who treats me like a sheep. But when I must bow my head before their majesty and hold my tongue no matter what they do, I know that my Church has sold its birthright for the scepter of a king. And a great body of thought, the decadent theology of the Catholic Church, has told her she is right. Catholic theology, which died somewhere between Thomas and Tarzan, permits the Pope to be as untouchable as an emperor, the bishop to be an independent lord, and even the pastor to rule without regard for the person that is man. Until Catholic theology ceases to be an archaic defense of obsolete forms, there cannot be persons in the Church.[10] There can be only quiet serfs who await the orders of a king. There can be no protests, no revolutions, no genuine reforms. The years of Vatican II will remain a superficial gesture by a frightened Church, until theology discovers it is dead.

What has Vatican II really done to make us persons? Has it really helped us by permitting our Mass in English when the prayers and ceremonies continue to leave us cold? Are we persons now that the bishops have voted to share the medieval powers of our Pope? Or do we only have a greater distribution of the same unyielding game? Are we persons now that we have finally freed the Jews and Protestants from our arrogance and wrath? Or have we only duped them into lesser anger when their children marry in our parish Church? Are we persons now that we have promised to respect the religious conscience of each man? Or have we only mumbled words whose meaning still escapes?

Ask the Catholic man whose wife had three affairs before he threw her out. Ask him if his conscience is free. Ask him if Vatican II gave him the permission to marry again, to replace a baby sitter with a wife, to make the decision he's made each night a thousand times. Ask the widow who fears another marriage, but cannot promise to live without the beauty of love and sex. Ask her if the bishops, gathered in august council, solved anyone's problems but their own. Ask the college graduate who hears the normal sermons in his Church and wonders if hell's loneliness could ever be as bad. Ask him if he is a person in his Church, and if the recent council fortified his faith.

Nothing has really changed. We are still as helpless and frightened as before. We will still stand back and watch the humanist struggle with the problems of man. We will continue to preserve the system that has paralyzed us and only offer reforms that are dull and out of date. The authority that forbids us to be persons remains untouchable. The theology that protects this authority is afraid to face itself. Biology did not die with Linnaeus or Lamarck, nor did medicine grow rigid with Harvey and Pasteur. But Catholic theology is a barely stirring corpse, too weak and frightened to leave the universities, too superficial to strike at roots, too timid to move among simple and honest men.

But honest men are not satisfied. They are raging and the world has just begun to hear their cry. They long to be persons more than they have been permitted to realize. Their personalism is not of yesterday. It looks back a hundred years. It is in their blood, in their culture, in the angry silence of their heart. Each decade the vision has grown a little clearer, each decade courageous voices have gained a little strength. Newman did not speak in vain from England, nor did the French priest Lammenais, who died without the Church. They are long dead, as are Blondel and Reusselot, who fought the Church's arrogance in France. Chardin is gone, and so is Buber, and Tillich, too, can speak no more. The simple man has never read them and might not even recognize their names. No matter! He has heard them in the ball parks and the barbershops, in the taverns and restaurants, in simple words, without deference to the author or the text. He has heard them and my Church will know his rage.

He will demand that the Church permit him to be a person, that it serve and not absorb him in his search for God. The Church has no choice. It will hear him, satisfy him, or become a museum for the timid and helpless few. Blondel, the French philosopher, wrote fifty years ago:

There are two ways of looking at the history of philosophical ideas. Either we remain outside the main stream which sweeps through the world of thought and radically exclude everything which is opposed to the system we have adopted . . . and that is to cut ourselves off . . . Or else we try to perceive the birth pangs of humanity and profit by this vast effort, to enlighten it, to bring it to fruition.[11]

Man will not long listen to a Church that ignores the person in a world that has changed superstition into science. My Church is not a big thing in Europe and struggles for its very life. Even in conservative America, the children of the immigrants have learned to read. The protests grow stronger and the smiling peasants start to frown. Man has listened long enough to the severe condemnations of birth control and steady dating, to financial plans which cater to suburban comfort and create schools of questionable value, when overpopulation, war, and the brutality of an industrialized society threaten the humanity he has. Man searches for direction and identity, and hears dull, doctrinal sermons which presume a loyalty that was never asked. He looks for a key to life in a world of pressure and speed, and he is scolded for his failure to receive the sacraments or tithe or support the men's club. Once he could be held by the pressure of his family or the threat of excommunication or the fear of hell. Now, however, if the Church does not reach him, respect him, hear him, he will search for God in his own way. Only a servant Church can assist him in his quest of self and God. He must be a person, because he was made a man.

6. THE CHURCH OF THE

LEGAL CODE

I had spent three months giving Doug instructions in the Catholic faith, and I could see that he pondered my words seriously. One night he told me that he wanted to join my Church and to marry Martha, the Catholic girl who sat with him during each conference. I liked Doug. He was twenty-eight, tall and intense, and three months from his degree in engineering. A place called Korea had postponed his education, a girl called Martha had given direction to his life. I heard him describe in simple language what the Christian vision meant to him. I saw Martha study his lips as he talked.

He told me that his parents had seldom gone to Church. He called himself a Methodist, but knew nothing of the simplicity and beauty of that faith. He had learned a few prayers, knew by heart a handful of scriptural texts, but abandoned all religion in the thrill of high school "sophistication" and sex. Once, he admitted, he had thought that financial success would quiet the rage of his heart. He had been ruthless in his ambition, cynical in his vision of the world. He had smothered the secret protests of his soul with drink and endless activity.

Religion had scarcely occurred to him again until he spent a couple of lonely and frightened nights on one of Korea's hills in the company of a young chaplain. Doug liked this man, and

68

learned from him that God could be found in the warmth of
friendship or in the struggle to draw meaning from the insanity of life. He experienced the same longing for God in his
love of Martha and could not be truly close to her until he
shared her simple faith. He said, with obvious embarrassment,
that he had never known that life could be so alive. His words
did not come easily, the pauses were punctuated by the agitation of his face. It was beautiful to see and hear, to know that
I had helped him in his search for God.

I looked at Martha and saw the eyes of youthful love. She
was twenty-four, a graduate of a Catholic college, a petite
beauty who had asked me to give religious instructions to her
man. She had dated a dozen others, traveled to Europe, held
a challenging job, and won the affection of many friends. Now
she had found the man who would not let her mind be quiet
until she pledged to him her body and her heart. She was one
of the joys of my priesthood, one of the complex creatures
who had penetrated my defenses and involved me in her life.
Her silence was eloquent and I could feel the force of her love.

Then, quietly, Doug told me that there was something else
I should know. He had been married before at eighteen and
lived with his bride for eleven months. He said that it had
really been no marriage at all, rather, the result of a young
man's fears when he discovered that his steady girl was pregnant. They had been married quietly in the Methodist Church
to appease her parents and the chagrin of his righteous father.
Doug had fought with her, slapped her, wept and slept with
her. But he didn't love her, and actually felt relieved when she
lost the baby at seven months. He wanted out, but his father
insisted that he live up to his vow. He tried a few months
more, to no avail, and by mutual agreement he and his teen-
age bride were divorced. Then it was service, school, and
Martha.

He looked for my reaction and waited for my words. I was
confused; the proper legal questions were biting at my lips.
I knew that if he and his first "bride" had been baptized in
their faith, there was nothing left for anyone to do. But I had

to ask the questions. I learned that Doug had been baptized at the age of twelve to please his father's mother, even though he and his father never went to Church. His bride, too, had been christened in her faith and was as ignorant of its meaning as he. But both had been baptized, exchanged "consent," and had marital intercourse, and this would make their marriage forever binding in the awesome courts of Rome.

Doug could beg for consideration because of youthful fear and parental force, and Rome might theoretically accept his excuse. But it could not be proved, and Roman lawyers only want the facts. My submitting his case would be tragically in vain. Doug had no case, only an honest story and a human heart, which would count for naught in the laws and canons of my Church. He could say that baptism had meant nothing to him, that he had not understood the meaning of a married love in Christ. That would not matter. Rome would only want to know if the water of baptism had flowed on his skin, if he had agreed to the marriage, if he had slept in fleshly union with his wife.

I was upset, but my mind continued to struggle with the law. Could I lie for Doug when I knew that he had every right to take Martha as his wife? I did not have the courage. Could I ignore his first marriage? No, the calls would come from the angry and wounded "sinners" who had been denied a marriage in my Church. Could I plead with the bishop, the Pope? No, I would be treated with disdain and would be asked to re-examine the clear and simple law. There was nothing I could do. Doug and his teen-age bride were locked in an eternal union by the canonists of Rome. Doug and his gentle Martha were destined to frustration and defeat. I was trapped, and so were they, regardless of the decision our personal consciences made.

Doug stared at me in unbelief as he read the answer in my eyes. He asked me "Why?" and heard my stupid answer with patient grief. He protested that he had never known what marriage meant, that the pregnancy had scared him half to death. I felt the knot in my stomach as I spoke, the knot that was always there when I defended arrogant and ignorant rulings I could not understand. I knew Doug was not now the boy who had released his adolescent passion in the body of his teen-age date. He was not the boy who let a minister splash him with water to please his grandmother or who let an angry father frighten him into a premature marriage. He was a serious young man who had discovered the meaning of life and loved a girl named Martha who agreed to share his dream. But Rome would not listen, my Church would not listen, and I sat speechless before this tragedy. I sat and watched them weep and walk away.

I had instructed Doug, told him the simplicity of my own faith, told him of a Christ Who spoke of mercy from a hill. I had watched his eyes grow soft, his mouth firm, as I read stories of the Gospel and reflected on their words. I remembered the night I spoke of the prodigal son, the boy who took his father's gift and squandered it in a land of emptiness and sin. I told him of the homecoming, when an aged father lifted a repentant man from his knees and held him in his arms, and called him "Son" again. I knew when I saw Doug's face that he was that "son" who had wandered in confusion and Korea until he found his Father's house. I knew the guilt that lurked in his memory and saw it relax when I spoke of Mary Magdalene. I loved the story and I told it with every passion I possessed. I recalled her loneliness, her morning sickness when she woke to find a stranger in her bed, the pain she felt at every hollow laugh, the longing for love, the ever-present fear of death.

And then I studied him when he heard that Magdalene discovered Christ, met a man who could love her without leering or clawing contemptuously at her body and her breasts, and she learned again to trust. And I knew Doug was Magdalene, the repentant Peter, the doubtful Thomas, the blind beggar, the leper in a cave, the dead young man who rose again to life. I saw him touch Martha's hand and knew that in his love for woman he had found his God. Without her my words were nothing, without her love there was no mystery of mercy and of Christ. He listened to me in the strength of her affection and heard me in the depths of her faithful love. And suddenly, in my office, on an evening I can't forget, I gave him the legal vision of my Church and murdered all his love. What could I say? "I'm sorry"? "Tough break, old man"? "Find another girl"? The prodigal son and Magdalene were frozen on my lips, and Doug and Martha turned and slowly walked away.

I do not exaggerate. I have stabbed a thousand brothers with the knife of law and watched the flowing blood. The names escape me in the mercy of time, but the faces, the expressions, the sad and despairing eyes remind me of the gore upon my hands. I remember the sallow introvert who grinned nervously in my office chair. He told me of his five-year marriage, from which he had recently escaped. His story came out haltingly as he told me of the wife who had made him impotent with her scorn and mockery. He had been married by a priest. But he had not had intercourse for fourteen months, not until one night after a parish picnic and half a case of beer. Then for three and a half years he had waited for her to come home with other men. He heard her laugh on the sofa downstairs, heard her moans of pleasure, heard her mock his vanished manhood as she settled in his bed.

Finally, he had left her before he would murder her in sleep. He had met another girl at work, a plain and gentle girl who made him know he was a man. He had felt the fire of passion for the first time in years and knew that he could have children of his own. He was in love, he could face himself again, and could begin to forget the wounds that had made him welcome death. So he came to his priest. He told his story and learned that one burst of semen had bound him to a whore. No priest could help him, no loophole could free him. He was just another baptized corpse to haunt me in my work. He left my office as sallow as he came, and paused politely at the door to thank me for my time.

No theology could support such madness. Theology, which once had tried to make the words of Christ a vital message in every age, had stood aside before the legal code. I knew no theology, I had never been taught. There was no theology in the seminary, only cubed thought, closed definitions, and narrow law. I was never asked to make a judgment; only a closed decision was handed me by men. I could not go to my bishop; he knew less theology than I. He had been carefully trained in canon law and protected his office by his knowledge of the minutiae of the legal code. He had surrounded himself with advisers who had completed graduate study in canon law. The degree of Doctor of Canon Law (JCD) is one of the most unusual examples of academic game-playing still to survive in our society. It has little to do with education and practically nothing to do with creative and theological thought. Yet the men who are trained in it would qualify any decision that I made.

I could not help the sallow man because Catholic theologians had been overrun by law. They did not speak out, and we can scarcely hear them now. They well know the horror of our legal-minded Church. They laugh at it in private, but they do nothing for the helpless parish priest and his suffering people who are too sad to laugh. They allow the vague rules, whose history tapers off in the twelfth century, to control the Catholic Church. They let a sallow and sorrowful man be destroyed by a rule that can be traced to a medieval scholar named Gratian, the honored Zeus of the canonical myth. They permit the sallow man to walk away in misery, bound by a law which says that semen seals a contract according to the ancient wisdom of Pope Alexander III or the mossy vision of one Hincmar of Rheims. And the legalist is so positive and so powerful, that the theologian prefers his words to Christ's.

God is not dead, Catholic theology is![1] And even the modern efforts are too feeble and too gentle to bring it back to life. The legalist rules! He is the man who solves every doubt by a new and narrow law. He insists on reducing every truth, no matter how complex, to the simple and manageable. He pouted at the Vatican Council and shackled the reformation of my Church. He frightens the bishops in their conferences and makes them quibble so they will not have to act. He binds the pastor, intimidates the parish priest. He can condemn a book without reading it, ban a movie without seeing it, and make a law without explaining it to men. And the theologian snarls in silence or is too frightened, too fond of preferment, too content to snarl at all. A bishop who has never read a book can force a theologian not to speak.

So the theologian is largely silent, or he deals with the simple and manageable truths that matter not to men. He, too, has become a legalist who runs from complexity, and gives the sallow man an answer which has no foundation in the testament of Christ. He lets the legalist rule and reduce every case of conscience to a clear and simple law. He lectures on the beauty of Christian marriage while the men of the streets hear nothing new but law. He lectures on the freedom of conscience while the simple sinners can't escape the law. He speaks of a democratic Church while the parishes flounder in grievances and pain. He asks for more time, for more thought, for deeper reflection, while the simple men, who cannot wait, are sentenced to misery and death.

Would he ask for time if his wife were weeping or his children driving him mad? Would he ask for time if he were losing the woman he loved, or living in fear of hell, or overwhelmed with bitterness he could scarcely control? Would he run from the legalist and ask for time if he could not pay his bills, or face his family, or quiet his screaming nerves? Christ did not ask for time to start a revolution, to challenge pharisees, to threaten the bullies who scandalized the troubled little ones. He called them "hypocrites," "vipers," "clean white coffins full of dead men's bones," and trusted men enough to let them love.

I hate the legalism of my Church. I hate what it has done to Catholics and what it has done to me. It tells me that I must pray my breviary an hour every day. It binds me under pain of sin, because it cannot believe that I will willingly give my time to prayer. But I hate the scheduled prayer that legalism imposes, the fat book of psalms and readings that I must complete. I am forced to read the dull and wordy speeches of men rather than to spend the time in silence with my God. I hate the loopholes that the legalist offers me to avoid this obligation, since such excuses only make me realize how unimportant is my prayer. He tells me that if I pay a few dollars to a missionary society, I will receive permission to say my rosary instead of my breviary when I drive a given distance in my car. But if I do not pay the money, I am bound to recite my boring breviary even if I drive my car. He told me this, and even as I hated him, I once assented to his words.

I hate the legalism that obliges me to anoint corpses with the holy oil of the last rites in hopes that a soul yet lingers in a cold body. I am embarrassed when the nurses pull back a sheet to reveal the withered flesh while I rub in my oil and whisper foreign words. It is superstitious magic, but the busy nurses soberly watch me out of pity or respect. In my heart I know I am wasting my time, that even if the body still nourishes life, the unconscious and dying man needs no oil of mine to lead him to his God. But I have forced myself to keep the law and to keep alive the simple ignorance that the Middle Ages handed modern Catholic men.

I condemn the legalist who can tell a Catholic that he must be married by a priest. I know the history of his law and realize that his kind once demanded, well into the eighteenth century, that even Protestants could only be married by a priest. I hate such arrogance, which forces Catholics to bring protesting Protestant spouses to the sanctuary of my Church, to ignore consciences and feelings, to blackmail simple men with the threat of no marriage unless they keep the smug, archaic rules. I hate the promises men of other faith must sign to take a Catholic bride. I hate the laws that can trample on Protestant tradition and wound the pride of Jews. But most of all I hate myself for keeping them.

I hate the legalism that tells a Catholic girl that her maid of honor must be a member of her Church. It is not enough that this witness to the wedding be a loyal friend who believes in marriage and the permanence of love. It is not enough that a best man be an honest man, but only that he be a Catholic no matter the weakness of his faith. I hate the law that tells Protestant grandparents that they cannot act as baptismal sponsors for their daughter's Catholic child. The very law of sponsors has no meaning, and in many cases, even an idle janitor will do. The priest's housekeeper can be summoned from her kitchen to witness legally the pouring of the water, and wonder what is happening to the pie that's in the oven. But a non-Catholic relative or friend cannot fulfill the law. Our legalists cannot even permit the parents to choose the child's name, but ask them to honor him with a proper patron saint. It does not occur to them that this tradition is outmoded, so loyal is their keeping of the law. To be called Mary is apparently more Christian than to be called Apple Blossom, unless, of course, "Apple" can be attributed to the saintly Apollonia, who died in innocence and peace.

I hate the legalism that teaches Catholics about indulgences and measures the amount of help that they can provide for purgatory's suffering souls.[2] It teaches that a three-word prayer is as valuable as seven years of public penance, so mighty is the spiritual treasury of the Church. And even though the theologian knows better, as does any man who thinks, the legalist controls our propaganda and leads our children on. He teaches them that prayers, said to gain an indulgence, must involve some motion of the lips. That will make them "public" as required by the law. He tells them that a series of indulgences can be gained only on successive visits to the Church, so obliges them to step momentarily outside the Church, then to return and pray some more. And the workmen obey, so do the nuns and priests, the doctors and professors, in loyalty to the legalism of their Church.

I hate the legalism that tells Catholics they cannot participate in the rites of another Church. I hate the narrowness and fear that forbid me to pray with Jews in their temple, to join the Methodists in their petitions and their hymns. I have not the nervous faith of the legalist who cannot look at the writings of other religions, who cannot challenge the doctrines of his Church. I can pray with any man, kneel with him, sing with him, share his communion or honor his belief. Only a legalist can ask me to love him with words while I shame him by the rudeness of my faith. He is as honest as I, and therefore as much in touch with God as I. And I will show him this by my respect for his faith even as I grow in the fulfillment of my own.

I despise the legalism that forbids a non-Catholic friend to receive communion in my Church.[8] I cannot call him brother if I will not share my food. The legalist tells me it would be sacrilegious for him to eat at my table, that this would make a mockery of God. The legalist runs a segregated restaurant, with a list of tawny rules, fixed firmly to the door. Only Catholics may come, only Catholics may eat, and they must be the Catholics whom he carefully approves. He stands as a snobbish headwaiter and ignores the hunger of the patrons who come without a tie.

I hate the legalism that preserves the ceremonies that have lost their meaning and explains the ancient rites that time has robbed of power to inspire men. I hate the legalistic wranglings in Rome that have made the prayers of Holy Week a bore. I watch the people on Good Friday and know their numbness as they listen to readings which are irrelevant and wearily say "Amen" to the endless petitions we should discard. I see them shuffle at the Easter Vigil as we chant over candles and water with dullness, and hurry through the dry selections from the Old Testament. I see them leave our churches in weariness and I detest the bureaucracy that will not give them what they need.

I reject the legalism that tells me I must support the Catholic schools to be loyal to my faith, the law that demands that Catholics support their Church while pastors erect expensive monuments to themselves. I despise the laws that tell a man to fast and do not permit him to select a penance that has some meaning in his life. And, most of all, I hate the legalism that forces Catholics to come each week to Mass, and then congratulates itself on the thriving life that packed pews and parking lots attest. It is this legalism that has forced hell to the fore of every Catholic conscience, that has muddled Catholic minds with the plenitude of sin.

And our poor, timid theology stands back and permits the

legalists to make madmen of us all. I hate the legalistic theology that can describe the angels and divide them all in choirs, that can name the devils and tell frightened men that evil spirits lure them into sin. It can make Adam's sin the source of sickness and death, his disobedience the cause of loneliness and unrestrained emotion. It can tell of limbo where the unbaptized babies go. It can package grace and measure all the mysteries that God has offered man. It can classify sins, enumerate the gifts of the Holy Spirit, order and arrange every virtue, name each attribute of God. It can make Christ so divine that he isn't human, his mother so marble that she cannot cry. It makes the Trinity into a course in logarithms, and turns the Apostles into a modern hierarchy. It tells me nothing new from eighth grade until I am ordained a priest, and does it with solemnity and dramatic frowns.

Legalism has drained our theology, enslaved our people, made hostile our non-Catholic friends. It permits bishops to stomp on priests, to ignore problems, to hoard money, to live in splendor, and to forget the poor. It permits pastors to destroy their assistants, to burden their people with the financial pressures born of personal appetite for prestige, to ignore the suffering of men, to mistreat nuns, to build a parish around their own convenience. It permits young priests to give sermons without preparation, to hear confessions with arrogance, to revel in undeserved praise, to escape blame, to remain immature, to grow ambitious, to avoid responsibility, to wither intellectually, to die emotionally, to drown in self-pity, to overlook the fears and feelings of men.

Legalism allows Catholics to feel holy when they are only docile, Christian when they are only the scrupulous observers of rules. It makes them proud that they are not Protestant, smug that they are free from sin. It causes them to boast about their mediocre schools, to exaggerate the evil in the world, to fear involvement, to take no action without the priest, to have no opinions without authority's support. It makes them suspicious, prejudiced, timid, blind to facts, disinterested in programs that do not serve the Church.

The legal mind is a restricted and impoverished mind which cannot move without a law to support each flicker of its brain. It is not satisfied to follow the norms of Christian love, or even to discover them in the romance of an involved life. The legalist laughs at such discovery, and calls an honest search for God a selfish and indulgent way of life. He only knows the way of law, and, for him, a Church which is not smothered in law is a religion without absolutes, a society without bones, a body without a spine. His way is the only way, even if millions tell him of their pain.

But we are Catholics, too, those of us who will not be bound by empty law. We will not abandon our Christ because a legalist says we must. We want living sacraments and not the tired forms that do not speak. We want a Mass that offers us food and love, and not a sterile ceremony that leaves us bored. We want to live by our conscience, to reflect on our experience, to hear the words of Christ, and not to be frightened into subjection by the cold force of law. We will not abandon our friends who feel obliged to practice birth control, who find peace in remarriage, who leave the priesthood for another way of life. We want a Church that will serve us in our search for happiness and fulfillment, and not smother us before we discover who we are.

We ask more of our Church than we ask of our government, more than we ask of industry, more than we ask of our parents and our home. We know that the Church is a society, that it must have its structure and law. But it cannot worship structures and multiply laws until man has no life or conscience of his own. Newman said it very well: "Conscience is a personal guide, and I use it because I must use myself; I am as little able to think by any mind but my own as to breathe with another's lungs. Conscience is nearer to me than any form of knowledge."[4]

Conscience is God's hand upon me, to restrain me, to lead me, to assure me that I am never lost, to convince me that I cannot live as every other man, to approve me when I do the honest thing. And my Church and I, my Church of the legal code, have labored long to tear men's consciences away.

I cannot heal the wounds I caused, nor calm the fears that I in honest ignorance forced upon the men I truly sought to help. I can only say I'm sorry, and promise never again to sell my conscience to the law. I cannot forget the woman of fifty who came to me in the parish church several years ago. She had been excommunicated from the Church because she had divorced her husband and married again. She had been living with her second husband, a non-Catholic, almost twenty years and heard from a friend that she could be reinstated if she promised not to have intercourse with him. She could cook his meals, wash his socks, make him laugh, share TV, but she could not join him in his bed. I told her that I would petition the bishop for this special privilege, called a "brother-sister arrangement," if she was sincere in her request. She thanked me with many tears and agreed to live this sexless life to know the joy of the sacraments of her Church.

Her petition was granted and she was informed that she could not receive communion in the parish Church, because there were people who knew the facts of her case. She insisted that this didn't matter and she would drive each Sunday to another town. She was also informed that this "privilege" could not promise her a burial in the Church. This hurt her deeply, and she made me promise that I would be at her funeral even if there was not a Mass to honor her in death.

For a few years I did not hear from her, and then one day she wrote me in the touching tones that indicate a fear of sudden death. She told me of the times that she had put her husband off when he came to her in bed. She told me of the confessions when the priest threatened to revoke her privilege if she broke her promise of celibacy again. She wrote of her longing to receive communion in the parish Church. But most of all she wanted the assurance that she could be buried from the Church. She did not want to die in disgrace or shame her children and her friends. So she wrote to me, the priest who got her the "privilege" she would never forget, the privilege that made her half a Catholic and half a wife.

I could not write her what my conscience suggested. I could

only give her the feeble comfort permitted by my Church. I told her she was not even sixty and death was most likely many years away. I told her that the Church might change its stand and that the modern debates in theology gave her a solid reason to hope. I felt sure that she could be buried in the Church.

But I could not tell her to be wife to the non-Catholic man who had lived with her for almost twenty years, who had fathered her two children and taken her out of town to Mass. I could not tell her to love him the way he wanted. I could not ask her to atone to him for the ignorance of her Church. I could only make promises for a funeral Mass when he couldn't have her any more. I could only make her his sister when he married her as his wife.

Now, however, I am not so frightened and I can write her from my heart:

I was wrong when I insisted that you make a brother out of that strong and noble man. I was wrong when I demanded that you abdicate his bed. Follow your heart and love him as your conscience will permit. I hope you can take him to yourself tonight, without guilt, without fear, and apologize for me, for you, for the arrogance of our Church. He is your husband if you believe he is, and the pen of a legalist cannot tear him from your side. Hold him close to you, he is kinder than most. Touch him gently, he has been wounded in his heart. If he has not taught you of God, then you will never learn. Make him your man, your husband, your strength, your contact with your God.

I will rest a little easier, knowing that you have joined him in his bed. But if you cannot be his wife until the Church offers you the chance, then so be it. But tell him that I wrote to you and read him what I said. And tell him I am sorry for the misery I caused. Then, at least, I may forget your tears, and his, and feel less a lawyer than a priest.

7. CONFESSION AND MORTAL SIN

Whenever I take non-Catholic visitors through a Catholic Church, nothing arouses their curiosity like the confessional. They see it as a secret little room hidden in the corner of the Church where Catholics come and whisper their sins and failures to the priest. They think of their own sins, and wince at the thought of revealing them to anyone. I try to move to other items of interest in the church, but the visitors' glance is fixed on the confessional. They remember the stories they have heard, the movies where priests confronted criminals or sinful women in dramatic confessions, and the fears of their Catholic friends who felt compelled to get to confession before a Saturday date.

Catholics, however, take the confessional in stride. They seldom question its value or significance, presuming that there is no other satisfactory way to find peace of conscience and freedom from sin. They love it and hate it, fear it and praise it, rush to it regularly or stay away for years. It has offered them peace and fulfillment, discouragement and bitterness, but it is at the heart of their Church's structure. Seldom do they forget it, no matter how far they wander from the Church. They know it is a sacrament, a sacred ritual which offers them God's forgiveness in tangible form. It is not merely the therapy of self-accusation, nor the comfort of vanished guilt. It is a symbolic contact with God, the sense of His presence and absolving hand. It is a mystery entrusted to sinful men to extend in time the love and mercy of God.

Catholics believe that Christ established this sacred ritual of forgiveness and encouragement. It is the court of appeals where the sinner's own honesty is the only jury, his own conscience the ultimate judge. The woman in adultery comes here to reveal the weakness that her husband would never understand. The angry adolescent comes to confess the contempt for his father he fears to admit to his closest friend. The alcoholic comes when his wife and children have turned their backs, when his employer has lost his patience, and his friends merely nod and back away. The single girl comes to explain the affair that would kill her mother if she knew; the homosexual comes when parents are disgraced and doctors cannot help; the little boy comes to whisper in fear his first awareness of the sexual urge. Young and old come to find forgiveness for their "mortal sins."

Mortal sin, to a Catholic, is a serious offense which severs man's friendship with God. It is "the greatest evil in the world," more serious than Vietnam, more final than death, more tragic than the murder of a child. It can descend like lightning into the life of peasant and president alike. It is not an infrequent occurrence in the lives of Catholics, although it usually reserves its fury for certain stress periods in life. Adolescence is such a period. The Catholic teen-ager lives in the shadow of mortal sin. He knows the three simple conditions for its fearful presence: a serious matter, sufficient reflection and awareness of the evil deed, and full consent of the will. When these three conditions are present, a single action leaves man in a state of rejection by God. Were he to die while in this state, he would know the pain of an eternal hell. He could utter no plea in his own behalf, the time for excuses and reforms would be over, and he would burn forever in misery and regret.

The conditions are not too easy to apply. But the sinner refuses to take a chance. The odds are too great. He might wonder if missing Mass or masturbating[1] is really very wrong. He might question the seriousness of his passionate fondling of his girl friend, or the drinking party that provoked the neighbors to summon the police. He might even debate with himself the extent of his awareness, or the freedom he possessed at the time of his sin. He might search for excuses, recall the state of mind that drove him, the circumstances that precipitated his behavior. Probably, however, he will run to confession as quickly as he can lest he risk the sudden death that would summon him to hell.

The average Catholic learns from his youth the agony of guilt, and will struggle with its pangs through college and business, through retirement and terminal illness. While he has heard that confession is a sacrament of gentle mercy, it is often to him a tense ritual of anxiety and guilt. While he comes as the prodigal son, he often faces an angry executioner instead of an understanding father. Theoretically, he knows what confession *should* mean in terms of confidence and peace, but practically it *does* mean a life immersed in guilt. The exceptional may well escape such suffering because they have conquered or repressed the human drives which make of confession the feeding ground of guilt. They are not living in conscious fear of hell, because their sins are the gentle violations of impatience and neglected prayers. They come to confession to receive a merit badge, to hear the congratulations of the priest. But the rest of us, the sinners, the weak and confused, the human and passionate, come to whisper our mortal sins to the priest. We sense his anger, feel his hostility, endure his sermons, and dare not question his naïve solutions to the temptations we face.

We come because we have learned from childhood that confession is the only safe way to escape mortal sin. We have been taught that God will indeed forgive us without confession—but on two conditions: if our sorrow is "perfect," that is, if it stems from our concern for the injury we have done God rather than our fear of going to hell; and if our delay in confession is not due to procrastination. We are never certain, however, of the "perfection" of our sorrow until we have received the forgiveness of the priest. I can remember as a boy, when I gave in to the weakness of my flesh, trying desperately to speak my "perfect" sorrow, only to live in misery until I went to confession. Then, for a moment, I knew exhilaration and hope, only to flounder in guilt when another temptation flattened me in "mortal sin."

I can well understand, as a priest, the college boy who called me at midnight and asked for confession before he dared sleep. He came to my office in a state of almost hysterical fear. He sobbed like a little child, tried to tell me what had happened, but only wept the more. Finally, he calmed himself enough to tell me his "mortal sin" with obvious regret. He had been petting with his girl friend. Usually she had pushed his hand away. This night, however, she had been as "weak" and curious as he. He assured me that they had not gone "all the way," but realized that they were now in "mortal sin." He had returned home, struggled with his conscience, and called me to free him from his sin. I knew the forgiveness I offered would give him a night's rest. I tried to talk to him, to assure him that he had done nothing so terrible, but the fears learned in childhood blotted out my words. He only wanted forgiveness, and begged for it, came too frightened to be ashamed of what I might think. He felt obliged to tell me each passionate motion of his hand, each fleshly sensation, to describe his ardor in each intimate detail. And when I forgave him, he sobbed his thanks, told me I was the "greatest," and strode happily away. But he would be back.

And this young man is no exception in our system. He is the preview of the anxious adult who rushes to confession to escape the fire of hell. He is one in a series of frightened sinners who come to reveal their "mortal sins." Most of the mortal sins they bring center around Mother Lust and her numberless children. There are the "impure thoughts" and "impure desires" which are "mortal" only if they are nourished and embraced. This distinction requires the sinner to decide precisely when they are "nourished and embraced." The Catholic conscience avoids the dilemma by "playing it safe" and confessing to the priest. Then there is "petting," which includes the sexual touch, and "necking," which covers untold varieties of abortive love-making. Again, the ordinary man dares not fool with the fires of hell, so he assembles his "sins" like a giant grocery list and checks them off in turn. Marriage brings its own "mortal sins," and the Catholic hardly returns from the honeymoon before the conscience wrangling starts again.

There are, of course, mortal sins on our books which do not center on sex. The only one that occurs with any frequency is that of missing Mass. In addition, each conscience will have its special sin that keeps it in turmoil. There are prepared lists of sins around many Catholic churches to help the sinner decide what separates him from God. Such lists dissect the commandments and challenge the want ads for compact information. Visits to fortunetellers are lined up with false oaths and superstitions. Then come profane speech, and warnings to the nagging wife and stubborn child, to brawlers, drunkards, and thieves, to the doubters, the despairers, and the suicide-seekers who lost their nerve. Even charity, which once was the motif of every Christian law, is perforated into a dozen little species of rancor and deceit. Not all the sins on the list are "mortal," but each Catholic seems to have his own version of the boundary between "mortal" and "venial" sin. No amount of instruction, for example, can convince Mike that it is not a "mortal sin" to say "God damn it" when the Yankees lose to Boston in the ninth.

Most Catholic Churches cater to the troubled conscience of their children. Confessions are heard with great regularity.[2] Some parishes offer confessions every evening; others, during morning Mass. Nearly every parish lines up its penitents on Saturday afternoon and evening to permit the guilt-ridden people to return to their weekend in peace. Each person is given approximately a minute, unless he happens to be a stray sheep who returns or a sinner who is involved in a problem of sex. The confessional is swamped at Christmas and Easter, and priests may well listen to the whisper of sin for a dozen hours a day. But no matter when the light of the confessional signals the priest's readiness to absolve the weakness of men, no matter the day or the hour, the people appear.

Some, however, do not come. Some are too terrified to recite their secret sins, so they live in guilt instead. Some grow discouraged and give up on confession. Others postpone it until a time when they hope they will be better able to live within the narrow boundaries of the Catholic conscience. They stay away and try to ignore the stinging reminders from the pulpit, hoping they will not be stricken with unexpected death. Many, indeed, do not come, but few escape the fear that was nourished in their mind from childhood and troubles them whenever they think of God.

It is hard to relate such routine guilt and organized forgiveness to the gospel of Jesus Christ. Our confessional becomes a travesty when we compare it to the Christian vision of pardon. Christ promised freedom and we offer imprisonment and guilt.[3] Christ spoke of joy and we offer only a break in tension to be followed by a more painful relapse. Christ gave us a new direction and we provide a sacred automaton which binds the very heart it promises to release. We don't offer hope or confidence or love. We don't help a man to understand his weakness or encourage him to be patient and to grow. We tell each man that he is uniquely sinful, and we urge him to produce an ideal self which is likely years away. We permit his guilt to mount on the strength of his repeated failures and we teach him to resolve with spiritual help[4] problems which are emotional in origin. We beat him down when he needs a hand to lift him from his pain. We ask him to be a robot when he tries to tell us he is a man of flesh and blood. He comes for understanding and the courage to endure; we treat him with coldness and routine dispatch.

And despite our abuse, he is helpless. We have carefully taught him, simple or sophisticated, that there is no place else to go. He is bound in the guilt we taught him, and held to the narrow forgiveness we provide. He comes to Christ and he hears an impersonal voice. I do not see him when I hear his confession. I do not know his background, his circumstances, his pain. I only hear his whisper and docile acceptance of everything I say. He dares not argue with me, he dares not even tell me of the progress he notes. He tells me his sins, waits for my judgment, and rushes out to admit another of the waiting sheep. He even thanks me as he leaves, because he has not the confidence to find peace without the comfort of my absolution. I am the only one who can free him from his mortal sins and make it possible for him to live without the ever-present fear of hell.

He does not know that theologians are presently questioning the very notion of "mortal sin."[5] He may not hear of such valid speculation for another dozen years. Yet the best of our theologians well know that we cannot justify our childish vision of mortal sin. It has been too easy to sever one's friendship with God. Such a vicious conception of God as we have known makes of our Creator a Prussian general or an angry Irish judge. It sees "mortal sin" everywhere and makes of life a tightrope on the brink of hell. The Catholic only knows that a single Mass not attended because of weariness can be a mortal sin. This makes little sense, though the average Catholic is too frightened to reflect.

Who can love the God of this theology, the God Who can dismiss His friends with such readiness and ease? Even weak men do not break their friendship with one another without long and serious cause. If God is so sudden in His judgment and so petulant in His anger, who could take Him seriously or hope to win His love? One argument does not break our relationship with a friend. Nor does a single act of greed or egotism or self-indulgence ordinarily tear our hearts apart. A friend accepts an excuse, and under no circumstances would he destine us to hell.

Our notion of mortal sin is as sick as any element of our theology. It presumes that when man acts he is in complete possession of himself, that he can contain his whole personality in a single act. But how often in human life can a single act build or destroy a friendship? How often does any man perform a "centered action," a truly "self-representing deed"? Love is built through a thousand experiences. It is compounded of laughs and tears, gentle forgiveness and secret fears, boredom, a new baby, a lost job, a miscarriage, a hundred midnight snacks, days when communication suffers, nights when a common pillow cannot create unity, and other days and nights when the flow of hearts is free.

A man cannot stand back after a week or ten days and say: "How is our love?" He cannot evaluate a marriage or a friendship by a temper tantrum or an occasional cycle of discouragement or emptiness. He can only rely on the thousand fibers that wove a love to sustain it from the wear of routine and rebuff. Love will fight closeness as often as it will seek it out. Man cannot even measure or chart his love; there is no way to reduce it to a list of rules or a graph with peaks and valleys. Only occasionally can he look back and sense that he and his wife have been growing apart or that his dread of failure has made him tense and irritable, or that his restlessness has taken him from his duties as husband and father. Only over a year or two can a couple recognize that artificial appetites for status and social prominence have cooled a friendship. Even then they do not panic, but attempt to move gradually onto another plateau of love. Not every argument can become a crisis and demand a formal retraction of angry words or selfish indulgence. Mature love has more confidence than that. It does not have to make "firm and sudden resolves" or "absolute promises of amendment." It has some respect for itself and simply takes a step forward without looking back. Least of all does it try to remember the name and number of each offense and to report it in a confession to be reviewed in domestic court.

Why should man's relationship with God be different? Why should confession have to be a detailed list of thoughts and actions, and not merely a calm and general appraisal of life with a burst of new hope for the future?[6] Why must a man report each serious sin in number and kind, and not merely indicate the direction and growing maturity of his love? Why must he be frightened from his childhood with the philosophy of "Better be safe than sorry"? It is only a moral theology steeped in legalism and casuistry that has required confession to be more like an income tax report than a personal contact with the holy God. If a person were only expected to make a private confession on rare and important occasions, and not after every individual "mortal sin," then confession could be truly personal. The priest could be a person and not an absolving machine. The penitent could be a person and not an irritating whisper in a long gray line. A kind of general confession could be held on regular occasions, whereby a man could confess his faults silently to God and hear the forgiveness provided for all the people in the name of Christ.

The format of private confession would change. There would be no need for anonymity (though it could be had), nor would there be any need for the production-line approach. The Catholic prefers anonymity because he is forced to list the details of embarrassing sins, and is made to think that his sins are unusual and sordid. He would not want anonymity if he could discuss the realities of his life and hopes, and talk with a priest who is human enough to understand. I have heard numerous private confessions in this "open" way during college retreats, and the numbers of penitents kept me busy far into the night.

Recently I gave a retreat at a Catholic college. I offered a new approach to confession which did not bother with lists of sins or embarrassing details. I told the students of my own struggles with the sins of the flesh that trouble every man. I insisted that each man shares our weakness and that no one of us can judge another's guilt. I asked that they not be too hard on themselves, that they not stay away from communion or confession because they could not achieve total reform. The results of such confessions were exciting. The students had formerly found confession as dull and meaningless as I. They hated to go as strongly as I hated to hear their lists of sins. Suddenly, confession began to make sense, and the students, long denied a hearing by the Church, continued to come for several days and nights.

The procedure was simple. We just sat and talked, and at times smoked a cigarette. It was far from a "Bless me, Father, here are my sins" approach. It was a conference about the things of the spirit and the hopes of a person. I asked for no details, although often enough they discussed comfortably even the problems of marriage and courtship, or their concern with the emptiness of modern life. I didn't sit as the judge of personal conscience, since no man has such a right. I was only the judge of sorrow and our presence together made such a judgment unnecessary. We merely talked about the goals of courtship and marriage, the secret dangers of self-deception and of self-indulgence masquerading as love. We talked of the difficulty of prayer in modern society, of the hunger for money and success, of the indifference which infects young minds faced with a term of duty in Vietnam. I shared with them some of my own experience, and that of the many people with whom I had worked. I did everything but read to them from the gory lists of traditional sins. Most of all, I listened,[7] and for the first time in my life, I began to understand what confession could mean. I heard young hearts screaming to find relevance in our Mass and sacraments. I heard honest doubts about the dogmas which had been inherited, but never embraced. After our confession, we knelt down together in the presence of God and I asked His forgiveness in the name of Christ.

I had not heard the confessions, for once, of the gentle girls whose only dates were with eagle scouts on tennis courts on sunny afternoons. Nor had I heard only of sex and anger for a change. I heard the doubts of those who wondered if communion could possibly produce a change in character. I heard valid questions about the worth of religious education. I heard about pressures from home and the secret fears of the lonely, the deep prejudices, the hatred for parents, the tales of honor students who came to school, and remained there only to please an ambitious father or mother. I heard men and women talking to a man and heard dozens tell me that they had rediscovered their faith.

Catholics are ready for confession in such a framework. They are sick of playing games and running to different confessors to whisper regularly their secret sins behind silent screens. They are tired of a morality which can chart their acts before they begin, and can treat extenuating, simply human circumstances as if they did not exist. Confession has become a public bath with a single bar of soap and a common towel, and modern young Catholics are growing to ignore it with maturity and experience. They are demanding a confession which offers them a chance to be a person.

I can hear the legalists tell me about the *objective* moral law. I can even watch the traditional theorems working in the pulsing of their veins. And yet I know that morality can never be universally imposed. It can only be the growing experience of an individual, and short of this is mere conformity.[8] Even the scholastics have seen morality as the "moral quality of a personal act," and, as such, it cannot be univocally enforced. Morality and moral views depend largely on knowledge and experience, and I cannot tell this young man or woman what intercourse before marriage means to every Christian. I can only ask what it means to him or her. If purity, in the legalistic and traditional sense, means nothing but a game to this person, then it is no longer purity, but only mute compliance with a law that belies experience. This does not mean that I agree with him, it does not even mean that he is certain of his own position. It only means that together we are attempting to measure this relationship in terms of God and human love. It only means that he has a chance to grow, to make mistakes, to become himself.

We have never been able to talk to Catholics about goals in confession. We have never been able to talk about anything except to comment on a tailored recitation of "sins." For this reason we have often not reached them where they felt, but only where they said they thought. We talked to them in quiet groups without dialogue, and even when we had them alone in confession, we were satisfied with a routine recalling of the accepted sins. We did not teach them to be responsible to God, only to be accountable to us.

A mathematical confession without dialogue permits the priest to absorb the conscience of the person. It prevents the individual from achieving honest self-knowledge. He may well be satisfied to confess the same way for twenty years, still accusing himself of "swearing thirty times," "fighting with his wife eleven times," and "thinking dirty thoughts about women a dozen times—more or less." Meanwhile he may be organized to keep Negroes out of his neighborhood, play at a golf course that blackballs Jews, and value every human relationship in terms of money or personal prestige. Simply to tell his sins and to promise reform can be a simplistic and self-centered search for "personal holiness." Man becomes holy with someone else, and only when he begins to recognize his responsibility to the "other," the "thou," is he even capable of the religious experience—no matter the frequency and the accuracy of his confessions.

Obviously, such a personal, truly individual confession as I propose could not be made frequently, nor would it be required. General confessions in a group would provide a man with the needed opportunity to express his sorrow regularly and to know the power of his victory in the risen Christ. In such a confession the person would confess his sins silently to God and hear the public words of forgiveness spoken in the name of Christ. The private confession could be held by appointment at special times (as it frequently is in the Episcopal Church). Sometimes it might not be needed for years, or at other times it might be needed every couple of months. The Catholic people, long trained in the fearful theology of mortal sin, would have to be conditioned for such new freedom, but it would not take as long as some may think. Recently, for example, I gave a day of recollection to a group of sisters. The superior and I had an honest talk. She told me her views on confession and they were surprisingly like my own. She told me of the painful routine of weekly confession and the indifference she felt toward the confessor who had heard her sins for almost four years. Gradually, she had grown old enough or wise enough to call a halt to this programmed boredom. Presently, she goes to confession only when she feels the need or comes in contact with a priest who can reach her in a special and human way. After years of indifference, confession has meaning for this honest nun.

Priests, of course, might object that they have neither the time nor the counseling ability for such an approach to confession. But the priest would have time—the endless hours he currently spends hearing the confessions of the fearful and guilt-ridden. He would have time if he were permitted to be a servant of the word and the sacraments, and not a fund raiser, a teacher of high-school Latin, a band director, a bazaar chairman, a bingo caller, and the emergency entertainer at the ladies' guild when Betty Crocker doesn't show up. The priest may well lack the techniques of dialogue, since his education taught him to be a part-time pope and sublime inquisitor. He could, however, be taught. He could learn something of the dynamics of personal interview and dialogue, and learn a great deal about human motivation and the ingredients that compose a person. He would have to discipline himself to learn to listen more than he talks. He would have to understand that no one can impose moral views on another, and that life is a process of growth and not a large vacuum that collects the infallible conclusions of medieval theologians. He would even have to acquire respect for the ideals of his own society, and if he ever assumed the role of prophet-critic, he would reveal that he was as much a man of his own day as a resounder of Christian tradition. Especially would he have to learn to believe in man and to know that the greatest asset in man's search for Christ is the very human heart that God has fashioned in His own image.

The priest could even have a better picture of man if he were not tied to a tired and impossible vision of the original sin of Adam. Original sin, in its traditional expression, is the sin of Adam which all men have inherited. The priest, and all Catholics, have learned that this inheritance made of the prize product of God's creation a limping and wounded lover living on the fringe of self-deception and divine fury. Man was not destroyed by Adam, in the accepted view of the Eden myth, but would be the eternal puppet of passion and ignorance. He was doomed to death, and even after baptism had put him on the road of life, he would wear the tearful scars of Adam's betrayal.

The theology of original sin has moved a long way from Augustine's view that it was passed through the union of parents who bore their children in the fire of carnal love.[9] Most of such progress in theological thought, however, has taken place within

the last five years. We are beginning to recognize that Adam is
only a symbol of man, the concrete embodiment of man's
struggle to discover love amid the feebleness of the flesh and
the loneliness of the spirit. Original sin is the sin of a world that
crucified Christ and rejects His way of peace for a life of anxiety and isolation.[10] It cannot point to a single pair of parents
nor blame a curious man and woman in a mythical garden. It
cannot be contained in a solitary act of disobedience, but can
only gradually be seen in the gathering anger and hatred of
men. One must stand back to see it in the wars and massacres
of man, in the violence of the cities and the pillage of the
countries. It can be seen in the father who loves his family even
as he runs from them, or hurts them, or draws their very blood.
It can be seen not as a static and historic offense, but as a
dynamic reality dividing man himself even as it divides the
world. It can grow when man teaches man distrust and hatred,
and can wane when man embraces man in love. It is the sin of
a world, not of a single parent, the groan of a creature who is
expected to be a creator even as he whines like an animal to be
left in isolation.

In a society of superstition and pseudoscience, the myth of
Adam's indulgence of Eve could answer each question about
the origin of evil and death. In such a world evil had to have
parents even as thunder and lightning were tied to some magi-
cal source. But we do not live in such a world. We know that
the authors of Genesis knew nothing of "original sin,"[11] but
only recognized sadly that man could deny bread to his hungry
brother and kings could sleep with maidens who had not the
freedom to protest. They knew that evil was in the world and
they only said that it was not the creation of the holy God.
They saw it as a kingdom to itself, with its prince of darkness
and its code and covenant and gods of metal and stone. Even
in Christian times, Paul would speak of evil as if it had arms
and legs and the crown of a perverted king.[12] He did not hesitate in his Letter to the Romans to borrow the Adam symbol
and to make of it a striking contrast to the liberating Christ.
Paul was not interested in tracing the family tree of sin and

hatred; he only wanted to announce that man had new causes to rejoice in the victory of the risen Christ. He, with all of his reputation for anti-feminism and sexual anxiety, was a herald of victory and not a messenger of sin's supremacy. Paul saw Christ as a beginning, the promise of triumph, the pledge of new growth, the bearer of "good news" to an unhappy world, the trumpet sound of victory.

After twenty centuries of "victory," the battle is not yet won. Nor will it be until the world is no more. The "original sin," man's fear of love, remains, and yet each new generation can sense a growing freedom from its power. Our parents have known its force and passed it on, but we live with the hope that it will not reign as actively in our own lives. We believe that our personal struggle to love will be reflected in the lives of our children, as "original sin" loses more of its fury with each step forward that man takes in creative love. No man can measure the evil of his generation, nor can he accurately compare it with a world in which he did not live. But if Christianity means anything, and is not merely a single and passing state of man's development, it must mean that we have edged forward a step with the love that our parents transmitted to us.

Our parents left us evil as well, such as the deep-seated prejudices which they acquired in fear and ignorance. They left us insecurities that we conquer only with difficulty. They left us intolerance and superstition, shortsightedness and insensitivity. They left us quarrels with our brothers, desperately unresolved. They left us distrust of the world and its joys. They left us "original sin," and we shall, unwittingly, pass it on to the children we have been called to love. We cannot look back and blame an historic Adam for his feeble resistance to a snake's request. We can only look to a kind of man that lives in every man, the man whose "demon" conquers his spirit, the man who knows even as he falls that he can and must rise. I am such a man, and so are you, and together we have crucified Christ when we ignore the power of His resurrection. This is the remnant of the "original sin."

Such a view of original sin makes the mystery of mortal sin

less obscure. The true "mortal sin," the true sin of death, is that human existence which approves Christ's death by the consistent refusal to love. Perhaps such a sin can be committed in a single act, but rarely is man so in possession of himself that he can endorse Calvary by missing Mass, or acting "impurely," or shutting out his wife and children. Perhaps after a year, or several months, he can look back on his life and know that his goal, his "ultimate concern" has been unworthy of a child of God. He must, however, recognize the "evil" he has done. We ask too much of man when we see a rejection of God in a burst of passion or fear or bitterness. And if man himself cannot agree that his action cuts him off from God, how can he be held responsible? How can a single act send him to hell? Love is not a single act, nor is its loss. The moral theology that handed us our view of mortal sin and forced us to run trembling to confession was based upon a medieval vision of man. Such a vision has passed, as should our archaic description of sin.

Catholic theology has made too much of Adam's sin and not nearly enough of Christ's victory.[13] We learned well enough that it might take us years to "grow up" in Christ, but we ignored the development necessary to be named one of Satan's recruits. No reasonable theologian would say that a single act of love binds us to God in eternal fervor. Even the great conversions of Christian history were the climax of a thousand victories. How can the same theologians be so facile in cutting off the creature from his Creator in the throes of a lonely act?

The Christian must know that he is a conqueror, a man of undiminished hope, the only son of a loving Father Who does not arbitrarily reject in pettiness and petulance. How many times have I heard the weariness of the world in hours of confession and known that these were not sons but slaves? How many times did I hear the people confess to "feel better" when I well knew that they would never feel anything but fear and temporary relief from fear until they learned that Christ had conquered Adam? To abstain from the communion table because there is no chance to confess a "mortal sin," to hurry to report each solitary sin and "impure embrace" is to make of the

Christ of Magdalene and Peter a pompous judge in a traffic court. To call "sinful" what one's own heart says is good and holy is to refuse to be a man. To count each sin and classify it in a moral computer is to make a mockery of a sacrament of mercy.

I cannot hear such confessions any longer. I cannot fight sleep and boredom as men file by and formally list their basketful of faults. I cannot bear their guilt over trifles, their repentant reports of the "sins" that are merely the story of a maturing soul. I am tired of taking away sins that I cannot be certain exist, of evoking promises that cannot be kept, of representing a God Who so easily sentences men to hell.

Once on a hillside in Galilee man saw another Man Who spoke of God. He did not multiply laws as the Pharisees, or wrangle in subleties like the Sadducees. He did not cross-examine or condemn like the courts of Rome. He seemed to understand, to believe in man, to realize that beneath this shy smile and wrinkled glance rested the image of His own Father. He carried neither pencil nor pad, nor adding machine to tabulate the offenses of men. He spoke of a son who could always come home, a helpless lamb that would tremble in fear until it heard His voice.

We need such a man in the Catholic Church today, a man who understands and bleeds to forgive, a man who will take our word even if we are only halfway to honesty, a man who will not call "sinful" what we can only see as a necessary step in the search of love. We need to find the light and joy that was lost in the legalism of history's dust and decay. We need to find priests again, priests who can make men's hearts glow with confidence in themselves, and not mere absolving robots who hand out green stamps to the frightened children. Then will the Church have something to say to the man of our generation, when the confession line dwindles and the invitation to the banquet reaches the poor, the weak, the truly human. Then can my Church, grown cold and formal, speak the words that made men follow: "Come to me, you that labor and are burdened, and I will give you rest."

8. THE RULES OF COURTSHIP

It is always disconcerting to hear the retreat questions of a senior in a Catholic girls' college. We could well discuss the new opportunities that modern psychology offers in raising well-loved children. We could talk about the signs of love or the breakdown in personal communication. We could even talk about the sorry preoccupation of the fair sex with bustlines and hiplines. There is so much to talk about with a sincere and sophisticated young lady approaching career and marriage. But we always seem to end up with an incredibly naïve and tiresome discussion about "French kissing" or "prolonged embracing." If the results of her formation were not so sad and unfortunate, the whole conversation would be comical.

Her education has taken her from the first suggestions of Euclid to the last offerings of Einstein. She has read Teller and Wittgenstein, Tillich and Graham Greene. Her vision, however, of the moral meaning of sex and love has hardly progressed since grade nine. Every date has been a natural, human exchange until the last drop of coffee has been drained from the cup and the bewitching hour approaches. Then the wheels begin to spin in their mathematical track. To kiss or not to kiss is hardly the question, though once it well may have been a decision matching marital consent in its gravity. To French kiss or not to French kiss is usually the question. Keeping the teeth closed becomes the ancient badge of the martyrs who refused to sacrifice to the pagan gods of Rome. She has undoubtedly heard from priestly lips that the "soul kiss" is a symbol of intercourse, and she has bowed to the logic of one who may have kissed no one other than his mother. At times she would like to spring loose from a system of morality which measures hugs and times kisses, but her fear of hell's fire sends her back into line.

One gentle touch of curious hands, one burst of passion that pulls her body too close to his, and she wonders about the next opportunity for confession. In a society in which the "French kiss" is a normal way to express affection, she firms her lips and guards her tongue with all the ardor of a convent under siege. From a quiet conversation over coffee, she has galloped to a state of scrupulous frenzy in twenty minutes. Maybe she shouldn't see him again; after all, they really haven't made plans for marriage. She likes him, but she is not yet prepared to commit herself for life. She's playing the field, and the only time she is comfortable is the very first date with a very shy young man. She has heard of men who take girls to their stereophonic apartments and the sad tales of pregnant friends who took a prolonged tour of "Europe." She had heard the retreat talks that start with the Immaculate Conception and end with drive-in movies and broken homes. She has heard so much more about sex than about love that love becomes an unattainable ideal and sex the forbidden path that leads to misery.

Since the age of twelve she has heard about the dangers of the hayride and necking parties where twelfth-grade boys threaten the virginity of giggling girls. She has been told that her body is a Temple of the Holy Spirit and that a kiss is a sacred symbol of deep affection. By the time she was in ninth grade she probably knew the difference between necking and petting, and wondered when her first encounter would threaten her faith and morals. For years she had been confessing regularly her "bad" thoughts and "impure desires," and the passage of time meant only that the cinema of imagination offered her more to worry about. She learned that she was a gentle daisy in a grisly, leering world. Her little Protestant friends, with their whispers and knowing grins, would soon enough discover the horrors of unprincipled living. They were not burdened with the great charter of sexual mores and their experiential approach to libido would punish them in marriage. Yet, because it doesn't always turn out that way, the Catholic system cannot afford to highlight the successful marriages of the morally unenlightened. Purity in the form of total abstinence is the proof of love, according to the Catholic view, even though "purity" can also be proof of neurotic guilt or fear of physical love. Augustine suggested to the violated virgins of his *City of God* that they were able to remain humbly pure, since savage barbarians had stolen their physical virginity. The Catholic ethos, however, is timid in drawing conclusions from such bold speculations. Since there are enough quotes from Augustine to enforce the most puritan system of morality, his advice to the blushing virgins has gone the weary way of his "Love and do what you will"— paraphrased out of existence.

In any event, Augustine has had little to do with the Catholic conscience, which has found nourishment enough in such Jesuitical offerings as Kelly's *Modern Youth and Chastity*. Here the rules are all laid out in handy fashion. Even the first kiss of the sweaty-fingered sophomore is categorized. Five rules, practically impossible of application, are listed to cover "every" situation. First, the Catholic has to know what "venereal pleasure" is. It would seem hard to define, but rather easy to experience. It is not a simple love glow or the moon-tingling sensation of dancing with a wind-blown pinafore of starched cotton. It is passionate, intense, violent! Venereal pleasure is always seriously wrong for the unmarried, whether "direct" or "proximately indirect." Try this for size on a fourteen-year-old conscience!

Venereal pleasure is distinguished from the more gentle varieties known as affection. Affection is legitimate if it is sincere. The violations of the rules on affection are not considered serious, and, for the confused Catholic conscience, this means, "Don't sweat it!" The line, however, between affection and venereal pleasure is the narrow boundary between dark white and light black. It is so easy to slip from the gentle brush of tender lips to the torrid embrace of locked arms. Prolonged kissing is usually presumed to be "passionate," and passionate kissing is the entryway to lust. The question that naturally flows from this profound speculation is: "When is a kiss prolonged?" A quick check of the medieval minds is not a great help. Some suggest that twenty seconds might be prolonged. Others, more practical, think that passionate kissing is marked by the gradual replacing of a love purr with a bearish growl. No effective formula has been devised to determine the moral quantity of a hug. Weary moralists, like myself, have usually ended all discussion with the weak assurance that "You'll know when it happens." At least, I hoped they would, since I had never known myself. The closest I came to a passionate embrace in my preseminary days was a ten-minute ride in the back seat of a crowded car after a football game. My formation was quite average in seminary circles.

Our intentions are not bad. People need much help in facing life's wonders. Sexual experience can be as dangerous as it is beautiful. We need goals, self-questioning, some understanding of the heterosexual dynamic. Girls need to know something about the psyche of man, as well as the inner activities of their own psyche. Young men need to know the characteristics that divide male and female, and the danger of calling a passionate experience an undying love. There is a lifetime of learning, but it cannot be contained in neat categories. In reducing a profound area of human experience to a set of rules, we somehow manage to take away the conscience of the young Catholic and substitute the sexual hangup.

Young Catholics learn to guard their thoughts and to banish lustful desires.[1] They often complain that such efforts are futile, and the more they banish, the more fruitful seems the supply. Teen-agers are of especial concern. They report their passionate kissing, their "almost petting," their brief and furtive touches, their moments of curious excitement. They want to be sure. They do not think this act is "mortal," but the odds are

too great to take a chance. The more conscientious torture us
with the stuttering distinctions that our moral code has made
so essential.[2] They want to know the borderline of mortal and
venial sin, they probe to discover how far they can go—to drain
each ounce of pleasure and experience without offending God.
Nothing seems serious in confession except matters of sex. We
hear of quarrels at home, struggles with sullen friends, bits of
theft and disobedience—but it is only sex that brings hoarse
fear to the voice and concern to the confessor's admonitions.

In such a world, "going steady" is the most fertile target of
our attacks. We condemn the steady daters whenever we can.
We expel them from school, call them in for private council,
telephone their parents, and dissect them in our religion class.
We try every new vaccine to end this blight, yet nothing seems
to work. We are nostalgic and tell them of our old gang, where
no one went steady. Why can't modern youth gather around
the piano, or linger around the redolent smoke of the autumn
hot-dog roast? We had so much fun in "our" day, when guys
and gals traveled in packs, and there was little time or place to
linger in private passion. We extoll the athlete and mock the
twisting teen who lets his id run wild in an orgy of discordant
sounds. We criticize the public schools, where skinny boys hold
hands with listless girls between classes. We whisper about the
scandals of the locker rooms and dark alcoves. We hear of
teachers who treat promiscuity as a joke. We are the enlight-
ened, and we demand that our young prepare themselves for
marriage with discipline and honor.

The results of our campaign have not been exceptional. We
still have our surprise pregnancies, our premature marriages, our
little parties that help make clear the distinction between affection and venereal pleasure. Some of our young come back to
us in confession and tell us of their exciting misdeeds. Some do
not, but instead postpone confession until such a time as their
repentance will have some roots. Few give up their new experience, even if it means shopping around for confessors who are
not so desperate about the rules of thumb. The lonely and timid
are our best customers, since they can only dream of sex, and

we are not so violent in our attacks on impure thoughts. This is
not to say that we are not kind or patient. Most priests are at
their best in the confessional, and seldom do they lose their
patience or compassion. But they can allow no recourse, no
court of appeal. The sexual struggle is cut and dried.

There is little difference in the treatment of a child of fourteen and a young adult of twenty-five approaching marriage.
We only grant that the adult has more reason to be flirting with
the dangers of sin. But sexual arousal is as forbidden to the
engaged as it is to the adolescents. All that is permitted anyone
before marriage is the "Frenchless" kiss and the gentle embrace.
Engaged couples are expected to appear at the altar as sexual
strangers and the same night to share a king-size bed.

We are opposed to long courtships, so any violators who are
not planning marriage within a reasonably short time are asked
to break up, or to stop dating for a specific time. The Catholic
soon finds out that he has a better chance of escaping confessional agony if the escapades are somewhat promiscuous than if
concentrated in one relationship. College students come and
tell us of the girl friend who fills the whole of their social life.
It is a social life without funds that grows on discussion and
deep affection. They have no immediate intention of marriage,
nor have they the money or the desire to play the field. Each
new girl means a series of expensive dates. She has to be
charmed before she will consent to friendly economy. Or, if
money is not the social problem, then shyness is. It takes some
boys three or four months to get up enough nerve to meet a
girl. Yet we demand that a relationship end as soon as sex
emerges.[3]

Our ideal is impossible. While asking two people never to
know anything but gentle affection before marriage, it asks
them not to marry too young, not to extend the dating period
for a prolonged time; also to get to know a great number of
possible mates, and to receive the sacraments frequently. What
our ideal achieves is one huge round of anxiety. Confession ends
with great sincerity and noble promises. Then a weekend comes,
a passionate exchange, followed by another encounter with a

priest who cross-examines the roots of the relationship. The ultimatum of give up the girl or give up God often makes little sense, because God has become close for the first time in years through the prism of the relationship. The young lover is asked to abandon the only person who can make God seem real. The priest does not enjoy his task; it tears at his mercy and manhood. He, too, is without recourse, and the weight of campus sex weighs heavily on his shoulders. More than once many of us have been tearfully accused of destroying a friendship. At other times we sit for hours with sullen couples who will not abandon the sacraments, but cannot sacrifice each other's friendship.

Somehow, ironically, such an approach to sex plays into the hands of a world that makes of sex the very pulse of life. The Catholic couple, warned so frequently of the tree of good and evil, often expects of sex far more than it can give. The exchange of vows transforms a courtship of sexual sins into a paradise of sacred delights. It is a shock to learn that what watered the mouth from its distant tree was only an apple after all, and not the ambrosial honey that banished human hunger.

Unwittingly, too, the Catholic mystique of sex pushes teenagers into marriage. Since the experience of sex is guarded by solemn law, the tortured couple has to choose between the agony of a sin-ridden courtship and the confusion of a premature marriage. And the confesser is in no position to balance the "sins" of adolescence against the crime of a youthful marriage. The blind emphasis on the sin of sex clouds the future horror of a marriage without love, of children without parents.

Some go away sad, some go away angry. Some do not go away; they submit and break off a friendship with tears and prayers. Some even thank us for the courage that we give. Most, however, shake their heads, and wonder how long they can last. It is only lately that they have rebelled, only of late that they have begun to talk back in confession or to ignore it entirely. In the past we could silence doctor and teen-ager alike with the firm and gentle stroke of our decision. Now they begin to talk back, and I for one am glad.

The young do not wish to ignore our directions for dating and courtship. They would even welcome them. The directions, however, must be those of one who is guiding a personal conscience, and not the decisions of one who has absorbed it.[4] They will not submit their romance to a slide rule, nor will they measure their kisses and touches with the impersonal theorems of a moralist. We can talk to them of goals and they will listen far into the night. When we speak to them of codified specifics, however, they tell us to mind our own business. We will be their servants again when we offer them the essential freedom to learn by their mistakes, when we help them to learn a moral law which measures guilt by the hurt done to other people and not by the crisply mathematical violation of an unequivocal law.

Our legalistic approach was not always a failure. Some had the capacity to see the wisdom that lurked beneath its law. They were not troubled by the narrowness of the rules, or they entered a marriage soon enough, or after a brief enough courtship, to avoid much of the problem. Some were able to channel the sacrifice into the dynamic of their friendship, some found it a protection from close encounter, some were just too afraid to deviate. There were those, unquestionably, who approached marriage in the innocence of childhood. But even though they were the marginal few, somehow they became the norm of universal behavior. Each of us can point to a parent, a friend, even, perhaps, a spouse, who lived the Church's law of courtship to the letter and yet was not marked by hostility, confusion, or pharisaic pride. These are the exceptional people who can maintain their balance in any system. But we do not raise our children in log cabins because Lincoln seemed to prosper there.

Man also was more tolerant of such a system in another world because he did not know so much about the dynamics of courtship. We have come to realize that sex can mean a thousand different things to a thousand different people. It can mean anything from the first experience of a man's tenderness to a complete rejection of the responsibilities of love. It can mean a selfish attempt to prove something, or a genuine expression of love. But while man has acquired this new knowledge about the dynamics of courtship, the Church does not honor it.

It is an impossible procedure to listen to a voice in a dark confessional say: "I let my boy friend go too far three times," and to attempt to understand what is involved in sin and psychology. There is no time or method to discover what sex means to this person, no chance to discuss the fear of being "an old maid" that frightens this girl as much as the fear of hell. "If he *really* loves you, he can be pure," we say, and our calm decision requires no evidence or justification. We say it so often we are certain of it. We can never ask: "What do you think? Does it seem wrong? Is this sincere friendship, or a fear of growth and communication?" We know the answer before we ask. It is impurity and impurity is irresponsible love.

But we cannot blame the priest too much, for, as I have said, he suffers in his role of judge without recourse. He has learned a morality of the "individual action," a morality which numbers and categorizes mortal sin. He cannot be satisfied with "general progress" or a "growing awareness"; he must know each sin and then receive the assurance that it will not recur.

The Church must replace its blind, arbitrary formulas with an intense awareness that each man must stumble to find his way in love. It must ask more questions than it answers. It must shift the responsibility from the unyielding decision of the priest to the individual conscience that is carving out a life. To build such a religion—and the theological ground is already laid [5]—means that men have to be trusted with the right of personal decision.

Perhaps the adolescent will need more pointed directions, but even he will know new freedom to make mistakes, and will not fear the independence of moral judgment that must attend age and experience. I have often wondered what would indeed result if we converted the massive efforts of our dating code into a vast educational program of self-knowledge and the dynamics of personal, responsible love. It is unfortunate that we have armed our charges with such precise distinctions in matters of sex, and have spoken to them so little of the nature of friendship. Perhaps we did not know about the love of friendship ourselves.

When I speak of a program of morality that rests the sexual decisions of dating on the responsibility of a personal conscience, I can anticipate the screams of a "morality without absolutes." I know, however, that absolutes live in books and scholars' heads, whereas life is a struggle of doubt amid certitude, shadow dotted with light. If a man tells me that he sees no harm in intercourse before marriage, I can question his emotional awareness, or even his sincerity. But I can be concerned with his decision only to the degree that he lets me be. And even then we search in dialogue; I cannot preach to him in absolutes I do not understand. Man is not absolute, either in mind or heart, nor can he possess or reveal all of himself in a single act or decision. His moral attitudes may change as he himself grows and changes, but my conscience must never speak for his. Direction, yes; dictation, never.

There will always be the simple and the fearful who will ask the church to make all judgments for them. They will need the more directive help of "Father's own opinion." Life for them must be clearly laid out, and each decision must not tremble with equivocation. The increasing multitude of men, however, must hear the responsibility of their own judgments. The community with its suggestions and its alternate opinions will be the constant test of their sincerity, the god that teaches them of love and pride.

Would not marriages be much the same if we only offered general advice and permitted the individual to follow the directives of his own conscience? Could we not, for example, reexamine the goals of Christian marriage and courtship? Could we not talk to him about the dangers of false love, the obstacles to communication, the seriousness of false commitment? Could we not beg him never to rest in stagnant assurance of moral rectitude, but to continue to evaluate and grow? Cannot the true sin of sex be the consciously selfish seduction which makes of man an object and not a person? What harm has the sincere man done who made love to a fiancée with whom he will sleep for forty years of marriage? Can people not be taught to measure the rights of sexual expression by the nature of the commitment? Do they not do this already in high school, in college, in the world of factory and office? Would man not mature if we offered him a plan of growth in love and not a judicial ultimatum? Could we not say "I think" or "it seems," rather than "you must" or "you can't"? Can we not learn from married couples about what happens during courtship and what actually hurts or helps a relationship?

I know from personal experience of dozens of couples whose marriage is as successful as their courtship was passionate. Did they sin so gravely in their preparation for the marriage which ultimately gave to past sex its present meaning? If a married couple can delay the birth of children for personal reasons and yet know the enjoyment of sex, is it wrong for honestly engaged couples to communicate in a similar way? If it is wrong, why? If a love affair, not leading to marriage, teaches a man about himself, teaches him consideration and confidence, helps him to be honest and to feel warmth and pity, is it a sinful affair or an essential step in his search for the capacity to love maturely? And of what value is the conscience wrangle that goes on in Catholic courtships? [6] Is the ordinary woman, flushed with her diamond, capable of denying sex to the man who will father her children? Is the sexual abstinence required in Catholic courtship not often the club which a woman refuses to relinquish in her lifelong struggle with her man for supremacy? Is not such abstinence as blinding as sexual indulgence? Cannot the one be as dangerous a cover for fear of sex or latent homosexuality as the other can be an indication of egotism and selfishness? Is it morally good to do the right thing for the wrong reasons?

These are questions which I cannot completely answer. But they are honest questions, real questions, and they cannot be ignored with simple conclusions of an unyielding law. Man the complicated cannot be dismissed with a quiet shrug and a nod in the direction of tradition. As anthropology grows, as man's view of himself is altered, he will continue to ask new and harder questions in practical theology. If we cannot answer them, we must not tell him that we can. Love is not afraid of discipline, it thrives on it, it learns to respect it even as it grows. It is, however, as unique in each case as the two people that make up the custom-made union. We in the Church do not have a corner on concern for happy marriages. We are not alone in our search for the meaning of morality in courtship. It troubles every parent, each church and school, it troubles society itself. Most of all, it concerns the maturing couple who have some awareness of what a lifelong commitment means.

The sexual morality of the Church was unquestionably right in seeking the marital union as its point of reference. Few would quarrel with that. Sex finds its meaning and fulfillment in the marital union. But why does sin have to be measured by the presence or absence of this or that act of pleasure? Since serious sin is determined, granting freedom, by the harm done, does not an honest theology have to point out the nature of this harm? What actual harm is done when two people, who think they are in love—and who would tell them certainly they are not—express their affection in the physical dimension? Whom did they hurt by this passionate exchange? God? One another? Society? A future child? If so, how? Is it the risk of pregnancy that makes it wrong? What if there is no risk? The traditional moralist would say that only the married have a right to sexual pleasure and this would end the discussion. Or he would point to the scriptural condemnation of "fornication" without deciding whether Scripture referred to promiscuous lovemaking or preparation for marriage, whether it was describing a single action or a way of life.

What if sexual experience were a necessary way of distinguishing between infatuation and serious love? Would it then be virtuous? If a courtship leads to a happy marriage, regardless of the sexual exchange, it is not a sound courtship? Is it not, in retrospect, a holy courtship since it produced sincere human commitment? Can a courtship, no matter how "pure" and undefiled, be called "good" if it led to divorce? Does a moral theologian have no obligation to examine his presuppositions about the virtue of premarital purity if there is positive evidence that many a courtship was both "pure" and ineffective?

We have not talked much about such matters in theological circles. We have little time to draw any support from the way in which most couples conduct their courtship. Is this not important? Can we call the conduct of society merely the influence of pagan amorality? Or could it also be the growing maturity of a society which has lost its Victorian obsession with the horror of the flesh? Have other religious groups, which have offered only general directives about premarital sex, failed to produce happy and holy homes? Perhaps they did not have enough of a hold on their members to offer such a program. But perhaps, too, they believed more in the individual and refused to involve themselves in the intimacy of private love. It may well be that we have not trusted man enough, that we do not recognize that God speaks to him in channels that stem from creation and not from allegiance to the Church. Each man is human before he is Christian. Will not God offer private revelations to every man He has made if the channels are not frozen by a system? Are we afraid to believe in man, to know that he wants a happy marriage far more than he wants an exciting Saturday night? Must we bind him with absolutes that deny circumstances and experience? Is there anything truly absolute short of God Himself? Even Christ could not carry the burden of the Godhead without shadows. Can the laws enacted in His name do more?

No man can say to the morally responsible person: "You cannot receive the Church's sacrament. You have offended God seriously." This is a decision a man has to make for himself. I have found, in retreat and counseling experience, that man is far harder on himself than an objective law could be. If given a chance, man will evaluate his courtship in terms of the person with whom he seeks love. He will center his attention on goals and meaning, not on a single action or a personal "state of grace." This takes a great deal more reflection and sincerity than any effort to "avoid the occasions of sin" or to limit the good-night embrace.

Such an approach to conscience means that you must believe in man. You must respect his right to make personal decisions and you must realize that he wants personal happiness with divinely sparked intensity. Is this a Protestant morality? A Jewish morality? A humanistic morality? I am not sure if any group offers the proper balance of personal freedom and well-defined goals. I only know what I try to offer is the personal understanding of Christian morality that study, experience, and prayer have offered me. It is the freedom of the sons of God, the opportunity to make of a systematic creed a personal faith. No system can ever absorb man, it can only serve and direct him in his search for honest commitment. Some will be certain that sex before marriage is wrong. Others will insist that it is noble and essential. Neither group must be barred from the sacraments in the name of some absolute that makes men the docile slaves of a system.

To learn a trade or to absorb an education is a series of successes and mistakes. It cannot be measured by income or scholastic records. To learn to love is a lifetime task; it cannot be measured by "purity" or "the keeping of the law." There is only one law, the Christian law of love, and no love affair of man and man, or man and God, can ever be the same. One woman asks of a man kindness in the name of love. Another loves him for his sensitive pride. Yet another loves a loud and boisterous man, while this one wants him quiet and pensive. One man goes to love with a volcano of locked hostility, another with a deep fear that he cannot be loved. One is passionate and impulsive, another talkative and philosophic, this one is shy and inhibited. Yet each must know love if he is to know God. Each will love another human being, and God Himself, in a unique and personal way. Who is to say which act will bring love, and which will tear a man from the core of himself and his God?

Love must ever be a quest, an experiment. It must have

THE RULES OF COURTSHIP

bounds, but only bounds that are broad enough to permit breath. Most of all, it must have freedom or it will die. In all my efforts as a priest, the purest girl I ever knew was a Mexican Negro who lived in the heart of the slums. Her mother was an alcoholic, her father perpetually unemployed. She was a beautiful girl, twenty years old, and of exceptional olive complexion. She was working part time to buy food for the family, attending college at night, and attempting a moderate social life. I gave her private instructions and got to know her well. She told me of her childhood, of the free exposure to sex, of the virginity that she had guarded for the man she would one day love. She came to the Church in innocence, and lived a life of purity before she heard mention of our rules. She knew nothing of our multiple laws, nothing of the harassing provided the Catholic conscience. She was baptized with tearful eyes, she received communion with joy she could not contain. She was open, honest, loving, pure. Somehow she found her purity with God in the slums—and she knew nothing of our rules.

9. CHRISTIAN MARRIAGE
AND DIVORCE

It is hard to hide the scars of an unhappy marriage. They are
visible when the smile fades, when a sudden burst of sadness
hits in the midst of a crowded room. The unhappily married
have a way of draining the meaning out of a remark that was
not meant to be profound. They question you, explore your
mind with too searching an intent, change your relaxed grin
into a serious and wrinkled look. They want answers, and the
time or place is not of great concern. That's why I was not
surprised when—why don't we call her Jean—asked me if I
had a few minutes to talk after a Parent-Teachers meeting one
evening. We walked from the auditorium to the rectory and before we reached my office, she had started to cry.

She apologized and told me that she had not been sleeping
well. I told her not to mind her tears, offered her a box of
Kleenex, and she lit up a cigarette. She and her doctor husband
had been married for seventeen years. They had two boys, Dick,
fifteen, and John, thirteen, both adopted. I knew the boys well,
since they stayed around the gym a lot, and each responded
vigorously to my least show of interest. She told me how much
they thought of me and I knew she was struggling to get to
her story.

She had met her husband, Don, when he was an intern at

a local hospital. Don was from a broken home, his father having disappeared when Don was in eighth grade. Jean had never felt close to Don's mother, but they lived far enough away so that she seemed no problem. They had visited her only twice during their courtship, and somehow she wasn't able to attend the wedding, which took place in Jean's parish. It was only two months later that she discovered Don was a homosexual.

I asked if he had given evidence of this during the courtship. She answered with a touch of bitterness that she had felt he was just being a good Catholic when he never got "carried away." After marriage they had had intercourse only twice, both times on their eight-day honeymoon. For a time Jean had been able to show Don affection, but after a few weeks he would move away whenever she touched him. For seventeen years Jean had never made love. He had brought his friends home in odd assortments, until she had "put her foot down" when she discovered him with one of his friends making love on the living-room floor. She said that she had prayed to forgive him, but never could. She had gone to the parish priest and he had listened with sympathy. He suggested that they adopt children and Jean had agreed that only this could give any meaning to her life. And while the two boys had not dulled the pain, they had given her a reason to go on.

Lately, it seemed, there was no reason to continue. The boys didn't need her as much, she was beginning to drink, she found it difficult to sleep. She had tried the hospital auxiliary, the Junior League, programs to establish mental health, to help the Negro, to provide entertainment for the aged. But none seemed to help, and presently she found herself longing to be held in the arms of a man who cared. She converted trifles into complicated fantasies. The touch of a postman's hand, a social dance with one of her husband's friends, even a glance from an attractive man—each set her flesh trembling and her mind echoing with confusion. She had never been unfaithful, she was not sure that she could be.

She found herself staring in the mirror, watching each new

wrinkle give emphasis to the one before. Every pound she gained seemed to speak of loneliness and death. Her figure had become almost the measure of her worth. Of late she was on the verge of tears every time her husband was obliged to take her out socially among associates. She was the female that accompanied him, the hired wife that gave him acceptability among his peers, the middle-aged woman who had never known the needs of a man. Her husband worked endless hours to amass money. They lived in a hundred-thousand-dollar home, each drove a new Cadillac, had twice as many clothes as anyone could want. But she would throw it all away to know a husband's love.

The boys, she told me, had never really had a father. They looked for substitutes and hung on every new priest or teacher that came into their lives. At that moment, the basketball coach and I were the constant subject of their conversation. Don had never spent time with them, and she was just as glad because she feared the company he kept. She had played ball with the boys, cheered at the little league games, praised and corrected them. Five years ago she had talked to a Jesuit who was giving a conference in the parish. He seemed to have the kind of heart that would understand and the kind of mind that would know some special court of recourse. He had studied in Rome and the resonant confidence of his voice gave her some new and strange hope. He had listened, and when she had finished the outline of her story, he only shook his head. He was moist around the eyes and his voice was not as resonant as before. He had nothing new to say, but he promised to write her. He signed his letters "With love," and for a time this was indeed her secret love. Of late, however, the letters were occasional, and the melody of his words had lost their impact. He spoke of suffering with the clear distinctions of a man who had never known its awesome power to torture memories and transform ideals. She was losing the language of the Christian dream, and words like "Cross" and "saint" no longer rang with the mystery of childhood.

The sacraments, once her contact with sanity, had become

empty forms, the sermons in church seemed the pious sentiments of untried boys. Only her sons were real, their hair damp
with sweat, their appetites eager for fun and food. Only her
sons gave her life and the thought of them kept the sleeping
pills bottled in the medicine cabinet. Her inflection under-
played the drama of her words, and after forty minutes she had
said it all. I had no questions, and all the answers I had were
forbidden by my Church.

This was a marriage in Christ, the law insisted, since it
fulfilled all the prescribed patterns. Two baptized Catholics
had been married by a priest. The marriage had been consummated—granted, only twice in seventeen years—and now it was
sealed in the iron ledger of some eternal apocalypse. They were
"two in one flesh," the manuals said, bound in the mysterious
intimacy of Christ and His Church. The nuptial blessing had
warned her to be "faithful to one embrace," "to flee unlawful
companionship," to emulate the faith of Sara, Rachel, and
Rebecca. She was the valiant woman who knew that beauty
was vain and fleeting, who watched it fade each morning and
wept for it each night. She had been told by Paul himself to
"obey" her husband since she would be cherished as his own
flesh. Time had told her that she could not love her husband,
despite Paul or Pope or Christ Himself. She could only stay
with him in barren union, afraid to leave him only because she
feared to lose her God.

Jean was not alone in the limping procession of married
martyrs that came to me for answers when I could give them
only a memorized text. There were hundreds more! There was
Harry, who married Sharon at eighteen, when sex seemed to
contain all that love promised. She had left him after two
years, left him and the house and the baby as well. She had
married again and gave him the child to care for in his Catholic
celibacy. I had talked with her, pleaded with her, but the iron
of her eyes had told me that she no longer listened to the
Church. One kiss from her new-found man would blot out a
thousand words from priestly lips. Harry was alone for almost
four years, and then he married again in love and need. His

parents would not attend the wedding or purchase a gift. They cut him off with all the courage of a canonical theology that knows no exceptions. He was not welcome in his father's house; his mother could kiss her granddaughter before her son's remarriage, and after close the door. Harry was excommunicated from the Church and ripped from the family that had raised him. He had protested that his marriage to Sharon was the decision of a boy, and the pressures of an unhappy home had pushed him into a premature union. Harry could protest, but no one listened. He heard the whispers of the Catholic community until the fury of the ghetto morality drove him to another town.

The litany I remember is endless: the spouses who watched a home disintegrate around an alcoholic, the teen-agers who thought marriage meant only freedom to make love in their own apartment. It includes the man married to a helpless psychotic, the woman bound to an angry beast, the couple who have not spoken a direct and personal word in twenty years. It embraces the nervous little ladies who make novenas for their husbands to abandon the barmaids or wait for their men to get out of jail and make them pregnant. There are sadists and masochists, beaters and brawlers, profane and rigid dictators who match Hitler at his worst. Yet the law says these men and women are united in Christ and that no power on earth can loose the bond. They are to choose between the distant hope of a miraculous reform or the lonely life of parents without partners. And while they debate the decision of divorce, they stay together long enough to have another child, to incur another time payment, to suffer another breakdown, to grow too old to care. If they finally leave their private hell, they are told never to date, never to kiss, never to linger near the "occasion of sin," and, ultimately, never to love.

And in all this fierce legalism, what does my Church propose to gain? It says that marriage is the human image of Christ's relationship with the Church. It says that every couple who are married in the Church are united in Christian love. The husband must cherish his wife as his own body, and she must treat him as her very blood and heart. The children must feel the overflowing warmth of this union and grow strong and secure in the patience and kindness that pervade the home. There will be quarrels, but forgiveness must be sought before the day is at an end. There will be sickness, a retarded child, financial pressures, a sense of failure that plagues the middle years. There will be trouble in school, fights at the dinner table, flareups and sullenness, jealousies and sleepless nights. But husband and wife must bear the burden of the day and seek to nourish love in the prayer and silence of the night.

Such an ideal cannot be questioned, and any Church does well to promulgate such hopes. I have seen such marriages in every parish that I served. I remember the tall businessman and his redhaired wife, and the houseful of children that welcomed my frequent calls. The husband's pride showed whenever his wife told an anecdote about the children, or when she insisted I eat a sandwich and drink a beer. She kidded him and he loved it, with even the children joining the good-natured banter. It was a happy home, the best of Christian homes, where love and interest lived in every room. The children were bright, enthusiastic, each with a dozen hobbies, each with a unique and obvious place in the parents' hearts. Jimmy was retarded, but in his bubbling joy for life, he didn't seem to know it or to mind. Ellen planned to be a nun, and her love for practical jokes could spark any community to whom she gave her vows. Dave could think of nothing but football in the fall, pestered me to throw him passes, and to show him how to block. There were dogs in the yard, rabbits in the garage, and snakes and guinea pigs in the basement. The house was a menagerie, a circus, a dormitory, a subway station, a sanctuary —a home. Here were parents, here were children, here was love!

Every home could not know such happiness, some could only remember it from years gone by. I remember the gray-haired father of fifty-five who called and told me he needed my help. I had known and admired him for several years. I had taught his children in high school and chatted with him and his wife at every parish function. But his call sounded like trouble, so I went as quickly as I could. He met me at the door and stopped me at the porch. He wanted to prepare me for the problem, to explain his alcoholic wife. He was embarrassed, confused, unable to tell me coherently what had happened in his home. She had just begun to drink excessively a few months ago. She had drunk socially and moderately for years, but suddenly had lost control. Her anger was violent, her language coarse and snarled, her tantrums made the younger children cry.

It was a miserable visit that only prefaced others twice again as bad. I don't know how he stood it, but he loved her and remembered the gentle days gone by. At times, as she lay in a drunken stupor and ceased her screaming for a time, he recalled their vacations, their fun with the children, the card games with friends, the closeness and confidence they shared. I listened to his stories, laughed at the funny things she'd done, and watched a man in love struggle to keep his sanity, his hope, his marriage. There was no talk of divorce; she needed him, he loved her, and that was all there was to say. But he needed me and the comforts of the Church. I prayed with him, watched him come more regularly to Mass, gave him the assurance that this crisis would pass. And it did.

This, too, was a permanent marriage; this, too, was an obvious union in Christ. It was not as carefree as the home of the businessman and his redhaired wife. But it was Christian. It was an enduring bond that held a suffering man to his alcoholic wife. It was not my Church that kept him at her side. It was not his vows, his children, his honor, his pride that held him faithful; it was his love. He loved her because he loved her in the sacrament of love. He was not a sullen martyr who fought to honor a promise made in youth. He did not want to hear of his nobility, his patience, his Christian fortitude. It was not the fear of hell that frightened him to save a marriage, but the love for his wife that offered him no other course.

This is marriage; this is the answer to easy and impulsive divorce. But what of the twenty-year-old girl who came barefoot in her robe to the rectory door one cold November night? She sobbed convulsively on the steps. Her face was swollen and bloody, her right eye was completely closed. I knew her and the angry boy she had married, who threatened her with death. She would not go back to him, she screamed for the baby that lay in a crib while a mad young man was raging through the house. I asked her what had happened, but she wouldn't answer until I called the police and brought the baby to her side. She told me that he had returned from a poker game and asked her for a cigarette. She didn't have one, and he demanded that she go out and get some. She refused and he began to beat her until she thought he would kill her on the spot. Now she was in my office. She held the baby close and the policeman drove her to her parents' home. What of her?

She was married in my Church. She exchanged her vows before her God. She knelt at the altar, received communion with her husband, and heard the priest describe the beauty that is married love. Her hopes were high, her resolutions intent, her love was young, but serious and strong. Three months later she was living in hell. He lost his job and refused to work. She supported him while he played basketball and drank. He slapped her, abused her, brought home lipstick on the shirts she washed. He didn't pray or go to Church, or speak a decent word. And when the baby arrived, he was only annoyed. But he was a Catholic, and so was she, and the priest had married them in Church. This, therefore, was an endless union in Christ, she only had to wait and try until she knew the joy of Holy Mary or the peace of St. Theresa. Or she could offer her suffering for the souls in purgatory and wait for the heaven promised to the patient miserable who do not kill themselves. She was married forever, and there was nothing more to tell her in my Church.

The Pope did not have to tell her this as he talked to diplomats or begged for world peace. I had to tell her. The Pope was worried about Vietnam, or nuclear war, or the Irish bishops who balked at reform. I was worried about her, and I carried her sorrow as I preached on Sunday or taught the teenagers about marriage. My bishop did not have to tell her as he worried about collections or hurried to confirm the docile children who nervously kissed his ring. My bishop did not take her to the Council, or explain her marriage to the theologians, or see her crumpled on the steps in the middle of the night. He told me to tell her that she had been joined in Jesus Christ, that she could not stop and start again. So I told her, like a coward, like an obedient Catholic priest, who could violate his conscience in fealty to his Church.

It was not only this little one I told. I told the lawyer who came to me by night. I heard him describe his marriage as a lasting cold war. There were no blows, no violent explosions, only ugliness and hate. His wife was a social climber who enjoyed each new and more expensive house until there were no more guests to impress, no more articles on the society page describing the parties held in her elegant mansion. She dragged him to parties he couldn't stand, pushed him to entertainment that depressed him, and brought him back to a home where he led a sexless life. Her taste in clothes and homes kept him working dangerous hours, and yet he was endlessly in debt. He liked simple things like conversation and an occasional outing with the children. He liked to read, to walk, to associate with friends who offered more than money and prestige.

He had conceded to her tastes for a time, hoping he could recapture the friendship that courtship had seemed to promise. At other times he had fought her, demanded that she be his wife, told her that nothing satisfied her and nothing short of an honest marriage ever could. She turned her back, lost herself in bridge and art, added more important people to her list. Finally, he had given up. Any suggestion he made was ridiculed, any effort he made was never quite enough. Suddenly he could take it no longer. He was tired of cajoling her, of indulging her, of living as a stranger in his house. There were no family meals, no laughs or simple fun. He loved his children but they were not enough. He could not bear to leave them, but he was only pushing them away in the bitterness of his marriage and hurting them in his hatred for his wife. He had tried everything. He had prayed, sought guidance from a counselor, even tried to make friends with the people who spoke artificially of opera and art. Now it was over; he had tried enough to make a marriage of a contract that only brought him misery and debt. He asked for an answer, and I gave him the party line. He asked for understanding, and I had nothing more to say. I could only make him feel guilty about leaving the children, or suggest that he was intolerant and rude.

So he went away, divorced her, and left the Church. Was this the marriage of which Paul in his epistle speaks, where wives are subject to their husbands and husbands love their wives? Or was this only hatred, only game-playing, self-destruction, and horror? But my Church had spoken, changing water into wine, by calling misery "marriage" and hatred "home." Nothing could permit him to leave his wife and try again. There was no hope, no excuse, no second chance, and with such a conclusion my Church had done its job. The Pope could sleep, my bishop could sip his wine and eat his evening meal. I could cry or curse or get busy and try to forget. But the Catholic man, the lawyer, the father, could only linger in his guilt.

And on Sunday, when he comes to Mass, we'll talk about divorce. We tell him that secularism, neopaganism, and hedonism have increased the incidence of divorce. We tell him that we are the valiant moral guardians in the garbage pile of civilization. We blame Hollywood, which has made light of marriage in its lives and its movies. But its lives evoke men's pity, not their imitation, and its movies only reflect the tensions in modern life. We blame freedom of the sexes, the modern fashions which seem to offend bishops, the early dating pattern of our youth. But every generation has had a scapegoat for its own weakness, and has blamed the young for what their elders taught them. We blame the laws that make divorce easy, and the lawyers and counselors who urge it on their clients. But we do not realize that divorce is never easy, save in the minds of the celibates, who do not understand what the loss of children, the legal wranglings, and alimony mean. We forget that divorce requires the great courage to face loneliness, society's disdain, parents' wrath, friends' criticism, and children's tears. We do not tell our people that divorce can be a martyr's way and the way of loveless marriage a concession to convenience.

We speak of divorce in the simple categories of defensive minds which have never loved. We do not recognize that divorce is a deep wound among the weak and ordinary men, an abiding sense of failure, a lost vocation, a shattered dream, a growing guilt, a secret fear that one may not be capable of giving or winning love. It well may be a relief, but it is seldom simple. And so, steeped in our callowness and inexperience, our smugness and ignorance, we condemn divorce and blame it on everyone but ourselves.

Why do we not blame it on the dullness of our religion, on a structure grown sterile and foreign, on sermons that didn't say anything relevant, on a Christ Who has been made as mute as steel and ice? Why not blame it on a theology that condemned adultery with eloquence, but couldn't say anything important about love? We spend time priding ourselves on the strength of our many-babied homes, but do not hear the groans of the babies grown to manhood. We are satisfied to call self-fulfillment "selfishness" and to rant with dishonest conservatives about a society saturated with sex, bikinis, and dashing Bond men. It does no good to rant of this, to condemn it, to threaten mothers with the premature pregnancy of their daughters. We need interpreters, not angry orators who lack the wisdom and experience to match their words.

Man wants interpreters, and is weary of our scolding and our misplaced blame. He does not want divorce, he merely accepts it when there is no other course. He is not concerned about the fearful statistics, he is concerned about himself. He wants to love, not to know the reasons why the selfish world never can. And what help have we given him? Has my Church encouraged him to be emotionally honest, or has it helped to bury his emotions in anger and fear? Has it given him a personal God, urged him to discover this God in the loving closeness of another human being, or has it only demanded that he keep the rules? Has it told him of the need for maturity and offered him a possible way of finding it, or has it only been rigid in its rules on sex and often forced him into a legal contract to quiet his scrupulous conscience? My Church can blame no one for divorce unless it as vigorously blames itself.

It has taught man less than psychology about love, less than group therapy, less than quiet discussions that bring men to bars and coffeehouses, less than the movies or TV. It has taught men rules, discipline, and endurance. It has not taught men friendship, marriage, love.

If my Church permitted divorce, it fears, every home would be threatened. This is an exaggeration. Catholics are not struggling to save a marriage simply because the Church threatens them with excommunication if they marry a second time. The divorce rate among Catholics is not lower than that among other honest men. Divorce is more often a reflection of an impossible marriage than a mirror of irreligion in the world. People stay together, with few exceptions, because they love each other, or because a broken home costs too much in personal effort, confused children, and social criticism. Only a minority are restrained by religious conviction when the chance for real love presents itself with reasonable convenience. A change in the Church's attitude toward divorce would free this miserable minority, and relieve the torturous guilt of those who have remarried without the blessing of their Church.

The Church is not keeping marriages together, people are. To say that men would lose their balance if the law governing the permanence of marriage were more humble and honest is to lose faith in man's capacity to love. Man wants to marry once, to remain married for life, to enjoy his children's children. We do not have to command this; we only have to show him how. But we cannot tell him that God demands that he live with a spouse he does not love. No honest man will listen, and only frightened men will obey.

Long enough has the legalist told us that Christ denied the possibility of divorce. No honest Scripture scholar can assert that Christ or early Christianity did more than uphold permanent marriage as the *ideal*, the fruit of Christian love.[1] He cannot say that a contract witnessed in the Church, any valid contract, makes a marriage as lasting as man's life. Modern Catholic theologians are more honest. They tell us that it is not the ceremony and consent that makes of marriage a permanent sacrament, but *the presence of Christian love.*[2] It is the presence of this unique love which distinguishes marriage from every other form of society. This special love gives marriage its meaning and determines whether this is a union born of God or a misfortune that should be remedied. Society's other forms, such as clubs or even fraternities, can well endure without personal love, but marriage is unique. Love is not merely one of its aims, but its very center and core. The man who cannot love cannot truly be married in Christ, no matter the sons he has fathered. He well may enter a contract that creates responsibilities, but to call this Christian marriage would make a mockery of the vision of Christ.

The canon law of my Church does not even mention married love in its description of the purposes of marriage. This is proper enough, since love is not a purpose of marriage but its creative cause. Even the children cannot move the husband from the center of his wife's heart, or the unique union of marriage is in jeopardy. Love for children must somehow be merged in the mutual love of husband and wife. When a man falls in love, he has found his other self, he has found the chance for fullness offered by the God Who made him empty. He will not be replaced in his beloved's heart by children or relatives, by the amusing or the profound, or even by his Church. It is the union of love which speaks to him of God. If you call him proud and selfish to search for such love, you condemn the Creator Who fashioned man in the very image of His jealous love.

The law does not deal with such mysteries. It mentions the purposes of marriage: the procreation of children, mutual help, and the calming of passion. Love, however, is the essence of marriage, even as love is the essence of Christianity, or any honest faith. Christ gave special meaning to marriage that this peak of human love might more clearly resemble His own.

Where there is not love, there is no sacrament, no Christian marriage. This does not even mean that the sacrament endures if once there was love. The contract endures until the rights of each party have been protected, until the children are provided for, but the permanent sacrament ceases when love is at an end. The legalist in my Church can call a hate-filled union a Christian sacrament of marriage; the honest theologian never can, he never should.

There is nothing to prevent my Church from declaring null any union which has lost its substance, that is, any marriage which has lost its love. This does not mean that divorce should be granted with ease. Nor does it mean that the innocent can be ignored, or the rights of children overlooked. It only means that a pregnant teen-ager will not have to pay for a mistake until the end of her life. It means that a man who married for sex at twenty may long for love at thirty, and we cannot tell him he is bound in a sterile union for life. It means that Jean, married to a homosexual, will not lose her place in the Church if she remarries. It means that the lawyer who lives with a social-climbing stranger will not be bound by empty form. It does not mean that men may run from marriage at the least pressure or provocation, but it does mean that they will not have to endure a relationship that is teeming with hatred and anguish.

There is no law, of course, which can measure the existence of love in marriage. We will have to trust a man when he tells us that he has no love. We will have to take his word, as we do in confession, and not make him prove the facts he only has to state. Canonists demand proof and require witnesses, legalists smother a man with forms to fill out and oaths to swear. A Christian takes his word and leaves judgment to his conscience and his God.

Locked in the memory box of my childhood is a sad face that I knew and loved in my youth. She was a middle-aged Catholic who sold candy to a little boy in a grocery store. She was kind to me, patient with my selection of four cents' worth of sweets. She always made me feel good, told me how handsome I looked when I served at the altar in Church. She said she would have liked a son as polite as I was, and I wondered why she couldn't have one. I knew little about her and only cared, as is the way with little ones, that she was kind and interested in me. One day I heard that she had divorced and remarried, and in my childish mind our friendship was over. I still bought candy, but I was painfully strained and different. She sensed it in my unspoken words and downcast eyes. One day she touched my hair and I pulled away. She looked at me with the saddest face I can recall, and said, "Someday I hope you'll understand!"

I do not know where life has taken her. I do not even know where it has taken me. But from my heart, I say to the sad face of my youth, "I do understand; forgive me!"

10. BIRTH CONTROL

"A dozen times I practiced birth control," a Catholic man says to me in my confessional. He tells me his name that I may better understand his problem. I know his children. They are a joy to have in school, a reflection of a man and woman's love. I know he has tried "rhythm" since the night he told me that he could name each of his last three children "Our Mistake." I know he has practiced abstinence until his wife was too edgy to live with, and he was masturbating twice a week. I have talked to him again and again, I have offered him all my solutions, described the homemade remedies hatched in a celibate's mind. Once I even suggested separate beds, so ignorant was I of a man's relationship with his wife.

And now he comes again, not to the Pope, not to the bishops, but to me in the confessional, and I have nothing more to say. My training tells me that he is living in "mortal sin," that without the forgiveness of confession he could die and go to hell. I cannot tell him this. He is among the best men I know. He is responsible, talented, sensitive, generous with money and time. His eyes are clear, his private life above reproach, his friends loyal, his wife still deeply in love, his children happy and full of life. But my Church accuses him and forbids him to receive communion until I take away his "sins." Tomorrow, first-communion Sunday for his seven-year-old boy, he cannot join his family at the table of Christ unless he is free from mortal sin. So I forgive him again with kindness and wait a month to forgive him yet again.

He goes back home to watch the children and to give his wife her chance to confess. She summons up her courage, holds back her tears, enters the confessional, whispers her guilt, and waits for the sermon that will make her feel dirty and ashamed. She takes me into the bedroom, tries to tell me what marriage is like, tries to explain the needs of her husband and her own desire for warmth. She recalls the calendar she threw away, the thermometer that lied to her about her ovulation, the confusion of charts and graphs and organized love. There are supposed to be several days a month, when intercourse might possibly be "safe." Yet she is not sure, and when these days come around, she is so tense that she fails at lovemaking. She ends up weeping and hoping her husband will somehow understand.

Lately she has noticed that he has grown a little cool. His expression has changed, he is drinking more. She herself has been increasingly nervous. If he puts his arm around her when he is watching TV, she fears he will lead her into sin. If he kisses her firmly on his return from work, she can feel her shoulders pull away. She tells me she is growing bitter and has lost much feeling for her Church. She asks permission to take the pill and wonders what I think. I hesitate. I know she will tell her friends what I said, if only to quiet her conscience, which has so long depended on the Pope. If I tell her to use the pill, then I will be swamped by the guilty who will ask to join my exodus. If I say "no," I will trample on my own conscience and send a sinner back to sin again. So I do not answer. I forgive her in the name of Jesus and leave her as wounded as before.

I do not answer because I do not agree with my Church, and I am hardly prepared to let my bishop tear the priesthood from my back. If I preach the conclusions I have reached by reflection and experience, I will be condemned to silence. If I forgive the couple who live in misery and suggest they use the pill, my rights to hear confessions will be revoked. So I turn to my fellow priests and ask for wisdom. The young are almost unanimous in their refusal to believe the Church, but they are too frightened to stand alone. The old tell me of their own dear mother who raised a family of ten, and boast of the happiness they enjoyed in their father's house.

These older men, vigorous in their opinions and usually Irish in background, deserve a special place in the annals of my Church. For years they prevented me from forming my own opinions, so strong were their sentiments, so firm their voices, so white and dignified their hair. I did not see the deep resentment in their blood, which somehow merged Margaret Sanger with the English Crown. I only saw the courage in their eyes and heard the lilt of deference when they greeted parishioners with a family full of children. They talked of Marie and her brood of ten, they extolled Louise and her six in seven years, they invited the bishop to baptize Helen's twelfth. But neither Louise nor Marie nor Helen could match their own Irish mothers, who chopped wood, kneaded dough, taught school, shoveled snow, nursed eleven babies, and attended daily Mass. All I could do was pant in the presence of such sacrifice and wonder if the world had not lost it pristine light. In the company of these priests, birth control was Communism, or Freemasonry, or the lust of Caesar's court.

No one dared question them, or ask them if they had read the modern arguments that justified the pill. They treated rhythm as a concession to weakness and urged newlyweds to let God and Mary shape the family size. They read nothing but the daily paper and the priestly journals, which confirmed their prejudices and gave fuel to their ancient arguments. They knew no theology and they dismissed fresh thought with a startled look, a puff on their pipe or cigar, and an abrupt change of subject. They were sure that nothing exciting had happened in religious thought since Christ surprised his Apostles on Easter Sunday morn. They rarely heard confessions, and when they did, the pious flocked to them, the "sinners" stayed away.

Such men are rarer now, but the power of their impact lingers in the Church. Even as I write, I think of the white-haired pastors who will hate me for my words. It is hard to hurt them, hard to oppose them in their declining years. They can point to the noble graduates of their schools, the prominent men who would not miss their Sunday sermons, the grown men and women who live only because parents listened to their priestly words on birth control. It is hard to hurt them because they are prayerful men, who read the Mass with dignity and simple, honest faith. It is hard to hurt the generation that they formed, the men and women who obeyed each sentence they uttered. These are my parents, my relatives, the loyal laity that gave me respect in the parishes I served. It is hard to hurt them, to meet their gaze, to know that I disturb the principles that have guided their whole life.

And yet it is harder to sit in my office and to hear the middle-aged doctor and his wife. He is not a Catholic, while she was trained from first grade through womanhood by nuns. She had even flirted with the convent, but recognized that marriage, too, is a dedicated love. Her husband does the talking in our conference. He speaks of six children and four miscarriages in a dozen years. His wife has spent over seven months in the hospital. They have always practiced rhythm, since her conscience would accept nothing else. Recently, she has had her fourth miscarriage and a solemn warning from her obstetrician that another pregnancy might take her life.

I wait for his question, and even as I wonder how he'll phrase it, I know the hollowness that will punctuate my words. He asks it simply: "What is wrong with birth control?" I reach in the grab bag of arguments handed me by my Church. I hear a voice that sounds like mine speak of primary purposes and natural law.[1] It says foolish things that only frightened men can hear. I hear the voice suggest abstinence or a new thermometer, or gratitude to God for all they have.

The doctor and I listen to the voice that sounds like mine, and we are not impressed. We think of six children, miscarriages, and a battered little wife. We think of the comfort she needs to care for the children she has, the recreation she needs to restore her energy and zest. We hear six children screaming for attention, we see clothes to be washed and sorted, housework to be done, food to be prepared. We do not believe that birth control is unnatural. It does not trouble the Jews and Christians, who love as much as we. Are they sinners? Pagans? Lusting and selfish men? We do not believe that sex is merely the bait to trick wives into another pregnancy, to lure husbands into feeding another mouth. We believe it is a road to tenderness, a special kind of conversation, the balm of loneliness, the sense of being needed and wanted amid rejection, the source of strength and comfort that teaches love. The doctor and I know that his wife needs his body that she may explore his soul, that he needs hers that he may penetrate the barriers to closeness, the sealed emotions, the secret sources of her pain.

He does not need her when her temperature is right. She does not need him when the calendar permits. He does not seduce her on a special evening like a man who dates a woman twice a month. She does not whisper as she kisses, "Yes, tonight!" She sleeps with him, studies him, notes the nervousness that attends his work, touches him to let him know she cares. He does not regulate his passion like a Stoic on display. Her sadness, a sick and sleeping child, evokes it. A song can send him to her bed, a special conversation, an evening of lightness and laughter, his hour of triumph or despair. The calendar can make of sex a duty and smother its spontaneity. Sex is a mystery never quite the same. It can uncover the hurts that preoccupation ignored, restore the closeness that routine and business wore away. All of this I know, as does the doctor and his wife. But we listen to the voice that sounds like mine, and hear it drone of selfishness and sin.

Suddenly the doctor stands, shakes his head, and takes his wife by the arm. It is only when he makes ready to leave that I realize the droning voice was mine. I want to tell him of my thoughts, but he does not want to hear any more. He has heard enough. He stands in the doorway and looks at me with sadness, with pity, with quiet, manly tears. He utters no protest, nor does he bombard me with biological arguments of his own. He only pauses to ask, "Have you ever loved a woman, Father, loved her enough to cry? Have you ever seen her bleed from a dead baby and wondered if she could live to mother the ones she had? Have you ever fondled her tired body, watched her breast heave as she lay asleep, and wondered how you'd live if she were gone? Have you ever held her when nothing else would do? Cried in her arms when you were afraid of life? Dried her tears when her duties drove her mad, then watched her smile?"

Now he is gone, his questions ringing in my ears. What do I tell him: "Obey the Church?" "Life is fleeting?" "You have not prayed?" Should I remind him of the suffering in Vietnam, or tell him that life is a valley of tears? Should I recite the arguments I've heard a thousand times, the arguments that nauseate me with their sordid view of sex, and amuse me with their puritan prejudice? Shall I tell the doctor about Onan in the Bible, who spilled his seed and was murdered by God? Or shall I tell him of Augustine's fourth-century views and his distorted references to sex? Or shall I recall the warnings of Pope Pius XI, the patron saint of the Church's present position, the warnings born of nineteenth-century theology and a medieval vision of man? Or maybe I should tell him that the Council Fathers are thinking of him in their annual meetings and the Pope will give an answer when all the facts are in.[2]

I told him *nothing* because there was nothing else to tell. Unless I told him that I was a coward who let my Church hide my conscience in the comfort of its skirts. Or told him that I was afraid to argue with my bishop, or place my priest's vocation on the block. Or told him I had been brainwashed in my training and was incapable of an independent thought.[3] Or maybe I should send him to Holland, where the theologians seem almost brave enough to tell the truth. Or best of all, tell him to inaugurate a rally in every diocese in our land, to make our people picket the rectories and gather on the bishops' porches, boycott schools, and deny parishes their weekly funds. Then maybe the Pope will hear in the silence of his chapel. Maybe he will not have to study so long, pray so fervently, if he finally hears the screams of men and women in the world.

I ask my Pope if he knows he is tearing homes apart, if he knows that Catholic men and women sexually grow apart. I see it every day, the frigidity caused by calendars, the anger and unfaithfulness of husbands, the anxiety and bitterness of wives. Some are strong enough finally to ignore the Pope when suffering is such that it threatens their sanity. The weak and docile, however, still count the days and run to confession when they violate our rules. They ask me when I see them on the streets: "When will the Pope tell us if we can use the pill?" "Do you think he'll permit it?"

Poor deluded children of the Pharaoh, making their bricks in Egypt without the straw that gives them strength. They come to me as Moses, or wait for the Pope to see a burning bush. I am Moses without charter, Moses without a single miracle, Moses without the guiding hand of God. I am a poor man's Moses, who has seen the foreign law which oppresses my people, and can only scream: "Let my people go!" Let wives go to their husbands and let husbands stop murdering their wives. Let my people go to the sacrament of communion when all they've done is love as human beings. Let my people go to confession without telling me what happens in their beds. Let Catholics go free from the consuming guilt that withers love.

The poor are made to play a vicious game when we bar them from the sacraments if they practice birth control. They come to Church each Sunday, but are forbidden to receive the bread which gives them life. They are in mortal sin, and everyone in Church can know. Even their children know as they stumble over their parents in the pews to approach the altar and share the food of Christ. But their parents stay behind and try to ignore the pressure from the pulpit: "Good Catholics receive communion every Sunday." They must sit there in shame, sit there separated by a pharisaic line. They are the "sinners" who live in lust and cannot share the banquet of their God.

The selfish woman can come to the altar if she begrudgingly gives her husband his bimonthly dose of sex. She has no problem with the Church's law. She loathes sex, and impassively endures it once or twice a month. But she keeps the law—not the law of love and concern, but the law of calendar and consummated sex. The sermons on birth control do not bother her, the Church's law protects her from the responsibility of tender love. She gives her husband her body to calm his physical hunger every other week, she only denies him the involvement of her heart. She does not practice birth control, she practices love control, and my Church is unconcerned. She keeps the law, controls her passion without a struggle, and smugly sits, without scruple, at the table of the Lord of Love. But the woman who loves her husband, who cannot keep the rules made by monks and celibates, must live in guilt till menopause.

One day, history will record the madness of my Church. Meanwhile, the weak and ignorant listen to the archaic arguments which support our views on birth control. They do not even sense the irony of our law. The Pope visits India, weeps for its poverty, and condemns the only sensible plan to control its teeming population. He comes to the United Nations to speak of peace and takes time for an irrelevant commercial to chastise birth control. For once he can let the world know that he can talk of peace without chewing the hand that passes out contraceptives. Instead he tells the politicians and the social workers, the diplomats and the welfare workers, even the religious leaders of the world, that they are selfish and immoral.

I might believe his concern for the warring world if he would relieve the misery of the weak and warring within his Church. We do not need his blessing, we need his openness to honest reform. He well knows how specious are our arguments against birth control, how they are merely wordy logistics which bind and frighten men. Men know nothing of the natural law;

they only know the pressure of hungry children and the tension of loveless lives. They cannot quote Augustine or Pius XI, they can only tell the clergy how little they know about marriage and sex. They would like to ignore the Church's law, but they cannot gamble with the fires of hell, so desperate have we left them in their fearfulness of sin and God. Somehow our law was broad enough to permit the nuns in the Congo to take the pill lest they conceive the child of the savage who was threatening to rape them. Why is it not broad enough to include the mothers of the world lest they lose the love of the men who married them?

There is not a solid argument that prevents the Church from permitting birth control. We only have to admit, as every man who loves already does, that sex means something other than conception. It is as simple as that. My Church does not need more time to make up its mind; it only needs the humility and courage to face facts. It does not need a special revelation; it only needs to admit that celibates developed our theology of marriage, and the ancestors of the rigid Irish monks enforced it. We have become the laughingstock of the world, the butt of a million jokes, the nineteenth-century Church in the age of space.

Our rhythm clinics still condemn the family-planning clinics and sincere researchers continue to study cycles and take temperatures of desperate women.[4] Several days a month, all circled in red and green, admit a husband to the body of his wife. Moods and family tensions defer to the calendar, and the creative and sensitive union of intercourse loses its human coloring of hunger and surprise. Man, the clock-puncher, the button-pusher, the computer-regulated, sacrifices his personal love to cycled demands of sex without any rhythm at all. The world watches, wonders, waits, but my arrogant Church ignores the weak who love her and resists the necessary change.

We do not ask the Church to change her concern that husbands love wives, or its concern that children learn to know they are unique and priceless. We realize that behind the charts and rhythm cycles lies a Church that wants the best for her children. That is why we can forgive the priests who invade bedrooms, the "theologians" who deny our parents their place at the communion table, even the Pope, who comes to America by air but condemns birth control as if he came with Columbus.

The home is, indeed, in jeopardy. The secular city has made us wonder where the picnic and the playground went. Fathers know that their work takes too much of their time. Mothers know that social commitments and car pools can easily exhaust them. Children feel the pressure of competition as soon as they enter school. The Church, ever a champion of the family, has a new and unprecedented job, a new chance to defend love in the nuclear age. But man does not need to hear of pills and passé problems; he needs to know the gospel that is for his peace.

I cannot see my world as lost and selfish. I cannot call the men who approve the pill the promoters of compromise, the immoral agents of crime. I can see them as the instruments of God. The pill is not nirvana, but neither is it sin. It is a help, certainly to be improved, to assist parents in co-creatorship with God. What is wrong if parents chose their children, plan their family, decide how far their love and energy can stretch? Must they guess at fertility or regulate love? Must they praise another generation, whose self-control might well have been more a product of prudery than of religious faith? Must they deny their spouse to pursue their God? I do not believe it. I do not accept my Church's stand on birth control, in conscience or in common sense.

I remember the young Mexican girl named María whose marriage I blessed some three years after she had first been married by a judge. She already had two children and I wondered how José could handle another one very soon. So I talked to María about rhythm, sensing that she knew little about calendars and charts. In the midst of explanation, she winked at me and said, "We won't have some kids for a while." Then, detecting my fear that she might be practicing sinful contraception, she grinned her special grin and said, "José says no more kids for now, *Padre*, but he still needs lots of love. So if the Church is mad, I tell her, 'You don't know José!' You see, *Padre*, I love the kids but José's the only man I got. I gotta love him, or he won't be happy and love María and the kids. And José don't look at the calendar when he makes love, but he don't want another kid right now. So . . . you know what I mean, *Padre*? That's all there is to it."

María seemed to have no dilemma. Her simple faith could solve the conscience problem built by Catholic theology. But millions are not as simple as María, millions have never learned the courage and independence born of her childlike trust in God. And somehow, tonight, after the angry arguments, and books, and papal statements, I think María has the problem resolved, and that's all there is to it.

11. CATHOLIC SCHOOLS

There is no modern folly to match that of the Catholic bishops who continue to erect Catholic schools. The Catholic school system, the pride of my youth and one of the landmarks of American history, deserves to be phased out. The Catholic school has drained the revenue of every parish, stolen the majority of religious vocations to staff its offices and classrooms, absorbed our energies and consumed our time. To sustain it we have neglected our parishes, ignored the poor, delayed renewal, and alienated our non-Catholic friends. Once upon a time such sacrifice made sense.[1]

The Catholic schools that cover our country are the valiant monuments of the zealous and weary pastors who built them to fortify their faith and the heroic people who sacrificed to pay for them. They were an emergency measure, a proof of the kind of determination that our fathers poured into our blood— the determination that would one day bring the freedom that would make these schools obsolete.

I attended such a school and I regret it not at all. I loved its old bricks and the railroad track that interrupted the classes with the hissing of its trains. I loved the sisters that taught me, and love them still. I was herded to Mass each morning and guided to confession each Friday afternoon. I did not murmur;

it was the only life I knew. It made sense to me because it made sense to my parents, and that was quite enough. I learned my religious "facts to remember" and gave a name to every sin or suggestion of the Holy Spirit. I knew that I would have to suffer for my faith, that Masons would get jobs denied to Catholics, that I was taxed for schools I didn't use. I was proud of my faith and would rather die than harm or deny it. I was convinced that I could read and spell better than my friends in the public schools, and attributed this to the special wisdom given me by God. I sold my raffle tickets with vigor, ransomed black babies from pagan lands, and had free days that my public school friends didn't share.

My school is a noble part of America's history, a witness to the accumulated bigots of Europe's religious wars. I was accused of idolatry and of orphanages filled with the babies of nuns. I was reminded of Galileo and Torquemada as if they slept with me at night. I was not alone in my suffering; I lived in a ghetto as did the Negroes and the Jews. I clung to my fellow Catholics when my countrymen called me ignorant and superstitious. My friends were the Polacks, the Dagos, the Hunkies, and the shanty Irish of America's bloody birth. I knew in my way what the Mexicans and Puerto Ricans know, what the Protestants in Spain have known, what man everywhere has known when he threatens the security and comfort of the party in power. And so my parish built my school, as Catholics throughout my country built their schools, when they were denied religious rights and self-respect. They built them with the meager income that an immigrant could make, with their own hands if there was no other way. They built them, and I, like all America, should be proud. They could do nothing else, given their background and the climate and culture of our land. They showed the Catholic world in Europe what the faith could mean to an American. They showed their fellow Americans that they were a part of America, a part possessed of fire and wisdom that America could not do without.

Catholics clung to each other because a man in a ghetto has no other choice. They clung together longer than was needed because, like frightened children in war, they could not believe that the bombs and screaming rockets had ceased. The echoes were still in their ears, the bitterness still in their mouths, the memories of Al Smith and Boston's Brahmins locked in their hearts. They were too proud of their victories, too defensive in their defeats, but it was not hard to understand their feelings if you saw their scars. Their pastors were sergeants who led them into battle and gave them courage and hope. They told them to build schools and they built them with the fury of a father building a shelter for his children. They told them to heed the bishop and the Pope, and they followed their words with the determination of a man in all-out war.[2] That war, however, is over, and another has begun, the war of civilized man to survive and live in peace. In such a world religious differences sound like the persistent whinings of a spoiled child. And still we build our schools and beg for funds to perpetuate an America which we have fought to bury in the past.

We build our schools like soldiers returning from the war who learned only to fight. We build them to honor the wisdom of another age. We build them to please our parents, to thank our pastors for their service and their love, to make our bishops happy, to postpone the religious problems that presently we face. We beg for more vocations to fill our schools with teachers, when we should begin to close them and send our priests and sisters to more important fields. We ignore our children in the public schools and offer them irrelevant programs of catechism that only leave them bored.[3] We ignore the state universities and the religious indifference that challenges our students there. We build schools to protect the Catholic children from the world in which they live, to smother them with religious information they do not really need. We build, we build, we build, even though the coming generation will find our schools obsolete.

No longer can we protect our children from their society, no longer will Catholics remain separate in the world in which they live. They need religion, they even want it, if their conversation is any indication of their appetite. They wonder about morality, ponder values, question the power of God, sense the sacred in the joy and the emptiness of life. They need religion, but they do not need our schools.

I have taught in parochial schools for more than ten years. I have taught children in grade school and young adults in the Catholic university. I have been a staunch defender of Catholic education and pressured many a student away from the state university, where he would be exposed to the "temptations of the world." I continued to sell Catholic education long after I personally questioned the defensiveness of its message and the quality of its religious formation. I argued that a sound education should include theology, even though I knew that Catholic schools only offer advanced catechism and largely irrelevant moralizing. I fought those who questioned Catholic schools. I spoke of the dangerous positivism that infected our universities, the pagan perspectives that soiled our lusting world. I saw Catholic schools as the hope of our civilization, the last fortress in a raging world of sin. Then, suddenly, I stopped defending and started to think.

What difference was there between the students I taught in the parochial high school every day and those from the public schools who attended my evening discussion once a week? The public-school students were as sincere and searching as any I ever taught. They were perhaps more tolerant than those in parochial schools, less indifferent about their faith, more mature in their awareness of the modern world. Their morals seemed as solid as the substance of their home. They brought their Protestant and Jewish friends to hear our discussions and encouraged them to state their views. They attended Mass, struggled to respect their parents, planned to attend college and to have loving families of their own.

They made me wonder if information is as important a part of religious training as I had been led to believe. What part does theology have in the building of a faith? Does any child need more than a smattering of theology unless he reveals an aptitude or interest in such a discipline? Is it not more important that a young person have a chance to practice religion, such as working with the poor, than to master definitions and to know the names of Abraham's wives? Religious instruction is one thing and religion quite another.

These children in the public schools were not concerned with the involved dogmas that occupied my class time in the parochial school. They did not care about the distinction between actual and sanctifying grace, the refined discussions about sacraments and angels, the gifts of the Holy Spirit, or the latest findings on the Galileo case. They were bored with the textbook I provided to cover the whole of our system in four years of Thursday evenings from seven till eight. They wanted religion; not facts about it, not involved studies about it, but something to give them courage and to provide meaning for their life. If I spoke of the "sacrament of initiation" they were fidgety, if I talked of "salvation history" they were bored. They didn't want to know that they were "prophet, priest and king"; they wanted to know that they were alive and capable of love. I could not tell them of the meaning of the Exodus, or rehash the story of Moses, or else they'd "turn me off." I had to begin with Kennedy to discover Moses, and to speak of novels and movies if Abraham was to live.

And yet, each morning for four long hours, I taught religion in the parochial school. For most of the students this was only tolerable because my classes were more exciting than the dull catechism they had had in the past. They were the victims of a Catholic grade school where untrained sisters taught a theology they themselves had never understood. I do not blame the sisters; I am in envy of their patient endurance. But most of them knew no theology, and a questioning hand could mean a stuttering effort to defend the Church. No wonder the students could tolerate my class. Some even liked it, just as some are fond of history or math. The majority, however, were bored and resentful of the discussions, which had little bearing on their lives. They had heard of the Trinity until it exuded from their ears. They had discussed the death of Christ until they knew the mark of every nail. They knew the pains of hell, the rights of marriage, the purpose of confirmation, the seven deadly sins, the beauty of Mary, and the heritage of Adam and Eve.

They were bored, and so was I. I was preparing little information boxes who could pass tests and challenge the evangelists who knocked on their doors. Of what value was this?[4] Did it make them more concerned with the horror of war, the suffering of the poor, the injustice to the Negro, the frantic pace of modern life which gave no time for self-knowledge and peace? Would it make them better spouses or citizens, would it make them more human, more attuned to the mystery of life? Or did it only make them smug and righteous, narrow-minded and afraid? I was giving them information when they wanted life. I was providing them with answers when they were not even open to the questions that honest men asked.

So I changed my approach and devised my own course. I abandoned the textbook and taught in seminar fashion. We read selections from *Time* and *Look,* pondered the meaning of *Catcher in the Rye* and *1984.* We examined Françoise Sagan, Hemingway, and William James.[5] We attended and discussed movies, and when I recommended *The Silence* by Bergman, I almost lost my job. I abandoned exams and quizzes, and marked them on a single essay on "The Search for Self in Modern Society." I marked liberally, paid little attention to rhetoric and spelling, encouraged freedom of expression, perhaps even rebellion. I discovered, however, that I was only trying to repair the damage done by the narrow Catholic ghetto and to create the experience that other students found in their public schools. Half of my time was spent in fighting intolerance or arrogance, or the bigotry of frightened parents. I was teaching students who had been trained by Catholic teachers, who had read largely Catholic books, and were immersed in Catholic experience. And yet they would go on to live in a world where men are only men.

Some of them would marry non-Catholics, some would lose their faith, some would find an answer in humanism, some would investigate another religion, some would settle into the routine observance of a dull Catholicism. Some would love their faith, some would grow to despise it. Girls would get pregnant and "have to get married." Boys would go in service and abandon religious practice. Some would practice birth control, others would shun it. Some would get divorced, others would know the beauty of a Christian home. But what did I contribute by my high-school classes? Was I solving any problems, or only postponing them? Was I forming their faith or had it been well determined by the family in which they lived?

Even the recent surveys cannot justify the money we spend for Catholic schools. And in effect, surveys are of little worth, because there is no possible way to measure what is mature faith and what is merely indoctrination. Surveys can tell us who goes to Mass, but they cannot tell us what happens to man in the center of his soul. They cannot reduce honesty to a graph nor chart the fire of charity nor distinguish between honest action and empty words. But even though surveys cannot justify our system of parochial schools, bishops and pastors continue to build their monuments.

How is a child better formed in a parochial school than in an intelligent program of part-time religious education after school? [6] We really don't know, since we have never had an intelligent part-time program. We spend millions of dollars on our Catholic schools and pennies on the greater number of Catholics who attend our public schools. Meanwhile, a few battered heroes try to convince our stubborn bishops that the Church faces a crisis in religious education.[7] These few recognize how little we have done for our students in public schools and how vastly their number is growing. Bishops continue to appoint diocesan directors of religious education who are "safe" and without professional training in the field, or who have accumulated sudden and unquestioned wisdom in a summer-seminar. Education is obviously among the most explosive problems we face, and I am convinced that if we developed a sound program for teaching religion to Catholic students in public schools, we could phase out the bulk of our own schools in twenty years.

You cannot possibly know the agony of this situation unless you have worked for the Catholic Church. Our leaders will not face the problem! They extoll our Catholic schools without having taught in one recently—if ever—and without any measuring stick of their effectiveness. They complain that public-school students will not attend our part-time classes, without realizing how niggardly have been our efforts to make such classes interesting and relevant. They only imagine that they face the problem when they gather a few sisters and overworked priests to develop a program. They join them with a few gifted professors and some interested publishers and ask them to improve the textbooks and outlines. This assembled body works for three or four days, glows with mutual admiration, and continues to provide us with more printed irrelevance. And why not? They have been asked to do a full-time job on a part-time basis. They have been asked to resolve a key and perhaps desperate situation without adequate authority or charter. When will we face the problem and gather the very best of our talent into authorized full-time teams to explore the psychology, the sociology, the theology, and the philosophy of religious education? When will we learn something of the modern techniques of communications? When will we be bold enough to experiment, to recognize decay, to realize that the forms which served our parents and grandparents have been outgrown?

Our bishops would not stumble so if the question were one of diocesan finance, if parochial income dropped 25 percent. But with education our frightened bishops hesitate. They continue to build more schools, when they should bury them because this is a new and exciting era in the Church. Pope John lived with us long enough to tell us that we can join the rest of the world in a search for vision and value. Even the fears of Pope Paul, the foot-dragging of Vatican II, and the largely irrelevant concerns of our American bishops in their recent conference cannot dull the memory of John. He changed our outlook, opened our hearts, quieted our fears, and in essence told us that we could close our "segregated" schools.

Some of our schools will always survive, but they will have

to be monuments to the best in private education and not the barricades that preserve fear, intolerance, prejudice, and weak inbreeding. We no longer want to hear the letters from our bishops each summer reminding us of the necessity of parochial schools. Nor will we ever jam our classrooms with every last child to save his soul from a pagan and faithless world. We must chisel out our faith in common with the rest of mankind, and our Church must offer us relevant programs of religious education independently of school. In fact, if we rejoined the world of our countrymen and showed them that we have the best interest of our nation at heart, there well might come courses of religion offered as electives in our public schools.

No longer must every religious order feel compelled to erect its special schools or colleges to shelter three or four hundred girls. To build such a school today is to erect a monument to a holy founder or to satisfy the ego needs of an order or a weary, nostalgic superior. We would do well gradually to sell many of our schools—not just one or two of them—to the public, and with the compensation we could give our talent and attention to the religious problems of our age. We could permit our gifted priests and sisters to teach in secular universities and to prove the fire of their commitment by the breadth of their open mindedness. We could even close most of our seminary colleges and encourage our fledgling priests to discover how the rest of the world thinks and lives. We could open our remaining universities to the scholars of other creeds and values in order to discover what are truly the questions of our times. Why are there only one or two Protestant theologians at Catholic universities? [8] Why are there so few theological schools at our state universities? Mainly because theology has been a frightened and defensive discipline, afraid to meet in open discussion the questions which a man must face in the barbershop or cocktail lounge. What are we afraid of? Truth? Or are we afraid that we will lose the man who wonders and doubts? If so, we have lost him already, because we do not have the confidence to admit that God can draw man in His own way. I can honestly say that I did not really believe in a mature manner until I read Barth and Tillich, Calvin and Luther, Kierkegaard, Buber, and Camus. Faith can grow in Freud and Nietzsche, Dewey and James, Sartre and Heidegger. It only ceases to grow in fear and narrowness and never in the energy of an honest search. Such a search is the very mark of our age, and we recognize it once we emerge from the ghetto of WASP and Catholic and discover that each man's blood is only red.

In a modern age, most of our schools will pass away, but they will not leave without a fight. The very money invested in them is the strongest motive involved in retaining them. This is a sad commentary on a great and historic Church which prefers to grow irrelevant rather than abandon the schools which only serve to tell weak men that their work has not been in vain. They need the symbols that indicate success, regardless of how unnecessary such symbols have become.

Actually, our grade schools should be the first to go, since the religious formation of the young is so obviously the product of home environment! The religious needs of children can well be handled in part-time religious programs. This would give us an immediate chance to reduce the strain on religious vocations, and to take the time to develop new methods of Christian service. We could, perhaps, attempt to transform some of our high schools into true models of the best in education and honesty, but preserve only those that can demonstrate their value. They should be servants of the community and the nation, and should admit a representative number of students and teachers of other faiths.[9] Short of this, ecumenism is just so much talk. With the demise of our grade schools we would have to come up with sound programs of part-time religious education, and not flounder as we have in the past. We should have the same courage to thin out our colleges and universities as we had in building them, and to erect a new college should never again be the prerogative of some local octogenarian or megalomaniac. No bishop or religious superior, acting with misguided zeal, should be able to impose upon an unaware people a financial drive to build an educational irrelevance. We have far too many already. Dioceses and religious institutions should have the courage and wisdom to assess their educational institutions of all varieties and ask the simple question: "Why?"

We must abandon our schools with the same historic insight that pushed us to erect them. Such dynamic change has ever marked the history of the Church. We have been stubborn and slow, as a giant body must ever be, but we have not been afraid to change. Once the monks did not hesitate to teach the people to farm, and then to build. They taught boys to read and to conjugate when there was no other way. They were willing to be beggars or soldiers and knights if the service of man seemed to warrant it. The sisters were willing to nurse soldiers or lepers, to gather orphans, to care for unwed mothers, to bathe the children of the poor. There were orders of preachers to stem religious ignorance and superstition, or to provide teachers for the growing universities of Paris, Salamanca, and Louvain. There were friars who taught the people to build roads, or who, in poverty, spoke without any words. They wrote books and they also burned them, they chided, scolded, and extolled. There were the special troops of the Pope and commandos of each council, ready to serve man as time and circumstances said he must be served.

Now the change must occur once again, and man must be served with new ways, and not with the services that he in his society has outgrown. There are special areas where no one has yet recognized the needs and pains of man. Here must Christianity come alive with the principles of creative love that helped to heal another generation. Perhaps we are expected to pour our energies into the world of poverty and the plight of the Negro. What would be the result if the Church of Bernard and Borromeo, Elizabeth of Hungary and Vincent de Paul began to channel its mighty forces into the education of the poor? What if our sisters were to walk among them in great numbers, to cook and clean for them, to fight for them, to teach and console without the obvious prospects of conversion? Would they fear the threat to a virginity which means nothing locked in a convent? And could not the Church teach us to live in a world of speed and machines, to find peace amid tension, culture amid leisure, simplicity and personal love in the midst of rising incomes?

Must we have a particular and special work that we do not share with others? Or has man, perhaps, moved so far in twenty centuries that we can only join with those who do the work that once was exclusively ours? Once we ran the hospitals, the orphanages, the homes for lepers, and the schools for children. Now man has matured to recognize his responsibility as man. Can we not be grateful that it is difficult to recognize a Christian in our society since so many men and women do Christian work? Is there no work for a parish without fences, for a Church without schools. Once we were the Church of the poor and the hungry. How came we to be the Church of the middle class? Can we not search for the modern men who are blind and deaf and lame in modern ways? Once man cried to us for schools and Catholic Youth Organizations and even boxing gloves. Now he cries for mental health and happy marriages and friendship in a world of computers and space.

Is it not time to abandon some of our inherited structures and to search and explore? Long enough have we ignored the religious problems of state universities, to teach innocent communicants how to fold their hands and to memorize meaningless prayers.[10] Long enough have we equated religion with education and lost our vision for the vast works that have not been done. I worked, for example, in a large parish in New York City teeming with the aged. The parish offered a lecture series, a parish mission, but nothing for the bored old folks who went to Mass, confession, and the park because they had nowhere else to go. Maybe we should run lunch counters or bars. Maybe we should run laundromats or coffeehouses and card rooms. Maybe we should work in television and on the stage.

I know a hundred places we should be, and you can tell me a hundred more. But we will never get there if we are afraid to abandon our inherited structures. We do not live in a world in which we can protect Catholics, not even one in which we can serve Catholics alone. We know that every man is our charge and we must serve him where he needs us. We must reexamine our goals, no matter the cost. We are not here to convert the world, but to serve it. We are not even here to save souls, but to love all men. God will convert and save in His good time.

It is a time to question and to surge ahead. It is time to search out the helpless and the weak and to go to them, no matter their poverty or affluence, no matter their faith or lack of it. It is a time to ignore statistics, which have hypnotized and impressed us. It is time to forget about finances, to canonize no form, to seek no credit, to work without ceasing. It is time to do almost anything except, please God, to build more Catholic schools.

12. LIFE IN THE

CONVENT

Several years ago a nun approached me with a serious problem of conscience. She had been struggling with a sexual temptation that left her tormented and confused. Although she had lived as a nun for twenty years, suddenly she could not work or sleep for fear that she had been unfaithful to her vows. It took courage and cunning for her to contact me, since such private consultations were not encouraged in her order. She was expected to receive permission for each and every visit with a priest and to travel with a sister companion between convent and rectory. It was apparently not safe for her to come alone. I had first learned of her problem when I dropped by her classroom one day after school to borrow a dictionary. She asked if it would be possible to see me privately sometime and then she began to cry.

I learned that she had struggled with her secret fear for almost three years, until she felt that she was living perpetually in "mortal sin." I asked her why she had not talked the matter over with a priest in confession. She informed me that the assigned confessor was always in a hurry and was not the kind of man with whom one discussed such a problem. Besides, as I later learned, it was not the kind of problem that one would want to discuss in the darkness of the confessional, but the kind that would have to be worked out gradually in a counseling situation. When I told her that I would be happy to see her at any convenient time, she laughed bitterly amid her tears. It was then she told me the special and difficult arrangements that would be necessary. She would have to approach her superior like a little girl and reveal in some detail the reason for her request. The mother superior looked upon such "special permissions" as a sad reflection on the happy community life for which she was responsible. If problems existed, they were to be kept within the convent walls and not to be televised to the world. The superior, a woman of sixty, without an ounce of psychology or human relations in her background, was the "mother confessor" of this group of sixteen nuns. The sisters were "called in" for private conferences, they were at times reprimanded for a lack of family spirit, for giddiness or individualism, for failure in the spirit of prayer or personal asceticism. Since they could bare their souls to such an interested "mother," there was really no need of outside help.

Finally, we did arrange a series of visits in my office while the sister companion busied herself in the waiting room with correcting papers and repairing her winter shawl. It was not long before I decided that the problem was out of my province. When I suggested that sister should see a psychiatrist, she wept without control. Such a recommendation was out of the question, not because she could not admit this need to herself, but because the mother superior, a sturdy and disciplined immigrant, would not be able to understand. Another nun in the convent had asked for such help, and she had never been permitted to forget it. So I ended up doing the best I could with the advice of a psychiatrist friend. In the course of our conversations it became clear that sister knew little or nothing about her own sexual makeup and it was hard to discuss "sexual sins" without some further education. I gave her a couple of books to read despite her protests, and she hid them like a child with dirty pictures. I asked a physician to prescribe tranquilizers without knowing the sister to whom they were given.

It was a mad arrangement in an incredible structure, which, unfortunately, was not an unusual exception.

Later that year the sister was moved to another parish and found it increasingly difficult to continue the visits. The new "mother superior" was a boisterous back-slapper who thought that the solution to every emotional problem was fresh air and a hearty laugh. When I did manage to see sister, I felt like I was preparing for some furtive affair, so carefully did our plans have to be laid. For a time I could not write to her since her letters were censored. When she wrote to me, she did it secretly and mailed the letters with surreptitious caution. Gradually she did show some improvement, but still needed a great deal of help when our paths became permanently divided.

I wish that such a case were atypical. It well may be dramatic and, today, of less frequent occurrence, but it is not exceptional or exaggerated. Sisters do occasionally have serious problems which have been obscured or ignored lest such bad public relations should impair the flow of vocations. I remember the sister who was having a problem with homosexuality calling me from a pay station in a drugstore, and I ended up hearing her confession in the library stacks of a state university so that she would not have to receive permission to go to confession. I have heard sisters' confessions while walking across the school yard, in an empty classroom, at an altar boys' picnic. Canon law tells me that I cannot hear such confessions validly outside of the confessional, but common sense tells me that no man or woman is bound to the impossible. Canon law also provides numerous freedoms for a sister who requires confession, but experience has made me know that such freedoms are often not worth the paper on which they appear.[1] I do not mean to imply that sisters are frequently troubled by serious moral problems. I merely state that they sometimes are, and the structure of convent life then puts them through the terrors of the damned.

Once upon a time the rules of convent life were, perhaps, not unreasonable. Once the great majority of nuns in our country were the peasant children of immigrants and pioneers. They had learned in their large and disciplined families to sacrifice feelings, to live without privacy, to prize unquestioning obedience as the supreme sign of humility and faith. They had been taught to work hard, to ignore personal needs, to bury emotions in silence and a nervous smile. The white-haired pastor of the parish was Moses on a mountain with his arms raised high, filled with the spirit of private and public infallibility. Their natural father was also a man of self-denial and few complaints. To such women, religious life was not really a unique challenge, but merely a continuation of the existence they had known in the structured family of their neat and theocratic world.

Many of these women became nuns because they were enlisted by the solemn and strong priest who controlled their lives. They had really never thought of marriage, they knew little if anything of sex, and many knew from life at home that matrimony meant merely discipline and self-denial. They had seen their fathers work a dozen hours a day in factory or field. They had known the weary mothers who scrubbed, baked, and rubbed their rosaries until they drifted off to bed. There had been no talk of personal and ecstatic love, no word about the drive and violent hunger of the flesh, no deep discussions about the need for fulfillment in life. These were the hardy daughters whose mothers fed the chickens the morning after they bore a baby. They were the daughters of the potato farmers and dock workers, the progeny of wagon trains and crowded ships that landed in New York.

I knew these women well, and know the few that linger still. They taught me and encouraged me in my vocation. They spoke of the Cross with shining eyes and carried it with the asceticism learned as children. They could bury feelings without obvious frustration. They could pass from a position of authority to a drone's job in the ranks without upset. They could live a life without privacy, perform a task for which they were neither suited nor educated. They could teach subjects they had never formally learned, teach when they wanted to nurse, cook when they longed to work among the poor. They could retire at an hour when the rest of the world was beginning to seek out entertainment and culture. They could rise when the rest of the world was resting for another day. They could teach children with only a vague idea of the life the children lived. Forbidden to visit private homes, they could miss their mother's funeral or a golden jubilee. They were content not to attend a wedding nor be seen in public after dark simply because they were not allowed to.

All of this they seemed willingly to do in the name of the Church and the holy founder who had devised their rule. Their "holy rule," too, was the product of culture and folkways long since dead. They somehow lacked the freedom to change the inspired words of this rule which well may have been modern in the days of surreys and kerosene lamps. They attempted to run schools without questioning a proud pastor's ignorant interference. They taught school all year and picked up a degree over ten or twenty summers. They went to Mass every day whether they wanted to or not. They made eight-day retreats without speaking a word. They guarded the pride of their order no matter the personal cost. They competed for vocations and nursed the special students who seemed to be destined for the convent life. They prayed far more than they studied, even though they had been called to an active life within scholastic halls. They accepted sixty children in a classroom in order to please the pastor or his parish, and sometimes believed the myth that a nun can handle such numbers because of her special touch. They were the marvelous women who taught our fathers, and their fathers, and even some of us.

But gradually, even suddenly, they were invaded by the young sisters who had not known the world of the washboard and sacrifice. Yet the rules were unwilling or unable to change.[2] The new breed were the daughters of doctors and insurance men, draftsmen, dentists, and factory foremen. They had known freedom and trust, dances and spending money. They had read modern authors, attended "B" movies, and even traveled to Europe. Their presence precipitated a clash and I witnessed it a thousand times.

I shall never forget the sister assigned in one parish to teach math. She had been a good student but had not a particle of interest in cosines and logarithms. In the four years I knew her she grew alternately fat and thin, pale, despondent, and wretched. She came to me one day to tell me that she wanted to leave the convent. I asked if she had taken the matter up with her superiors. She informed me that her request had not been taken seriously since the order was short of teachers and had trained no one else to teach math. She told me, haltingly, as one quite unaccustomed to honest and personal communication, that once she had wanted to be a nun who labored among the sick and poor. She had made her request known on several occasions, but had repeatedly been told that God wanted her for another work. Before she entered the convent officially, she had been assured that she would be able to do the work that had filled her dreams. After her training, however, it had been suggested that she deposit her personal judgment in a superior's hands. So she continued to say her prayers and teach her math until she almost lost her balance.

In many ways she was afraid to leave the convent. The superior could make her departure so complicated and guilt-ridden that it would hardly be worth the personal strain. It was easier, in some ways, to drift along and call her life a "cross," when her whole being cried out for something else.[3] The really frightening thing was that there was actually no honest avenue of recourse. She could go to the pastor of the parish, but he was most likely baptized in the same system of "devotion to duty" and "God's will" that stifled communication with her own superior. Besides, he needed a math teacher and sisters come a whole lot cheaper than lay teachers. Her own superior would not offer much sympathy, since dissatisfaction within the community would threaten the superior's own prominence and authority within the order. Each superior must run a "happy family" or headquarters would likely take the matter amiss. It may happen, too, that the superior has some doubts about her own vocation, and the distress of a young sister can threaten her personal security. This was true in the case under discussion, and every visit to the superior produced more confusion and guilt, as the young sister was told of her selfishness and her stubborn rejection of "God's many graces." She was further told not to make her dissatisfaction known to the other sisters, since this, too, could upset the equanimity of a happy home.

Perhaps you, a product of a world of personal responsibility and decision, would ask: "Why doesn't she just walk out?" You, however, do not understand. "God's will" and "sacrifice" are words of deep meaning within the system and can frighten even the most independent and courageous. Besides, where would this sister go and what would she do? Her family would, most likely, mourn her departure. They had seen her as the flowering of their own faith and personal sacrifice. She was the daughter that they had given to God, their "bargaining point" at Heaven's gate. In addition, she had been sheltered from the world for a dozen years, and I do mean sheltered.[4] She had no friendships, she was not trained to make personal decisions, she had not a penny of income nor the money even to buy clothes. She would likely leave the convent like a convict, wearing the clothes she brought in or a simple outfit that some recent recruit had abandoned in the dressing room. She did not know how to go about getting a job or renting an apartment, nor would the order feel the least responsibility to make her leave-taking pleasant, or even untraumatic. She would be asked not to say good-bye to her fellow sisters, she would be hurried out of sight like an embarrassing relative, and the children she taught would be told that she was moved to another assignment. All the while she would not be sure that she had done the right thing, since her mind was confused and unsettled. She still was not sure that she did not have a "vocation," so carefully had the mystique of a "religious vocation" been buried in pious nonsense. She was only sure that she had been unhappy and lost. One understanding hand stretched out to help her might well be enough to lead her to peace, but she could well linger in years of misery before she found it. She was permitted to talk to no one who might understand, no one who was not conditioned by the system or personal frustration and fear. All she would hear would be: "Hang on and God will provide!" And if some priest or doctor were to make the exit smooth and easy, he would likely never receive a referral from this order again. I know, because I gave her the money to leave, and found her a respectable job.

I am not giving archaic examples. I had a very similar case a year ago in one of the most "modern" and "renewed" orders. I had taught theology to this young lady, and she had come to me a year later hoping that I would understand. When she finally had summoned up the courage to demand her release from "temporary" vows, a process which can be simple or vastly complicated, she was "forced" to take a teaching position in a distant state for five months. While she was preparing to leave for her new assignment, she was locked in a room so that she would not make contact with any of her sister friends. She wrote me from her new assignment to tell me of her utter misery. She did not want to be a nun and yet she was forced to live the life for several months while her "case" was being pushed through channels. The "channels" could have been opened in ten minutes, but a teacher was needed and she was unwillingly sent. Her letter ended with the words: "I don't know how long I can hang on. I just don't know!"

There are many sisters who would like to leave the convent. They came to convent life in obedience to some mysterious and "divine" command, or in fear of marriage or spinsterhood. They came to win a parent's love, to feel important, to avoid personal decisions, to fulfill a youthful vow, to prevent a sensitive conscience from tearing them apart. They came in youthful daydreams or unable to resist the pressures of a pastor, a parent, the nun who knew them for several years. Or perhaps they came searching for peace, which seemed to elude them everywhere. They came to escape confusion or decision, or to create a goal. They discovered after a year or ten that they should not remain, and they tried to summon up the courage to be honest to themselves. Many, perhaps most, could not leave, so they settled into the busy routine that alternately soothes and tortures them. After a time they do not question or think, they just drift along knowing that life can no longer offer them anything else.

There are thousands, too, who came and remained because they had found the life for which they were apparently destined. They accepted its difficulties even as they looked forward to renewal. They found in it a life of fulfillment and meaning. They grew in love and peace, they moved each person they met with admiration and a strange awareness of the presence of God. My close friend Sister "Jean" is such a nun, sensitive, intelligent, open, and totally feminine. She can talk as easily about the joys as about the difficulties and empty formalism of convent life. She is not afraid to love individuals and to tell them of her love. She was not afraid to tell me. She is not defensive about her habit, her rule, or her total way of life. She can laugh at the uniform which marks a nun as one who is obviously out of contact with the world. She can ridicule the changes in dress, adopted after many meetings and prayers, which hardly alter the medieval image. She can dream of the convents of the future, in which the sisters will be able to make friends easily and will be trusted to live as mature and independent women. She admits the diminishing number of vocations without "contrived" explanations, and sees in it a sign of progress. She approves the programs which teach a young sister about personal motivation, hidden sources of guilt, and the latent fears of sex and marriage.

She can speak of a convent life in which each nun does not have to walk alike and hide her hands or bury her personality in the rules provided by a well-meaning foundress.[5] She speaks of the need for freedom and privacy, if the sister is truly to be an active woman in the world. She looks forward to the day when the sister will not be locked from the world's sight once darkness falls, and will not be forced to rise in group conformity for Mass and morning prayers. Community has to mean more than compulsory programs of prayer and girlish recreation. The nun of the future should be able to know the joy of personal decision and to establish her own rule of life within the framework of the religious family.

Sister "Jean," like many other sisters, feels the need for personal friendships. She told me of a convent in which she was assigned where there was no sister who shared her age or interests. She was obliged to share her free time with the "community," although the "community" was only four other nuns. The superior of the convent was well past sixty-five, kind, gentle, and completely out of touch with the world. Her idea of real fun was to sew or to surprise "Father" on his feast day. Two of the other sisters were extreme introverts incapable of speaking personally at all. They lived as if they had no feelings. The other sister, who did most of the cooking and housework, was in her dotage, and spent her free time humming Christmas carols or saying her rosary while watching TV. This was "Jean's" home for four years, and her contacts with lay people were restricted to chats with mothers after Mass or school. She was not permitted to attend a movie theater (unless *Bambi* was being rerun) or a private home, since the mother superior did not consider this "prudent" behavior for a dedicated nun. (Mother Superior was not required to explain what "prudent" actually meant.) On one occasion "Jean" was visited by a young bachelor who taught in the public high school, and the superior told her to discourage any further calls.

Life in the convent needs renewal more desperately than any form of Catholic life.[6] Nowhere in the Church have the personnel invested more of themselves. Nowhere in the Church are they quite as lacking in avenues of recourse. For years, we priests were able to treat nuns as disembodied spirits who somehow did not need the vacations, the outlets, the relaxation demanded by the clergy. We could ask of them working and living conditions that we would never expect of ourselves. When I suffered most from an irate and impossible pastor or an overwhelming work load, I could always get away. I could chase the golf ball, have a few beers, or relax for three weeks in Miami. The sisters, however, must return to the convent and

join in the common prayer or common meals or common recreation. It has often not been important how they feel, or how
they like their job, or to what extent the "community" can
tear them apart. They have been the "dear nuns," the "good
sisters," the gentle little anachronisms without feeling. The
standard procedure in many parishes has been to ignore their
complaints until they disappear, or at best to offer some token
and fleeting redress.

Once upon a time the sisters were able to say that they were
the "brides of Christ" in a kind of spirituality fashioned before
Freud. They could fix upon the contrived image of some misty,
historical Christ who was a product of their dreams and not the
healthy vision of a living and relevant Christian. They could
linger before the tabernacle as a patient spouse waiting for
her "man" to come home or to communicate with a Christ
born in a stable of sugar and spice. They could make of Christ
whatever kind of bridegroom they wanted Him to be and hide
their frustrations in their "personal love" for Him. At times
they could find a "father" in the pastor, a "mother" in the religious superior, in a superb and involved effort to avoid maturity and growth. Once such innocence and childlike deference
was acceptable, even touching, in the simplicity that it produced. Of late it has grown pathetic and out of date.

Christ took no spouse except the Church,[7] nor did He
need a bride to keep Him "company" in the morning or at
night. He needed free and healthy laborers in His vineyard,
women whose life, and even whose garb and attitude, is modern and meaningful. No girl can account for her every thought,
her every minute, her every dime, and become a woman. She
must be free enough to make mistakes, modern enough to be
a real woman, and human enough to form male and female
friends outside the convent walls. She must have money to
spend,[8] time to travel, a chance to be alone, and to be, at times,
anonymous in a crowd. She must not hide behind her robes,
must not be led to believe that she walks on the streets as a
symbol of dedication when she is only a sign of an outmoded
tradition. She must not bury her personality in the tired rules

of some long-dead foundress. She must be free to enter the convent and must be given both encouragement and tangible support when she chooses to leave. She must know that she is first a child of God and only then a daughter of her parents, her pastor, her religious community.

It would do her good to have dinner with a man, to speak personally to him. It would do the world good to know that she can accept human love and still want to be a nun. Presently, most nuns would be forbidden to ride in the front seat of a car with a priest or embarrassed to have a snack with him in a quiet café. A vocation cannot be a burial from the world as once it was. It must spring from a mature love, a dedication, and not from a high wall of protections and fears. There are women in the world who know a virgin's dedication without knowing a nun's inhibited existence. There are nurses and teachers, social workers and cooks in rest homes who live without marriage in peace and honest fulfillment.

We do not have to "crowd" our young women for vocations or force the religious life on the frightened and the passively docile. There may not be so many nuns in a world which permits them to live as free women, but there will be more than enough to do the work. Their very life will be attractive enough to continue to draw the courageous and deep woman who seeks more than marriage can give in terms of service and human concern. Then the world will not wonder about them and check them off as the frustrated virgins who march without "oil" or "lamps." They will not be the oddities that wander through our streets with their umbrellas and black bags. They will not be the conversation stoppers that hear only half of the world's ways. They will be the magnificent women that some have managed to be despite unbelievable obstacles, the mature and relevant sisters who search out the lonely and the poor, who speak of God without uttering a pious phrase or handing out a single "holy card," who know even more about this world than they do about the next. Then they can begin to speak of "community," and even I will know what they mean.

13. THE MAN WHO IS A NON-CATHOLIC

From childhood through my priesthood, I have learned that every non-Catholic is a potential Catholic. He has no other meaning. The hope of his conversion is the reason for the smile I offer him, the kind word I whisper when I pass. If he lives in my neighborhood, I must convert him by my example; if he lives in China, I must convert him by my prayers. The non-Catholic is the target of a never-ending conspiracy to drag him unawares to Rome. If he resists my efforts, time will undoubtedly tell him of the heresy that blinds and fetters him, and I will ignore him and search out his more docile children.

A non-Catholic is not a Jew who holds dear the faith and history of his people. He is simply not a Catholic, and I must lead him patiently to truth. The non-Catholic is not a committed Protestant who loves his neighbor and worships his God. He is not a Catholic, and is deprived of the strength and comfort of the Church. A non-Catholic is not an honest searcher who lives without the structure of organized faith. He is a pagan, a cripple, who will never learn to love until he finds the path to Rome. All of this I learned in my parochial school, in the seminary which trained me to be a priest. I learned it from my fellow priests in serious conversation and seminars, in the talk over beer, in the treatment of non-Catholics by the rulings of my Church.

I learned my lesson well and practiced it carefully in my labors as a priest. I remember the sad-faced lady who used to wait for me each Sunday after the final Mass. She was well-dressed, lived in a beautiful home, had two bright and healthy children, was married to an interesting and thoughtful husband. Yet she was a tragic figure, and I helped to make her so. It was not her health or her job that upset her. It was the husband who did not share her faith. He was a non-Catholic who stubbornly resisted the power of her prayers and the charm of my approach. She waited after Mass because she knew her husband would soon be there to pick her up. She would delay me that he might have another chance to know the hypnotic influence of the Catholic priest. Maybe this time he would see the folly of his ways, and know the mystery and joy he missed. So we stood there, the sad-faced lady and I, waiting for her husband to return from the golf course, that we might invite him by our presence to the sacred rites of Rome.

He always drove up to the back door of the Church with a style all his own. He bounced from the car with a special exuberance, shook my hand with a big grin, and said, "Think my old lady will ever amount to anything, Father?" We all laughed, but the lady and I wondered if God would ever hear our prayers, or if only the threat of death would move this non-Catholic to join the one, true Church.

He was a good husband, an involved and loving father, but a heartache to his wife. My Church had made him her heartache, and so had I, by pushing her to struggle for his conversion. And when he resisted, in his kind and manly way, she questioned her prayers, her daily example, the sincerity of the penances she offered in his behalf. And in her eyes each Sunday after Mass I saw her pleading and her hurt. She was counting on me because her husband liked my personality and my interest in their children. I was her new hope, her last champion, the strong knight who could challenge her husband in the battlefield of religion and lead him to the Church. She invited me to dinner. She telephoned me, to recount each religious suggestion that slipped from his unsuspecting lips. She prayed ceaselessly and told the children that they must storm heaven with the fervor of their requests. She sent money to missionaries, who promised to help her with their labors and prayers in another land. She had Masses said for a "special intention," exulted when he joined her on Christmas and Easter in the pew, rejoiced when he glanced at the Catholic literature she had strewn carefully through the house.

But somehow he resisted, read his Bible almost every day, and continued to love his family without the guidance of my Church. Now I wonder how he could smile when we badgered him with the pressure of our frantic attack. We had forced him to sign promises that he would raise his children in the Catholic faith. We had embarrassed his parents when we refused to marry him at the altar of our Church. He had submitted to the instructions provided to explain our "position" and to hasten his "conversion." He had endured the requests of his little children when they asked him to join them in their first communion and to pray with them at Mass. He had tried to answer their questions of why he was not a Catholic, or how he would get to heaven without the priest. Yet he smiled, this man that we had made a stranger in his house.

His wife had signed no promises to respect his honor and dignity in the home he built. She was not required to tell the children that men could serve God in many different ways. She was not obliged to explain that his loyalty was the product of faith and his love its inner core. She had only promised to convert him, to lead him from the folly of his simple and incomplete religion, and to see that he did not win the children to the poverty of his own, misguided state.

Once, history tells us, Omar and his Muhammadan hordes forced conversions at the tip of the sword. They threatened Christians and dragged frightened Catholics to pray and worship in the mosque. And when we read such bloody and bar-

baric accounts we shudder, somehow forgetting the swords we wield in Spain and the daggers we thrust in the heart of the non-Catholic husband with the sad-faced wife. Our daggers are everywhere, and we use them with artistic skill. We poise them before each non-Catholic who hopes to take a Catholic spouse, before Protestant parents who watch their children marry in our Church. We poise them before the Jews, even as we smile at them and ignore their traditions, which are as sacred and deep-rooted as our own. We poise them before the millions who find Churches a sham and organized religion a study of hypocrisy. We poise them before the world, at the United Nations, at welfare conferences, at the ecumenical gatherings where we feign brotherhood and are not prepared to budge an inch. Our daggers, perhaps, are more secret than Omar's sword, but not less painful. The non-Catholic feels their sharp steel in every contact with the Catholic Church.

We might fool the Protestant observers who attended Vatican II, or lull to sleep the Jews who receive a blessed medallion in an audience with the Pope. But we do not fool the college student who hopes to marry a Catholic girl. He comes to me and tries to tell me that he will not raise his children in the Catholic Church. He is not bitter or angry, only honest and open in his search for faith. He will not force a religion on his children, nor sign promises that he can't in conscience keep. Colleen is with him, watching my eyes as he talks, fearful lest I drive her non-Catholic fiancé from her love. She does not want to leave her Church, but she cannot make her man alter his beliefs. She has been afraid to tell him about the instructions he must take, about the nature of the promises I will ask him to sign. So we talk, hoping to change his honest views and undermine his faith. I approach him gently, calmly, not raising my voice or playing the authoritarian that he has learned to expect in dealing with my Church. But he is stubborn and direct. He wants no double talk, no wily meanderings that only say an uncompromising "No!"

Colleen is listening in fear and Catholic guilt. She attended my classes in school when I told her to marry a Catholic. She has heard since childhood that she is baptized in the one, true Church, and that to abandon her faith is to "go to hell." She senses the futility of our conversation, for she knows the determination of her man and loves him for it. But she watches me, pleading with me to give her love a chance, begging for an exception to our inexorable rules, trying to tell me with an eloquent glance that I am the finality of her hope. She wants to be married at Mass, she wants to grow in the only faith she has ever known, she wants her children to know the comfort of her belief. But this is her man, the man who will father her children and fortify her life, the man who has faith and principles of his own. Can she ignore his rights so as to please her Church? Can she leave him to find a husband who will not compromise the unyielding law of Rome?

Her man talks and listens with dignity. He is a Lutheran, the product of a religious home, independent in his judgment and honest in his dealings with other men. He has friends, a promising future, great hopes for his future children, a warm and abiding love for his future wife. He worked his way through college, served for fourteen months in Vietnam, and has been offered an exciting job. But he is a non-Catholic, not a man, an honest American, a successful student, or a loyal Lutheran. And since he is a non-Catholic, he must follow my dictates or leave!

So he left and Colleen went with him. He could have signed the promises like a thousand others and refused to keep them. He could have taken the instructions and resisted my attempts to snatch away his faith. But he was too honest to pretend, so he left my presence in anger and disgust. I was angry, too, not at Colleen or her courageous young man, but at my arrogant Church and its obsolete law which could attempt to force a man against his conscience in order to marry the woman he loved. It was a coward's law, a despot's law, a law which made a mockery of God.

But I kept the law, and I must keep it still. I must wait for the Pope to change it, or the bishops to seduce the papal court. I must be satisfied with the crumbs that trickle bit by bit from Rome. I can now invite non-Catholics to marry Catholics at Mass, and ask a minister to give a blessing to this union in my Church. I can waive the written promises as long as I get permission and exact these promises with solemn words. I must be satisfied with such meaningless crumbs when I am screaming for a loaf of bread!

Dear God, who will obliterate the arrogance of my Church? Have I not watched a non-Catholic raise his family Catholic, support our Church, and send his children to our schools? Have I not watched his endurance of the religious gibes of his own children, his tolerance of his wife's insistence on rhythm in their bed, his charity to the poor, his honesty in business, his respect in the community? Then have I not seen us refuse to bury him in our Church because he was not a member of our faith? Have I not whispered a pathetic handful of prayers over his body in a mortuary, forbidden to bring his body into my Church, to bless his last remains, even to wear a single vestment of my priesthood? Have I not spoken the few comforting words to the six Catholic children he raised, to the widow and the nineteen grandchildren who loved him and kissed his cold hand until the coffin was sealed, ignoring their pleas for a more decent burial, and explaining my Church's rules to his weeping wife.

She had no answer to my learned theology and canon law. She could only tell me of his love, his gentleness, his kindness to the children. She could only recall the Sundays he shoveled snow to bring the children to Mass. She could only tell me of the times he taught the children their religion, of the days he struggled to support the large family that her Catholic convictions produced, of the nights she turned her back on him to honor a law he did not understand. She knew nothing of history or bigotry or Roman law. She only knew that her husband had died and she wanted to honor her memories of him with the liturgy of her Church. But he was a non-Catholic, an outsider, a non-participator in the privilege of my faith. So we honored him in a funeral parlor with its professional sympathy and its impersonal dismissal of the dead.

Nor could she have Masses said to honor his name. She could offer Masses for a "special intention," but his name could not appear in the lists that were printed in the parish bulletin. I explained all this to her and she thanked me in her tears. I wish she would have turned her back, screamed at me, hated me. But she thanked me, and left me cursing the heartlessness of my Church. I had eaten in this man's home, played golf with him, worried with him about his children, but I could not honor his body with the ritual of my Church. Had I been able to pour a bit of water on his head before he died, to extract a dying wish to be a Catholic, even to hear a nurse say that he had requested a priest, then perhaps I could have buried him from the Church. But he had died a non-Catholic, and I could not reward his family's failure to convert him with a solemn *Requiem*.

The man who is a non-Catholic has known the pride of my Church. The Protestant knows that Catholics are forbidden to worship in his Church lest they be contaminated by heresy. A Catholic can attend a wedding or a funeral in a Protestant Church, but he cannot join in prayer. He comes as a silent spectator, paying his respects to his non-Catholic friend even as he insults his friend's faith. The Catholic can attend a bar mitzvah, if a broad-minded pastor gives his consent. But he cannot pray with the Jews or receive their blessings or share the sacred traditions which antedate his own Church. Jews are especially pitiable because they rejected Christ, especially hard to convert because they take pride in their family.

The man who is a non-Catholic has suffered from the narrowness of the Catholic mind. Catholics do not listen; they have only been taught to defend. They refuse to question what they learned in childhood. They can defend pious superstition with the same ardor with which they embrace key doctrines of their faith. They can uphold a Roman ruling with the fire of a martyr's conviction and ignore it once the bishop pronounces that Saturday, at midnight, it does not apply.

They can criticize non-Catholics as indulgent sinners who dilute the teachings of Christ. They can ridicule ministers and rabbis as unworthy prophets or frauds, laugh at the ceremonies of non-Catholic sects, condemn the vagueness of other moral teachings without recognizing the rigidity of their own. Catholics can attack the non-Catholic's stand on birth control as "selfish compromise" and his position on divorce as "moral chaos." No one escapes our wrath or righteous condemnation. Our papers attack the divorces of Ford and Rockefeller without knowing the circumstances of their private lives. Catholic leaders can question their moral fitness for office, and defend with fervor an alcoholic bishop or a greedy priest. They can scorn welfare programs which attempt to solve a problem without upholding the moral opinions of the Church.

We have alienated our public schools by our criticism of their efforts, by dumping our problem children in their laps, by attacking the teachers who attempted to tell Catholic children there was more than a Catholic view of life. We have attacked professors in our state universities who upheld moral systems different from our own, who described the brutality of the Church in history, who questioned Catholic opposition to the democratic way of life. And in areas of our country where Catholics were in the majority, we have even driven such professors from their posts to shield our students from unpleasant truth. And thus refusing the freedom of speech to others, we have screamed when our own freedoms were put in jeopardy.

We have boycotted movies when our censors were offended, forbade literature which questioned our infallibility or impugned the motives of our Pope, lured advertisers away from magazines which printed articles hostile to us. We could criticize the entire world, mock its standards, ridicule its goals, and not bear the least attack on the policies and programs that we enforced. We made fun of the archaic laws which questioned our bingo and gambling, and were indignant when moderns suggested that our marriage laws were obsolete. It has been our way or no way, and the non-Catholic has suffered from the authoritarian arrogance that characterizes our defense of the Catholic Church.

I am guilty of the wounds that my Church inflicted on the man who is a non-Catholic, because I did not battle or openly protest. And I should have known better as I walked among my fellow men. My optometrist was Jewish, loyal to his relatives and honest in his work. Yet he is a non-Catholic, and I was forbidden to share the bar mitzvah to honor his son lest I give scandal to my calling and my Church. I might give approval to his religion by my presence at his Temple. I might fortify his blindness or delay his conversion to the Catholic Church.

A generous friend was Jewish, married to a Catholic, but married without the permission and blessing of my Church. I was expected to ask him, therefore, to renew his vows in my presence. He was in serious error since he was not married in the Church. His Catholic wife was forbidden the sacraments, and I was expected to insult him by asking him to go through a religious ceremony required by laws that neither he nor I could understand.

Another close friend was a Mason. I used to drink beer with him, to ask his help with programs for the teen-agers, to hear him tell me what Masonry had done to make of him a man. Yet I was expected to convert him, even though I knew he was closer to God than I, more tolerant of sinners, more loyal to his calling.

I toured Europe with religious teachers of every denomination, enjoyed their friendship, laughed and ate with them, marveled at their sincerity, noted the seriousness of their quest. But they were heretics, potential converts, men who knew but half the truth until they joined me in my Church. And yet how could they so embody the fullness of charity if they were so severed from the truth? What did they lack if they worshiped God and loved their fellow man? What could I offer them in the restricted quality of my own love? Did they need to know of purgatory, honor Mary, obey the Pope before I could relax and join with them as friend?

They had more to offer me than I could ever give to them. They had learned tolerance and lived it in their life. Their conscience was free and so was their childlike openness to God. I was the narrow one, the man stuffed with unchanging dogmas and unyielding codes. I was the intolerant priest, the fierce judge, the subtle searcher for converts. The man who is a non-Catholic was the better suited to talk to men of Christ.

And yet I have wounded him and we wound him still. We invite him to share our friendship when secretly we try to win him to our side. We enter with him in dialogue, but we anticipate any motion to come from him. We insult him with our feigned learning, and lure him with the better public relations which only hide the same narrow theology.

But no longer will I call him "non-Catholic" to reveal that I divide the world between my kind and his. I will not even call him "Christian," so varied has this common word become. Nor will I call him "Jew." I will call him "brother" and hope he will forgive and understand.

My brother, who does not believe as I, I apologize. I apologize for the pain I have caused you, for the indignity I have forced upon your children. I apologize for imposing my laws upon you, for the arrogance of my public statements, for the smugness that made me always right. My brother, I denied you my sacraments and made a mockery of yours. I called my family loyalty "faith" and called your faith a sham. I laughed at your ministers, slurred your rabbis and bishops, criticized your conferences, and undermined your reputation. And for all this I apologize.

And, my brother, I lied to you when I told you the certainty of my faith. I live in doubt and shadows as do you. I struggle to believe amid pain, search to find amid confusion, often touch a phantom when I try to hold my God. I sound cocky when I recite my doctrines and confident when I resolve the dilemmas of moral law. But I am only a child in search, a weak and frightened one, who struggles with the mystery of faith. I do not believe, I only try to. I do not love, I only make a feeble effort to begin. I am your brother, or want to be, if you will forgive me for the wall I built to separate our hearts.

My brother, I need you, I miss you. I need the loyalty of Israel, the fire of Luther, the discipline of Calvin, the warmth of Wesley, the wisdom of the humanists to speak to me of man. I have lived in suspicion, in tension, in anger, in bitterness, in calumny and righteousness, in narrowness and fear. I have hidden from you my weakness and exaggerated my strength. Now I ask to be your brother, not in simulated love, but in the depths of my own loneliness to join you in the search for the Father Who loves us both alike.

I cannot atone for the injuries of the past. I cannot bring together the many couples whose religious differences tore them apart, the differences I fostered. It only helps to reveal to you how miserable and inhuman I have felt in loyalty to my job. It helps to look forward to the day when my Church will have abandoned its arrogance, when it will not offer its Catholic code to force the conscience of the world. Then there will be no "non-Catholics," there will be only persons, struggling to be honest to themselves. Then I can call you "brother," not Jew or Protestant or non-Catholic, and hope that you will forgive my narrowness and call me "brother," too.

EPILOGUE

One Christmas Eve when I was a little boy, I wandered alone through the darkened streets of my city. It was cold and a softly falling snow was cleaning the sidewalks for an Infant's birth. I was holding my rosary in the pocket of my jacket and whispering the thousand "Hail Marys" that the Irish often say on Christmas Eve. I was at peace with the world and full of joy in the exuberance of my youth. I remember coming home, flushed with the cold, still absorbed in the reverie of that unforgettable night. My mother was playing Christmas carols, my father was reading the paper in his chair. I did not feel like talking, I did not want to disturb the quiet magic of the spell. A couple of my brothers were wrapping packages, one was struggling with a stubborn set of lights. It was a quiet time in a home that seldom stood so still.

I do not know why that night is etched in my memory, I do not know why its music haunts me. Perhaps it is because I knew that night that I belonged to God and that peace is all I want. Perhaps it is because I knew that night that I must be myself. Even now, nothing has changed, the child has grown, and the peace I sought in praying through the snowy streets, I pray and search for still.

I still believe in the power of the priesthood, where sinful

176

men are helped by sinful men. I believe in an authority that stoops to wash a poor man's feet. I believe in a banquet where sinners learn to love, eating in company with their God. I believe in parents who teach their children the beauty that is life. I believe in the words that God has left for men, words that can fashion hope from darkness and turn bitter loneliness into love. And I believe in man, fashioned in mystery by God. I believe in the beauty of his mind, the force of his emotions, the fire and loyalty of his love. I know his weakness, his cowardice, his treachery, his hate. But I believe in him and his thirst for acceptance and love.

Most of all I believe in God and the power of His victory in Christ. I believe in a Resurrection that rescued man from death. I believe in an Easter that opened man to hope. I believe in a joy that no threat of man can take away. I believe in a peace that I know in fleeting moments and seek with boldness born of God. I believe in a life that lingers after this, a life that God has fashioned for His friends.

I believe in understanding, in forgiveness, in mercy, in faith. I believe in innocent children whose eyes are messages from God. I believe in teen-agers, carefree or sullen, whose struggles presage the tempest that is man. I believe in man's love for woman, and hers for him, and in the fervor of this exchange I hear the voice of God. I believe in friendship and its power to turn selfishness to love. I believe in lasting love and the painful growth that it requires. I believe in death and the mystery that it unveils. I believe in eternity and the hope that it affords.

I do not believe in arrogance or pride. I do not believe in the haughtiness of man. I do not believe that laws can crush man's confidence or smother the spirit of God. I do not believe that any ritual can limit divine love or seal the channels that lead a man to God. I do not believe in the unerring judgment of men that ignores the conscience of the simple and sincere.

I am sorry if, in writing this book, I hurt my family, although they are, for the most part, likely to approve. I am sorry to hurt the sisters who taught me from childhood, who asked my blessing as a priest. I am sorry to hurt the priests who forgave me as a child, the priests with whom I labored in the field, the priests whose confidence I shared. I am sorry to hurt the people who listened to my words, who received my absolution, who welcomed me to their homes and offered me their hearts. Their faces swim before me as I write. I am sorry for the pain I may cause, and only the pain I may relieve provides me with the courage and patience to write.

You have heard my story, told as honestly and carefully as I can. You may say that I seek a way of indulgence and compromise, but you are wrong. I do not live without worry or responsible concern. In fact, I have never felt so responsible since I discovered that the Church cannot absorb my conscience, nor replace my mind. Life was easier when I knew where everything fit, when I could lose myself in the structure of a massive organization. There heaven and hell were governed by careful laws. There God's friendship was certain and manageable, and I was satisfied when I kept the Church's rules.

Now I am lost, but free; honest, but afraid; certain, but ever in doubt. I do not fear hell because I cannot fathom it. I do not seek heaven because it offers no image I can grasp. I only struggle to find myself, to love my fellow men, and to hope that in this way I am truly loving God. And in my struggle, I would like the Church to be my servant as Christ promised that it should. I need to know the wonder of the Mass and the comfort of confession amid the perils of my search. But I will not be absorbed, or crowded, or refused permission to be a man. I do not look for the Church to agree with me, for the Church is as various as the feeble men it serves. I only ask that it not refuse to help me because I refuse to be as every other man.

I prize the uniqueness that is mine, and you must do the same. I am God's own child, and no man can tell me that I must live and die as alien. I can respect the Church's goals even as I formulate my own. I can listen to her directives even as I decide how I must live my one and only life. I can pray with brothers who do not agree with me, eat with brothers who find me bold and independent, speak with brothers who regret I ever ceased to be a child. I can do nothing else, for I am a man, designed by God. I need my family, my friends, my Church, but none of these shall forbid me to be myself.

No longer can I stand before my bishop and smile in shy assent when I know he is wrong. No longer will I bow before a pastor when I know his mood has formed the policy of his Church. No longer will I accept in silence the travesties that a dishonest theology has imposed on simple and unsuspecting men. Nor will I leave the Church, even if they demand it of me, for it is my Church.

I shall be a Catholic, a vocal and honest one, even if my superiors forbid me to be a priest. I shall be a Catholic who follows his conscience, demands meaning and relevance from his Church, and will not permit his God to be reduced to empty ritual and all-absorbing law. I shall be a Catholic until one day, perhaps sooner than I think, I shall return to ashes and to God. He will judge me as He must, but I can say to Him as honestly as I say to you: "I have tried to be a man!"

NOTES

PREFACE AND DEDICATION

1. March 12, 1966, Father Stephen Nash (pseudonym), "I Am a Priest—I Want to Marry."

2. Actually, the greatest number of non-Catholic respondents in any given "group" were Mormons, followed by Episcopalians and Baptists.

INTRODUCTION

1. The recent (January, 1967) news of Father Charles Davis, British priest and theologian, Council *peritus*, and spokesman for England's Cardinal Heenan, who left the priesthood and the Catholic Church, is a violent sign of what is taking place within the Catholic Church. My personal opinion is that Father Davis is actually wrong in considering himself disassociated from the Church. He is but one type of "Catholic" who exemplifies the change *within* the Church. A man cannot abandon his tradition and past so easily. Actually, Charles Davis has been produced in the framework of a changing Church, and in a very real sense remains a member of it.

2. Declaration on Religious Freedom, paragraphs 9 and 10.

CHAPTER ONE *The Ideal Becomes the Law*

1. Romans 3:21–28. See S. Lyonet, "De Epistolis Paulinis" pp. 79–87; (Rome: PIB, 1957), Lucien Cerfaux, *The Church in the Theology of St. Paul* (New York: Herder and Herder, 1963), pp. 59 ff. and *passim*.

2. The Catholic scholar begins every argument with a set of presuppositions which make further discussion impossible. See Hans Küng, *The Council, Reform and Reunion* (New York: Sheed and Ward, 1961), pp. 14 ff., wherein he points out that the Church is made up of men and not ideas.

3. The textbooks we used to study theology were the same textbooks that men twice our age had used. There was no room for speculation, only for memorization and conformance.

4. See John McKenzie, *Authority in the Church* (New York: Sheed and Ward, 1966); Marc Oraison, *Love or Constraint?* (New York: Deus Press, 1959), pp. 13 ff.; see also Roger Aubert, *Le probleme de l'acte de foi* (Louvain: Warny, 1958), pp. 677 ff. and *passim*.

5. The discussion on celibacy has grown loud and angry. A good scholarly treatment of the issue is contained in R. J. Bunnik, "The Question of Married Priests," *Cross Currents*, XV (1965), pp. 407–31, and XVI (1965), pp. 81–112. Bunnik, a well-known Dutch theologian, shows the mistaken identification of celibacy with priesthood in the Catholic Church. For an opposing view, see E. Schillebeeckx, "Priesthood and Celibacy," *Documentum Centrum Concilie*, No. 111. Schillebeeckx pursues his theology independently of any empirical evidence, such as Father Fichter's recent study on the problem of clerical celibacy (*National Catholic Reporter*, December, 1966, and January, 1967). See also Leslie Dewart, "The Celibacy Problem," *Commonweal* (April 22, 1966), pp. 146–50, wherein celibacy is seen as a barrier between the priest and the secular man.
For a more ethereal view of celibacy and one revealing the author's unawareness of the realities of priestly existence, see Ida Gorres, *Is Celibacy Outdated?* (Westminster, Md.: Newman, 1965). A more honest view is contained in Pierre Hermand, *The Priest, Celibate or Married*, (Baltimore: Helicon, 1966). Since Hermand is an ex-priest, some Catholic minds can readily dismiss his arguments as mere rationalizations.

6. There is no story more pathetic in its lack of charity than the way the Catholic Church treats its ex-priests.

7. See Yves Congar, *Power and Poverty in the Church* (Baltimore: Helicon, 1964), pp. 111 ff. and *passim*.

8. See J. Ratzinger, "Free Expression and Obedience in the Church," *The Church* (New York: Kennedy, 1963), pp. 194 ff., 212 ff., where he speaks of the "servility of sycophants."

CHAPTER TWO *The Man Who Is a Priest*

1. Will Herberg, *Protestant—Catholic—Jew* (Garden City: Doubleday, 1956); Gerhard Lenski, *The Religious Factor* (Garden City: Doubleday, 1963), pp. 35 ff.; Herve Carrier, *The Sociology of Religious Belonging* (New York: Herder and Herder, 1965), pp. 117 ff.; Edward Wakin and Joseph F. Scheuer, *The De-Romanization of the American Catholic Church* (New York: Macmillan, 1966), pp. 17–54.

2. John Courtney Murray, *The Problem of Religious Freedom* (Westminster, Md.: Newman, 1965), pp. 7–17.

3. See Michael Novak, *A New Generation* (New York: Herder and Herder, 1964), pp. 59 ff.; E. L. Mascall, *The Secularization of Christianity* (New York: Holt, Rinehart and Winston, 1965), pp. 23 ff.

4. See John McKenzie, "Law in the New Testament," a paper delivered to the Canon Law Society of America, October 12, 1965, and to be found in the "Proceedings" of that group.

5. Joseph Fichter, *Religion as an Occupation* (Notre Dame, Ind.: Notre Dame Press, 1961), pp. 220–70.

6. John McKenzie, *Authority in the Church*, pp. 110–22; William DuBay, *The Human Church* (New York: Doubleday, 1966), esp. Chapter 7; Gerhard Lenski, *op. cit.*, pp. 293–304.

7. See Gabriel Marcel, *Creative Fidelity* (New York: Farrar, Straus and Co., 1964), pp. 147–94; Teilhard de Chardin, *The Divine Milieu* (New York: Harper and Row, 1960), pp. 57–66.

CHAPTER THREE *The Man Who Is a Catholic*

1. John McKenzie, *Authority in the Church*, passim; *Theology in the University*, John Coulson, ed. (Baltimore: Helicon, 1964), pp. 25–46.

2. Recently, theological developments have begun to consider the so-called "anonymous Christian," i.e. the sincere searcher of every faith. See Karl Rahner, the great German theologian, in *The Church* (New

York: Kennedy, 1963), pp. 112 ff.; see also Charles Davis, *Theology for Today* (New York: Sheed and Ward, 1962), pp. 65 ff.

3. Daniel Callahan, *The Mind of the Catholic Layman* (New York: Scribner, 1963), pp. 79 ff.

CHAPTER FOUR *The Catholic Parish*

1. Vatican II simplifies this process: *Decree on Bishops' Pastoral Office in the Church*, paragraph 31 (October 28, 1965).

2. Vatican II offers other norms to determine a pastoral appointment, but such a change in attitude will take a long time to enforce: *Ibid.*

3. Congar-Dupuy, *L'épiscopat et l'église universelle* (Paris: Les Editions du Cerf, 1964), pp. 240 ff.

4. See Canons 451 ff.

5. Bishop Steven Leven, "Priests Without Power," *National Catholic Reporter* (October 27, 1966), p. 10. The *National Catholic Reporter* has, in my mind, been the greatest single publication in America to spark renewal. It has been of special assistance to priests and nuns. The "Sisters' Forum" is an unparalleled effort in journalistic dialogue.

6. *Decree on Bishops' Pastoral Office*, esp. paragraphs 4–10.

7. Gerard Sloyan, "The Parish as Educator," *Commonweal*, special issue (March 25, 1966), p. 20. This entire issue was an outstanding treatment of the problem of parochial renewal. See also Aloysius Church, "Preach the Word," *The Way* (January, 1965), pp. 33–44.

8. *The Word*, ed. by the seminarians of Canisianum, Innsbruck (New York: Kennedy, 1964), pp. 171–248; Charles Davis, *Theology for Today*, pp. 12–24, 44–64; Gregory Baum, "Word and Sacrament in the Church," *Thought* (1963), pp. 199–200; Vatican II, *Dogmatic Constitution on Divine Revelation* (November 18, 1965), esp. Chapter VI.

9. *Martin Luther*, ed. John Dillenberger (Garden City: Doubleday Anchor, 1961), pp. 229–32.

10. Davis, *op. cit.*, pp. 53–55.

11. "DePauw Presents His Case—Rome, Mary, Mass," *National Catholic Reporter* (February 9, 1966), p. 7.

12. See the special issue of *Commonweal*, entitled "Reforming the Parish" (March 25, 1966); Herve Carrier, *The Sociology of Religious Belonging*, pp. 167 ff.

13. Vatican II, *Decree on Bishops' Pastoral Office*, paragraph 30, 2.

14. Charles Davis, *Liturgy and Doctrine* (New York: Sheed and Ward, 1960), pp. 75–92; see the classic letter of Romano Guardini, *Herder Correspondence*, special issue (Spring, 1964), pp. 24 ff.

CHAPTER FIVE *The Loss of Personalism*

1. See John Macquarrie, *Twentieth Century Religious Thought* (New York: Harper and Row, 1963), pp. 193–209, 210–25, 351–70.

2. Jean Moroux, *I Believe* (London: Sheed and Ward, 1955); Romano Guardini, *The Life of Faith* (New York: Deus, 1960), pp. 72 ff.; Joseph Pieper, *Belief and Faith* (New York: Pantheon, 1962), pp. 43 ff.; Richard Butler, O.P., *Themes of Concern* (Garden City: Doubleday, 1966), pp. 15–30.

3. Karl Rahner, *Theological Investigations*, Vol. II (Baltimore: Helicon, 1963), pp. 89–107; also *Moral Problems and Christian Personalism*, Vol. V of Concilium Series (New York: Paulist Press, 1965).

4. J. H. Newman, *Grammar of Assent* (1870) (Garden City: Doubleday Image, 1955), p. 90.

5. See Max Scheler, *On the Eternal in Man* (London: SCM Press, 1960), pp. 281 ff., pp. 297 ff.; Maurice Blondel, *Letter on Apologetics* (New York: Holt, Rinehart and Winston, 1964), *passim*.

6. Ollé-LaPrune, a quote from *La Certitude Morale*, found in Roger Aubert, *Le problème de l'acte de foi*, p. 269.

7. Blondel, *op. cit.*, p. 196.

8. See Emile Poulat, *Histoire, dogma et critique dans la crise moderniste* (Paris: Casterman, 1962); in English, see the Introduction to Blondel's *Letter on Apologetics*, by Trethowan and Dru; also Alec Vidler, *Prophecy and Papacy* (New York: Scribner, 1964); and Gustave Weigel,

"The Historical Background of the Encyclical 'Humani Generis,' " *Theological Studies*, XII (1951), pp. 212 ff.

9. See Cirne-Lima, *Personal Faith* (New York: Herder and Herder, 1965), *passim*; G. Phillips, "Deux tenances dans théologie contemporaire," *Nouvelle Revue Theologique*, 85 (1963), pp. 227 ff.

10. See Karl Rahner, *Theological Investigations*, Vol. II, pp. 235 ff.; Charles Davis, *Theology for Today*, pp. 12 ff.

11. Blondel, *op. cit.*, p. 147.

CHAPTER SIX *The Church of the Legal Code*

1. This is not to deny the efforts of Europe's Karl Rahner, Edward Schillebeeckx, Bernard Haring, or Canada's Gregory Baum, or even America's John Courtney Murray. But even the best of our theologians seem to fear the essential conclusions that should courageously follow their speculation. Rome has made cowards of them all.

2. Karl Rahner's more sophisticated approach to indulgences can be seen in *Theological Investigations*, Vol. II, pp. 175 ff. The people, however, are fed the same involved myths born of medieval superstition.

3. The theologian can admit the honesty of a non-Catholic's faith, but denies him the right to share in the Catholic communion.

4. Newman, *op. cit.*, p. 304.

CHAPTER SEVEN *Confession and Mortal Sin*

1. Hagmaier and Gleason, *Counseling the Catholic* (New York: Sheed and Ward, 1959), pp. 73–93, offers a somewhat balanced view of the problem of masturbation, but "legalism" still leers through the treatment. It is a case of good psychology inhibited by mediocre theology. More balanced approaches are contained in Von Gagern's *The Problem of Onanism* (Westminster, Md.: Newman, 1955), pp. 53–114, and in Marc Oraison, *Love or Constraint?* chapters II–V.

2. Much of the Catholic emphasis on frequent confession is the product of myth and guilt, and not sound theology. See Bernard Leeming, *Principles of Sacramental Theology* (London: Longmans, 1962), pp. 485, 595 ff., and *passim*; Louis Monden, *Sin, Liberty and Law*, pp. 44 ff.

3. See the involved "double-talk" in Ford and Kelly, *Contemporary Moral Theology*, Vol. I, pp. 174–276, wherein man's freedom is taken for granted and obstacles to freedom are considered an exception rather than the normal human condition. Compare this, for example, with Jean Mouroux's *The Meaning of Man* (Garden City: Doubleday Image, 1961), pp. 151–81.

4. See Emmanuel Mounier, *The Character of Man* (New York: Harper, 1956), pp. 268–314; Henri Niel, "The Limits of Responsibility," *Sin* (New York: Macmillan), pp. 33–60; Frederick von Gagern, *Mental and Spiritual Health* (New York: Deus, 1954), pp. 64–76.

5. Piet Schoonenberg, *Man and Sin* (Notre Dame, Ind.: Notre Dame Press, 1965), pp. 25–39; Monden, *op. cit.*, pp. 34–40; Henri Rondet, *The Theology of Sin* (Fides, Notre Dame, Ind.: Fides, 1960), pp. 87 ff. Rondet proposes the right questions, but answers them with legalistic simplicity. For an example of the kind of Catholic scholarship which can find our legalistic view of "mortal sin" in ancient texts, see Hubert Motry, *The Concept of Mortal Sin in Early Christianity*, a dissertation (Washington, D.C.: Catholic University, 1920). Motry can make the Shepherd of Hermas and Justin sound a whole lot like Ford and Kelly.

6. Monden, *op. cit.*, pp. 45 ff. It also should be indicated for the non-professional that the Church omits a detailed or "integral" confession for a serious reason. Thus servicemen entering battle can be given a kind of "group absolution." Scrupulous penitents would also be freed from the obligation of a detailed confession. What better reason could there be for a confession without the listing of sins than an effort to restore relevance and personalism?

7. Hagmaier and Gleason, *op. cit.*, pp. 31–50.

8. Marc Oraison, *Love or Constraint?*, pp. 120–39; Vincent P. Miceli, "Marcel: The Ascent to Being," *Thought* (1964), pp. 395–420; John McKenzie, *Authority in the Church*, pp. 162–74.

9. Schoonenberg, *op. cit.*, pp. 150 ff.

10. *Ibid.*, pp. 98–199; Charles Davis, *Theology for Today*, pp. 139–152; Karl Rahner, *Theological Investigations*, Vol. I, pp. 347 ff.

11. E. A. Speiser, *Commentary on Genesis*, Vol. I of *Anchor Bible* (Garden City: Doubleday, 1965).

12. S. Lyonet, *De Peccato et Redemptione*, Vol. I, *De Notione Peccati*, Chap. VI, "De Epistolis Paulinis," pp. 79–87 (Rome: PIB, 1957); Henri Rondet, *The Theology of Sin*, pp. 29–35.

13. F. X. Durwell, *The Resurrection* (New York: Sheed and Ward, 1961), pp. 202–359; Gabriel Marcel, *Homo Viator* (New York: Harper Torchbook, 1962), pp. 29–67.

CHAPTER EIGHT *The Rules of Courtship*

1. Marc Oraison, "Psychology and the Sense of Sin," *Sin*, pp. 1–32.

2. See Ford and Kelly, *Contemporary Moral Theology*, Vol. I, pp. 141–73.

3. Bishop J. Reuss, *Modern Catholic Sex Instruction* (Baltimore: Helicon, 1964), makes some attempt to recognize the pressure of real-life situations, such as those he calls "situations of dependence." The Bishop, however, believes his title page and ends up giving us the same old ideas with a gentle disposition.

4. Any personal approach to morality is always called by its Catholic opponents "situation ethics." This is a broad term which is supposed to end all discussion. See Ford and Kelly, *op. cit.*, pp. 104–40. Joseph Fletcher's *Situation Ethics* (Philadelphia: Westminster Press, 1966), is a refreshingly new approach to moral problems and it gives a positive place to the individual and the supremacy of love. Fletcher really believes that man is basically good and offers him the chance to become a person. See also the fine chapter "Legal Ethics or Situation Ethics" in Louis Monden's *Sin, Liberty and Law*, *op. cit.*, pp. 73–144. Also Jules Toner, "Focus for Contemporary Ethics," *Thought* (1965), pp. 5–19.

5. Bernard Haring, *The Law of Christ*, Vol. I (Westminster, Md.: Newman, 1963), pp. 35–134.

6. Catholics unquestionably share this "game playing" with others. See the excellent chapter "Sex and Secularization," in Harvy Cox, *The Secular City* (New York: Macmillan, 1965), pp. 192–216, especially pp. 206–208.

CHAPTER NINE *Christian Marriage and Divorce*

1. Rudolph Schnackenburg, *The Moral Teaching of the New Testament* (New York: Herder and Herder, 1965), p. 267.

2. See Enda McDonagh, "Recent English Literature on the Moral Theology of Christian Marriage," in *Moral Problems and Christian*

Personalism, Vol. V of Concilium Series, pp. 130–54; also Bernard Haring, Marriage in the Modern World (Westminster, Md.: Newton, 1965), pp. 75–77. Haring supplies the principles which would permit a change in the Church's divorce law, but, typically, hesitates to draw conclusions. John McKenzie, Authority in the Church, p. 168, offers an explanation for the Church's fear of change, no matter how urgent the need.

CHAPTER TEN Birth Control

1. There have been solid treatises which show the futility of the Church's efforts to base its policy on birth control on the natural law. See Louis Dupre, Contraception and Catholics (Baltimore: Helicon, 1964), or Leslie Dewart "Casti Connubii" in Contraception and Holiness (New York: Herder and Herder, 1964), pp. 202–310.

2. Actually the Constitution on the Church in the Modern World from Vatican II, paragraphs 47–52, reveals that a progress in the Church's thought and in the minds of some theologians has already resolved the birth control problem by casting a giant doubt on the Church's "traditional" stand. See Gregory Baum, "Can the Church Change its Position on Birth Control" in Contraception and Holiness, pp. 311–44.
Another important work which shows that the Church will obviously change its present position is the exceptional work of John T. Noonan, Jr., Contraception (Cambridge, Mass: Harvard University Press, 1965). Noonan shows the historical effort of the Church to protect certain values in marriage and leaves little doubt as to the necessity of a change in the present birth control "law." Since our understanding of the place of sex in marriage has grown, the marriage "value" reveals that sex has meaning in the lives of married persons even if such sexual expression is "contraceptive." See also Noonan's article "Contraception and the Council," Commonweal (March 11, 1966).
An increasing number of priests are giving Catholic women "permission" to use the pill.

3. Perhaps the clearest expression of the Church's traditional stand against birth control is contained in Ford and Kelly, Contemporary Moral Theology, Vol. II (Westminster, Md.: Newman, 1963), pp. 235–429. To one who has studied any modern moral theology, the Ford-Kelly position has only historical interest. For a clear exposition of the method of modern theology, see the late Kieran Conley's "Procreation and the Person" in Contraception and Holiness, pp. 60–71.

4. See John Marshall, The Infertile Period (Baltimore: Helicon, 1963). Dr. Marshall's efforts are sincere and sophisticated. For an incredible attempt to defend the Church's traditional stand and to en-

courage rhythm, see F. J. Ayd, Jr., "The Oral Contraceptives and Their Mode of Action," National Catholic Welfare Conference, pamphlet publication (Washington, D.C.: 1964).

CHAPTER ELEVEN Catholic Schools

1. Andrew Greeley and Peter Rossi, The Education of Catholic Americans (Chicago: Aldine, 1966). The Notre Dame study appears to be no more strongly supportive of our educational system than the Greeley-Rossi research.

2. Vatican II's remarks are just as defensive and "unaware" in the school problem as are those of Pius XII's Encyclical on Christian Education. See Declaration on Christian Education, paragraph 5 ff.

3. Mary Perkins Ryan, Are Parochial Schools the Answer? (New York: Holt, Rinehart and Winston, 1964).

4. Herve Carrier, The Sociology of Religious Belonging, pp. 138–53.

5. Anthony T. Podovano, The Estranged God (New York: Sheed and Ward, 1966), makes an outstanding effort to relate the search of man for God to the best in modern drama and novels.

6. Michael Duclerq, "The Church and the Question of Catholic Schools," Cross Currents (Spring, 1965), pp. 200–12; Daniel Callahan, "The Schools," Commonweal (January 8, 1965), pp. 473–76.

7. Shaping the Christian Message, ed. Gerard S. Sloyan (New York: Deus, 1963).

8. Theology and the University, ed. John Coulson (Baltimore: Helicon, 1964), pp. 107–88.

9. Vatican II seems to offer some approval of this; see Decree on Christian Education, paragraph 9.

10. The Church's neglect of the Newman apostolate on the state university campus has filled volumes of periodical literature in the last few years. Newman Club chaplains are among the most talented and hardworking of the priests in the Church. Their apostolate is surely among the most neglected.

CHAPTER TWELVE *Life in the Convent*

1. See Canons 520–27.

2. Vatican II asks for generous adaptations: *Decree on the Appropriate Renewal of Religious Life*, paragraph 3.

3. Arturo Paoli, "Obedience," *Cross Currents* (Spring, 1965), pp. 275–94.

4. Sister Maureen O'Keefe, *Christian Love in Religious Life* (New York: Regnery, 1966), wherein a sister is encouraged to enjoy the human experiences which are a part of any mature life. It is hard to believe that such a book would have to be written, but it actually does.

5. See interview with Margaret Mead, "Sisters in Modern Society," *National Catholic Reporter* (March 30, 1966), p. 11. The religious need many such interviews before they decide on the value of their "witness."

6. The problem of the renewal of religious life, so vital to aggiornamento, was treated with platitudes by Vatican II, and most orders are giving the Council the response which it deserves. The sisters are generally as defensive about their "irrelevance" as was Vatican II, and they continue to trouble themselves with much concern about trivial changes.

7. Christopher F. Mooney, *Teilhard de Chardin and the Mystery of Christ* (New York: Harper and Row, 1966). Christ assumes meaning in the world of men in Chardin's view. He must be found in a Christian's love for others and not in a self-centered form of hypnosis amid personal frustrations. The "life of Christ" spirituality which has filtered through the sisters' meditation books is simply bad theology. We have no biography of Christ, only one of Christ in His Church.

8. Sister Charles Borromeo, "Poverty and Property in Religious Life," *National Catholic Reporter* (June 1, 1966).

THE VOYAGEUR

THE VOYAGEUR

BY

GRACE LEE NUTE

ILLUSTRATIONS BY
CARL W. BERTSCH

Reprint Edition
MINNESOTA HISTORICAL SOCIETY
St. Paul, 1955

TO

HELEN BIGELOW MERRIMAN

"SAID ONE OF THESE MEN, LONG PAST SEVENTY YEARS OF AGE: 'I COULD CARRY, PADDLE, WALK AND SING WITH ANY MAN I EVER SAW. I HAVE BEEN TWENTY-FOUR YEARS A CANOE MAN, AND FORTY-ONE YEARS IN SERVICE; NO PORTAGE WAS EVER TOO LONG FOR ME. FIFTY SONGS COULD I SING. I HAVE SAVED THE LIVES OF TEN VOYAGEURS. HAVE HAD TWELVE WIVES AND SIX RUNNING DOGS. I SPENT ALL MY MONEY IN PLEASURE. WERE I YOUNG AGAIN, I SHOULD SPEND MY LIFE THE SAME WAY OVER. THERE IS NO LIFE SO HAPPY AS A VOYAGEUR'S LIFE!'"

PREFACE

It is time to write the story of the voyageur. His canoe has long since vanished from the northern waters; his red cap is seen no more, a bright spot against the blue of Lake Superior; his sprightly French conversation, punctuated with inimitable gesture, his exaggerated courtesy, his incurable romanticism, his songs, and his superstitions are gone.

In certain old books and in many unpublished manuscripts, however, he still lives. Read the diaries of Montreal fur-traders and the books of travelers on the St. Lawrence, the Saskatchewan, and the Great Lakes in the eighteenth and early nineteenth centuries. From their pages peals the laughter of a gay-hearted, irrepressible race; over night waters floats the plaintive song of canoeman, swelled periodically in the chorus by the voices of his lusty mates; portage path and campfire, foaming rapids and placid fir-fringed lake, shallow winding stream and broad expanse of inland sea, whitewalled cottage of Quebec hamlet and frowning pickets of Northwest post—become once more the voyageur's habitat; the French *régime* comes to its tragic close on the Plains of Abraham; the British rule lasts but a brief half-century in a large portion of the fur country; Washington supersedes London in the allegiance of many of the red children of the far western waters—still the

PREFACE

voyageur places his wooden crosses by dangerous *sault* and treacherous eddy, sings of love in sunny Provence, and claims his dram on New Year's morning, undisturbed by wars, treaties, and the running of invisible boundary lines.

Though he is one of the most colorful figures in the history of a great continent, the voyageur remains unknown to all but a few. This little book seeks to do justice to his memory for the romance and color he has lent to American and Canadian history, and for the services he rendered in the exploration of the West.

My thanks are hereby offered to the many persons who have given me assistance and encouragement in the preparation of this study. I am especially indebted to several members of the staff of the Minnesota Historical Society, who have called my attention to data relating to the voyageurs; and to my sister, Virginia Beveridge, who typed the manuscript for me. Mr. Marius Barbeau, of the National Museum, Ottawa, has been both generous and very helpful in supplying me with the airs and words of "La belle Lisette" and "Voici le printemps," as well as with some material that does not appear in this volume. To Mr. J. Murray Gibbon I also wish to extend my thanks for his generosity in translating several songs especially for this volume. I am also grateful to Miss Constance A. Hamilton for permission to use her translation of "Voici le printemps," and to Mrs. William H. Drummond for permission to use her late husband's poem, "The Voyageur."

G. L. N.

CONTENTS

I

FURS AND FUR-TRADERS

I

THE term *voyageur*, a French word meaning "travel-er," was applied originally in Canadian history to all explorers, fur-traders, and travelers. It came in time to be restricted to the men who operated the canoes and batteaux of fur-traders, and who, if serving at all as traders, labored as subordinates to a clerk or proprietor. Even as late as 1807, however, the famous Beaver Club of Montreal, a group of prominent and, usually, success-ful fur-merchants or traders, balloted to determine whether its name should be changed to the Voyageur Club. Thus the term was somewhat vague, though always referring to men who had had actual experience in the fur trade among the Indians. In this book the term is restricted to French-Canadian canoemen.

The French *régime* was responsible for the rise of this unique group of men. From the days of earliest explora-tion until 1763 a large part of what is now Canada and much of the rest of the continent west of the Appalachian Mountains was French territory. In this vast region lived the several tribes of Indians with whom the French settlers about Quebec and Montreal were not slow to barter furs. Beaver, marten, fox, lynx, bear, otter, wolf, muskrat, and many other furs were obtained. Furs were in great demand in Europe and Asia, and both the Eng-lish colonists along the Atlantic seaboard and the French

3

in New France supported themselves in large part by means of a very flourishing fur trade.

At first the Indians took their skins and furs down the St. Lawrence to Quebec and Montreal, whither annual fairs attracted them; but in the process of time ambitious traders intercepted the natives and purchased their furs in the interior, thus gaining an advantage over fellow traders. The enmity between the Iroquois and the Algonquin also tended to prevent the Indians from making their annual trips to the lower St. Lawrence, since the western tribes, who brought most of the furs, feared to pass down the river through enemy territory.

When traders began to enter the Indian country, the voyageur may be said to have been born. Farther and farther up the St. Lawrence, up the Ottawa River, into lakes Huron and Michigan, the traders ventured. Erie and Ontario were explored, and finally Lake Superior. From these lakes more venturesome traders entered the rivers emptying into them and reached the Ohio and Illinois countries and the region about the Mississippi. They even found the rivers emptying into Lake Superior from the west and marked out the route by way of Rainy Lake into Lake Winnipeg. When Canada was lost to the English in 1763, French posts were established far up the Saskatchewan, and French traders had seen the Rocky Mountains and knew of the "Oregon" River. On these trips westward the birch-bark canoe was almost the sole vehicle of transportation, and men from the hamlets on the lower St. Lawrence were the canoemen.

Naturally the French Government found it necessary as time went on to establish rules and regulations for this lucrative business. Licenses (*congés*) to enter the Indian country were required; certain articles were prohibited in the trade; and only a specified number of traders might be licensed in one year. A man with sufficient capital to purchase a season's outfit acquired a license and hired men of his neighborhood to take the goods in canoes to the point at which the trader wished to sell his wares to the Indians. After bartering knives, beads, wampum, blankets, vermilion, and numberless trinkets and other articles for furs worth infinitely more in monetary value, these subtraders returned to their proprietor with the results of their transactions. The French term for the proprietor was *bourgeois*, and for the subtrader *voyageur*. The latter in time became a general term covering the *mangeur de lard* ("pork-eater") and the *hivernant* ("winterer"). The former were the novices, the men who could be entrusted only with the management of the canoes and who for that reason returned home each season. The *hivernants* were experienced voyageurs who spent the winters at posts in the interior, exchanging trade goods for furs under the direction of a *commis*. The latter was a clerk who was training to become a *bourgeois* and who was frequently a son or a near relative of a *bourgeois*. These terms came into use in the French period, but they and the system described were retained by the British after 1763 and by the Americans after 1816, when the British abandoned their posts in the American Northwest. French remained the "official" language as long as the fur trade flourished. Some of the terms are still in use in the forts of the Hudson's Bay Company in northern and western Canada.

Because this system developed under the French *régime* and about Quebec and Montreal, the fur trade continued to its last breath to be dependent to a great degree for canoemen and winterers upon the French Canadians in the country about these two cities. Just as the sailing vessel could be managed best by men in whose families was the seafaring tradition, so the fur-trading expeditions into the Northwest proved most lucrative when carried out by men from Sorel, Three Rivers, L'Orignal, and other Quebec hamlets, where babes grew into manhood with the almost certain knowledge that they would some day paddle canoes for the Northwest Company, the Hudson's Bay Company, the American Fur Company, or a rival firm or trader. John Jacob Astor, the prince of American fur-traders and the organizer of the largest American fur company, is said to have remarked that he would rather have one voyageur than three American canoemen.

Though the voyageurs were usually unlettered men and unambitious as well, Fate has decreed that even their individual names should not be lost. When a trader made application for a license, he was required to state the names of all his men. Hundreds of these licenses are extant, especially in Montreal, Quebec, and Ottawa, and from them one learns to recognize whole families of voyageurs who were enrolled year after year in official records. Doubtless many of these visitors to the West in the seventeenth, eighteenth, and early nineteenth centuries will remain forever unknown, but hundreds of others are becoming better known year by year as these old records are investigated.[1]

The number of voyageurs in any given year is truly surprising. The West was not the unknown, uninhabited region that the imagination of writers has pictured. To dispel any doubt on this point one has only to refer to the lists of licenses already mentioned. In the year 1777, for example, 2,431 voyageurs are recorded in the licenses obtained at Montreal and Detroit. Add to this number the men already in the interior as *hivernants*, the employees of the Hudson's Bay Company, and the traders from the new states on the coast, and five thousand is a conservative estimate of the men who were sprinkled from Montreal to the Rocky Mountains, from Hudson Bay to the Gulf of Mexico.

Voyageurs formed a class as distinct in dress, customs, and traditions as sailors or lumberjacks. They had the further unifying characteristic of speaking a language which was not the native tongue either of their employers or of the people with whom they did business. They were termed voyageurs by all who had occasion to speak of them, and the word was used with the implication that a distinct and easily recognizable group of men was meant. Later writers have sometimes confused the terms *voyageur* and *coureur de bois*. The latter term was used in referring to illicit traders of the French *régime*, men who ventured into the wilderness without licenses. It is incorrect, therefore, to make it synonymous with *voyageur*. The only other term by which voyageurs were commonly known was *engagés*, a loose expression which might be translated as "employees."

In American and Canadian history these voyageurs played a significant rôle. The fur trade was for genera-

7

tions the chief industry of the continent. Unfortunately, no thoroughgoing history of the industry has ever been written, and so its significance has not been fully revealed. When such an account shall have been completed, it will become plain that several of the struggles between France and Great Britain were occasioned by a desire to reap the rich profits of the fur trade of the West; that the large fur-trading companies exercised powerful influence over English, French, and American statesmen; that England's manufacturers realized the importance of the Indian country as one of their chief markets; and that the control of the western fur-trading posts was one of the chief objects of the War of 1812 between Great Britain and the United States.[2] When these and other salient facts about the fur trade are made clear, the significance of the voyageurs will be seen, for without them the industry could hardly have flourished and attained the importance that it assumed. A peculiar set of circumstances produced a unique group of men.

Though the voyageur was the product of the French period, he attained his highest degree of individuality and usefulness in the years between 1763 and 1840, the period mainly to be considered in this volume. After Canada had been wrested from the French in 1763, British and American merchants took over the entire trade formerly conducted by the French, and great companies were soon formed with large capital and many resources. Since the employers of the voyageurs were, in the main, the three great fur-trading companies of the continent, it may be useful at this point to describe them briefly. The Hudson's Bay Company was chartered in 1670, largely as a result of the recommendations of two great French explorers, Pierre Esprit Radisson and his brother-in-law, Medard Chouart, Sieur des Groseilliers. It soon had posts at various places on the shore of Hudson Bay. Until the period of the American Revolution it "slept by the bay," having the Indians bring furs to its forts. Then the activity of Montreal traders in the interior forced the company to undertake a more strenuous policy and to erect forts in the interior. These traders from Canada, usually Scotch, had experienced a period of excessive competition from the time of the conquest till towards the end of the American Revolution. Then they began to pool their resources and profits and to be known as the Northwest Company. It was a loose organization, never a corporation like its great rival. Generally speaking, voyageurs were employees of the Northwest Company, or of a closely allied organization, the Southwest Company, for the Hudson's Bay Company, at least till about 1815, used Orkney men as their "servants." However, an American corporation soon developed which employed voyageurs in much the same manner as the Northwest Company. This was the American Fur Company of New York, chartered by John Jacob Astor in 1808. In 1821 excessive competition forced the two Canadian companies to coalesce and to assume the name of the one possessing charter rights. The American Fur Company was reorganized in 1834, but maintained its existence till it failed in 1842. After 1816 it took over most of the trade that the Northwest Company had been enjoying since the Revolution about the Great Lakes and in the region of the upper Mississippi and Missouri rivers.[3]

Licenses were no longer for the few, and an ever increasing number of voyageurs were required to man the numerous canoes to the interior. Posts dotted the wilderness along the Great Lakes and on practically every navigable river and lake in the area now embracing Michigan, Ohio, Indiana, Illinois, Wisconsin, Minnesota, Iowa, North and South Dakota, Montana, Idaho, Wyoming, Washington, Oregon, and all of western Canada. The writer has mapped the sites of the more important posts within the area of Minnesota and has located not less than 125.[4] At every fort were a number of voyageurs. They, with their traders, were thus the first white settlers of most of these areas. It was they, too, who did the actual exploring of the interior, for the great explorers, like Alexander Henry, Jonathan Carver, and Alexander Mackenzie, relied on their canoemen for knowledge of navigable streams, portages, wintering grounds, and other topographical features. Moreover, they or their descendants remained when the fur-trade era gave way to the period of actual settlement and thus supplied part of the stock from which the inhabitants of these regions are derived. They named the lakes and rivers, prepared the Indians for the incursion of the whites, and made it possible for missionaries to go among the tribes and convert and civilize them. They were humble, unassuming men, but this fact should not obscure their services and importance in American and Canadian history.

II

PORTRAIT OF THE VOYAGEUR

II

My man dressed himself in the habit of a voyageur, that is, a short shirt, a red woolen cap, a pair of deer skin leggins which reach from the ancles a little above the knees, and are held up by a string secured to a belt about the waist, the aziōn ["breech cloth"] of the Indians, and a pair of deer skin moccasins without stockings on the feet. The thighs are left bare. This is the dress of voyageurs in summer and winter." [1] Add a few items which the worthy missionary, Sherman Hall, neglected to mention—a blue capote, the inevitable pipe, a gaudy sash, and a gay beaded bag or pouch hung from the sash—and you have the voyageur as he appeared speeding over lakes, advancing cautiously up narrow creeks, toiling over portages, cracking his whip over the heads of his dogs, laughing down rapids, fiddling in log forts, and singing wherever he was.

One would expect voyageurs to be men of heroic proportions, but usually they were not. The average voyageur was five feet six inches in height. Few were more than five feet eight inches. Had they been taller, they would have occupied too much of the precious space in a canoe already overcrowded with cargo. But though the voyageur was short, he was strong. He could paddle fifteen—yes, if necessary, eighteen—hours per day for weeks on end and joke beside the camp fire at the close

13

of each day's toil. He could carry from 200 to 450 pounds of merchandise on his back over rocky portage trails at a pace which made unburdened travelers pant for breath in their endeavor not to be left behind. A distinguished traveler on the Great Lakes in 1826, Thomas L. McKenney, later of the United States Bureau of Indian Affairs, wrote how his men took the canoe out of the water, mended a breach in it, reloaded, cooked breakfast, shaved, washed, ate, and reëmbarked—all in *fifty-seven* minutes! "Some estimate may be formed from this," says McKenney, "of the celerity of the movements of these voyageurs. I can liken them to nothing but their own ponies. They are short, thick set, and active, and never tire. A Canadian, if born to be a labourer, deems himself to be very unfortunate if he should chance to grow over five feet five, or six inches;—and if he shall reach five feet ten or eleven, it forever excludes him from the privilege of becoming voyageur. There is no room for the legs of such people, in these canoes. But if he shall stop growing at about five feet four inches, and be gifted with a good voice, and lungs that never tire, he is considered as having been born under a most favourable star." [2]

One result of the voyageur's mode of life was the overdevelopment of arms and shoulders at the expense of other parts of the body. This fact is brought out in a description by Dr. John J. Bigsby, the secretary of the commission that marked out the international boundary between Canada and the United States according to the provisions of the Treaty of Ghent of 1814. His portraits of the canoemen of his party as he saw them first at

Lachine are probably more realistic than those of any other contemporary writer.[3]

"I was disappointed and not a little surprised at the appearance of the *voyageurs*. On Sundays, as they stand round the door of the village churches, they are proud dressy fellows in their parti-coloured sashes and ostrich-feathers; but here they were a motley set to the eye: but the truth was that all of them were picked men, with extra wages as serving in a light canoe.

"Some were well made, but all looked weak in the legs, and were of light weight. A Falstaff would have put his foot through the canoe to the 'yellow sands' beneath. The collection of faces among them chanced to be extraordinary, as they squatted, paddle in hand, in two rows, each on his slender bag of necessaries. By the bye, all their finery (and they love it) was left at home. One man's face, with a large Jewish nose, seemed to have been squeezed in a vice, or to have passed through a flattening machine. It was like a cheese-cutter,—all edge. Another had one nostril bitten off. He proved the buffoon of the party. He had the extraordinary faculty of untying the strings of his face, as it were, at pleasure, when his features fell into confusion—into a crazed chaos almost frightful; his eye, too, lost its usual significance; but no man's countenance . . . was fuller of fun and fancies than his, when he liked. A third man had his features wrenched to the right—exceedingly little, it is true; but the effect was remarkable. He had been slapped on the face by a grisly bear. Another was a short, paunchy old man, with vast features, but no forehead—the last man I should have selected; but he was a hard-working creature, usually called 'Passe-partout,' because he had been everywhere, and was famous for the weight of fish he could devour at a meal. . . . Except the younger men, their faces were short, thin, quick in their expression, and mapped out in furrows, like those of the sunday-less Parisians."

Now and again one found a giant among these dwarfs. Nicholas Garry, deputy-governor of the Hudson's Bay Company from 1822 to 1835, mentions as one of his voyageurs "a Man six Feet high and of herculean make, who was called in consequence 'La Petite Vierge.' " [4] Nicknames were common among these men. Frequently, too, as in the case of Garry's "little maiden," the nickname was in exact contradiction of some characteristic of the man. Stephen H. Long, an explorer in the valley of the Red River of the North in 1823, gives an example of this trait in describing how his men had no sooner seen his black man Andrew "than they immediately agreed among themselves to apply to him the term Wapishka . . . which means white." [5]

McKenney, in the letter already quoted, points out an essential characteristic of the voyageur—his pride of profession. He was class conscious; he considered himself favored by fortune to belong to his group; he took a happy pride in doing his work in such a way as to bring credit to his fellow workers; and he considered the toil and hardships of his chosen work incidental to the profession and was seldom known to pity himself. An example of this attitude is given by McKenney in describing a man on Lake Superior whose business it was at the time to catch fish. He was sixty-nine years of age and

16

active as a boy, though radically diseased. "On his legs, and arms, and breast," writes McKenney, "are tatooed, the marks of superiority in his profession, which has been that of a voyageur, and it seems he excelled in carrying packages across the portages, both on account of their weight and the celerity of his movement. He is now sallow, and dropsical, but active as stated. On questioning him as to his former life, he said, with a slap of the hands, 'he had been the greatest man in the northwest.' It is questionable whether Bonaparte ever felt his superiority in all the departments of mind which so distinguished him, or in his achievements, to an extent of greater excitement, than does this poor man on Michael's island, in the animating and single belief in his supremacy as a *north-western voyageur*." [6]

The voyageurs gave proof of this joy and pride in their work by decking themselves and their canoes in color. "The voyageurs," again to quote McKenney, "are engaged, and on the spot, each with a red feather in his hat, and two others, in possession of the steersman, one for the bow, and the other for the stern of the canoe. These plumes in the canoe are intended to indicate that she has been tried, and found worthy." [7]

The young Chicago scientist, Robert Kennicott, who made a study of flora and fauna of the Canadian Northwest in the fifties and sixties, describing his guide as one of the best runners in America, remarks that he "seemed to feel much more pride in being a good voyageur than a famous runner." And to show how seriously these men took their work he relates that once on the voyage his canoe grazed a rock by accident. "Then, though not

17

the least harm was done, and it was not altogether his fault, old Baptiste our guide was cross till the day after, when he recovered his good humor in the pleasure of running some difficult rapids." [8]

Whether in canoes or with dog trains the voyageurs were ever trying to outdo one another in speed and endurance. Kennicott relates how the agreeable change from working against the current to moving with it put his voyageurs in excellent humor: "the canoes were constantly contending for the lead, the relative cleverness of the bowsmen in cutting off bends in the river . . . causing much excitement and sport." Canoe racing was, indeed, one of the chief delights of voyageurs. [9]

With pride in their own ability went its usual concomitant, ridicule of lesser powers in others. To have the laugh on a greenhorn or to be able to taunt a fellow voyageur of weakness or slowness was to relish life thoroughly. "In an hour we were in still water," writes McKenney, "when our voyageurs, all wet . . . began to chatter again, and pass their jokes upon the bowsman, in whose face many a swell had broken in making this traverse." [10] With dog trains fear of this ridicule showed itself characteristically. Many a warming did Kennicott's dog No-gah get because he would not *mouche* ("go fast") when it was his spell ahead. When a sled could not keep up and take its proper place in the brigade at each spell, it was said to be *planted*, "which is considered something very disgraceful; and a good voyageur will push (i.e. help his dogs by pushing with a long pole always attached to the top of a loaded sled) till he is nearly knocked up, rather than be planted, even though his dogs are known to be weak, or his load extra heavy." [11] When the advance party with Kennicott arrived at Peel's River, they gave the dogs a *festin*, ate two suppers themselves, sat comfortably before the fire, and "boasted of our dogs; while the three unfortunate owners of poor trains lay in their windy camp that night and the next." When the laggards came up, the fortunate owners of good dogs laughed at them, much to their indignation. "Anyone who expects much sympathy for such trifling misery in this country," observes the author, "will be left to wipe his own eyes. If one gets frozen, starved, . . . he may expect ridicule, not condolence. . . . It is very comical, sometimes, to see the pains taken by the old voyageurs to cache a frost bite, or any fatigue." [12]

The boasting of which Kennicott makes mention was characteristic of the voyageurs. The speed of their dogs, the lines of their canoes, the heaviness of their burdens on portages, their skill in shooting rapids, and similar topics were points discussed soon and late before blazing camp fires. Pulling the long bow did not arise when the first Paul Bunyan story was told. For a century and more its counterparts had made animated many an encampment of gesticulating French-Canadian voyageurs. The difference lies in the fact that the hero of every voyageur's yarn was himself instead of a mythical giant embodying the same exaggerated traits and abilities as those of which he boasted.

One of the most interesting traits of the voyageur was his extreme courtesy. His Gallic ancestry was nowhere so evident as in the deferential ease with which

19

he addressed his superiors, the Indians, ladies, or men of his own class. The French language came to his aid here, for though he could neither read nor write, his by birthright were the graceful French phrases and expressions which mean little and yet are so effectual in establishing cordial relations. Many of the vulgar, beastly phases of the voyageur's life are offset by the refinement of his bearing and his speech.

III

THE VOYAGEUR'S CANOE

C.BERTSCH

III

WITHOUT the birch-bark canoe the history of inland North America would have been altogether different from that which is on record. Dugouts, batteaux, rafts, and other clumsy craft could have replaced the canoe in many instances and on many waterways; but dugouts cannot be carried easily on men's shoulders over the scores of portages which made tedious the explorers' and traders' routes; batteaux and rafts cannot shoot rapids skillfully; and a dozen other objections to such water conveyances could be advanced to prove that the canoe was the only practicable vehicle for a large part of the fur-trader's frontier.

Disassociated from his canoe the voyageur can hardly be imagined. As well separate him from his pipe! It was his carriage by day, his house by night, the topic of fully half his conversation, and the object of his pride. His clothing, his food, his songs, his family life, his very stature were all conditioned by a frail basket which he could carry on his shoulders.

In what dim age the Algonquian tribes learned the secret of making canoes from the rind of the yellow birch tree is not known. Generations, perhaps even centuries, witnessed the perfecting of the art, for it is no slight task to build a vessel that weighs less than three hundred pounds and yet can sustain the burden of five tons of crew and freight. Moreover, no nails or other metal substances were used in its construction, all the building materials being found in the forests. And the reason for the use of the canoe by the Algonquian tribes and not by more southern bands was the fact that the canoe birch grows only in northern latitudes. One of the most potent arguments used by the British in their efforts before 1795 to retain control of the Lake of the Woods–Grand Portage water route was that birch-bark canoes were indispensable to British control of western Canada and that these were made by the Indians on the southern shore of Rainy Lake.[1]

This unique craft, this essentially native American product, has been described by numberless travelers. It varied in size according to the extent of the body of water on which it was to be used. Generally speaking, three types of canoes were in use among the white people of Canada and the United States. The "Montreal canoe," or *canot du maître*, which was thirty-five to forty feet long, was used on the Great Lakes and on large rivers like the St. Lawrence. The "North canoe," or *canot du nord*, about twenty-five feet in length and carrying only about three thousand pounds besides the crew, was used on smaller streams and lakes, particularly on those beyond Grand Portage—whence its name. Between these two in size was the *bâtard*, or "bastard canoe," which was propelled by ten men. Fourteen were usually required for the *canot du maître* and eight for a North canoe. A canoe about twenty feet long, called a "half canoe," was sometimes used; and Indian canoes, ten to fifteen feet, were sometimes termed "light canoes." Or-

dinarily, however, a "light canoe" was merely one dispatched without freight.[2]

Either Indians or voyageurs were employed to build
the canoes, in use in the fur trade. The rind of one birch
tree was often sufficient to construct a canoe. *Wattape*,
the fine root of some coniferous tree, usually the red
spruce, was used in lieu of rope or thread to sew together
the strips of bark. When a covering of sufficient size had
thus been manufactured, it was placed over a framework
of thin white-cedar boards shaped to form a structure
twenty to forty feet long, four to six feet wide at the
center, and narrowed to a point, or *pince*, at either end.
Over the gunwales the bark was lashed with *wattape*,
and four to nine narrow thwarts or bars were placed
across the top at more or less regular intervals to hold
the canoe in shape. In front of these thwarts and depend-
ing several inches from the gunwales were boards about
four inches wide which served as seats for the voyageurs.
The canoe was now ready for gumming. This substitute
for calking was achieved by applying melted gum from
pine trees with the aid of a torch; the process must be
repeated daily or oftener throughout the voyage to keep
the craft watertight.

Not all canoes were painted, but it was usual to depict
a flag, a horse, an Indian head, or some similar object on
the high prow and stern. One traveler describes his Lake
Superior canoe thus: "The canoe would be an object of
interest any where, even without paint; but now, ornamented as it is, it is really striking. . . . Around the
sides, and upon a white ground, is a festoon of green and
red paint. The rim is alternate green, red, and white. On

each side of the bow, on a white ground, is the bust of an Indian chief, smoking, even larger than life. . . . In the bow is an enormous wooden pipe. . . . This is the canoe that was made at Fond du Lac; and on both sides, and against the swell of the middle, is painted in large letters, Fond Du Lac." [3]

Three sizes of paddles were used: the common paddle, about two feet long and three inches wide, which was used by the middlemen (*milieux*), or men in the center of the canoe; a longer kind, about five inches wide, which was used by the steersman (*gouvernail*), who stood in the stern; and a still larger paddle, which the bowsman or foreman (*avant de canot*, *devant*, or *ducent*) employed when running rapids or leaping small falls. These paddles were made of red-cedar wood and were very light. The blades were usually painted red and ornamented still further with some markings of black and green.

For other equipment the canoe carried an oilcloth which could be used both for covering the cargo and for improvising a sail when *la vieille*, or "old woman of the wind," was propitious. On such occasions a block was placed in the bottom of the canoe to receive the foot of a mast carrying a pole at right angles which served as a yard for the sail. The sail was trimmed by lines attached to the ends of the yard. Sometimes, instead of a single mast with its horizontal yard, two poles were erected at the center of the canoe between which the sail was hung.

Another essential article in the equipment of every well-stocked canoe was a large sponge capable of taking up two to four quarts of water. When the canoe sprang a leak, this sponge was used for bailing. A rope for cordelle, or towing purposes, sixty yards in length, also found a place in every canoe. When rapids were not of such magnitude as to require portaging the canoe, it could be towed by means of this rope.

"The proper crew of such a [North] canoe is eight men," writes Kennicott, "a *bowsman, steersman,* and six *middlemen.* The bowsman, who is the guide, sits alone in the bow; the six middlemen occupy three seats placed about five feet apart in the middle of the canoe; and the steersman stands in the stern, never sitting down while the canoe is in motion. . . . All, except the steersman, keep perfect stroke in paddling. . . . [They] paddle with great rapidity, making about forty strokes per minute, . . . dipping the paddle a foot or eighteen inches into the water and pulling with very considerable force. When it is considered that this is kept up, exclusive of several short resting spells of ten or fifteen minutes each, and of the stops for breakfast and dinner, from twelve to fifteen hours per day, some idea may be formed of the extreme powers of endurance possessed by these voyageurs." [4]

Another traveler betters Kennicott's statement, for he found by precise count that his voyageurs in a Montreal canoe made just a stroke a second. [5] Four to six miles per hour was the average speed of canoes propelled thus in calm water. When head winds or untoward weather of any sort were encountered, the voyageurs generally put ashore, for even though their strength was sufficient for the task, they knew that their frail bark could be broken

27

in two by a wave of unusual size. Reading the many available diaries kept on such canoe trips, one finds again and again on almost every voyage the entry, "Wind bound—forced to remain at last night's encampment." The voyageurs' term for this state of affairs was *degradé*, and "degraded" soon became a part of the vocabulary of English-speaking travelers. On the other hand, if a favoring wind arose, the sail was hoisted and with wind and paddles eight to ten miles an hour could sometimes be attained.

While paddling, the voyageurs sang. Songs were chosen whose rhythm was such that the paddles could keep time to the music. Ordinarily the steersman chose the song and gave the pitch. Sometimes he sang the stanza and the others joined in the chorus. In the parlance of his fellows he was the *solo*. Voyageurs were chosen partly with respect to their vocal abilities, and the effect of six to fourteen of them in full song was quite impressive. Of course, they sang in French—of their canoes, of their country, of their life, of their loves, of their church— sentimental romances, old ballads, humorous jingles, lofty poems, and obscene versifications. Many of the songs were inheritances from the *trouvères* and *troubadours;* some were of the voyageurs' own composition. They lightened the work and were the natural expression of such an effervescent race of men as the French Canadians admittedly were.

Here is one of their songs in honor of the birch canoe, *"Mon canot d'écorce."* [6] It is an indigenous product, a voyageur's own composition, telling much of his attitude toward his canoe.

MON CANOT D'ÉCORCE

Dans mon ca-not d'é - cor - ce, as-sis à la frai-che'du temps, Où j'ai bra-vé tout' les tem - pê - tes, les grandes eaux du Saint Lau-rent; Car j'ai bra-vé tout'les tem - pê-tes les grands eaux du Saint Lau-rent. Mon canot est fait d'é -cor-ces fi - nes qu'on pleum' sur les bou-leaux blancs; Les cou-tur'sont fait' de ra - ci - nes, Les a - vi-rons de bois blanc.

Dans mon canot d'écorce, assis à la fraîcheur du temps,
Où j'ai bravé toutes les tempêtes, les grandes eaux du Saint-
Laurent. (bis)

Mon canot est fait d'écorces fines
Qu'on pleume sur les bouleaux blancs;
Les coutures sont faites de racines,⎫ (bis)
Les avirons de bois blanc.⎭

Je prends mon canot, je le lance
A travers les rapides, les bouillons.
Là, à grands pas il s'avance.⎫ (bis)
Il ne laisse j mais le courant.⎭

C'est quand je viens sur le portage, je prends mon canot sur mon
dos.
Je le renverse dessus ma tête: c'est ma cabane pour la nuit. (bis)

THE VOYAGEUR

J'ai parcouru le long des rives, tout le long du fleuve Saint-
Laurent
J'ai connu les tribus sauvages et leurs langages différents. (bis)

> *—Tu es mon compagnon de voyage!—*
> *Je veux mourir dans mon canot.*
> *Sur le tompeau, près du rivage,*⎱ (bis)
> *Vous renverserez mon canot.* ⎰

Le laboureur aime sa charrue, le chasseur son fusil, son chien;
Le musicien aime sa musique; moi, mon canot, c'est [tout] mon
bien! (bis)

TRANSLATION

MY BIRCH-BARK CANOE

In my birch-bark, canoeing, in the cool of evening I ride
Where I have braved every tempest St. Lawrence's rolling tide. (*repeat*)

> My canoe's of bark, light as a feather
> That is stripped from silvery birch;
> And the seams with roots sewn together,⎱ (*repeat*)
> The paddles white made of birch. ⎰

> I take my canoe, send it chasing
> All the rapids and billows acrost;
> There so swiftly see it go racing,⎱ (*repeat*)
> And it never the current has lost.⎰

It's when I come on the portage, I take my canoe on my back.
Set it on my head topsy-turvy; it's my cabin too for the night. (*repeat*)

Along the river banks I've wandered, all along St. Lawrence's tide
I have known the savage races and the tongues that them divide. (*repeat*)

> —You are my voyageur companion!—
> I'll gladly die within my canoe.
> And on the grave beside the canyon ⎱ (*repeat*)
> You'll overturn my canoe. ⎰

His cart is beloved of the ploughman, the hunter loves his gun, his hound;
The musician is a music lover—to my canoe I'm bound. (*repeat*)

*By permission of J. Murray Gibbon.

30

The French of this song is very illiterate, and the tune appears to be a variant of an old English sea song or ballad. The French ballad writer may have picked it up at Quebec or Three Rivers where the lumbermen, after rafting their logs down to the seaport, helped to load the logs on the ships. Mr. Gibbon remarks that Ralph Connor gave him a song, which he picked up from a half-breed in the Northwest, in which the solo part was in French and the chorus an old sea-chanty called "Blow Ye Winds of Morning."

So frail were the bark canoes that, once in them, the voyageurs could hardly shift their positions for fear of breaking the gum. Thus they sat, hour after hour, in one posture without so much as moving their feet. Passengers unaccustomed to the tedium found the cramped position almost unendurable, especially for the first few days. Because of the brittleness of the gum a curious way of taking on and putting off passengers was customary. This was none other than a brief ride on the broad back of a voyageur. As contact with sand on the shore would be likely to break off bits of the gum, the canoe was anchored off shore. Before the momentum given by the last paddle stroke had been lost, every voyageur was out of the canoe with a swift, graceful spring. One held the bow and one the stern, and the others loaded their backs with freight or passengers as the case might be. Such novel transportation was rather startling even to male passengers; what, then, must have been the emotions of the missionary's little wife who was faced with a ride pickaback? She confessed her feelings in a letter to a relative: "When we came to a good place [to disembark] the waves were so high that it was unsaf[e] to run the canoe ashore but one or two men held it with their oars while two others jumped into the water & began to unload as fast as possible. One offered me his back to take me ashore. Though my feelings revolted there was no alternative & I was soon safely landed." [7]

IV

VOYAGING

IV

To understand the voyageur completely one must accompany him on one of his trips from Montreal into the *pays d'en haut*, as he termed the Northwest. Thereby one learns his numberless little customs, his superstitions, his method of handling a canoe, and a thousand other phases of his mercurial nature.

Any year between 1770 and 1840, Montreal Island above the Lachine Rapids was the scene of much commotion on the May morning set for the departure of a brigade of canoes for the Northwest. During the winter months an agent of the fur company had been engaged in canvassing the hamlets and parishes round about for voyageurs. Experienced *engagés* were preferred, of course, but in every brigade there were certain to be *mangeurs de lard*, the butt of many a practical joke.

The region from which the voyageurs were drawn may be determined by the bonds given by the *bourgeois*, which included the names of voyageurs and the parishes from which they came.[1] In the years from 1774 to 1776 the following places were mentioned: Montreal, Laprairie, Lachine, Châteauguay, Sorel, Ile-Perrot, Pointe-Claire, St.-Philippe, Chambly, Boucherville, Ile-Jésus, Batiscan, St.-Laurent, Varrenes, Terrebonne, Lachenaie, Longueuil, St.-Ours, Yamaska, Trois Rivières, Contrecoeur, Berthier, Quebec, Vaudreuil, St.-Leonard,

Mascouche, L'Assomption, Ste.-Geneviève, St.-Pierre, St.-Joseph, Rivière du Loup, Pointe-aux-Trembles, St.-Michel, Lavaltrie, St.-Sulpice, Gentilly, Verchères, and St.-Denis. Thus the St. Lawrence from above Montreal to Quebec ran its majestic highway through a voyageur country. The Richelieu and St. Maurice rivers nourished a less numerous race of canoemen.

As soon as the agent had come to terms with his *engagé*, an *engagement* was signed. Many of these papers have come down to us and show the terms of the agreements. They were printed in French, with spaces left for the voyageur's name, his home, the wages he was to receive, and any special provisions. One to three years seems to have been the usual term for which the voyageur contracted to remain in the service. If he were a foreman or a steersman, he ordinarily received twelve hundred livres per annum,[2] but if he were a pork-eater, he got only four hundred livres. He agreed not to desert his master and not to give aid or encouragement to his master's rivals during the period of his engagement. At the bottom of the sheet one usually finds a cross instead of a signature, showing that a formal education was not one of the assets of these men.

Of course, such irresponsible persons as the voyageurs confessedly were often broke their engagements, and much of the confusion of the departure was due to the fact that Henri, Amable, Pierre, Hypolite, or some other renegade had failed to put in his appearance, though already supplied, as was the custom, with a third of his wages and his equipment. This equipment consisted usually of a blanket, a shirt, a pair of trousers, two handkerchiefs, several pounds of carrot tobacco (a carrot-shaped twist of tobacco weighing one to two pounds), and a few miscellaneous items for pork-eaters, and nearly twice the number of each item for winterers.

One of the chief agents of the American Fur Company found himself one day in May, 1817, in the usual situation of the person responsible for the voyageurs of a departing brigade. To his superior, John Jacob Astor, he wrote in his usual correct manner, but between the lines one can detect his exasperation: "All our Boats are off from Lachine in charge of Mr Matthews, but in consequence of a number of Engagés being still absent he has advanced only a short distance and remains on an Island waiting their arrival. I am in hopes this day will produce every one we expect . . . there are upwards of twenty five men missing [*sixty were engaged*], and of these I am sure at least a dozen will not come; indeed I shall consider ourselves lucky if we do not lose more than fifteen, of which number very few will have the honesty to return the money advanced them at the time they engaged." [3]

The agent, finding himself short of men, must prosecute the offenders and secure substitutes, a task not always easy to perform, especially during the periods of intense rivalry between fur companies. But worse could and frequently did happen: a voyageur could desert *en route*. Sad was his fate if he were recaptured. One of the missionaries to the Chippewa Indians relates how he prevented an angry *commis* from giving the regulation flogging to a deserter.

While the agent was filling up the quota of *engagés*,

the men themselves were down by the water's edge, gumming the canoes, making up packages, loading the canoes, bidding farewell to friends and families, and talking and weeping vociferously. Each package, or *pièce*, was made up to weigh ninety pounds, and two ears were left at the top by which the voyageur could lift it easily in the manner of a modern flour bag. Two of these *pièces* made an ordinary load for portaging, but emulation among the men in proof of unusual strength or endurance caused many an *engagé* to carry three or four. A member of a famous Negro-Indian family of voyageurs, the Bongas, is said to have had such strength that he could carry five. And the voyageurs before their camp fires told in awed tones of voyageurs who had carried eight. In such packages were arranged the blankets, scarlet cloths, strouds, calico, gartering, pins, beads, flour, pork, silver earbobs, and numberless other articles which were to be bartered in the interior for furs. Guns and ammunition were also packed into convenient packages; and intoxicating liquors and shot were packed usually in small kegs. When we read of such things as pigs and cookstoves being carried beyond Lake Superior in such brigades of canoes, we can but marvel at the ingenuity and perseverance of the fur-traders, and especially of their employees.

Having loaded each canoe with a cargo whose weight had been equalized by placing it on poles laid on the bottom of the canoe, the men and their clerks were ready to embark on their long and tedious journey. As many as thirty canoes or as few as two or three formed the brigade. Sometimes there was even a squadron of brigades. Flags were flying from sterns, feathers waving in caps, red oars flashing, and voices ringing out in a spirited canoe song as the shore receded.

But the voyageurs did not consider the journey begun as yet, for Ste. Anne's help and protection had not been implored. So the brigade proceeded up the river to where Ste. Anne's church, the chapel of the voyageurs, stood on the westernmost point of Montreal Island, the last place of worship that would be seen for months, perhaps for years. "This Church," writes Peter Pond, one of the earliest traders and explorers of the Northwest, in a perfect phonetic rendering of his own Connecticut dialect, "is Dedacated to St. Ann who Protects all Voigers. Heare is a small Box with a Hole in the top for ye Reseption of a Little Money for the Hole [holy] father or to say a small Mass for those Who Put a small Sum in the Box. Scars a Voiger but stops hear and Puts in his mite and By that Meanes they Suppose thay are Protected. . . . After the Saremony of Crossing them selves and Repeating a Short Prayer" they were ready to depart.[4] Even the Protestant clerks and *bourgeois* traveling with the brigade put coins in the box.

And now the hazardous expedition had begun. The route lay along the St. Lawrence to its confluence with the Ottawa and up that stream to the point where the Mattawa River joins it from the west. In this distance on *la grande rivière* there were eighteen portages. There were also approximately as many *décharges*. At these places the canoe and usually a part of the load were towed over the obstruction. To the numerous falls and rapids on their route the earlier voyageurs gave such curious names as *Les Chats* ("the cats"), *La Chaudière* ("the kettle"), *Les Allumettes* ("the matches"), and *Le Calumet* ("the peace pipe"). As early as the last quarter of the seventeenth century these names were already in use.

When the voyageurs passed from the St. Lawrence into the Ottawa and again when they entered the Mattawa, they performed one of the many rites that were traditional with them on their journeys. They pulled off their red caps and a man in each canoe uttered a prayer. A little later, when they left the Mattawa River, they performed another rite. Up to this point they had used "setting poles" as well as paddles wherever the current was too swift for the ordinary method of propelling the canoe. This system was called "tracking." At Lake Nipissing, however, they left the streams running east and entered one, French River, whose current was with them. For that reason they chose to express their joy of labor ended by going through a formal ceremony of throwing away their setting poles to the accompaniment of loud huzzas.

Another custom had already manifested itself on their trip. Near dangerous *saults* and rapids they had caught sight of tall wooden crosses on the banks. Whenever such a cross was passed, red caps came off and a prayer was uttered. For were not these crosses the rude but tender memorials of the voyageurs to mates who had perished at these spots, caught in the treacherous swirl and eddies of the stream? As many as thirty crosses on one bank are recorded by a clerk who entered the country in the summer of 1800.[5]

Soon after leaving Ste. Anne's all clerks or *bourgeois*

who had never before accompanied a brigade into the interior were given to understand that they would be "baptized" in the chilly waters of the river if they did not moisten the whistles of their men. Accordingly high wines (brandy) was produced, kegs were broached, and soon the red plumes in the Northmen's caps waved at more uncertain angles, and the sorrows of leaving home were forgotten.

On the second evening after the departure from Montreal, when the *campément* had been made in a pine-sheltered nook on the bank of the river, when *souper* had been eaten around the blazing fire, and whilst the smoke from many pipes lay like a cloud against the dark forest trees, the call for *la ronde* was issued. This dance was another customary part of the journey, and it was entered into heartily despite the moralizing tone of the verses.[6]

Two sacks were placed some ten feet apart in an open space, and on them two singers were seated facing each other, one an old man, the other a youth. Each carried an empty kettle under his arm. About these two the rest of the voyageurs formed a circle. The dance began with the singing of the first stanza by the young man, in his shirt sleeves, a feather in his cap, holding his head high and prancing about in a swaggering manner:

> *Ce sont les voyageurs*
> *Qui sont sur leur départ;*
> *Voyez-vous les bonn's gens*
> *Venir sur les remparts?*
> *Sur l'air du tra, lal-déra:*
> *Sur l'air du tra, lal-déra:*
> *Sur l'air du tra, déri-déra:*
> *Lal-déra!*

41

When he had ended, the old voyageur, dressed in his big
blue capote, wearing his *ceinture fléchée* (sash) and his
sac-à-feu (beaded bag), and shaking his head wisely,
sang in a staid manner a couplet of advice to the young
people who were leaving for the *pays d'en haut:*

> *Mets d'la racine de patience*
> *Dans ton gousset;*
> *Car tu verras venir ton corps*
> *Joliment sec,*
> *A force de nager toujours*
> *Et de porter:*
> *Car on n'a pas souvent l'crédit*
> *D'se sentir reposer!*

And thereupon the voyageurs grasped hands and commenced to turn, dancing and singing the refrain, whilst
the two singers beat on their kettles:

> *Lève ton pied, ma jolie bergère!*
> *Lève ton pied, légère!*
> *Lève ton pied, ma jolie bergère!*
> *Lève ton pied, légèrement!*

Three times they turned, repeating the strain. The remainder of the song runs as follows:

Young Man

> *Au revoir père et mère,*
> *Soeur, frère et toi Fanchon;*
> *Vous reverrez bientôt*
> *Votre cher Siméon!*
> *Sur l'air du tra, lal-déra:*
> *Sur l'air du tra, lal-déra:*
> *Sur l'air du tra, déri-déra:*
> *Lal-déra!*

VOYAGING

Old Man

Embarque-moi dans ton canot,
Prends ton paquet
Car tu vas laisser ton pays
Et tes parents,
C'est pour monter dans les rivières
Et dans les lacs
Toujours att'lé sur l'aviron,
Ainsi que sur les sacs!

Chorus

* * * * * * *

Young Man

Ce sont les voyageurs
Qui sont de bons enfants;
Ah! qui ne mangent guère,
Mais qui boivent souvent!
Sur l'air du tra, lal-déra, etc.

Old Man

Si les maringouins t'piq' la tête,
D'leur aiguillon
Et t'étourdissent les oreilles,
De leurs chansons,
Endure-les, et prends patience
Afin d'apprendre
Qu'ainsi le diable te tourmente,
Pour avoir ta pauvre âme!

Chorus

* * * * * * *

43

THE VOYAGEUR

Young Man

Quand on est en voyage,
  Le saque sur le dos,
On s'écrie, camarade,
  Camarade il fait chaud!
Sur l'air du tra, lal-déra, etc.

Old Man

Quand tu seras dans ces rapids,
  Très dangereux,
Prends la Vierge pour ton bon guide
  Fais-lui des voeux!
Et tu verras couler cette onde, ⌐
  Avec vitesse,
Et prie bien du fond de ton coeur
  Qu'elle coule sans cesse.

Chorus

\

* * * * * * *

"We are voyageurs starting on our way," the young
man announces. "Don't you see the townsfolk watching
from the walls?" But the old man replies in admonition,
"Put some patience in your wallet, for you will get dry
from paddling constantly and from portaging, for rest
comes seldom." Then all sing a refrain from a familiar
song (*En roulant*), "Dance, pretty shepherdess, dance
lightly," etc. "Goodbye, Father and Mother," sings the
pork-eater, "you, too, Brother and Fanchon. You will
soon see your dear Simon again." But the old man is
relentless. "Embark in your canoe and take your pack,
for you are about to leave your country and your rela-

44

tives to go upstream and through lakes, always harnessed to your paddle and your pack." Nothing daunted, the young man breaks forth again, "We are voyageurs and good fellows. We seldom eat but we often drink." The old man then moralizes, "If the mosquitoes sting your head and deafen your ears with their buzzing, endure them patiently, for they will show you how the Devil will torment you in order to get your poor soul." This seems to chasten the tenderfoot, for he replies in serious vein, "When we are voyaging, pack on back, it will be, 'Comrade, how hot it is!'" As his parting bit of advice the Nor'wester preaches, "When you are in the worst rapids let Mary be your guide. Make your vow to Her and you will see the waves recede. And pray from the bottom of your heart that they may ever recede." Snatches from other *chansons* are recognizable.

Only two meals were eaten ordinarily, the breakfast and the evening meal. An hour was allowed, as a rule, for breakfast, but if portages were numerous or especially difficult, less time was permitted for the morning meal. Hard portages usually necessitated a third meal, for no human being could have labored more arduously than the voyageur on a difficult portage.

Nearly everyone who has written of canoe travel remarks on the laboriousness of portaging. One author describes a portage scene thus: "As soon as a canoe reaches a portage, a scene of bustle and activity takes place, which none can picture to themselves but such as have seen it. The goods are unloaded, and conveyed across, while the canoe is carried by the stern and bowsmen. As soon as they have reached the end of the portage, it is launched and reloaded without any loss of time. An obstruction of one hundred yards does not detain them more than twenty minutes. We had occasion, however, more than once, to regret their speed, which caused them to toss our baggage very unceremoniously, using it as they would packs of furs, which are so made up as not to be injured by this rough treatment. The whole care and attention of a voyageur seems to centre in his canoe, which he handles with an astonishing degree of dexterity and caution." [7]

The length of a portage was computed by voyageurs in a characteristic way. The canoe and goods were carried about a third of a mile and put down, or *posé*, two or more trips often being required to transport all the load to this point. Then, without resting, the men shouldered their burdens and went on to the next *posé*. And so on till all the *posés* had been passed. One long portage of forty-five miles in Wisconsin was divided into one hundred and twenty-two *poses*.[8]

Across these portages the men dogtrotted at a pace which kept passengers running. A missionary, William T. Boutwell, relates how he had merely a musket and two umbrellas upon his shoulder, and yet he could not keep in sight of the greater part of the voyageurs unless, as he says, "I *ran* faster than I chose." [9] So much lifting and carrying proved a strain to all but the toughest, and many a bruised foot and wrenched ankle were the result of nearly every portage. Hernia was very prevalent among voyageurs and not infrequently caused death. On the other hand, the voyageurs, though nearly amphibious, seldom had colds, and so, like the lumberjacks, they are good proof that exposure and wet feet bear no relation to respiratory infections.

For portaging, a sort of harness, called the "portage collar," was used. This consisted of a strap of leather about three inches wide, to which smaller straps were attached of sufficient length to tie around the packages. The straps were first tied around each end of a *pièce*, which was then swung upon the back, the lower part resting on the small of the back. The collar was then brought over the top of the head. The voyageur, taking a load, inclined a little forward, so that the load rested on the back and drew only gently on the collar on the head. After the first *pièce* was swung on the back, the second was taken up and laid on the top of it, reaching, if it was bulky, nearly to the top of the head. "I was surprised," adds the writer whose description of a portage harness has just been given, "to see with what ease these men, after they had suspended the first *pièce*, would raise up the second and place it on the top of it." [10]

The same observer was much impressed with the docility, strength, and good humor of the voyageurs in this "hard business" of portaging. "They appeared generally in good spirits, though some of them said it was hard business. One man in particular, I could not but feel a deep sympathy for. This was his first year in the country, and this probably the first time he had converted himself into a horse and baggage waggon to transport goods from the manufacturer to the far distant consumer. His back had become so heated and chafed by his loads, that several large boils had formed and which of themselves were very painful; yet his loads rested on them when he carried. He said in the morning when he first commenced his daily task, he could hardly endure the pain he suffered, notwithstanding he continued to carry his quota of goods with his companions." Very probably, when the missionary observer was not in his vicinity, the poor wretch expressed himself with many a *sacré* or even a *saccajé chien*, the favorite profanity of these men.

Sometimes it was not necessary to portage around an obstruction, but merely to remove some of the lading from the canoe. Such spots were termed *décharges*, which promptly became "discharges" in the English vocabulary of the clerk, proprietor, and passenger. To pass a *décharge* it was necessary to *cordelle*, that is, to tow the canoe by means of a rope (*cordelle*) or cable. Bad accidents happened occasionally when a towing rope broke and the canoe was precipitated down rapids or over falls, with loss or wetting of baggage and, not infrequently, loss of life. Often the current at the rapids was so violent that two or more men must accompany the canoe, wading waist deep in ice-cold water and over treacherous rocks. At the end no fire was made to dry the men's clothes, but all was hurry and away to the camping ground.

When the baggage became wet, or even damp, it was necessary to delay a day or even longer in order to dry the goods. Bales were unrolled, and blankets, cottons, clothes, and what not were hung on the bushes to dry. One traveler describes such a scene in delightful detail: "Left our encampment about 9 a.m. and proceeded to portage Coteau. Our private baggage was removed about one pose from the foot of the port[age]. The bales that were in the canoe which broke upon the large stone in the Rapids yesterday, were also brought up and opened. Our encampment looks not a little like a clothier's establishment from the rolls of cloth, and pieces of stroud nailed to the sides of trees and spread upon bushes. It might, however, be mistaken for a laundress establishment in seeing the shirts, blankets, vests. &c. In addition to the 5 bales that were drenched, was a box containing sundries, such as knives, forks, siedlitz powders, sulphur, starch, saltpeter, snuff, and numerous other articles, all of which were soaked. Five or six of us have been employed the remainder of the day in hanging out and drying wet goods. I have labored in wringing shirts and spreading clothes until I am quite tired. We shall not be able to get half through today with this unpleasant work." [11]

Sometimes, however, even the worm turns. A few instances are recorded of mutiny among voyageurs. Duncan M'Gillivray, a renowned trader and explorer of the Saskatchewan plains, on his trip into the interior from Grand Portage in 1794, records such an instance. At Rainy Lake he found a strike in progress among the men of a brigade already there. "A few discontented persons in their Band, wishing to do as much mischief as possible assembled their companions together several times on the Voyage Outward & represented to them how much their Interest suffered by the passive obedience to the will of their masters, when their utility to the Company, might insure them not only of better treatment, but of any other conditions which they would prescribe with Spirit & Resolution. . . . They all declared with one voice that

unless their wages would be augmented, and several
other conditions equally unreasonable granted them they
would immediately sett off to Montreal." Here, then, is
material for students of labor history, and where one
would least expect to find such an early instance of
"walking delegates" and strikes. Of course the tractable
voyageurs were unable to carry the strike to a successful
conclusion. "Their minds were agitated with these scruples at the very time that they insisted on a compliance
with their demands, and tho' they endeavoured carefully
to conceal it, yet a timidity was observed in their be-
haviour which proved very fortunate for their Masters,
who took such good advantage of it, that before night
they prevailed on a few of the most timid to return to
their duty, and the rest, being only ashamed to abandon
their companions, soon followed the example." [12] It is
refreshing and buoys up one's faith in human nature to
read that "a few of the most resolute were obstinate
enough to hold out . . . and were therefore sent down
to Montreal in disgrace." Explorers like Fraser and
Franklin found that there were limits even to voyageurs'
endurance, and they were obliged to drive on their men
where they refused to go.[13] Indeed, there was a prison at
Fort William for "refractory voyageurs." [14]

We have seen that the voyageurs had their own method
of measuring portages. They were not less original on the
water. Here the *pipe* was the standard of measurement.
This was the distance covered between respites, when the
luxury of resting and smoking was indulged. The order
"*Allumez*" was given by the guide when he deemed that
the usual time between smokes had elapsed, and no

second command was needed. Paddles were laid in the canoe, tired shoulders rested back on the thwarts or baggage, *sacs à feu* were opened, pipes were taken from *ceintures* and lighted, and jokes and stories were told for ten or fifteen minutes. The command to resume work given, the little craft moved on to the strains of another *chanson à l'aviron*.

Nightfall usually brought the toil of the voyageur to an end. A landing was made, the camp fire was lighted, the unloaded canoes were turned over on the shore, the clerk's tent was set up (in many brigades custom decreed that he must do this without aid from his men), the supper was cooked and eaten, and preparations were made for a night in the open. Though the clerk could indulge in such luxuries as tea, a voyageur's rations were almost invariably a quart of lyed corn [15] (dried peas were frequently used until Mackinac was reached) and an ounce or two of grease, pork, or bacon. From this last item, called *lard* in French, the class name, *mangeur de lard*, "pork-eater," was derived. The manner of cooking this monotonous but seemingly adequate diet was quite in keeping with the voyageur's other customs. "The men's practice in the culinary art was very simple, but good," writes a clerk in reminiscent mood. "The tin kettle, in which they cooked their food, would hold eight or ten gallons. It was hung over the fire, nearly full of water, then nine quarts of peas—one quart per man, the daily allowance—were put in; and when they were well bursted, two or three pounds of pork, cut into strips, for seasoning, were added, and all allowed to boil or simmer till daylight, when the cook added four biscuits, broken up, to the mess, and invited all hands to breakfast. The swelling of the peas and biscuit had now filled the kettle to the brim, so thick that a stick would stand upright in it. It looked inviting, and I begged for a plate full of it, and ate little else during the journey. The men now squatted in a circle, the kettle in their midst, and each one plying his wooden spoon or ladle from kettle to mouth, with almost electric speed, soon filled every cavity. Then the pipes were soon brought into full smoke." [16] This clerk became a trader of importance on the upper Mississippi.

It must not be supposed that the voyageurs did not add to their rations whatever berries, game, birds' eggs, or other "wild" items could be picked up in the day's "march." They were ever on the alert to catch a fish, turtle, or muskrat, to find a bird's nest full of eggs, to kill a deer or bear, or to locate a honey tree. A beaver's tail was considered an especially dainty morsel, and the story is that the voyageurs in the French period ate it even during Lent. To determine how far they were sinning, the matter was referred to the Sorbonne, and, no doubt because the aquatic habits of the beaver so closely resemble those of fishes, the privilege of eating the tail in Lent was permitted.[17]

Ingenuity came to their aid oftentimes when the voyageurs sought to add to their larder. One traveler describes the following scene as an illustration of their resourcefulness: "The Frenchmen here found a turtle, which they esteem as one of their luxuries. They were unsuccessful for a long time in getting its head from under its shell in order to kill it, when one of them put its tail to the fire, a second ready with two sticks, siezed its head as it thrust it from under its covering, and a third cut it off. So much for French wit." [18]

The same writer, however, had not such an exalted opinion of the cleanliness of the men, and his comment on that topic is worth noting: "It is perhaps difficult to determine which are the most squalid in their habits, the Indians, or some of the French voyageurs, who, as often as any way, recieve [*sic*] their rations in their pocket-handkerchief, or hat." [19]

Of the same opinion was the scientist Kennicott. He describes some of their culinary methods thus: "Near this lake Mr. Hubbard found the nest of a ruffed grouse containing five eggs. These our cook used in making our *galette*, thereby giving us quite a treat. This galette is the only form of bread used on a voyage, that is, when voyageurs are so fortunate as to have any flour at all. It is made in a very simple style:—the flour bag is opened, and a small hollow made in the flour, into which a little water is poured, and the dough is thus mixed in the bag; nothing is added, except, perhaps some dirt from the cook's *unwashed* hands, with which he kneads it into flat cakes, which are baked before the fire in a frying pan, or cooked in grease. . . . There is no denying that voyageurs are not apt to be very cleanly, either in their persons or in their cooking." And later he tells even more of the gustatory eccentricities of his voyageurs: "During the day I found the nest of a Canada goose. . . . It contained seven eggs. . . . Though the eggs mentioned had been incubated for some time, the voyageurs ate them. . . . It is very rarely that the voyageurs reject anything in the shape of fish or bird. A crow and pair of pigeon hawks, which I shot a few days before, were eaten, and I think they would eat eggs so nearly hatched that the chick could almost *peep*." [20]

Pemmican was used on voyages in the far interior. This was a kind of pressed buffalo meat, pounded fine, to which hot grease was added, and the whole left to form a mold in a bag of buffalo skin. When properly made, pemmican would remain edible for more than one season. Its small bulk and great nutritional value made it highly esteemed by all voyageurs. From it they made a dish called rubbaboo. "Rubbaboo," says Kennicott, "is a favorite dish with the northern voyageurs, when they can get it. It consists simply of pemmican made into a kind of soup by boiling in water. Flour is added when it can be obtained, and it is generally considered more palatable with a little sugar. Pemmican is supposed by the benighted world outside to consist only of pounded meat and grease; an egregious error; for, from experience on the subject, I am authorized to state that hair, sticks, bark, spruce leaves, stones, sand, etc., enter into its composition, often quite largely." [21]

Another writer, a native missionary, goes into the details not only of the manner of cooking rubbaboo, but also of the approved manner of eating it. Peter Jacobs' remarks are as follows: "The food that is generally prepared and eaten in these regions by voyageurs is what is called 'ahrubuhboo.' I do not know what the word itself means. I spell it as I hear it pronounced. All *pork eaters* from Canada do not know how to make it; I shall here tell my readers how I proceeded to make it; for it was this sort of food we had in the voyage. After I had got the wood in order, and made a good blazing fire, I took my kettle, went to the lake, and put in it about two quarts of water. While this was getting to boil over the fire I took a two-quart hand dish half full of water, and put into it some flour, and stirred it till it looked like *mush*. The pan was now full. As the water in the kettle was now boiling, I took my pan-dish, and put all that was in it in the kettle, where it became thinner. I then took a stick and stirred. This, of course, took some time to boil. When it boiled I kept stirring it in order to prevent the dregs of the flour-soup (if I may so call it) from sinking and sticking at the bottom of the kettle and burning. If it burned, the dinner would be spoiled. This frequently happens with bad and indolent cooks. I myself succeeded very well, as I was determined to be a good cook on this occasion. All depends upon the faithful continuance of stirring the flour-soup with a stick, until such a time as it is cooked. I carefully attended to this. When the flour-soup was quite cooked, I removed the kettle from the fire, and while my soup was boiling hot I jumped at my hatchet or tomahawk, and cut to pieces about a pound weight of *pemmican*, after which I threw this into the kettle. I stirred this quickly, so that the grease of the *pemmican* might be dissolved in the hot flour-soup. Thus ends the cooking. The time it takes to cook this is less than half an hour. It is very much like what is called in some countries *burgoo*. This 'ahrubuhboo' is first-rate food for travelers in this country. At this time I poured it out in dishes for my men and myself, and made a good dinner out of it. Very often the

men, when they are in a great hurry, instead of using
dishes and spoons, pour out their 'ahrubuhboo' on the
smooth hollow rocks, where it becomes cooler in a short
time, and eat it; those who have no spoons generally eat
it in the dog fashion, licking it up with their tongues." [22]

The nightly encampment was made about nine o'clock
in the long twilight of the northern spring. McKenney,
who became so deeply interested in the voyageur on his
trip through Lake Superior in 1826, asked his men one
evening at seven o'clock if they did not wish to go ashore
for the night. "They answered," he relates, "they were
fresh yet. They had been almost constantly paddling since
3 o'clock this morning. . . . 57,600 strokes with the paddle,
and 'fresh yet!' No human beings, except the Canadian
French, could stand this. Encamped . . . at half past nine
o'clock, having come to-day *seventy-nine miles*." [23]

Encampments meant a tent and a sweet-smelling bed
of fir boughs for *commis* or *bourgeois*. For the men, however, they connoted a canoe turned on its side as roof,
the rocks of the shore as bed, and a single blanket as
coverlet. Clerks often found these nights *à la belle étoile*
full of romance and poetry, but the voyageurs were ordinarily too weary to observe the brilliance of the stars or
to give heed to the soughing of winds in the pines or to
the music of waves and *sault*. Despite myriads of mosquitoes, drenching thunder storms, blistering heat, or un-
seasonable cold they slept like the dead beneath their
canoes.

One lone figure stood out darkly silhouetted against
the blazing fire that he tended so assiduously. It was the
cook, preparing food for the following day. Dr. Bigsby

brings one of these men out from the general obscurity of their lives in the following story.

"The evening had been lowering, but afterwards became partially clear and starry. I left the tent at about eleven o'clock, and was much struck by the picture before and around me.

"Our men were asleep at the fire—all, save the cook on duty, who was feeding it with wood, and stirring the soup. The cool wind was shaking the birch trees, and the waves were whispering and rippling among the reefs below. . . .

"After a time I went and sat on a stone by the side of the cook, and watched his stirrings and tastings.

" 'Monsieur le Docteur,' said he breaking silence, 'these vile rocks and morasses remind me of a mishap of mine long ago in the Indian countries, which would have put an end to me, *"ici bas,"* had it not been for a tin-pot and a gull's nest—things very simple, Monsieur le Docteur.

" 'Our *bourgeois* took me and an Indian to look for a new beaver district on the Black River, which runs into the Mackenzie.

" 'Two days from the Fort, while crossing a pond, I saw a gull's nest, with four little gaping chicks in it, on a bare rock. I had lifted up my foot to kick the whole hatch into the water, according to our notion, that if you kill a bird, a deer, or what not, ten will come instead, when the *bourgeois* forbade me.

" 'Well, one day, three weeks afterwards our canoe capsized in a rapid, and we lost all—every thing, except a tin-pot, which stuck in one of its ribs. Of course we turned back, and lived on dead fish, green bilberries, now and then a young bird, *tripe de roche*, and Labrador tea, which fortunately our pot enabled us to boil. . . .

" 'When we were near spent by many weary days' travel, the *bourgeois* told us that if we would work like gallant men, he would give us a meat-supper on the morrow's night. We wondered but somehow believed the *bon homme*.

" 'Sure enough, on the next evening, we reached a pond. I knew it immediately. Above a bare rock two old gulls hovered and sported in the air. Trusting the young birds had not flown, but fearing they had, we rushed to the nest and found four large plump pullets, which I certainly think, blessed be God, saved our lives. The next day we fell in with some friendly Indians.' " [24]

Dawn came, and before the first glimmerings of light the call of *"Alerte!"* or *"Lève, lève, nos gens"* ("Get up, get up, men") resounded through the camp. No time to hear the sweet songs of birds or to watch the silver sheen of mist rising from the water. All was bustle and confusion. Canoes were launched and loaded, and within fifteen minutes a *chanson* was struck up as the shore receded. Scant courtesy was shown to tardy risers, even though they were "dwellers in tents," for the tent poles were needed in the bottoms of the canoes to equalize the weight of the loads. It was always a race, therefore, between those in the tent and those outside, and the voyageurs considered it a tremendous joke to be able to pull down the tent and reveal a half-clad *bourgeois*.

Trois pipes, some twelve miles, of lusty paddling in the cool morning brought respite and breakfast. The canoes were moored offshore by long poles laid one end on the beach and one on the gunwale, the fire was lighted, and for the *commis*, *bourgeois*, or passenger a cloth was laid on the rocks. Should the traveler be a lady, as sometimes chanced, the never-failing *galanterie* of the voyageurs displayed itself in a little bunch of flowers before the plate, plucked from the numberless wild roses, red columbines, and other flowers that embroidered the clefts in the rocks of this north country in May and June. It was characteristic of this race of men who slept four hours a day in order to shorten their tedious journeys that they should spare time to gather wild roses to grace a lady passenger's breakfast table.

Perhaps they enjoyed, in their own mute way, the freshness and beauty of the scenes through which they passed. How could any human being remain untouched when such scenery as that described by Nicholas Garry presented itself:

"Our Dinner Table was a hard Rock, no Table Cloth could be cleaner and the surrounding Plants and beautiful Flowers sweetening the Board. Before us the Waterfall, wild romantic, bold. The River Winnipic here impeded by Mountainous Rocks appears to have found a Passage through the Rocks and these, as if still disputing the Power of Water, show their Heads, adding to the rude Wildness of the Scene, producing Whirlpools, Foam loud Noise and chrystal Whitness beautifully contrasted with the Black Pine . . . The Wildness of the Scene was added to by the melancholy white headed Eagle hovering over our Board." [25]

Thus the voyageurs spent their days in paddling, smoking, and singing, and their nights in making camp and sleeping, till Michillimackinac, near modern Mackinac, was reached. Just before reaching this, or any fort, the voyageurs, who were great dandies in their own way, must stop and, on a great rock or beach, literally *plume* themselves. For the *crowning* touch of their toilettes, destined to impress all beholders, was the colored feathers which Northmen, as distinguished from pork-eaters, had a right to wear. In such regalia and at top speed with ringing song they paddled vociferously to the landing.

At Mackinac a long halt was made, for *commis* and *bourgeois* must conduct negotiations with other traders, attend to supplies for their men in the big warehouses along the water front, and determine the destination and route of each of the canoes. It was here that the supply of Indian corn was shipped, to take the place of the peas eaten on the route thither from Montreal. From this point many routes diverged. Brigades for the lower Wisconsin and Illinois countries went south through Lake Michigan, but those for the region about Lake Superior and the "Northwest," that is, all of northern America beyond Grand Portage, took the hard route over the portage at the Sault de Sainte Marie and entered the greatest of the lakes.

At Mackinac and again at the Sault the voyageurs had respite while their masters attended to business matters. Gay were the sashes and plumes that were donned to win the favors of dusky maidens, and many the *piastres* spent for high wines, candles, and food. Carnival was the order both of day and of night, and he was an alert *commis* who could keep his men within bounds and round them up on the day of departure in condition to paddle his canoes. Here, as elsewhere when stops were made after arduous paddling and portaging, the men put on weight with amazing rapidity, so much so that one traveler in the far West after a three days' stop remarked, "Some of them became so much improved in looks that it was with difficulty we could recognize our voyageurs." [26]

Once again the long *marches* were resumed as the little hamlets on either side the rapids at the Sault faded from sight. Now the dangers of an immense stretch of water were added to the voyageurs' troubles. *Traverses* must be thought of, yes, prayed over. These crossings of wide stretches of water were hazardous in the extreme, mainly because of treacherous winds and storms which might arise suddenly while the canoes were far out from land. Ordinarily the men kept close, skirting the rocky northern coast or the picturesque southern shore of Lake Superior. But now and again a wide stretch of waters must be crossed. Auspicious weather might not be encountered for several days. Meantime the voyageurs lay in their encampments fretting to be thus delayed. Finally, when the command to move was given, every muscle was strained as the canoes were pushed with utmost speed across the dreaded expanse. Successful prediction of weather was naturally an acquired trait of this class of men whose life was a long struggle against the elements, and disasters in these crossings were not common; yet now and then a storm arose which left only a survivor or two and a wrecked canoe.

When the waves ran high on the lake, the voyageurs, with skill born of long experience, no longer plied their paddles incessantly, but suspended them just as a big wave was met. The object of this manœuver was to avoid sending the sharp nose of the canoe under the succeeding wave, which would have drenched them. When all precautions were unavailing and great waves swept over the canoe, it was necessary to bail with the large sponge kept for that purpose. Two quarts of water could be taken up at a time in this manner.

There were compensations, however, in traveling on Lake Superior. When the wind was soft and light and blowing from the proper quarter, sails were improvised from oil cloths or blankets, and the little vessels sped along while the voyageurs took their ease, smoking, singing, or sleeping. It was *La Vieille*, or "the old woman of the wind," who thus blessed the voyageurs with favoring breezes and lightened their toil; and so, sacrifices to her were always in order. The ritual consisted of throwing a little tobacco into the waters, or scattering a little water from the blades of the paddles, and uttering the formula, *"Souffle, souffle, la vieille"* ("Blow, blow, old woman"). This ceremony was doubtless borrowed from the Indians, whose customs were often appropriated by the voyageurs.[27]

A long spit of land on the southern shore, Keeweenaw Point, necessitated either a circuitous route around it or a portage. As early as Radisson's time the voyageurs had made their choice, for he recounts in the narrative of his first trip on the lake, about the year 1660, how he followed the portage route already well marked by the feet of the "commers and goers." [28] This epithet was sometimes used as the English equivalent of *mangeurs de lard*.

Did voyageurs then precede Radisson in the exploration
of the Lake Superior country? So it would seem from this
evidence produced by the great explorer himself.

Those who took this route along the southern shore of
the lake were bound as a rule for either the northern Wisconsin or the Minnesota region. Two streams gave access
to the interior, the Bois Brulé and St. Louis rivers. Both
were famous highways into the fur country, and thousands of human feet packed the soil of the portages so
firmly that even yet traces of the trails are discernible.
When the voyageurs reached the Mississippi, they often
met the traders who had entered by another route—*via*
Green Bay, the Fox River and portage, and the Wisconsin River. And if they went far north, to the headwaters of the Mississippi, they often found *engagés* who
had entered by still another way.

This last route was the most famous of all. It began
at Grand Portage, the easternmost tip of soil in modern
Minnesota, passed up the rivers and through the lakes
that make the natural boundary between Canada and the
United States in this region to the outlet of Rainy Lake,
where an important fort had been located since the days
of La Vérendrye; then through Lake of the Woods,
down Winnipeg River to Lake Winnipeg, and up the
Red River of the North and its tributaries to the headwaters of the Mississippi. At Lake Winnipeg the Red
River traders parted company with the most hardy and
venturesome of the Nor'westers, the men who passed up
the Assiniboine and Saskatchewan rivers and on to the
Rocky Mountains, the coast, and even to Great Bear
Lake. Here, too, the menu changed. The corn of the pre-

ceding weeks was supplanted by pemmican, which thence-
forth was the chief article of diet.

Grand Portage, the gateway to this vast country until
shortly after 1800 (when Fort William was substituted),
was reached *via* the rocky northern shore of Lake Superior, where the winds were so violent that canoes were
often lost. It was a post of the first importance, being the
meeting point every June and July of hundreds of traders and voyageurs from interior posts. This was the destination of the Montreal canoes. Here the *mangeurs de
lard* turned back, having unloaded the cargo of manufactured goods from France or England and reloaded
with packs of furs and skins from the uttermost parts of
the wilderness. Here novices who wished to become experienced hands left the ranks of the pork-eaters and became *hivernants*. Here, too, the smaller canoes were procured for the shallower waters beyond Lake Superior.
And here life was so picturesque and unusual that Irving
found a place for a description of it in his *Astoria*.[29]

But even with all their endurance and speed the
voyageurs from the Athabasca country could not reach
Grand Portage during the short northern summers and
return before ice had choked the passages through rivers
and lakes. Accordingly, some of the Montreal men went
on to Rainy Lake, and at the fort there they met the far-
famed Athabasca men, delivered to them their annual
supplies, and reloaded the Montreal canoes with packs of
furs and skins. A special house, called the Athabasca
House, was erected within the stockade of the fort at
Rainy Lake to accommodate the travelers from the north.
Here, if the Athabasca men were delayed, the voyageurs

resorted to one of their rites for speeding the arrival of the expected brigade. This was the erection of crosses with one of the arms pointing in the direction from which the travelers were expected.[30]

The Athabasca men were the Gascons of the "voyaging" class. They looked down with pity mixed with scorn on the mere pork-eaters and even the winterers on the Fraser River and the Columbia were too inexperienced in their eyes to be treated seriously. Naturally the men of other regions resented their superior airs. Duncan M'Gillivray was an amused—even biased—onlooker in the competition which inevitably resulted from this attitude: He wrote of them: [31]

"The Athabasca Men piqued themselves on a Superiority they were supposed to have over the other bands of the North for expeditious marching, and rediculed our men *a la facon du Nord* for pretending to dispute a point that universally decided in *their* favor. Our people were well aware of the disadvantages they laboured under (being about ¼ Heavier loaded than their opponents) but they could not swallow the haughtiness and contempt with which they thought themselves treated, and tho' they could flatter themselves with no hopes of success from the event yet they resolved to dispute the Victory, with the greatest obstinacy that their opposers might not obtain it without the sweat of their brows. In consequence of this determination the two Bands instead of camping according to orders, entered the Lake at sunset, the one animated with the expectation of victory, and the other resolved, if possible, not to be vanquished. They pursued the Voyage with unremitting efforts without any considerable advantage on either side for 48 hours during which they did not once put ashore, 'till at length, being entirely overcome with labour and fatigue, they mutually agreed to camp where we found them, and cross the rest of the Lake together."

M'Gillivray understood the seriousness of this contest for the voyageurs. He goes on:

"Tho' this dispute will appear trifling to you, yet to shew you how much it interested the Parties concerned it will only be necessary to mention a circumstance, which clearly proves their emulation but will do no honor to their humanity. On the second night of the Contest one of our steersmen being overpowered with sleep fell out of the Stern of his Canoe which being under sail advanced a considerable distance before the people could recover from the confusion that this accident occasioned; in the mean time the poor fellow almost sinking with the weight of his cloathes cried out to 2 Canoes that happened to pass within a few yards of him to save his life *pour l'amour de dieu;* but neither the love of God or of the blessed Virgin, whom he powerfully called to his assistance, had the least influence on his hard hearted Countrymen who paddled along with the greatest unconcern, and he must have certainly perished if his own Canoe had not returned time enough to prevent it."

Grand Portage was left with regrets for the end of rest and conviviality. The carrying place there was nine miles in length, and the voyageurs earned six *livres* extra for every *pièce* carried over the bitterly toilsome way. Now the current was against the voyageurs until the height of land was reached near Rainy Lake. On this eminence, whence water flowed northward to Hudson Bay, east to the Atlantic, and south to the Gulf of Mexico, the voyageurs halted for another of their many ceremonies. Here every novice, be he *bourgeois*, clerk, or pork-eater, must be made a Northwester. The ceremony consisted of sprinkling the candidate with a cedar branch dipped in water. He then gave certain promises, among others, never to allow anyone to pass that way without initiation into the ranks of Nor'westers, and never to kiss a voyageur's wife without her consent. The rites were completed with a dozen gunshots fired in rapid succession and a treat of high wines by the new members.[32]

Another custom practiced in this region was the construction of a lob stick. It was customary to make one of these Maypoles in honor of any gentleman who might be a passenger in a canoe. A tall pine, standing out on a point in the lake, was climbed by one of the voyageurs, who, with an ax, cut off all the branches except a tuft at the top, thus rendering it very conspicuous. The name of the passenger was then carved on the trunk, and ever after the spot was called after him. As the crew paddled off, the lob stick was saluted with three cheers and the discharge of guns, the honored passenger, of course, being expected to acknowledge the compliment by a treat at the first opportunity.[33]

On the route from Rainy Lake to Lake Winnipeg, as earlier on the French River, the voyageurs had ample opportunity to display their skill in shooting rapids. The thrill of such dangerous sport appealed powerfully to these French Canadians. To the uninitiated it seemed incredible that such frail structures as bark canoes could remain intact among such rocks and seething waters. It was very exciting to travelers to see how easily and perfectly the voyageurs managed their canoes on the rapids —the bowsman and steersman using their long paddles with wonderful celerity and effect, often turning sharp angles while shooting down bad runs at full speed. The guide very rarely spoke to the steersman, giving his orders merely by a nod of the head or leaving the other to find the course by observing his motions, to every one of which a good steersman responded instantly. "During our first day among the rapids old Baptiste, the guide, was constantly in great glee," writes Kennicott, "and always laughed when entering a bad rapid." [34] To avoid concealed rocks the most perfect skill and coolness, as well as great strength, were required of the guide. To strike a rock while shooting down a rapid with great velocity would almost certainly break or upset a canoe, and in the dashing water any other than a practiced eye and ear would fail to distinguish the hidden boulders. Any attempt at checking the velocity of the canoe when in such danger would be worse than useless, and it was never made; on the contrary, the men all paddled as hard as possible when running a rapid. "When on bad rapids," says the same writer, "I repeatedly saw our guide turn our canoe aside in less than a second, by a stroke of his big paddle, when detecting a sunken rock within two or three feet of the bow, and that, too, when he knew that within several seconds after he must pass in dangerous proximity to other rocks. . . . Still I think he would have dreaded the disgrace attending an accident on a rapid more than the personal danger."

In this stretch many rapids were interdicted to the voyageurs of the Northwest and Hudson's Bay companies because of the great danger to life and property; but voyageurs were not famous for obedience when proprietors and clerks were absent, and so they were often run. Nicholas Garry, who passed that way in 1821, tells in his diary how his crew disobeyed orders: "A few minutes paddling brought us to the Portage de Petite Roche which is a dangerous Rapid but the Water being high we run it, which was great Folly as it is seldom run and we certainly touched. . . . At 2 we embarked, at 5 we arrived at the Portage de l'Isle. This is a very dangerous Rapid, and so many fatal Accidents have attended the Sauting of it that it has been interdicted to the Servants of both Companies. Our Men forgetting Orders and wishing to avoid the Trouble of carrying the Canoe run it and we escaped, though an Absolution of Sin in a severe Ducking would not have justified this Rashness. . . . In half an Hour we arrived at a Décharge but our Steersman preferred running it and we had a narrow escape having just touched. A harder Knock would have broken our Canoe." [35]

When such a blow was sustained and the canoe injured, a sickening sensation was experienced, which one traveler describes as "your Feeling when under the Hands of an unskilful Dentist." [36] Sometimes the danger was not alone to one canoe but to all those following in the brigade. Garry, who had escaped so many accidents, at length had his experience: "entered the Hill River which is full of Rapids and Cataracts the water so low that we struck at every Moment and at last about two o'clock when going down a Rapid we struck upon a rock and broke our Canoe. Our Situation was very perilous. Our Canoe immediately began to fill and Mr McGillivray who was following us close was bearing down upon us, and had he struck us both Canoes would have been knocked to pieces and all of us thrown into the violent Rapid below us. By the great Skill of the Steersman and a wonderful Effort he brought the Canoe alongside and we remained on the Rock. . . . We found four Feet of Bark had been knocked to Pieces. . . . If we had been alone many of us must have perished or if we had escaped a watery Grave we should have been exposed to Starvation and a miserable Death. The Day was fortunately very fine and dry and with several fires we soon dried our Papers, Linen, Beds, &c., for everything was wetted. Our Encampment had a singular Appearance, the Trees covered with our Linen, Sheets, Beds, &c., and the Earth covered with Papers." [37] Wettings were especially detrimental to packs of fur.

When such a hole had been made in the canoe, it was necessary to cut away all the injured bark and patch with new. In such a case as Garry's it might have been impossible to get a piece sufficiently large, for such a wound was larger than the usual patches kept rolled in the front of every canoe. Here Garry pays his tribute to the voyageur: "It now became necessary to consider how we should get on but the Canadian Voyageur soon finds a Remedy and our Men were immediately occupied in repairing the Hole. The Woods furnished the material. Bark from the Birch Tree Wattape from the Root of the Pine, Splints made from the Cedar Tree and the Cross-bars. In the Evening all was ready to start in the Morning." [38]

Even the voyageur had nerves, however. The next day, when another dangerous rapid was reached, the hero of the previous occasion found himself so unnerved that he gave up his post at the most dangerous point. "We escaped in Safety," remarks Garry, "having struck against a flat Rock, in going down, which almost upset us." [39] One day, however, sufficed to restore the guide's confidence in himself. "At 4," continues the same author, "we arrived at the last Rapid before the Rock Depôt, a most dangerous Rapid, where we were nearly lost. Our old Guide, who had before resumed his Situation and Courage, and who had conducted us through many dangerous Rapids, with admirable Skill, was now at the Bows, and directing the Canoe. At once, when in the most dangerous Part, his Pole broke. Two Seconds would have dashed us over the Rocks into the deep Rapid, when the most of us, if not All, must have perished. With an admirable Presence of Mind, he took another Pole and in a Second guided us through the Channel." Garry then goes on to reflect, "How singularly the Mind of Man is framed, how unnerved at one Moment, the next showing Heroism and Presence of Mind, and never has there been a greater proof of this, than in our Guide, at this perilous Moment, and when he gave up the Steering."

Beyond Grand Portage the method of portaging was slightly different from what it had been earlier in the route. After the canoe had been emptied, instead of being turned over and carried upturned by four men at the ends and two in the center, it was now left in its normal position and carried by two men.[40] This change was due to the smallness of the North canoes. Here, too, it was sometimes necessary to use the bedding in carrying the canoe over steep rocks. The beds were placed in the recesses of the rocks as steps or supporting places for the canoe. The bow of the canoe was placed on the bedding as it was lifted from step to step up the rock; in very much the same manner it was let down as carefully on the other side.

With such difficulties and dangers as those described, it is small wonder that orders were not carried out as precisely as some of the clerks in distant posts could have desired. Gabriel Franchere, the famous Astorian and later a clerk of the American Fur Company at Sault Ste. Marie, was able to understand, as many less experienced clerks would not have been able to do, why his brigade from Montreal in the spring of 1837 was so long in arriving and why so many articles were missing. Indeed, there is more than an accent of censure in his letter for the stupidity of superiors in New York who so little realized the burdens of the voyageur. He writes: "The reason of their long passage was owing to an accident which occurred on the Otawa River. They broke one canoe, drowned 1 man, had to run back to Fort Colonge for other canoes and provisions which they procured from Mr. Sicought [Siveright?], and thereby lost 8 men by desertion. Of the articles sent up, all the portage collars were lost, 65 prs shoe-packs, 8 side leather and 6 stoves; that is they brought sundry stove plates here, but only one of the smallest kind was complete. It is to be regretted that such heavy articles should be sent by Grand

River & in such weak vessels as a bark canoe. However, I suppose you followed instructions from New York. It will teach us a lesson for the future." [41]

Do not imagine that these long trips were accomplished in the company of only one's own canoemates. On a certain trip in the early twenties, to mention only one instance to the contrary, the voyageurs in one light canoe encountered five groups of canoes, some forty or so in all, between Montreal and Lake Huron. The parties not only met or passed one another on the water, but at times they camped together. Then the leaders needed to exercise their utmost control, for quarreling was likely to result. An artist with an eye for the picturesque has left us a word sketch of one of these encounters at an encampment: "Here we found waiting for the morn seven loaded canoes and eighty *voyageurs* belonging to the Hudson's Bay Company. . . . It was an uncouth scene. There was a semi-circle of canoes turned over on the grass to sleep under, with blazing fires near them, surrounded by sinister-looking long-haired men, in blanket coats, and ostrich feathers in their hats, smoking and cooking, and feeding the fires. I particularly noticed one large square man, squat on the wet ground, with a bit of looking-glass in his hand, intently watching his wife, as she carefully combed out his long jetty hair. . . ." [42]

The long hair to which the traveler refers was a protection against the hosts of mosquitoes which beset all who *voyaged*. It was an object of great pride, and voyageurs bestowed much time and energy in dressing it. In truth, voyageurs were great dandies in their own fashion. They were even known to wash their garments occasionally.

They dried them with just that difference of method which characterized everything they did—they spread them on the sands to dry, even when bushes were available.

Even though they did not subscribe to the tenet that cleanliness is next to godliness, the voyageurs usually took excellent care of their few articles of wearing apparel. If rain overtook a canoe, the passengers vanished under oilcloths or tarpaulins. The voyageurs pulled off their garments to keep them dry, while the cold rain coursed down their powerful, naked backs. Of course, this precaution was fully as much in the interest of comfort later on as in desire to preserve the garments themselves.

By early autumn most of the brigades had reached their destinations, sometimes a large important fort, like that at Rainy Lake, sometimes an insignificant wintering post on an inland lake. But wherever the voyageur went in the fur country, his life was very much like that of every other voyageur. Hence, though details might differ in such widely separated posts as Mackinac and Astoria, the everyday routine was very similar. It is possible therefore to describe this fort life accurately in a general way.

V

FORT LIFE

V

THE first duty of voyageurs on reaching their wintering ground was to erect a fort, unless, of course, the post was already established and supplied with buildings. A consultation was frequently held with the chief Indians as to the best site. When this was determined, a clearing was made, trees were cut and hewed in proper lengths, and a storehouse and "shop" were erected. Next came the clerk's house, then a house for the men, and finally a high stockade, the *fort* in local parlance. The day on which the great gate was hung and locked for the first time marked the completion of the post in the eyes of the men. Other buildings, such as a roothouse or a magazine, might be added, and a flagstaff was always put up in the enclosure. Often a well was dug within the stockade. Chimneys of mud and sticks or mud and stones were put up at the ends of the dwellings, and roofs were thatched with boughs held down by poles or sticks. Nails were expensive and heavy to bring into the interior, and so the logs were held in place in a unique way. Grooves were cut in logs set upright at each corner of the foundation. Down these grooves were slipped the ends of the wall logs, which were cut to fit exactly between the uprights. Thus one log lay in place above another, all being held in position by the vertical logs.[1] A certain kind of white clay served admirably in place of plaster and whitewash and gave a neat appearance to the interiors. A puncheon floor was laid, bunks were constructed against the walls, rough tables and stools were made, and a window or two was filled with oiled deerskin in lieu of glass. Such a cabin, filled with the odors of game roasting on a blazing grate which flung fantastic shadows over guns, knives, and snowshoes on the walls, was not an unhomelike place, and it was the prototype of many a pioneer's home as the frontier moved westward.

From a diary kept during the winter of 1804-05 on a branch of the St. Croix River, within the present boundaries of Minnesota, something of an idea of the time required for building a fort may be drawn.[2] Three, possibly four, buildings were erected in three weeks. Four chimneys are mentioned; these required four days. The "masonry" of them, however, to use the clerk's term, was completed in two days. A few weeks later one of them caught fire and had to be repaired. The "covering" of the houses apparently took two days. The "flooring" of both houses and the plastering of the clerk's residence consumed five days. Three weeks after the first tree was felled the clerk wrote in his journal, "This evening entered my dwelling House." It must have been unfinished within, however, for two evenings later he recorded, "Men finished my Bed Room." At this point All Saints' Day with its "enchanting Weather" caused a temporary halt. The usual dole of rum, one gallon in this case, was made, and the voyageurs "did no Work of course." On Sunday, November 4, twenty-six days after work was begun, the clerk recorded, "My Men entered their dwellings." The cutting of the stockade was begun on the seventh of November, and by the thirteenth the "Men began raising the Stockades." This was evidently a long process, for it was not till the twentieth that the clerk could enter in his diary that "the Doors of the Fort were fixd & Shut this Evening." All this time, apparently, the *commis* was doling out a dram morning and evening to each voyageur, for at the very outset he recorded: "men perform'd a great Days Work gave them each a Dram morning & Evening & promised to do the same till our Buildings are Compleated provided the[y] exert themselves."

The site of a fort was chosen with several requirements in mind. It must be near Indian villages; it must be readily accessible from the highways of trade; usually it must be on a stream or lake well stocked with fish, the staple diet of the wintering fur-traders; and wood for building and fuel purposes must be at hand. In the region beyond the Mississippi the feeding grounds of the buffalo were also taken into account, both because of food and robes which could be obtained from them and for the additional reason that buffalo "chips" could serve as fuel.

Once settled in their fort, the men must prepare for the long winter. Seines were set in the water just before the ice "took" on the lake or river. Whitefish and trout were taken in the bigger lakes, and tollibees, sturgeon, pike, and other varieties in the smaller lakes and rivers. The method of preserving the winter's supply of fish was the same throughout the wilderness. Each fish was pierced with the point of a knife about two inches from the tail and strung on a twisted willow branch. Groups of ten

79

were thus made and hung heads down in a shady place. If they did not undergo too much warm weather before they froze, the fish were excellent all winter; otherwise a strong, rank taste developed. Approximately four fish per person was reckoned the daily ration. Hence, many hundreds were required in the course of a winter for a fort of a dozen or fifteen persons. The following entry in a clerk's diary may be taken as a good fish story, but so it stands on the yellowed pages: "Took a Pike of 37[lb] Weight in our Net the largest I ever yet saw." [3]

Wild rice was another staple item in the larder of every fort in the regions where this plant grew. It was usually called "oats" by the traders and was bought by the sack from squaws, who gathered it in the lakes and marshes in the late summer. In the spring maple sugar was also bought by the *makuk* (a birch-bark vessel) from the squaws. At Connor's fort in the St. Croix valley five kegs of sugar were secured in one season, four of which were cached under the fireplace in the clerk's house for the next year's use.

In the buffalo country the traders' chief reliance was on the "cows," as the female buffaloes were almost invariably called. These were hunted in the fall and spring. A part of the meat was preserved by drying or "jerking" in summer and by freezing in winter. Much of the remainder was made into pemmican. At Archibald Norman McLeod's fort at Alexandria, on the Assiniboine River in modern Saskatchewan, there were stored away in March, 1801, the meat of about eighty-five buffalo cows, sixty-two bags of pemmican weighing ninety pounds each, and nine kegs of grease, each of seventy pounds. It must be added, however, that this fort was a depot for supplying the western brigades of canoes with pemmican and grease.[4]

In the autumn the clerk chose as hunter for his fort an Indian who was reliable and a good marksman. It was the business of this man to keep the fort supplied with fresh meat or wild fowl. It was everyone's business, however, to assist in this work whenever other duties did not prevent. Thus Connor records at various times during the winter of 1804-05: "At Sun rise the Men that went for Meat came back"; "the 2 Men that went Yesterday with Mr Seraphin to Lodges arrived before day light with the Meat of 6 Deers"; "This afternoon Desève arrived with 2 Beavers & the Meat from Pierro &co"; "This evening my Men came home with the Meat of 5 Deers."[5]

Yet with all these precautions the forts at times were as bare as Mother Hubbard's cupboard, and starvation was by no means unknown. The following are typical entries from the diaries of clerks: "We have now thirty people in the fort, and have not a supply of provisions for two days"; "During the last three days we have subsisted on tallow and dried cherries"; "I really begin to fear we shall starve this winter, at any rate we'll be oblidged to make use of the little dry provisions the Indians may bring to the Fort, & G—d alone knows whether we'll be able to scrape together what will make a little Pimican to bring us all to the Point."[6]

Two meals a day, breakfast and the evening meal, were customary everywhere in the fur country. The voyageurs were prodigious eaters, for, says Harmon, "a

Canadian, with his belly full of fat meat, is never otherwise" than happy."[7] To supplement this rather meager
diet, most of the clerks at posts of any size planted
gardens, where potatoes, turnips, beans, peas, and other
vegetables were raised. At a time when the world believed that these hyperborean regions (the adjective was
often used in contemporary references) were capable of
producing only icicles and furs, the traders were producing one thousand bushels of potatoes at Leech Lake,
near the source of the Mississippi River, and six hundred
bushels of potatoes, besides barley and peas, at Sandy
Lake a little farther south.[8] Nor were vegetables the only
products of these pioneer farms. There were horses at
Leech Lake in 1807; cows which had been driven overland were not uncommon on the Red River of the North
in the twenties; and even the humble hen and pig could
be heard within the stockades of some forts. An interesting reminiscent article written by an erstwhile missionary to the Chippewa Indians of the St. Croix valley in
western Wisconsin appeared in the New York *Evangelist*
in 1860 under the title, "Stray Leaves from an Old
Man's Portfolio." [9] Here is told with a humor which one
does not expect the story of how pigs were driven into the
region in 1834. Doubtless the same ludicrous methods of
transportation—canoes on the lakes and chase through
the forests—were used in introducing the swine that
were found earlier at Leech and Sandy lakes. Dogs, of
course, were numerous at every post.

One suspects that these gardens and animals were
raised not alone for food, but with some such motive as
prompts the modern city dweller to plant his sterile back

yard to vegetables which he could buy infinitely cheaper in the markets. Harmon, more articulate than most traders, hints at the underlying reason: "We are preparing a piece of ground for a garden, the cultivation of which, will be an amusement; and the produce of it, we hope, will add to our comforts." Then, without pause, he adds as his next sentence, "Mr Goedike plays the violin, and will occasionally cheer our spirits, with an air." [10] How easily a few words like these two sentences, especially their juxtaposition, produce the homesick atmosphere of those little, isolated posts of the "western waters."

The voyageurs, however, had their own ways of cheer, which the clerks and *bourgeois* wisely countenanced. Christmas and the New Year were celebrated with vastly more acclaim and spontaneity than in most civilized countries, and there were many other gala days which no voyageur ever passed up without the celebration prescribed in the *pays d'en haut*. Harmon's first Christmas in the interior came as somewhat of a shock to him, accustomed to the proprieties of the New England mode of celebration, for he says, "This day being Christmas, our people have spent it as usual in drinking and fighting." [11] Kennicott, however, was alive to the picturesqueness of this class of men and more in sympathy with their methods of self-expression. Consequently his remarks on a Christmas celebration in the Northwest are more detailed and full of interest. "The day after Christmas, Flett gave a Christmas ball. . . . The dancing was, I may say without vulgarity, decidedly 'stunning.' I should hardly call it graceful. The figures, if they may be called

such, were only Scotch reels of four, and jigs; and . . .
the main point to which the dancers' efforts seemed to
tend, was to get the largest amount of exercise out of
every muscle in the frame. . . . The music consisted of
a very bad performance of one vile, unvarying tune, upon
a worse old fiddle, accompanied by a brilliant accompaniment upon a large tin pan." [12]

Perhaps one may ask of the dusky partners of the men
in these gala affairs. Sir John Franklin, the Arctic explorer, recorded their conduct with some interest. He
noted at a dance in a northern post how fond of dancing
the half-breed women were, though a stranger would
imagine the contrary on observing their apparent want
of animation. On such occasions, he said, they affected a
sobriety of demeanor which was the very opposite to
their general character.[13] Another traveler found worthy
of even more detailed description the female portion of
an assembly which celebrated a certain Christmas with
a dance in a far northwestern post. The great hall was
lit up by means of a number of tallow candles, stuck in
tin sconces round the walls. The men, in their Sunday
jackets and capotes, sat on benches and chairs. Around
the stove, which had been removed to one side to leave
space for the dancers, a strange group was collected.
"Squatting down on the floor, in every ungraceful attitude imaginable, sat about a dozen Indian women,
dressed in printed calico gowns, the chief peculiarity of
which was the immense size of the baloon-shaped sleeves,
and the extreme scantiness, both in length and width, of
the skirts. Coloured handkerchiefs covered their heads,
and ornamented moccasins decorated their feet; besides

which, each one wore a blanket in the form of a shawl, which they put off before standing up to dance. They were chatting and talking to each other with great volubility, occasionally casting a glance behind them, where at least half a dozen infants stood bolt upright in their tight-laced cradles." [14]

On both Christmas and New Year's the men were given a *régale* with which to have a feast; in other words, they were served with flour to make cakes or puddings and with rum, usually a half pint. Perhaps no finer picture of the celebration of New Year's Day is afforded than in James McKenzie's amused and tolerant account: "Great preparations going on here this night for to-morrow, which is New Year's Day. Dusablon, with hands which have not seen a drop of water since last New Year's Day, made a large kettle full of *boulettes* of fish, each as big and as ill-shaped as his own head. Lambert made fish cakes, *alias 'pêtes,'* boiled for an hour with dried meat. Masquaro made the fire, drew water and cleaned shoes, &c. Mr. Wentzel and I were continually running from the shop to the *hangard*, from the *hangard* to the garret, from thence to the kitchen; in short, every body in the house had a finger in the pie and were as busy all night as *une queue de veau*. This morning before day break, the men, according to custom, fired two broadsides in honor of the New Year, and then came in to be rewarded with rum, as usual. Some of them could hardly stand alone before they went away. . . . After dinner, at which every body helped themselves so plentifully that nothing remained to the dogs, they had a bowl of punch. The expenses of this day with fourteen men and women are: 6½ fathoms spencer twist [tobacco], 7 flagons rum, 1 ditto wine, 1 ham, a skin's worth of dried meat, about 40 white fish, flour, sugar, &c. Felix Labrie, whose beard, from *chagrin* for his brother's death, is as long as my pen, was the first that began to drink and sing, and the last who gave up that farce. He is a gentleman who stands upon no ceremony; he was not backwards in taking along with him to his own house the punch which remained in the bowl, and, there, drink it." [15]

Many of the *bourgeois* and clerks in the interior were Scotch, and the voyageurs, with their typical Gallic courtesy, never failed to remember St. Andrew's day. Of course, their pure goodwill was mixed with the alloy of self-interest, for the customary presentation of a St. Andrew's cross was always rewarded with a quart or so of high wines in the morning and in the evening with another gift of wine or rum. Dancing was the entertainment of the evening. In the year 1800 at Archibald Norman McLeod's post on the upper waters of the Assiniboine they danced "till three oClock in the morning to Frise's singing." [16]

As the descriptions already quoted will show, the orchestras for these balls were not uniform. Music oozed from every pore of the voyageur, and when a fiddle was not handy, substitutes could always be found. In fact, musical instruments were far from uncommon in the interior, even excepting tin pans from the category. Many of the voyageurs carried fiddles with them to their wintering posts, and even on their winter jaunts from post to post. The arrival of such a man at a post where no musical talent was boasted was always the signal for a ball, which not infrequently lasted all night.

These accounts of festivals and balls must not be taken to indicate that the life at a fur post was a round of pleasure. The duties of the men were legion, even if their main task be excepted, which was, of course, the procuring of furs from the Indians. Before describing these trips afield, however, let us observe the everyday life in a typical fort. The diaries kept scrupulously by the clerks afford the best material. In them one reads of daily chores, of arrivals of Indians, of hunting and fishing, of illnesses, of deaths, and even of marriages. It must be explained, however, that marriages were "according to the custom of the country"; that is, they were rather informal and often temporary, judged by civilized standards. It would be too much to suppose that the hundreds of voyageurs who passed their young manhood in the Indian country lived ascetic lives. On the contrary, they made alliances with Indian girls, much to the gratification of the girls' parents, who received gifts of considerable value in return. Harmon, whose scorn for such unions was intense on his arrival but who later succumbed to the inevitable, describes such a wedding: "This evening, Mons. Mayotte took a woman of this country for a wife, or rather concubine. All the ceremonies attending such an event, are the following. When a person is desirous of taking one of the daughters of the Natives, as a companion, he makes a present to the parents of the damsel, of such articles as he supposes will be most acceptable; and, among them, rum is indispensable; for of that all the savages are fond, to excess. Should the parents

87

accept the articles offered, the girl remains at the fort with her suitor, and is clothed in the Canadian fashion. The greater part of these young women, as I am informed, are better pleased to remain with the white people, than with their own relations. Should the couple, newly joined, not agree, they are at liberty, at any time, to separate; but no part of the property, given to the parents of the girl, will be refunded. . . . Payet, one of my interpreters has taken one of the daughters of the Natives for a wife; and to her parents he gave in rum, dry goods, &c. to the value of two hundred dollars." [17]

Thus the forts were occupied not only by traders, but by their wives and children. The Indian women seem to have been very adaptable and to have been not only willing drudges but good mothers. Harmon, in fact, became so attached to his *femme* that he took her back to civilization with him in his later years. History does not record her reactions to her new surroundings. In general, however, the alliances were more or less temporary, though the children took their father's name and as a rule were acknowledged and cared for by him. Garry tells the following laughable tale of a half-breed boy who thought he knew who his father was: "A very nice Canadian Boy, moitié noir et moitié blanc, presented himself at our Tent and enquired for Mr. McGillivray. The elder Mr. McGillivray answered. After a short Preface the Boy said, 'Monsieur, vous êtes mon Père.' Mr. McGillivray, 'Comment, Coquin,' and his Look with it I shall never forget, and it set his Brother and Myself laughing in such a manner that I thought we should never have ceased. However the Laugh was a good deal turned against Mr.

Simon McGillivray on the Boy stating that Simon was his name. However after a few more Questions the poor enfant trouvé was dismissed without finding his Père. I could not but admire the Ruse de Guerre of the old voyageur Mr. McGillivray turning the Tables on his Brother who was not less expert in Expedient, as he took me aside afterwards saying it was an odd Adventure but added 'I see how it is,—it is my nephew Simon's Son.' So the poor Boy must go to the Athapascan for a Father and when he arrives the Nephew will be as ready in throwing the charge from his Shoulders. The Mr. McGillivrays intend enquiring out the History of the Boy." [18]

From these unions with Indian women developed the large class called indiscriminately half-breeds, *métis*, *bois brulés*, which formed such a large percentage of all American and Canadian frontier settlements. Many of their descendants are men and women of distinction and social standing in the modern cities that have developed from old posts, such as Detroit, Milwaukee, St. Paul, Winnipeg, and St. Louis.

With such a personnel, therefore, the fort was a busy place. The *commis* or resident *bourgeois* directed the work of all his numerous dependents and planned the winter's campaign for furs. A typical entry in such a *bourgeois'* journal may, perhaps, give the flavor of the setting better than any attempt at paraphrase. Such an entry is McLeod's for Tuesday, November 25, 1800: "A very mild day, the most of the Snow melted today I sent E. Ducharm for the Red Deer that the hunters kill'd Sunday La Rose & H. Ducharm I sent to look for Birch to make chairs, Vallé went to get wood for a Sledge, Roy took a

Doze of Physic, I scolded Girardin, for some stupid observation of his, to Mr Harmon & Collin. he is making me a pair of Deer skin trowsers. old Parant, is busy making a Slay to haul the fire wood home with, Danis is making a Couple of window Shutters."

A little later in the winter of 1801 McLeod's diary shows some other interesting occupations of the men: "Monday 2^d [February, 1801] Sent off, Roy, Giradin, Dannis, & Plante with 120 sk[in]s value of Goods, Rum, &c. to trade with the Indians   Tuesday 3^d· A very boisterous day. Blows prodigiously. Some of the men at work making horse sledges, others melting or Boiling back fat to put in the Pimican. All the women at work sewing Bags to put the Pimican into. Roy, Giradin &. E. Ducharm came home with the last of the meat & brought home the Lodge & now we have finished hauling meat, for this Season. We have now about eighty five Buffaloe Cows in the Meat house Collin very busy making kegs to put Grease into, old Parrant, making nails for the Sledges, &. Plante hanging up the meat &. tongues he put in salt ten days ago, today. Wednesday 4th I got the last Pounded meat we got made into Pimican, vizt 30 bags of 90^lb so that we have now 62 Bags of that Species of provisions &. of the above weight. I likewise got nine kegs filled with Grease, or Tallow rather each keg nett 70^lb. . . . the men &. women danced till twelve oClock at night."

Kane, a Canadian artist, with an eye for the picturesque, wrote in his memoirs of a winter sojourn at the fort at Edmonton a sketch of the ordinary life of the place. The fort, says he, presented "a most pleasing pic-

ture of cheerful activity." He describes the occupations
of both voyageurs and squaws, and then goes on: "The
evenings are spent round their large fires in eternal gos-
siping and smoking. The sole musician of the establishment, a fiddler, is now in great requisition amongst the
French part of the inmates who give full vent to their
national vivacity, whilst the more sedate Indian looks
on with solemn enjoyment." [19]

The men were not often sick, but when illness did occur, the clerk must assume the rôle of physician or sur-
geon. Cox, an Astorian and a trader on the Pacific
Coast, says of the men that they enjoyed good health
and, with the exception of occasional attacks of rheuma-
tism, were seldom afflicted with disease. "The principal
trading establishments," he says, "are supplied with well-
assorted medicine chests, containing books of directions,
lancets, &c. An assortment of the more simple medicines
is made up for each out-post; and as each clerk must learn
how to bleed, we generally manage, between low diet,
salts, castor-oil, opodeldoc, friar's balsam, and phlebo-
tomy, to preserve their health unimpaired, and cure any
common accident." [20] Several doctors were traders at one
time or another in the interior, and their professional skill
made them great assets to their whole regions. Thus, Dr.
John Munro was at Grand Portage in 1797. Dr. John
McLoughlin was at the same post in the early twenties;
about 1806 he had spent a winter on Vermilion Lake,
close to Rainy Lake fort, and in 1808 he was on Sturgeon
Lake in the Nipigon Department; in the year 1823-24
he was at Rainy Lake post. Dr. Charles W. W. Borup
traded in Michigan in the later twenties, and in the

thirties he was the trader at Yellow Lake in western Wisconsin and, later, the manager of the very important post at La Pointe, on the south shore of Lake Superior. Dr. Bell was a rival of the American Fur Company's man on Leech Lake near the source of the Mississippi in 1833. All of these men are known to have rendered medical service to the voyageurs and to the Indians.[21]

Communication between forts and with the Indians of a vast outlying area was not as uncommon as might be supposed. Voyageurs and clerks became almost as expert as Indians in their ability to cover ground rapidly. They adopted not only the Indian's canoe, but also his snowshoes, his dog trains, and his ponies as well. One gets the notion from reading the diaries of such men as McLeod, Harmon, Malhiot, and McDonell that scarcely a day passed without the arrival of Indians, other voyageurs, or clerks from neighboring posts.[22]

Indians were by far the most numerous guests, but they were seldom allowed within the stockade except in small groups, and then only on business. The fear of them was great, even though they appeared friendly. When they succeeded in getting the clerk to issue fire water to them, they became so quarrelsome and committed murder so easily that they became very unwelcome guests. Connor writes, as the culmination of a long series of entries on the turbulence of his Indians in the St. Croix valley: "Yesterday Evening the Indians began their usual Custom of Stabbing no less than 7 got wounded: 2 of them I believe are Mortally so. they are still Drunk." [23]

Several times in the course of a winter it was usually

necessary to send groups of voyageurs to distant bands to collect either furs or food. Such trips were usually made by *traîneaux de glace*, or long, toboggan-shaped sleds, drawn by dogs, sometimes by horses. Such a trip was termed a *dérouine* by the traders and voyageurs.

The dogs used to draw the trains were of the well-known Eskimo or huskie stock, though teams of fierce wolf dogs were sometimes employed, so wild that only their master and his guide could control them. The dogs of one team of this kind in the far north had to be chained up every night and kept in a stockade like wild animals in the summer. Finally they had to be shot, after they had attacked an Indian who had entered their stockaded yard. It was customary to put these dogs in "pensions" for the summer. Garry mentions such a dog hotel on the lower Red River in 1821. It contained "at least 100 Dogs" and was kept by a man who received two dollars per day for each dog. He had chosen "an excellent Fishing Place" in order to provide food, but from the fact that some twenty dogs followed Garry's canoe for some distance in the hope of getting food, he concluded that the poor beasts were not deriving the full benefit of the two dollars.[24]

The dogs were driven in tandem style in the forest regions, but on the prairies each animal pulled on his own traces. They were decked out with gaudy saddle cloths, fringed and embroidered in the most fantastic manner, with innumerable small bells and feathers. Many of the voyageur's hard-earned *piastres* were squandered on the trappings of his train of dogs. Usually four dogs constituted a train, pulling five or six hundred pounds and traveling forty to seventy miles per day. Their sleds were made of two oak boards securely fastened by cross pieces and planed thin at one end. By a process of steaming this end was rolled to enable the dogs to pull it more easily over rough country. These sleds were about ten feet long and sixteen to eighteen inches wide. The guide usually preceded the leading train, and on him rested the responsibility for keeping to the route.

The dogs, accustomed to fend for themselves about the fort, were hard to catch when wanted for a trip. The artist Kane relates how he was awakened one morning in a western fort by a yelling and screaming which made him rush from his room in great alarm. "There," says he, "I saw the women harnessing the dogs. Such a scene! The women were like so many furies with big sticks, thrashing away at the poor animals, who rolled and yelled in agony and terror, until each team was yoked up and started off." [25]

Much has been written of the unerring instincts of these guides, but from reading contemporary diaries one is forced to the conclusion that they were by no means infallible. In fact, the instances of voyageurs lost on the prairies and in the woods are legion. One of David Thompson's companions on a trip from the Assiniboine to the Mandan villages on the Missouri in 1797 owed his life to a chance discovery by his associates.[26] The clerk at the great fort on Rainy River recorded in his diary for the winter of 1804-05 how some of his voyageurs, sent on a *dérouine*, were lost and had to return to the post.[27] The wonder is that more were not lost.

On the road the dogs were fed but once daily. After

the encampment had been made, chunks of poor pemmican or two frozen whitefish for each dog were laid by the blazing fire to thaw. In their nervous eagerness to get these the dogs often fell to fighting amongst themselves, one team setting upon another. Seldom did the dogs of a train set upon one another, for there seemed to be an *esprit de corps* among those which pulled together. Unless watched, the dogs would eat anything of animal origin, including their own harness and their master's snowshoes. After eating, the dogs were allowed to settle themselves in the snow to shiver through the long winter night. Only dogs of such hardy stock and such woolly coats could endure this life. Even they often suffered from rough ice and stubble. Their paws would become sore, and then they were unfit for service. For such emergencies their masters carried many sets of little leather shoes which were pulled on like gloves and tied with thongs of deerskin. The dogs often became very fond of these accessories and would whine piteously for them. Frequently they would lie on their backs pawing the air to attract their master's attention to their feet in the hope of having their shoes put on.[28]

Often the men rode, but usually they followed on snowshoes. "Riding and running" was the expression used for swift traveling by dog train. Then only a light burden was carried, and the voyageur himself rode until so chilled that he must jump off and run for a time to get warm again.

If the thermometer registered between ten degrees below zero and ten above, five hundred pounds of baggage could be drawn by three dogs. At that temperature the friction that hindered the dogs in colder weather was absent. On the other hand, neither dogs nor men could travel well if the mercury mounted to more than ten degrees above zero.

The voyageur had his own method of reckoning distance by dog sled just as he coined his own phrases for computing the length of portages and stretches of water. Every five miles or so a halt was made to rest the dogs and to allow the men to smoke. These stops were termed "spells" or "pipes," and the voyageurs spoke of a day's journey as of so many spells or pipes. On a well-known road the spelling places were the same spots on every journey.

Customs developed in this kind of travel just as in canoeing, and the voyageur built up his own vocabulary. Thus, to *"mouche"* meant for a dog to increase his speed. "To spell ahead" referred to the custom that decreed that each train must take its turn in leading the procession of sleds. As the first *traîneau* had to beat the track for those following, the foremost dogs tired most easily. Consequently, after a period of spelling ahead the foremost train went to the rear of the procession, just as the leading gander in a flock of wild fowl is often seen to drop to the rear, presumably to get respite from the friction of the leader's position.

To "give track" was another expression used by these men. "Not to 'give track' is another disgrace," says Kennicott. "When the dogs of one sled keep so close to the one in advance that the foregoer's traces slacken, the sled ahead is said not to *give* track." [29] To call a dog the voyageur cried, *"Mon chien, vien ici."* To stop was *"wo"* or "*who*"; to turn right "*Yé*" or "*y'uî*"; to turn left "*chaw*" or "*cha*"; and to start was "*marche*." When dog trains passed, the air was rent with a succession of French expressions of vexation or praise, for the ability of his dogs meant much to the voyageur. Thus one would hear the following epithets hurled at slow dogs: "black frog," "little black dog" (especially if he were large and white), "geddie," "pig," "carcajou," and, most severe of all, "*sacré chien mort*" ("damned dead dog"). But if the speaker were proud of his dog, it was "good man," "flyer," "the fool," or, best of all, "that's a *dog*." Sad to relate, the voyageur frequently mistreated his dogs, beating them as well as flinging obnoxious language at them.

The men often suffered from *mal de racquet* on these winter trips. This snowshoe lameness was a painful inflammation, at the ankle, of the tendon that flexes the great toe. Like most muscular inflammation, it increased with exercise, so that the only remedy was rest. Tenderfeet nearly always suffered heroically from this malady on their first trip on snowshoes. Another discomfort often endured on expeditions across wide expanses of snow-covered country was snow blindness. Even experienced guides were kept in encampments for days recovering from a bad attack. Old voyageurs boasted much of taking few if any provisions on a trip afield. It was only pork-eaters, in their estimation, who could not live off the country.

Encampments had to be made every night, and long experience taught the voyageurs just how to make themselves most comfortable when spending the night in the open with the thermometer at zero or below. A contemporary description of a journey through the region just south of Lake Superior makes the whole process clear: "We generally stopped for the night about sundown. In the winter, it is of the first importance, to find a place for encamping where there is the best fuel for a fire. The second item of encampment, is the balsam tree, the branches of which are generally used for the foundation of a bed. On stopping for the night, the collars are stripped from the necks of the dogs—one man plies the axe in chopping wood for the night, cutting it from eight to ten feet long; another carries it on his shoulders to the camp; another, if there is a third, with a snow shoe, clears away the snow for a place for a bed and a fire, and a sufficient distance around for the baggage and dogs. We then break off the twigs of the balsam to prepare for a bed: or if these cannot be obtained, we search for dry grass or rushes. Sometimes pine boughs, and even little bushes a half inch in diameter are used, when nothing better can be obtained. When the foundation of our bed is laid, a fire is kindled, and one hangs on a kettle of snow or water for cooking our supper. We now gather before a cheerful fire, pull off our leggins and moccasons, and hang them by the fire to dry, putting on dry socks and moccasons. The cook urges forward the supper, which when ready is eaten with a keen relish. Supper ended, and dogs fed, preparations are made for lying down. Having spread our skins and blankets upon our foundation of boughs, with a bag of rice or meal, or our folded coats for a pillow, we . . . lie down, all in one bed, with all our clothes on except our coats; and even them, and caps and mittens too, sometimes. We lie at right angles with the fire, and put our feet as near it as we can and not burn them. When the weather is very cold, we are obliged to get up two or three times during the night, and renew our fire. When the wind blows cold we stick up bushes, or branches of the balsam, to break off the force of it. Traveling under the circumstances we do, it is impossible to carry bedding enough to make us comfortable in extreme cold weather—we consequently occasionally suffer much during the night." [30]

In the western mountains a "regular" winter encampment meant one made where the snow was very deep. Green logs eighteen or twenty feet in length were necessary for the hearth, for the snow melted to the depth of six to ten feet even beneath these poles. The length of the logs prevented them from falling into the well formed by the heat of the fire. The green logs seldom burned through in a night. Incautious voyageurs, however, sometimes rolled in their sleep into the pit, much to the amusement of their companions. The depth of the snow in these regions could be easily gauged by the height of the stumps of trees cut for previous encampments. In the summer or in open winters these stumps rose fifteen to twenty feet above the trail, though their tops were on the snow level when the voyageurs' axes were put to them. Around the fires made from these trees the old voyageurs amused themselves by telling the pork-eaters that the Indians in those parts were giants from thirty to forty feet in height and that fact accounted for the trees being cut off at such an unusual height. [31]

For respite on these, as also on canoe trips, the mer sang, played cards, threw quoits, and boasted to one an other. "All their chat is about horses, dogs, canoes, women and strong men, who can fight a good battle," wrote Harmon.[32] Boasting was as much a part of their make-up as it is of most grown-up children. They boasted of all their deeds, relatives, possessions, masters, friends, canoes, and dogs; and when they summed up all these, they announced to an admiring world that they were "Northwesters," or merely "*Je suis un homme*," and as such they could "live hard, lie hard, sleep hard, eat dogs." It was commonly remarked of them: "*les voyageurs n'avaient jamais vu de petits loups*" ("voyageurs never see little wolves").

Winter finally passed. All the labors of the season were to be seen finally in the packs of furs and kegs of grease, castoreum, and sugar that lay waiting for news to come that the streams and lakes were free of ice. The first duck or goose was sighted and the news sent hither and yon. Most of the squaws moved to their sugar bushes for their sugar-making. A few, accompanied by voyageurs, went to the woods to "raise" birch bark for canoe-mending or to gather gum. The canoes were brought out, mended, and gummed, and all was made ready for departure. On a bright May morning the canoes were packed and manned, a few men were left in charge of the fort, and the others paddled blithely off, singing in anticipation of the balls, wines, and *camaraderie* of Grand Portage.

VI

VOYAGEUR SONGS

VI

FAINTLY as tolls the evening chime
Our voices keep tune and our oars keep time.
Soon as the woods on shore look dim,
We'll sing at St. Ann's our parting hymn,
Row, brothers, row, the stream runs fast,
The rapids are near and the daylight's past.

Why should we yet our sail unfurl?
There is not a breath the blue wave to curl,
But, when the wind blows off the shore,
Oh, sweetly we'll rest our weary oar.
Blow, breezes, blow, the stream runs fast,
The rapids are near and the daylight's past.

Utawas' tide! this trembling moon
Shall see us float over thy surges soon.
Saint of this green isle! hear our prayers,
Oh, grant us cool heavens and favoring airs.
Blow, breezes, blow, the stream runs fast,
The rapids are near and the daylight's past.

THOMAS MOORE

Moore tells us in a letter appended to this poem, written in 1804, that it was adapted to the music of a song his voyageurs sang to him on a trip that he made from Kingston to Montreal. "The original words of the air," he writes, "to which I adapted these stanzas, begin:

'*Dans mon chemin j'ai rencontré*
Deux cavaliers très bien montés.'"

103

Moore was not the first—nor the last—to enshrine in verse the appeal of the voyageurs' songs, but probably this poem has done more than any other bit of writing to preserve the memory of an almost forgotten class of men. Scores of writers have recorded the impressions made on them by the haunting melody of these folk songs, but unfortunately only a few took pains to record either the words or the airs. Consequently, a century later, we are obliged in the main to hear the voyageurs of our imaginations singing the folk songs that were current among *all* Canadians. Probably it is true that sooner or later the rocks of the Ottawa and the pines of the *pays d'en haut* heard most of the airs that the *habitants* of the little hamlets on the lower St. Lawrence were accustomed to sing; nevertheless, we should like to know the favorites —the songs that had special appeal to this special group of Canadians.

Some clues are given now and again, though usually in a garbled French which defies analysis. It is certain that "*A la claire fontaine*" was the general favorite. It was sung from coast to coast, not only in canoes, but wherever the voyageur was found. Kennicott, for example, tells of singing it in the snowbound Northwest; atop his *traîneau à lisse* (dog train), he gave a yell, which, he says, "started my dogs off on a gallop, and [I] rode down the mountain singing *La Claire Fontaine* and other voyaging songs, to encourage my dogs, for dogs, and horses, seem to like singing." [1] Just why this song should have been the universal favorite of voyageurs is hard to say. Certainly the subject matter bore no relation to any phase of their existence, and the rhythm and lilt are not so

pronounced and catchy as those of many other *chansons*.
The music and words are as follows:

A LA CLAIRE FONTAINE

A la clai-re fon-tai-ne M'en al-lant pro-me-ner,

J'ai trou-vé l'eau si bel-le Que je m'y suis bai-gné.

Lui ya long-temps que je t'aime, Jamais je ne t'oublierai.

> A la claire fontaine
> M'en allant promener,
> J'ai trouvé l'eau si belle
> Que je m'y suis baigné.
>> Lui ya longtemps que je t'aime,
>> Jamais je ne t'oublierai.
>
> J'ai trouvé l'eau si belle
> Que je m'y suis baigné;
> Sous les feuilles d'un chêne
> Je me suis fait sécher.
>> Lui ya longtemps, etc.
>
> Sous les feuilles d'un chêne
> Je me suis fait sécher;
> Sur la plus haute branche
> Le rossignol chantait.
>> Lui ya longtemps, etc.
>
> Sur la plus haute branche
> Le rossignol chantait.
> Chante, rossignol, chante,
> Toi qui as le cœur gai.
>> Lui ya longtemps, etc.

THE VOYAGEUR

Chante, rossignol, chante,
Toi qui a le cœur gai;
Tu as le cœur à rire,
Moi je l'ai-t-à-pleurer.
    Lui ya longtemps, etc.

Tu as le cœur à rire,
Moi je l'ai-t-à-pleurer:
J'ai perdu ma maîtresse
Sans l'avoir mérité.
    Lui ya longtemps, etc.

J'ai perdu ma maîtresse
Sans l'avoir mérité,
Pour un bouquet de roses
Que je lui refusai.
    Lui ya longtemps, etc.

Pour un bouquet de roses
Que je lui refusai.
Je voudrais que la rose
Fût encore au rosier.
    Lui ya longtemps, etc.

Je voudrais que la rose
Fût encore au rosier,
Et moi et ma maîtresse
Dans les mêm's amitiés.
    Lui ya longtemps que je t'aime,
    Jamais je ne t'oublierai.

TRANSLATION *

At the Clear Running Fountain

At the clear running fountain
  Sauntering by one day,
I found it so compelling
  I bathed without delay.
    Your love long since overcame me,
    Ever in my heart you'll stay.

VOYAGEUR SONGS

I found it so compelling
　I bathed without delay;
Under an oak tree's umbrage
　I dried the damp away.
　　Your love, *etc.*

Under an oak tree's umbrage
　I dried the damp away.
There where the highest branch **is**,
　Sir Nightingale sang hey!
　　Your love, *etc.*

There where the highest branch **is**,
　Sir Nightingale sang hey!
Sing, Nightingale, keep singing,
　You sing with heart so gay.
　　Your love, *etc.*

Sing, Nightingale, keep singing,
　You sing with heart so gay.
You have the heart a-ringing;
　My heart—ah! lack-a-day!
　　Your love, *etc.*

You have the heart a-ringing;
　My heart—ah! lack-a-day!
I lost my lovely lady
　In such a blameless way.
　　Your love, *etc.*

I lost my lovely lady
　In such a blameless way.
For one bouquet of roses
　Which I must say her nay.
　　Your love, *etc.*

For one bouquet of roses
　Which I must say her nay—
I wish that now the roses
　Bloomed on their tree today.
　　Your love, *etc.*

I wish that now the roses
　Bloomed on their tree today,
And I and she, the lady,
　Were friends the same old way!
　　Your love long since overcame me,
　　Ever in my heart you'll stay.

* From *Canadian Folk Songs: Old and New,* by J. Murray Gibbon, by permission of the publishers, J. M. Dent & Sons, Ltd., London, Toronto and Vancouver, and E. P. Dutton & Company, New York.

In another version the final wish of the singer is,

Et que le rosier même
Fût à la mer jeté.

"and that the tree itself were thrown into the sea."

Another *chanson* commonly sung by the voyageurs was that to which Moore refers. There were many variations of it. In his letter Moore mentions the refrain, which differs considerably from the commonly accepted form in "*J'ai trop grand' peur des loups.*" James Lanman in an article on the fur trade published in *Hunt's Merchants' Magazine* gives still a third rendering.[2] The music and the French form as given by Ernest Gagnon follows:[3]

J'AI TROP GRAND' PEUR DES LOUPS

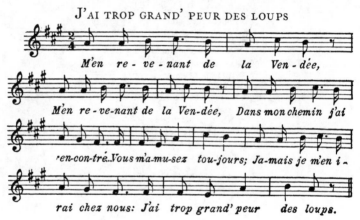

M'en re-ve-nant de la Ven-dée,

M'en re-ve-nant de la Ven-dée, Dans mon chemin j'ai

'en-con-tré..Vous m'a-mu-sez tou-jours; Ja-mais je m'en i-

rai chez nous: J'ai trop grand' peur des loups.

M'en revenant de la Vendée, (bis)
Dans mon chemin j'ai rencontré. . . .
Vous m'amusez toujours;
Jamais je m'en irai chez nous:
J'ai trop grand' peur des loups.

Dans mon chemin j'ai rencontré (bis)
Trois cavaliers fort bien montés.
Vous m'amusez, etc.

Trois cavaliers fort bien montés, (bis)
Deux à cheval et l'autre à pied.
  Vous m'amusez, etc.

Deux à cheval et l'autre à pied; (bis)
Celui d'à pied m'a demandé. . . .
  Vous m'amusez, etc.

Celui d'à pied m'a demandé: (bis)
—Où irons-nous ce soir coucher?
  Vous m'amusez, etc.

Où irons-nous ce soir coucher? (bis)
—Chez nous, monsieur, si vous voulez.
  Vous m'amusez, etc.

—Chez nous, monsieur, si vous voulez; (bis)
Vous y trouv'rez un bon souper.
  Vous m'amusez, etc.

Vous y trouv'rez un bon souper, (bis)
Et de bons lits pour vous coucher.
  Vous m'amusez, etc.

Et de bons lits pour vous coucher, (bis)
Les cavaliers ont accepté.
  Vous m'amusez toujours:
Jamais je m'en irai chez nous:
  J'ai trop grand' peur des loups.

TRANSLATION *

They Have Me Scared, Those Wolves

On my return from la Vendée, (*repeat*)
Coming along met on my way. . . .
  You make me laugh, you do;
Never shall I bid home adieu:
  They have me scared, those wolves.

Coming along met on my way (*repeat*)
Three cavaliers in fine array.
  You make me laugh, *etc.*

Three cavaliers in fine array, (*repeat*)
One of them walked the footpath way.
  You make me laugh, *etc.*

One of them walked the footpath way; (*repeat*)
He that was walking made me say. . . .
  You make me laugh, *etc.*

He that was walking made me say: (*repeat*)
—Where shall we sleep tonight, I pray?
  You make me laugh, *etc.*

Where shall we sleep tonight, I pray? (*repeat*)
—If you so wish, with us you may.
  You make me laugh, *etc.*

—If you so wish, with us you may; (*repeat*)
Supper you'll like when done our way.
  You make me laugh, *etc.*

Supper you'll like when done our way, (*repeat*)
Cosy the beds for you we lay.
  You make me laugh, *etc.*

Cosy the beds for you we lay, (*repeat*)
And they accepted without delay.
  You make me laugh, you do;
  Never shall I bid home adieu:
    They have me scared, those wolves.

* By permission of J. Murray Gibbon.

Lanman mentions also another boat song which he heard sung by the voyageurs. His version is not complete, and so the fuller form, as found in Mr. Marius Barbeau's collection of folk songs, is given here.[4]

VOICI LE PRINTEMPS

Voici le-prin-temps, les amours se renouvel-lent, Et tous les amants vont

charger de maîtresse. Le bon vin m'en-dort—, l'amour m'y réveil-le.

Voici le printemps, les amours se renouvellent,
Et tous les amants vont changer de maîtresse.
  Le bon vin m'endort, l'amour m'y réveille.

Changera qui voudra, moi je garde la mienne.
Elle a les yeux doux, et la bouche vermeille.
  Le bon vin, etc.

Ah! qu'il serait doux d'être aimé de la belle;
Encore bien plus doux d'avoir un baiser d'elle.
  Le bon vin, etc.

Encore bien plus doux d'avoir un baiser d'elle,
Le long d'un ruisseau, d'une claire fontaine.
  Le bon vin, etc.

TRANSLATION *

IN THE GAY SPRING TIME

See the Spring is here,
Our loves we are a-waking,
And lovers all now
New mistresses are taking.
  Good old wine makes me doze,
  But love keeps me a-waking.

And all lovers now
New mistresses are taking,
Let all those change who may,
I keep to my old mistress.
  Good old wine, *etc.*

Let all those change who may,
I keep to my old mistress,
So soft are her eyes
And so tender are her kisses.
  Good old wine, *etc.*

* By permission of Constance A. Hamilton.

Bela Hubbard, a fur-trader who was well acquainted with the voyageurs about Mackinac, Detroit, and Chicago in the thirties of last century, gives the words of two songs.[5] One of them is the well known *"Frit à l'huile,"* but with so many variations from the ordinary form that it may be well to give it as he wrote it down.

FRIT À L'HUILE

Mon père a fait bâ-tir mai-son, Ha, ha,
ha, frit à l'hui-le, Sont trois char-pen-tiers qui la
font, Fri-tai-ne, fri-ton, fir-tou, poi-lon, Ha, ha,
ha, frit à l'hui-le, Frit au beurre et à l'o-gnon.

Mon père a fait bâtir maison,
Ha, ha, ha, frit à l'huile,
Sont trois charpentiers qui la font,
Fritaine, friton, firtou, poilon,
Ha, ha, ha, frit à l'huile,
Frit au beurre à l'ognon.

Sont trois charpentiers qui la font,
Ha, ha, ha, frit à l'huile.
Qu'apportes-tu dans ton giron?
Fritaine, etc.

Qu'apportes-tu dans ton giron?
Ha, ha, ha, frit à l'huile,
C'est un pâté de trois pigeons,
Fritaine, etc.

C'est un pâté de trois pigeons,
Ha, ha, ha, frit à l'huile,
Assieds-toi et le mangeons,
Fritaine, friton, firtou, poilon,
Ha, ha, ha, frit à l'huile,
Frit au beurre et à l'ognon.

The full song as given by Gagnon is much longer and tells how the youngest of the three carpenters who have built a house for the singer's father is her favorite, and how he and she sat down to eat the pigeon pie that she had in her skirt, he with such a bound that it frightened the fishes and made the sea and the rocks tremble.

The other song given by Hubbard is called *"La jeune Sophie."* His version differs somewhat from Mr. Barbeau's *"La belle Lisette,"* which was obtained from M. François Saint-Laurent, a folk-singer of Ste.-Anne des Monts. Hubbard and his printer failed to coöperate in the matter of French spelling and diction, and so the more correct version is given here.[6]

LA BELLE LISETTE

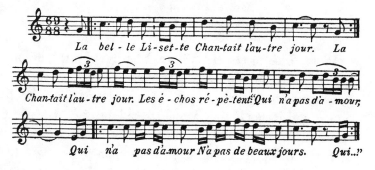

La bel - le Li-set-te Chan-tait l'au-tre jour. La Chan-tait l'au-tre jour. Les é - chos ré-pè-tent: "Qui n'a pas d'a - mour, Qui n'a pas d'a-mour N'a pas de beaux jours. Qui..."

La belle Lisette
Chantait l'autre jour. } (bis)
La belle Lisette
Chantait l'autre jour.
Les échos répétent:
"Qui n'a pas d'amour,
Qui n'a pas d'amour
N'a pas de beaux jours." } (bis)

Son berger l'appelle, } (bis)
Le berger Colin.
Le berger Colin.
Veillent à la chandelle,
La main dans la main } (bis)
Du soir au matin.

"Si gente, si belle, } (bis)
Dedans tes atours,
O ma tourterelle!
Répétons toujours,
Répétons toujours } (bis)
Nos serments d'amour.

"Unissons ensemble } (bis)
Ton cœur et le mien!
Ton cœur et le mien."
"Ne puis m'en défendre,
O berger charmant,
O berger charmant, } (bis)
A toi je me vends!"

Pretty Lisette (or Betty) was singing recently, according to this song. The echo sang back, "Who has no lover knows naught of happiness." Her shepherd, Colin, calls her. Hand in hand they watch the night out. "So sweet, so beautiful in your fine clothes, O my turtle dove! Let us renew our pledges of love. Let us join your heart and mine." "I can not resist, O charming shepherd. To you I give myself."

Dr. John J. Bigsby, who accompanied the British commissioners on their trip through the boundary waters in the early twenties, secured from one of his voyageurs the following variation of the old slumber song of Cambrésis, *"Une perdriole."* [7] It is substantially like Gagnon's version, and, as in his, each day adds a new gift to the previous donations of the lover. This fact accounts for the addition of a bar to the music of each succeeding stanza and for the change in the second word in each stanza, successive ordinal numbers being used to represent the days of May as they come. Gagnon's music for the first stanza is as follows; the words are Bigsby's:

UNE PERDRIOLE

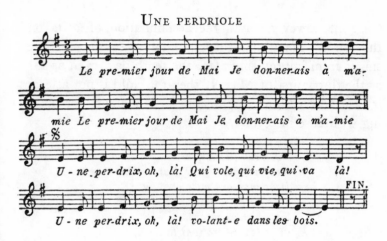

Le pre-mier jour de Mai Je don-ner-ais à m'a-mie Le pre-mier jour de Mai Je don-ner-ais à m'a-mie U - ne per-drix, oh, là! Qui vole, qui vie, qui va là! U - ne per-drix, oh, là! vo-lant-e dans les bois.

TRANSLATION *

THE OP'NING DAY OF MAY

The op'ning day of May,
What shall I give my dear one?
One, a little partridge, who comes, who goes a-flying,
One a little partridge a-flying in the wood.

* By permission of J. Murray Gibbon.

Only three days are accounted for in Bigsby's version:

Le premier jour de Mai
Je donnerais à m'amie
Une perdrix, oh, là! qui vole, qui vie, qui va là!
Une perdrix, oh, là! volante dans les bois.

Le deuxième jour de Mai
Je donnerais à m'amie
Deux tourterelles, une perdrix, oh, là! qui vole, qui
    vie, qui va là!
Une perdrix, etc.

Le troisième jour de Mai
Je donnerais à m'amie
Trois rats de bois, deux tourterelles, une perdrix, etc.

Gagnon, however, gives the accumulation of gifts on the tenth,[8] remarking that nothing is to prevent the singer from improvising after the tenth day, even as far as the thirty-first of May. If then the child is not asleep, it is useless to think of paregoric or laudanum, for nothing will close his eyes.

Dix veaux bien gras,
Neuf chevaux avec leurs selles,
Huit moutons avec leur laine,
Sept vach's à lait,
Six chiens courant,
Cinq lapins grattant la terre,
Quatr' canards volant en l'aire,
Trois rats des bois,
Deux tourterelles,
Une perdriole, etc.

Ten fatted calves,
Nine apparelled saddle horses,
Eight fat sheep with woolly fleeces,
Seven milking cows,
Six running dogs,
Five young hares that scrape the earth up,
Four wild ducks a-wing in air,
Three woodland rats,
Two turtle dove birds,
One a little partridge, *etc.*

116

The music for the second and third donations is the same:

Deux   tour - te   rel - les.
Trois   rats des   bois.

The gifts for the fourth and fifth days are also sung to similar notes:

Quatr' ca - nards vo - lant en l'ai - re.
Cinq   la - pins grat-tant la ter - re.

The notes of the sixth and seventh couplets are like-wise similar:

Six   chiens cou - rant.
Sept vach's   à   lait.

The notes of the ninth are a repetition of those of the eighth:

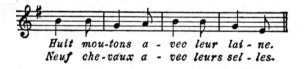

Huit mou-tons a - vec leur lai - ne.
Neuf che-vaux a - vec leurs sel - les.

The music of the tenth day goes back in form to that of the second. Each new bar of music is inserted after the repetition of the opening clause, so that the gift for the new day is always given first in the series of donations.

McKenney recounts how "the bowsman pushed the canoe into the current, and a chaunt was struck up, called the 'White Rose.' " [9] Many other travelers make mention of it, among them Robert Ballantyne in his *Hudson's Bay*, published at the middle of the century, which tells of six years spent in the North during the forties. He characterizes it as "the lively air of 'Rose Blanche,' sung by the men as we swept round point after point and curve after curve of the noble river." [10] Garry in 1821 took down the words, which differ slightly from Mr. Gibbon's version given here. Gibbon's, in turn, differs from Gagnon's version. [11]

J'AI CUEILLI LA BELLE ROSE

J'ai cueil-li la bel-le ro - se, J'ai cueil-li la bel-le ro - se, Qui pen-dait au ro-sier blanc, La bel-le ro - se, Qui pen-dait au ro-sier blanc, La bel-le ros' du ro-sier blanc.

J'ai cueilli la belle rose,
J'ai cueilli la belle rose
Qui pendait au rosier blanc,
    La belle rose,
Qui pendait au rosier blanc,
    La belle ros' du rosier blanc.

Je l'ai cueilli' feuille à feuille (bis)
Mis dans mon tablier blanc,
  La belle rose,
Mis dans mon tablier blanc
  La belle ros' du rosier blanc.

Je l'ai porté' chez mon père, (bis)
Entre Paris et Rouen,
  La belle rose,
Entre Paris et Rouen,
  La belle ros' du rosier blanc.

Mr. Gibbon has used "*Qui pendait au rosier blanc*" as the fifth line in every stanza after the third. Gagnon, however, continues the scheme of the first three stanzas, that is, the fifth line a repetition of the third in every stanza.

Je n'ai pas trouvé personne (bis)
Que le rossignol chantant,
  La belle rose,
Qui pendait au rosier blanc,
  La belle ros' du rosier blanc.

Qui me dit dans son langage: (bis)
Mari'-toi, car il est temps,
  La belle rose,
Qui pendait, etc.

Comment veux-tu que j'm'y marie? (bis)
Mon père en est pas content.
  La belle rose,
Qui pendait, etc.

Ni mon père ni ma mère, (bis)
Ni aucun de mes parents.
  La belle rose,
Qui pendait, etc.

119

THE VOYAGEUR

Je m'en irai en service, (bis)
En service pour un an.
   La belle rose,
Qui pendait, etc.

Combien gagnez-vous, la belle, (bis)
Combien gagnez-vous par an?
   La belle rose,
Qui pendait, etc.

Je gagne bien cinq cents livres, (bis)
Cinq cents livr's en argent blanc.
   La belle rose,
Qui pendait, etc.

Venez avec nous, la belle, (bis)
Nous vous en donn'rons six cents.
   La belle rose,
Qui pendait au rosier blanc,
   La belle ros' du rosier blanc.

TRANSLATION *

I HAVE CULLED THAT LOVELY ROSEBUD

I have cull'd that lovely rosebud,
I have culled that lovely rosebud
   Hanging on the white rose-plant,
      That lovely rosebud,
   Hanging on the white rose-plant,
   That lovely rose from white rose-plant.

I have cull'd petal by petal, (*repeat*)
Fill'd my apron with its scent,
      That lovely rosebud,
   Fill'd my apron with its scent,
   That lovely rose from white rose-plant.

I have brought it home to father, (*repeat*)
From Rouen to Paris went.
      That lovely rosebud,
   From Rouen to Paris went,
   That lovely rose from white rose-plant.

I found none—no, not a person (*repeat*)
Save the thrush who sung his chant.
    That lovely rosebud,
    Hanging on the white rose-plant,
    That lovely rose from white rose-plant.

Who informed me in his own tongue: (*repeat*)
"Marry now, ere time prevent."
    That lovely rosebud,
    Hanging, *etc.*

"Why your will that I should marry? (*repeat*)
Father would not be content."
    That lovely rosebud,
    Hanging, *etc.*

"Neither father nor my mother, (*repeat*)
Nor my kin would give consent."
    That lovely rosebud,
    Hanging, *etc.*

"I will now go into service, (*repeat*)
Service till a year is spent."
    That lovely rosebud,
    Hanging, *etc.*

"What the wage you gain, fair lady? (*repeat*)
What the wage per year you want?"
    That lovely rosebud,
    Hanging, *etc.*

"I gain quite five hundred shillings, (*repeat*)
Shillings silver-white I meant."
    That lovely rosebud,
    Hanging, *etc.*

"Come with us, and we, fair lady, (*repeat*)
Will six hundred then present."
    That lovely rosebud,
    Hanging on the white rose-plant,
    That lovely rose from white rose-plant.

* From *Canadian Folk Songs: Old and New,* by J. Murray Gibbon, by permission of the publishers, J. M. Dent & Sons, Ltd., London, Toronto and Vancouver, and E. P. Dutton & Company, New York.

Garry's version lacks the final stanza which makes the interrogator offer the girl a hundred shillings more than she will earn by going into service as she threatens to do.[12] Presumably she accepts.

Garry gives the words of two other songs and mentions many. Thus, he writes in his diary on September 6, 1821: "In the Morning the Voyageur sings 'Bon Jour, Jolie Bergère,' &c. 'Brave Capitaine,' 'Vin blanc,' 'Champagne,' &c., at Dinner. 'A terre, à terre' in the Evening at the Encampment." The words for one of the three songs given in full below are but slightly different from Gagnon's version.[13]

QUAND J'ÉTAIS CHEZ MON PÈRE

Quand j'étais chez mon père, (bis)
Petite Jeanneton,
   Dondaine, don,
Petite Jeanneton,
   Dondaine.

M'envoi' t-à la fontaine, (bis)
Pour pêcher du poisson,
   Dondaine, don, etc.

122

La fontaine est profonde, (bis)
J'me suis coulée au fond,
    Dondaine, don, etc.

Par ici-t-il y passe (bis)
Trois cavaliers barons,
    Dondaine, don, etc.

—Que donneriez-vous, belle, (bis)
Qui vous tir'rait du fond?
    Dondaine, don, etc.

—Tirez, tirez, dit-elle, (bis)
Après ça, nous verrons . . .
    Dondaine, don, etc.

Quand la bell' fut tirée, (bis)
S'en fut à la maison,
    Dondaine, don, etc.

S'assit sur la fenêtre, (bis)
Compose une chanson,
    Dondaine, don, etc.

—Ce n'est pas ça la belle, (bis)
Que nous vous demandons,
    Dondaine, don, etc.

C'est votre cœur en gage, (bis)
Savoir si nous l'aurons,
    Dondaine, don, etc.

—Mon petit cœur en gage, (bis)
N'est pas pour un baron,
    Dondaine, don, etc.

Ma mère me le garde, (bis)
Pour mon joli mignon,
    Dondaine, don,
Pour mon joli mignon,
    Dondaine.

THE VOYAGEUR

WHEN I WAS HOME WITH MY FATHER

When I was home with my father, (*repeat*)
Little wee Jeanneton,
   Ding a ding dong,
Little wee Jeanneton,
   Dong dain-a.

Off to the spring he sent me, (*repeat*)
So am a-fishing gone,
   Ding a ding dong, *etc.*

Deep in the spring a-sunken, (*repeat*)
Tumbled the whole way down,
   Ding a ding dong, *etc.*

There by the way came passing (*repeat*)
Three knights of proud renown,
   Ding a ding dong, *etc.*

"What would you give him, fair one, (*repeat*)
Who pulls you out anon?"
   Ding a ding dong, *etc.*

"Pull out, pull out," her answer, (*repeat*)
"We'll see when all is done."
   Ding a ding dong, *etc.*

When the girl out was lifted, (*repeat*)
Straight to the house was gone,
   Ding a ding dong, *etc.*

Sat down beside the window, (*repeat*)
There she composed a song,
   Ding a ding dong, *etc.*

"It is not that, my fair one, (*repeat*)
Which we from you would dun,"
   Ding a ding dong, *etc.*

"It is your heart in guerdon, (*repeat*)
Say, shall we have our own?"
   Ding a ding dong, *etc.*

124

"My little heart in guerdon (*repeat*)
Is for no baron grown."
   Ding a ding dong, *etc.*

"My mother keeps it for me, (*repeat*)
Sweetheart shall win alone."
   Ding a ding dong,
"Sweetheart shall win alone."
   Dong dain-a.

* By permission of J. Murray Gibbon.

Probably Garry's "Bonjour, jolie bergère" was "*La bergère muette.*" The salutation comes in the second stanza.[14]

LA BERGÈRE MUETTE

    Ecoutez la complainte,
      Petits et grands,
    D'une bergère muette
    Qui, dans ses champs,
    Gardait ses brebi-ettes,
      Le long d'un pré.
    Jésus, par sa bonté,
      L'a fait parler.

125

Un jour, la sainte Vierge } (bis)
  Lui apparut.
"Bonjour, joli' bergère,
  Grande Isabeau.
Voudrais-tu me donner
  Un des agneaux?"

—*"Ah non, certes!" dit-elle,* } (bis)
  "Sont pas à moi.
A mon père, à ma mère
  J'en parlerai.
A mon père, à ma mère
  Je leur dirai."

Ell' s'en est retournée } (bis)
  Bien promptement.
"Mon père, y-at une dame
  Dans mon troupeau.
Grand Dieu! ell' me demande
  Un des agneaux."

Son père, aussi sa mère, } (bis)
  Fur' bien surpris
D'entendre la muette
  Parler ainsi.
A Dieu firent prière
  Qu'il ait merci.

"Va lui dire, ô bergère, } (bis)
  Dans ton troupeau,
Qu'ils sont à son service,
  Grands et petits,
Que tous sont pour lui plaire,
  Jusqu'aux plus beaux."

La bergère, elle est morte } (bis)
  Avant trois jours.
Ell' tenait une lettre
  Dedans sa main,
Ecrite du grand maître,
  Dieu souverain.

Son père, aussi sa mère,} (bis)
    N'ont jamais lu.
A fallu que l'arch'vêque
    Y soit venu
Parler à la muette,
    Grande Isabeau.

"Ouvre ta main, bergère,} (bis)
    Ouvre ta main,
De la part du grand maître,
    Dieu souverain!"
A bien lu la lettre,
    A bien compris.

Qu'en chante la complainte} (bis)
    Le vendredi
Gagne les indulgences,} (bis)
    Le paradis.

TRANSLATION *

THE DUMB SHEPHERDESS

Hark ye to the complaint,
    Grown and little,
Of a dumb shepherdess,
    Who in her fields
Did guard her little sheep
    Along the mead!
'Twas Jesus, out of goodness,
    Made her speak.

One day the holy Maid} *(repeat)*
    To her appeared.
"Good day, sweet shepherdess,
    Big Isabeau!
And would you give to me
    One of the lambs?"

"Ah, no indeed," she said,} *(repeat)*
    "They are not mine.
To father, to my mother,
    I'll speak of it;
To father, to my mother,
    I'll tell of it."

127

She came back to her home⎱ *(repeat)*
  Straightaway. ⎰
"My father, there's a lady
  In my flock.
O God! she asks of me
  One of the lambs."

Her father, mother too,⎱ *(repeat)*
  They were amazed ⎰
To hear the speechless maiden
  Speaking thus;
To God they made a prayer
  For his mercy.

"Go tell her, shepherdess,⎱ *(repeat)*
  In thy flock, ⎰
That they are at her pleasure,
  Big and little,
That all are for her pleasing,
  Even the best."

The shepherdess was dead⎱ *(repeat)*
  Before three days. ⎰
A letter she was holding
  In her hand,
Writ by the sovereign master,
  Mighty God.

Her father, mother too,⎱ *(repeat)*
  They could not read. ⎰
It had to be the bishop
  Came to them
To speak to the dumb maid,
  Big Isabeau.

"Open, shepherdess, ⎱ *(repeat)*
  Open thy hand, ⎰
For the sake of the sovereign master,
  Mighty God!"
And well he read the letter
  And understood:

"Whoever sings on Friday ⎱ *(repeat)*
  This complaint, ⎰
Is freed of sinful taint, ⎱ *(repeat)*
  Gains Paradise." ⎰

* From *Folk Songs of French Canada,* by Marius Barbeau and Edward Sapir, by permission of the publishers, Yale University Press.

Another of the songs that Garry quotes from his voyageurs is a variation of the well-known "A-Rolling My Ball." Garry's men sang *"Ye, ye ment"* in place of *"En roulant ma boule"* in the second line of every stanza, *"Tous du long de la Rivière"* in the fourth line, and *"Légèrement ma Bergère Légèrement, ye ment"* in place of the last two lines.[15]

EN ROULANT MA BOULE

Voix seule, puis la reprise en chœur. FIN.

En rou-lant ma bou-le rou-lant, En roulant ma bou - le.

Voix seule, reprise en chœur.

Der-rièr' chez nous, ya - t-un é-tang, En roulant ma bou-le.

Voix seule.

Trois beaux canards s'en vont baignant, rou-li, roulant, ma boule roulant.

> *En roulant ma boule roulant,*
> *En roulant ma boule.*
> *En roulant me boule roulant,*
> *En roulant ma boule.*

> *Derrièr' chez nous, ya-t-un étang,*
> *En roulant ma boule.*
> *Derrièr' chez nous, y'-t-un étang,*
> *En roulant ma boule.*
> *Trois beaux canards s'en vont baignant,*
> *Rouli, roulant, ma boule roulant,*
> *En roulant ma boule roulant,*
> *En roulant ma boule.*

129

Trois beaux canards s'en vont baignant,} (bis)
  En roulant ma boule.
Le fils du roi s'en va chassant,
Rouli, etc.

Le fils du roi s'en va chassant,} (bis)
  En roulant ma boule.
Avec son grand fusil d'argent,
Rouli, etc.

Avec son grand fusil d'argent,} (bis)
  En roulant ma boule.
Visa le noir, tua le blanc,
Rouli, etc.

Visa le noir, tua le blanc,} (bis)
  En roulant ma boule.
O fils du roi, tu es méchant!
Rouli, etc.

O fils du roi, tu es méchant!} (bis)
  En roulant ma boule.
D'avoir tué mon canard blanc,
Rouli, etc.

D'avoir tué mon canard blanc,} (bis)
  En roulant ma boule.
Par dessous l'aile il perd son sang,
Rouli, etc.

Par dessous l'aile il perd son sang,} (bis)
  En roulant ma boule.
Par les yeux lui sort'nt des diamants,
Rouli, etc.

Par les yeux lui sort'nt des diamants,} (bis)
  En roulant ma boule,
Et par le bec l'or et l'argent,
Rouli, etc.

Et par le bec l'or et l'argent, ⎫ (bis)
  En roulant ma boule. ⎭
Toutes ses plum's s'en vont au vent,
Rouli, etc.

Toutes ses plum's s'en vont au vent, ⎫ (bis)
  En roulant ma boule. ⎭
Trois dam's s'en vont les ramassant,
Rouli, etc.

Trois dam's s'en vont les ramassant, ⎫ (bis)
  En roulant ma boule. ⎭
C'est pour en faire un lit de camp,
Rouli, etc.

C'est pour en faire un lit de camp, ⎫ (bis)
  En roulant ma boule. ⎭
Pour y coucher tous les passants.
Rouli, roulant, ma boule roulant,
  En roulant ma boule roulant,
  En roulant ma boule.

TRANSLATION *

A-ROLLING MY BALL

On, roll on, my ball I roll on,
  On, roll on my ball, on!
  On, roll on, my ball I roll on,
  On, roll on my ball, on!

'Way back at home there is a pond,
  On, roll on my ball, on!
'Way back at home there is a pond,
  On, roll on my ball, on!
Three bonnie ducks go swimming 'round,
  Roll on, my ball, my ball I roll on.
    On, roll on, my ball I roll on,
    On, roll on my ball, on!

Three bonnie ducks go swimming 'round, ⎫ (*repeat*)
On, roll on my ball, on! ⎭
The prince goes off a-hunting bound,
  Roll on, *etc.*

131

THE VOYAGEUR

The prince goes off a-hunting bound, ⎱ (*repeat*)
On, roll on my ball, on! ⎰
His gun so big with silver crown'd,
  Roll on, *etc.*

His gun so big with silver crown'd, ⎱ (*repeat*)
On, roll on my ball, on! ⎰
The black he saw, the white he down'd
  Roll on, *etc.*

The black he saw, the white he down'd, ⎱ (*repeat*)
On, roll on my ball, on! ⎰
O prince, that was a wicked wound!
  Roll on, *etc.*

O prince, that was a wicked wound, ⎱ (*repeat*)
On, roll on my ball, on! ⎰
To kill the white duck that I own'd,
  Roll on, *etc.*

To kill the white duck that I own'd, ⎱ (*repeat*)
On, roll on my ball, on! ⎰
Each eye becomes a diamond,
  Roll on, *etc.*

Each eye becomes a diamond, ⎱ (*repeat*)
On, roll on my ball, on! ⎰
Silver and gold her beak surround,
  Roll on, *etc.*

Silver and gold her beak surround, ⎱ (*repeat*)
On, roll on my ball, on! ⎰
Beneath her wings a bloody wound,
  Roll on, *etc.*

Beneath her wings a bloody wound, ⎱ (*repeat*)
On, roll on my ball, on! ⎰
The feathers in the wind fly 'round,
  Roll on, *etc.*

The feathers in the wind fly 'round, ⎱ (*repeat*)
On, roll on my ball, on! ⎰
Three dames to pick them up are bound,
  Roll on, *etc.*

Three dames to pick them up are bound, ⎱ (*repeat*)
On, roll on my ball, on! ⎰
They make a camp bed on the ground,
  Roll on, *etc.*

132

They make a camp bed on the ground, } (*repeat*)
On, roll on my ball, on!
That passers-by may slumber sound,
   Roll on, my ball, my ball I roll on,
   On, roll on, my ball I roll on,
   On, roll on my ball, on!

*From *Canadian Folk Songs: Old and New*, by J. Murray Gibbon, by permission of the publishers, J. M. Dent & Sons, Ltd., London, Toronto and Vancouver, and E. P. Dutton & Company, New York.

One suspects that Garry had in mind one song only when he wrote, "The Voyageur sings. . . . 'Brave Capitaine,' 'Vin blanc,' 'Champagne,' &c., at Dinner," though he wrote it as though there were three. The text of the following song includes most of the words he quotes: [16]

NOUS ÉTIONS TROIS CAPITAINES

Les reprises en chœur.

Nous e - tions trois ca-pi - tai - nes,

Nous é - tions trois ca-pi - tai - nes De la

guer-re re-ve - nant, Bra-ve, bra - ve, De la

guer-re re-ve - nant Bra-ve - ment.

Nous étions trois capitaines (bis)
De la guerre revenant,
  Brave, brave,
De la guerre revenant
  Bravement.

THE VOYAGEUR

Nous entrâm's dans une auberge: (bis)
—Hôtesse, as-tu du vin blanc?
  Brave, brave,
Hôtesse, as-tu du vin blanc?
  Bravement.

Oui, vraiment, nous dit l'hôtesse; (bis)
J'en ai du rouge et du blanc,
  Brave, brave,
J'en ai du rouge et du blanc,
  Bravement.

Hôtess', tire-nous chopine, (bis)
Chopinette de vin blanc,
  Brave, brave,
Chopinette de vin blanc,
  Bravement.

Quand le chopine fut bue, (bis)
Nous tirâm's trois écus blancs,
  Brave, brave,
Nous tirâm's trois écus blancs,
  Bravement.

—Grand merci! nous dit l'hôtesse, (bis)
Revenez-y donc souvent,
  Brave, brave,
Revenez-y donc souvent,
  Bravement.

TRANSLATION *

WE WERE THREE YOUNG TROOP COMMANDERS

We were three young troop commanders (*repeat*)
From the war returning home,
  Bravely, bravely, [*or* brawly]
From the war returning home,
  Bravely done.

134

In we went into a tavern: (*repeat*)
"White wine, hostess! have you some?"
  Bravely, bravely,
"White wine, hostess! have you some?"
  Bravely done.

"Yes, indeed," the hostess told us; (*repeat*)
"Both of red and white have some,"
  Bravely, bravely,
"Both of red and white have some,"
  Bravely done.

"Hostess, draw us now a flagon, (*repeat*)
With a flask of white wine come,"
  Bravely, bravely,
"With a flask of white wine come,"
  Bravely done.

When the flagons all were emptied, (*repeat*)
With three florins paid the sum,
  Bravely, bravely,
With three florins paid the sum,
  Bravely done.

"Many thanks," remarked the hostess, (*repeat*)
"Come again and often come,"
  Bravely, bravely,
"Come again and often come,"
  Bravely done.

* By permission of J. Murray Gibbon.

One of the most observant of the many travelers in the
interior was Mrs. Jameson. Her favorite among the many
songs that her voyageurs sang on discovering her fondness for their *chansons à l'aviron* was one which is still
sung by tiny maidens spinning their tops along the steep,
narrow sidewalks of Quebec. "After dinner," she writes,
"the men dashed off with great animation, singing my
favourite ditty,

'Si mon moine voulait danser,
Un beau cheval lui donnerai!' " [17]

It has a jolly tune, and our translator has been successful in rendering the pun on the word *moine*, which ordinarily means "monk" but which has an added meaning
of "top" in Canada. A slightly different version of these
two lines is ordinarily given in anthologies of French-
Canadian songs. The following is probably the standard
version: [18]

AH! SI MON MOINE VOULAIT DANSER

Ah! si mon moi-ne vou-lait dan-ser! Ah!
si mon moi-ne vou-lait dan-ser! Un ca-pu-
chon je lui don-ne-rais, Un ca-pu-chon je lui
don-ne-rais. Dan-se, mon moin', dan-se! Tu
n'en-tends pas la dan-se; Tu n'en-tends pas mon moulin, lon, la, Tu n'en-tends pas mon mou-lin mar-cher.

Ah! si mon moine voulait danser!
Ah! si mon moine voulait danser!
Un capuchon je lui donnerais,
Un capuchon je lui donnerais.

Danse, mon moin', danse!
Tu n'entends pas la danse,
Tu n'entends pas mon moulin, lon, la,
Tu n'entends pas mon moulin marcher.

Ah! si mon moine voulait danser! (bis)
Un ceinturon je lui donnerais. (bis)
Danse, etc.

Ah! si mon moine voulait danser! (bis)
Un chapelet je lui donnerais. (bis)
Danse, etc.

Ah! si mon moine voulait danser! (bis)
Un froc de bur' je lui donnerais. (bis)
Danse, etc.

Ah! si mon moine voulait danser! (bis)
Un beau psautier je lui donnerais. (bis)
Danse, etc.

S'il n'avait fait vœu de pauvreté! (bis)
Bien d'autres chos' je lui donnerais. (bis)
Danse, mon moin', danse!
Tu n'entends pas la danse,
Tu n'entends pas mon moulin, lon, la,
Tu n'entends pas mon moulin marcher.

TRANSLATION *

IF MY OLD TOP WERE A DANCING MAN

If my old top were a dancing man!
If my old top were a dancing man!
A cowl to fit I would give him then,
A cowl to fit I would give him then.
  Dance, old top, then, dance in!
  Oh! you don't care for dancing,
  Oh! you don't care for my mill, la, la!
  Oh! you don't care how my mill runs on.

If my old top were a dancing man! (*repeat*)
A sash to fit I would give him then. (*repeat*)
Dance, *etc.*

If my old top were a dancing man! (*repeat*)
A cap to fit I would give him then. (*repeat*)
Dance, *etc.*

If my old top were a dancing man! (*repeat*)
A gown of serge I would give him then. (*repeat*)
Dance, *etc.*

If my old top were a dancing man! (*repeat*)
A psalter fine I would give him then. (*repeat*)
Dance, *etc.*

Had he not vowed he would poor remain, (*repeat*)
A lot more things I would give him then. (*repeat*)
Dance, old top, then, dance in!
Oh! you don't care for dancing,
Oh! you don't care for my mill, la, la!
Oh! you don't care how my mill runs on.

* From *Canadian Folk Songs: Old and New,* by J. Murray Gibbon, by permission of the publishers, J. M. Dent & Sons, Ltd., London, Toronto and Vancouver, and E. P. Dutton & Company, New York.

Mrs. Jameson mentions other favorites: "This peculiar singing has often been described: it is very animated on the water and in the open air, but not very harmonious. They all sing in unison, raising their voices and marking the time with their paddles. One always led, but in these there was a diversity of taste and skill. If I wished to hear 'En roulant ma boule, roulette,' I applied to Le Duc. Jacques excelled in 'La belle rose blanche,' and Lewis was great in 'Trois canards s'en vont baignant.'" [19]

F. A. H. La Rue, who made a special study of these songs, declares that " 'La belle Françoise,' is the song *par excellence* of our boatmen." There are several versions, but the one that he describes is as follows.[20] Only six stanzas are sung as a rule.

LA BELLE FRANÇOISE

C'est la bel-le Fran-çoise, lon, gai, C'est la bel-le Fran-çoi-se Qui veut s'y ma-ri-er, ma lu-ron, lu-ret-te, Qui veut s'y ma-ri-er, ma lu-ron, lu-ré.

C'est la belle Françoise, lon, gai,
C'est la belle Françoise
Qui veut s'y marier, ma luron, lurette,
Qui veut s'y marier, ma luron, luré.

Son amant va la voire, lon, gai,
Son amant va la voire
Bien tard, après souper, ma luron, lurette,
Bien tard, après souper, ma luron, luré.

Il la trouva seulette, lon, gai,
Il la trouva seulette
Sur son lit, qui pleurait, ma luron, lurette.
Sur son lit, qui pleurait, ma luron, luré.

—Ah! qu' a' vous donc, la belle, lon, gai,
Ah! qu' a' vous donc, la belle,
Qu' a' vous à tant pleurer? ma luron, lurette,
Qu' a' vous à tant pleurer? ma luron, luré.

THE VOYAGEUR

—On m'a dit, hier au soire, lon, gai,
On m'a dit, hier au soire
Qu'à la guerr' vous alliez, ma luron, lurette
Qu'à la guerr' vous alliez, ma luron, luré.

—Ceux qui vous l'ont dit, belle, lon gai,
Ceux qui vous l'ont dit, belle,
Ont dit la vérité, ma luron, lurette,
Ont dit la vérité, ma luron, luré.

Venez m'y reconduire, lon, gai,
Venez m'y reconduire
Jusqu'au pied du rocher, ma luron, lurette,
Jusqu'au pied du rocher, ma luron, luré.

Adieu, belle Françoise, lon, gai,
Adieu, belle Françoise!
Je vous épouserai, ma luron, lurette,
Je vous épouserai, ma luron, luré.

Au retour de la guerre, lon, gai,
Au retour de la guerre,
Si j'y suis respecté, ma luron, lurette,
Si j'y suis respecté, ma luron, luré.

TRANSLATION *

BEHOLD THE FAIR FRANÇOISE

Behold the fair Françoise, ah! lon, gai,
Behold the fair Françoise, ah!
She would wed if she may, maluron, lurette,
She would wed if she may, maluron, luré.

Her love comes late a-calling, lon, gai,
Her love comes late a-calling.
Supper long cleared away, maluron, lurette,
Supper long cleared away, maluron, luré.

He found her all so lonely, lon, gai,
He found her all so lonely.
In bed weeping she lay, maluron, lurette,
In bed weeping she lay, maluron, luré.

"What ails you, then, my fair one, lon, gai?
What ails you, then, my fair one?
Why do you weep this way, maluron, lurette?
Why do you weep this way, maluron, luré."

"They told me yestereven, lon, gai,
They told me yestereven,
Off to the war you're away, maluron, lurette,
Off to the war you're away, maluron, luré."

"Who told you that, my fair one, lon, gai,
Who told you that, my fair one,
Told but truth as they say, maluron, lurette,
Told but truth as they say, maluron, luré."

* By permission of J. Murray Gibbon.

The full song carries on the conversation between the lovers to the point where Frances' lover begs her to accompany him to the foot of the cliff, where he bids her adieu and promises to marry her on his return from the war.

La Rue took down from the mouths of voyageurs themselves seven songs which he characterized as the ones most in vogue at the time he was writing. It is obvious that many of them are parodies of older songs. Gagnon says of the first that it is "very remarkable" and that he regrets he does not know the air.[21]

C'EST DANS LA VILLE DE BYTOWN

C'est dans la ville de Bytown
Mon capitain' je rencontrai;
Il a tiré son écritoire
Du papier pour m'engager.
Hélas! j'ai eu la promptitude,
Hélas! Je me suis engagé.

M'y promenant dedans la ville,
Ma maîtresse j'ai rencontrée.
Et qu'a'vous donc jolie maîtresse,
Et qu'a'vous donc tant à pleurer?
Et tout le monde dedans la ville
Dis'nt que vous êtes engagé.

Ceux qui vous ont dit ça, la belle,
Vous ont bien dit la vérité;
Mais nous irons dans l'écurie,
Nous trouverons chevaux sellés;
Mais les brides sont sur les selles,
Nos amours il faut nous quitter.

Quand vous serez dedans ces îles,
Mon cher amant, vous m'oublierez;
Mais si vous fait's un long voyage,
Pensez-vous bien de m'épouser?
En attendant de vos nouvelles,
Mon cher amant je languirai.

Pour t'épouser, charmante belle,
Tu ne m'en as jamais parlé;
Mais tu y as fait difficile,
Le plus souvent tu m'as r'fusé.
A présent j'en ai t'une autre
Qui y est bien plus à mon gré.

This dialogue between a voyageur and his mistress in the outpost of Bytown, the modern Ottawa, is all the more interesting because it reveals something of the life of the *engagés*. Thus the "captain" who induces the voyageur to engage early and who produces writing materials to make the engagement certain was no small factor in the life of the ordinary canoeman. Probably the little scene here described between the lady and her lover was enacted frequently when it came time for the men to leave. The girl weeps and begs to be remembered when her lover is *en route* and reminds him of his promise to marry her. Thereupon he reminds her that she has refused him so often that now he has another sweetheart more to his taste.

The next song that La Rue gives shows the class-consciousness of the voyageurs, as well as some of their customs.[22]

PARMI LES VOYAGEURS

Parmi les voyageurs, lui y a de bons enfants,
Et qui ne mangent guère, mais qui boivent souvent;
Et la pipe à la bouche, et le verre à la main,
Ils disent: camarades, versez-moi du vin.

Lorsque nous faisons rout', la charge sur le dos,
En disant: camarades, ah! grand Dieu, qu'il fait chaud!
Que la chaleur est grande! il faut nous rafraîchir;
A la fin du voyage, on prendra du plaisir.

Ah! bonjour donc, Nannon, ma charmante Lison,
C'est-i toi, qui porte des souliers si mignons:
Garnis de rubans blancs, par derrièr' par devant,
Ce sont des voyageurs, qui t'en ont fait présent.

As one may see from the following literal translation, the song is strongly reminiscent of *"La Ronde"* given in the chapter on "Voyaging":

Among the voyageurs, there are some fine fellows, who seldom eat but often drink. Pipe in mouth, glass in hand, we say, "Comrades, pour me some wine." When we are marching pack on back, saying, "Comrades, Heavens! but it is hot! The heat is terrible!" it will be necessary to

refresh ourselves. At the end of the voyage we shall have
our fun. Then it will be, Nannon, my charming Lison,
there you are in your neat little shoes, decked front and
back with white ribbons, given you by the voyageurs.

The third of La Rue's songs is probably more accurately a shantyboy's song than a voyageur's and is omitted
here. The fourth, given below, shows the joy of the voyageur on returning to his home, where his mother greets
him tenderly, happy to have him again to solace her in
her old age.[23] The word *François* (Francis) might be
substituted for the *Français* (French) of this version of
the song to give it a more personal meaning.

SALUT À MON PAYS

Salut à mon pays, après un' longue absence,
De mes anciens amis. O douce souvenance!
Dans ce désert affreux, où malgré moi je nage,
L'aurore des cieux vient bénir mon courage.

Salut, Français, salut,
Après un long séjour
Le laurier sur mon front
T'annonce mon retour.

Sur ses genoux tremblants, je vois ma bonne mère
Sortir de sa chaumière, venir en chansonnant;
Et elle a reconnu l'objet de sa tendresse,
Mon fils est revenu pour calmer ma vieillesse.

There were Enoch Ardens among the voyageurs, too,
if the next song is good evidence. The music and accompanying stanza are from *"Le retour du mari soldat,"*
from Barbeau and Sapir, although La Rue's slightly dif-

ferent version given below, beginning "voilà les voyageurs qu' arrivent," can be sung to the same tune. The
characters in La Rue's version are voyageurs and a hostess, instead of the hostess and the soldier of Mr. Barbeau's version. The voyageurs announce that men of their
class drink without paying, whereas the soldier pawns his
old hat, his belt, and his cloak. Otherwise the stanzas are
very similar.[24]

LE RETOUR DU MARI SOLDAT

Quand le sol - dat——arrive en vil - le
Bien mal chaus-sé, —— bien mal vê - tu:
"Pau-vre sol - dat, —— d'où re-viens-tu——?"

Voilà les voyageurs qu'arrivent, (bis)
Bien mal chaussés, bien mal vêtus,
Pauvre soldat, d'où reviens-tu?

Madam', je reviens de la guerre (bis)
Madam', tirez-nous du vin blanc,
Les voyageurs boiv'nt sans argent.

Les voyageurs s' sont mi t'à table, (bis)
Ils s'sont mi t'à boire, à chanter,
Et l'hôtesses s'est mi t'à pleurer.

Ah! qu'avez-vous, jolie hôtesse? (bis)
Regrettez-vous votre vin blanc?
Les voyageurs boiv'nt sans argent.

145

THE VOYAGEUR

C' n'est pas mon vin que je regrette, (bis)
C'est la chanson que vous chantez,
Mon défunt mari la savait.

J'ai t'un mari dans le voyage, (bis)
Y a ben sept ans qu'il est parti,
Je crois que c'est lui qu'est ici.

Ah! taisez-vous, méchante femme, (bis)
Je n'vous ai laissé qu'un enfant,
En voilà quatr' dès à présent.

J'ai donc reçu de fausses lettres (bis)
Que vous étiez mort, enterré,
Aussi je me suis mariée.

TRANSLATION *

THE RETURN OF THE SOLDIER HUSBAND

One day the soldier comes to town, *(repeat)*
His clothes in rags, his shoes are worn:
"Whence is it, soldier, you return?"

He sought him room within a tavern: *(repeat)*
"Hostess, have you wine to drink?"
"And have you silver, man, to clink?"

"And as for silver, I've little enough. *(repeat)*
Take my old hat to pay for wine
And take this belt and cloak of mine."

And when he'd sat him down to table, *(repeat)*
Filling glass and singing strong,
She wept to hear him sing the song.

"Oh, what is wrong, my little hostess? *(repeat)*
Is it your wine that you regret,
The soldier drinking in your debt?"

" 'Tis not my wine that I regret; *(repeat)*
It is the lusty song that you
Are singing and my husband knew.

146

"I have a husband traveling; (*repeat*)
He's been for seven years from me.
I well believe that you are he."

"Oh, wicked woman, be you still! (*repeat*)
I left two children in your care,
I see that four are playing there."

"Lying letters came to me (*repeat*)
To say that you were in the ground;
Another husband I have found."

"In Paris there's a mighty war, (*repeat*)
And all the torturings of Hell.
My wife and children, fare you well!"

* From *Folk Songs of French Canada,* by Marius Barbeau and Edward Sapir, by permission of the publishers, Yale University Press.

La Rue gives a version of the song of the famous voyageur Cadieux, who, during the French régime, saved his party from the Iroquois near the Grand Calumet on the Ottawa route. Separated from his party in performing this valorous deed, he became exhausted by hunger and fear. When a searching party returned to find him, he was so overjoyed that he could not cry out to them from where he lay, and so the men passed on up the river. When they returned, a few days later, they found his body lying in a grave which he himself had dug. In his hands, crossed over his chest, was a piece of birch bark, on which were written the words of the song which was so popular thereafter among the voyageurs. Whenever a brigade of canoes passed the spot, one of the older *engagés* always told the story of Cadieux to the porkeaters. The version La Rue gives is slightly different from Gagnon's, which follows: [25]

THE VOYAGEUR

PETIT ROCHER

Pe-tit ro-cher de la hau-te mon-ta-gne,

Je viens i-ci fi-nir cet-te cam-pa-gne!

Ah! doux é-chos, en-ten-dez mes sou-pirs;

En lan-guis-sant je vais bien-tôt mou-rir!

Petit rocher de la haute montagne,
Je viens ici finir cette campagne.
Ah! doux échos, entendez mes soupirs,
En languissant je vais bientôt mourir.

Petits oiseaux, vos douces harmonies,
Quand vous chantez, me rattach' à la vie:
Ah! si j'avais des ailes comme vous,
Je s'rais heureux avant qu'il fût deux jours!

Seul en ces bois, que j'ai eu de soucis!
Pensant toujours à mes si chers amis,
Je demandais: Hélas! sont-ils noyés?
Les Iroquois les auraient-ils tués?

Un de ces jours que, m'étant éloigné,
En revenant je vis une fumée;
Je me suis dit: Ah! grand Dieu, qu'est ceci?
Les Iroquois m'ont-ils pris mon logis?

Je me suis mis un peu à l'ambassade,
Afin de voir si c'était embuscade;
Alors je vis trois visages français! . . .
M'ont mis le cœur d'une trop grande joie!

148

Mes genoux plient, ma faible voix s'arrête,
Je tombe . . . Hélas! à partir ils s'apprêtent:
Je reste seul . . . Pas un qui me console,
Quand la mort vient par un si grand désole!

Un loup hurlant vint près de ma cabane
Voir si mon feu n'avait plus de boucane;
Je lui ai dit: Retire-toi d'ici;
Car, par ma foi, je perc'rai ton habit!

Un noir corbeau, volant à l'aventure,
Vient se percher tout près de ma toiture:
Je lui ai dit: Mangeur de chair humaine,
Va-t'en chercher autre viande que mienne.

Va-t'en là-bas, dans ces bois et marais,
Tu trouveras plusieurs corps iroquois;
Tu trouveras des chairs, aussi des os;
Va-t'en plus loin, laisse-moi en repos!

Rossignolet, va dire à ma maîtresse,
A mes enfants qu'un adieu je leur laisse;
Que j'ai gardé mon amour et ma foi,
Et désormais faut renoncer à moi!

C'est donc ici que le mond' m'abandonne! . . .
Mais j'ai secours en vous, Sauveur des hommes!
Très-Sainte Vierge, ah! m'abandonnez pas,
Permettez-moi d'mourir entre vos bras!

TRANSLATION *

O LITTLE ROCK

O little rock of the mountain I stand on,
I venture here my campaign to abandon.
   Ah! echoes sweet, give ear unto my sigh,
   Languid with wounds I come here but to die.

O little birds, with your sweet sounds of harmony,
Bring in your song all my life once again to me.
   Ah! would that I had only wings like you!
   Happy I'd fly ere another day were due.

THE VOYAGEUR

In yonder woods have I harboured a lonely fear,
Thinking the while of my friends all I hold so dear.
  This was my doubt: "Alas! if drowned are they,
  Or Iroquois should have ended their day!"

Not long ago on a far trail I dared to roam,
And coming back there was smoke rising from my home.
  This I have thought: "Great God! What does it mean?
  Do Iroquois hold my humble demesne?"

I then prepared myself as if for an embassy,
So as to find if in ambush the Indian lay.
  Then I espy French faces as I peep—
  With wondrous joy all my pulses do leap.

My knees succumb, nor can I any voice retrieve,
I fall—alas! they are now just about to leave.
  Lone I remain, not one left to console
  When death shall come with his desolate toll.

Howling a wolf round my shanty is turning,
Looking for smoke, if the fire still is burning.
  I said to him, "You'd better leave this spot,
  Or, by my faith, I shall shoot through your coat."

One black old crow, flying round at a venture,
Perched on a branch just close to my shelter;
  I said, "Oh, you, who feed on human flesh,
  Begone, nor think my blood will you refresh.

"Go over yonder in these woods and marshes,
There you will find more than one Indian corpse is,
  There you will find their flesh as well as bones.
  Get farther off and let me have repose."

Say, nightingale, to the wife I'm bereaving,
Just an adieu to my children I'm leaving,
  Still I have kept my love and loyalty,
  And from this time she must give up hope of me.

Here then it is that the world me abandons,
But I seek aid in the Saviour of mankind.
  Most Holy Maid! ah, do not me forsake,
  Let me but die in your arms I refuge take.

* From *Canadian Folk Songs: Old and New* by J. Murray Gibbon, by permission of the publishers, J. M. Dent & Sons, Ltd., London, Toronto and Vancouver, and E. P. Dutton & Company, New York.

Another voyageur song that La Rue has preserved is
very similar to the one already quoted in describing *la
ronde* which occupied one of the first evenings on the
lower Ottawa. Since La Rue's version differs considerably
from Taché's, it may be well to give it here.[26]

QUAND UN CHRÉTIEN SE DÉTERMINE À VOYAGER

Quand un chrétien se détermine
A voyager,
Faut bien penser qu'il se destine
A des dangers.
Mille fois à ses yeux la mort
Par son image,
Mille fois il maudit son sort
Dans le cours du voyage.

Ami, veux-tu voyager sur l'onde
De tous les vents?
Les flots et la tempête grondent
Cruellement.
Les vagues changent tous les jours,
Et il est écrit:
Que l'image de ton retour
Est l'image de ta vie.

Quand tu seras sur ces traverses,
Pauvre affligé,
Un coup de vent vient qui t'exerce
Avec danger.
Prenant et poussant ton aviron
Contre la lame,
Tu es ici près du démon,
Qui guette ta pauvre âme.

Quand tu seras sur le rivage,
Las de nager,
Si tu veux faire un bon usage
De ce danger,

THE VOYAGEUR

Va prier Dieu dévotement,
  Avec Marie.
Mais promets—lui sincèrement
  De réformer ta vie.

Si, le soir, l'essaim de mouches
  Pique trop fort,
Dans un berceau tu te couches,
  Pense à la mort.
Apprends que ce petit berceau
  Te fait comprendre
Que c'est l'image du tombeau,
  Où ton corps doit se rendre.

Si les maringouins te réveillent
  De leurs chansons,
Ou te chatouillent l'oreille
  De leurs aiguillons.
Apprends, cher voyageur, alors,
  Que c'est le diable
Qui chante tout autour de ton corps
  Pour avoir ta pauvre âme.

Quand tu seras dans ces rapides
  Très-dangereux,
Ah! prie la Vierge Marie,
  Fais-lui des vœux.
Alors lance-toi dans ces flots
  Avec hardiesse,
Et puis dirige ton canot
  Avec beaucoup d'adresse.

Quand tu seras dans les portages,
  Pauvre engagé,
Les sueurs te couleront du visage,
  Pauvre affligé.
Loin de jurer, si tu me crois,
  Dans ta colère,
Pense à Jésus portant sa croix,
  Il a monté au Calvaire.

152

Ami, veux-tu marcher par terre,
Dans ces grands bois,
Les sauvages te feront la guerre,
En vrais sournois.
Si tu veux braver leur fureur,
Sans plus attendre,
Prie alors de tout ton cœur,
Ton ange de te défendre.

As a translation will show, this extremely moralizing piece was prepared by one thoroughly conversant with the technicalities of voyaging. The voyageurs' own terms are employed—traverses, voyaging, portages, rapids, marching, the great woods, etc. It suggests the priest giving advice to his voyageur flock about to start on a trip to the *pays d'en haut,* perhaps a priest who has accompanied a brigade and learned at first hand to sympathize with the men. "When a Christian decides to voyage," he warns, "he must think of the dangers that will beset him. A thousand times Death will approach him, a thousand times he will curse his lot during the trip. Friend, do you plan to travel on the water amid the winds and where the waves and tempest menace cruelly? The waves are different every day, and it is written that the appearance of your return is that of your life. When you are on traverses, poor soul, the wind will come up suddenly, seizing your oar and breaking it and putting you in grave danger. You then are close to the demon, who is lying in wait for your soul. When you have reached the shore, exhausted from swimming [after your canoe has been broken in the traverse], if you wish to profit from this experience, go, pray God devoutly, and Mary also. But promise them sincerely that you will re-

form. In the evening if the swarms of mosquitoes assail
you unbearably as you lie in your narrow bed, think how
this couch is the likeness of the grave where your body
will be placed. If the mosquitoes waken you with their
buzzing and tickle your ears with their stings, think, dear
voyageur, how like to the Devil they are, who is singing
about your body, ready to seize your soul. When you are
in those very dangerous rapids, pray to the Virgin, make
your vow to her. Then take the waves boldly and guide
your canoe with skill. When you are on portages, poor
soul, sweat will drip from your brow, poor *engagé.* Then
do not swear in your wrath, rather think of Jesus bearing
his cross. He mounted to Calvary. When you are traveling in the great forests, the Indians will attack you from
ambuscade. If you wish to brave their fury, wait no
longer, but pray to your guardian angel to protect you."

Examples of voyageurs' songs might be multiplied. It
is enough here to cite some of the most common *chansons*
that illustrate the various types. The manner of singing
needs to be mentioned in more detail. Sometimes all sang
in unison. Again, one of the voyageurs, usually the steersman, sang a solo part and his companions joined him in
the chorus. The effect in general seems to have been good.
Long's companion, Keating, wrote of them in 1823:
"As we proceeded along these rapids our canoe-men enter-
tained us with songs more remarkable for the wildness
and originality of their notes than for the skill and
method with which they were sung. It is one of the delights of these men to sing in unison as they proceed, and
the effect is very fine." [27] Dr. Bigsby mentions the method
of ending the song: "Thus commanded, Mr. M——— sang

it as only the true *voyageur* can do, imitating the action of the paddle, and in their high, resounding, and yet musical tones. His practised voice enabled him to give us the various swells and falls of sounds upon the waters, driven about by the winds, dispersed and softened in the wide expanses, or brought close again to the ear by neighboring rocks. He finished, as is usual, with the piercing Indian shriek." [28]

One traveler mentions that the voyageur who could sing had a greater economic value than the average man: "This done, he called for a song; and many were gleefully carolled—each verse in solo, and then repeated in chorus, north-west fashion. Of such use is singing, in enabling the men to work eighteen and nineteen hours a-day (at a pinch), through forests and across great bays, that a good singer has additional pay." [29] McKenney, like the Norwegian trader of the far Northwest, W. F. Wentzel, mentions the indecorous quality of some of their songs. It is a great pity, nevertheless, that Wentzel's large collection of these songs has not survived. His musical gifts added to his unusual command of languages would surely have made the collection invaluable. [30]

VII
THE VOYAGEUR AS SOLDIER

VII

AMONG the services rendered by voyageurs was that of the soldier. During the American Revolution it is certain that they played a not inconsiderable rôle in the country lying between the Appalachians and St. Louis and about the Great Lakes. As they were usually mentioned by some other epithet than that of their calling, however, it is difficult to single them out from the "French," "Canadians," "traders," and others for whom many contemporary references can be found. It is especially difficult to distinguish them from the *habitants* of such settlements as Detroit, Vincennes, Green Bay, and Prairie du Chien. Some voyageurs were doubtless recruited from these settlements every year.

The editor of a well-known book depicting the Revolution in the Northwest includes voyageurs, apparently, in a statement concerning the general attitude of westerners during the war. She says: "The news of the French alliance, which reached Pittsburgh on May 26, 1778, heartened the defenders of the frontier, and gave them hope of relief from hostile attacks. The little clusters of French-Canadian settlers scattered throughout the Indian country and the French-Canadian traders and half-breeds in the Indian villages had unbounded influence over the red men, and the news that their French 'father' was giving aid and comfort to the American colonists

159

tended to check the inimical propensities of our fiercest enemies. That this influence was not more effective, however, was due to the counteracting efforts of the American Loyalists whom General Hand had allowed to escape from Pittsburgh in the spring of 1778, and who had established themselves in the more important villages of the Ohio tribesmen." [1]

Thus many of the voyageurs gave their support to the Americans. From the correspondence of such frontiersmen as David Zeisberger and Daniel Boone, on the other hand, it seems perfectly apparent that a great many adhered to the British. Thus Zeisberger on June 9, 1778, sent Colonel George Morgan the following information: "There is a small army of French 150 or 200 men that is for the frontiers, commanded by one Mr Lemot [Guillaume LaMothe]. I imagine he is for his old hunting ground on Red Stone." Boone in the same year addressed Colonel Arthur Campbell in a dispatch telling of a Mr. Hancock "who arrived here Yesterday and informed us of both French and Indians coming against us to the number of near 400 which I expect in 12 days from this." [2]

A trader by the name of Jean Marie Ducharme, who had traded through the Illinois and Wisconsin countries prior to the outbreak of the war, seems to have held an important position in the British expedition against St. Louis in 1780. Other voyageurs also are known to have taken part in this important campaign. As a brother and a cousin of Ducharme's were voyageurs, it may be assumed that he was also in that category. His services to the British cause, however, seem to be in doubt. At the outset of the war he was suspected by the British of furnishing provisions to the colonists. In 1780 he was accused of sympathy with the Americans and of causing the expedition to miscarry.[3]

The numerous references made by British partisans to disloyalty among various persons in the Indian country who purported to be pro-British provide further evidence that many of the voyageurs must have upheld the American cause. Even at Grand Portage disaffection was rampant, and in 1778 Lieutenant Thomas Bennett was detailed to take a force thither to protect the British merchants there, and incidentally to secure their loyalty, which was in some cases considered doubtful.[4]

Both sides evidently relied again and again on the information that only traders and voyageurs could offer concerning the topography of the country and the Indians. It is difficult in many cases to distinguish between the trader and the voyageur. Thus the man sent by the British to the upper Mississippi to prevent the Sioux from attaching themselves to the Spanish, Augustin Rocque, was not far removed, if at all, from the voyageur ranks.[5]

In this contest, as later in the War of 1812, both sides were to discover that voyageurs were not always to be relied upon when the odds seemed going against them. Like so many effervescent, fun-loving natures, they lacked stamina. Thus Colonel A. S. De Peyster wrote to General Haldimand on August 23, 1779, that Lieutenant Bennett's "Canadians" and Indians had grown homesick and were desirous of turning back from a certain expedition.[6] Indeed, as a soldier the voyageur, it must be admitted at the outset, had his disqualifications. He must have been the despair of officers accustomed to implicit obedience, and to a deliberate assumption of fearlessness on the part of their men, whatever the threatening danger. The voyageurs were as naïve in war time as in peace and presumed the same easy tolerance on the part of their army superiors as on that of their trading *bourgeois*. Moreover, when danger threatened, they were afraid and said so as unmistakably as they expressed their joys in their *chansons*. And they positively could not accustom themselves to doing without their pipes for sometimes as many as three or four hours! Yet they served well and won distinction in the War of 1812.

In the fall of 1812 the Northwest Company patriotically offered their *engagés* to Canada and their king.[7] The offer was accepted, and in October the Corps of Canadian Voyageurs came into existence. It served in at least two engagements and was disbanded at Lachine on March 14, 1813. A translation of the essential portions of the governor-general's proclamation ordering this corps to be enrolled is as follows:[8] "It has pleased His Excellency, the Governor-General, to order John M'Donell, Esquire, to enroll the names of all residents of the parishes of La Pointe Claire, &c.; and Messrs. A. N. M'Leod and James Hughes, Esquires, to enroll the names of voyageurs in the parishes of St. Ours, &c., &c.; and Mr. William M'Kay, Esquire, to enroll the voyageurs in the parishes of La Norraye, &c.; and Mr. Pierre de Rocheblave, Esquire, to enroll the names of the voyageurs in the parishes of La Prairie, &c.; Those who are now or have been voyageurs, and to see that they are in Montreal on the first day of October in order to form a corps, which shall be named the Voyageur Corps, under the command of William M'Gillivray, Esquire."

A uniform was adopted, and twenty-seven officers were appointed, among whom one recognizes many of the men who opened up the Northwest.[9] William M'Gillivray was lieutenant-colonel and in command. His is such an outstanding figure in the fur trade in the period of the Northwest Company's greatest activity that no account of his life need be given here. It is sufficient to mention that he had served for years with voyageurs in the region beyond Grand Portage and knew them intimately. Fort William is named for him.

Angus Shaw was made a major, and so also was Archibald Norman McLeod. Both were experienced fur-traders whose exploits in the Northwest are well known. The reader has already become acquainted with McLeod through his diary, kept on the Assiniboine River in what is now Saskatchewan. It is a remarkably intimate picture of the voyageur at home. A man who had directed the life of such a post could be relied on not to be shocked when Private Jean-Baptiste appeared on parade with his pipe in his mouth.

Among the six captains were Alexander Mackenzie, Kenneth Mackenzie, and John McDonell. The last is known to the reader ere this, for not a little of the description of the voyageur in this book has been derived from McDonell's unpublished diary. The two Mackenzies were outstanding figures in the fur trade and in the exploration of western Canada.

James Stanley Goddard's name among the six lieutenants recalls that famous expedition up the Mississippi to Grand Portage in 1767 for which Jonathan Carver has claimed all the glory, but of which Captain James Tute was the leader and Goddard second in command. Surely Goddard learned much of voyageur temperament on that ill-fated journey.

M'Gillivray's son Joseph was one of eight ensigns. To him we are indebted for an insight into the temperament and morale of soldiering voyageurs: [10]

"When on duty in company with the regular forces or the militia they were guilty of much insubordination, and it was quite impossible to make them amenable to military law. They generally came on parade with a pipe in their mouths and their rations of pork and bread stuck on their bayonets. On seeing an officer, whether general, colonel, or subaltern, they took off their hats and made a low bow, with the common salutation of *Bon jour*, *Monsieur le Général*, or *le Colonel*, as the case might be, and, if they happened to know that the officer was married, never failed to inquire after the health of *Madame et les enfans*. On parade they talked incessantly, called each other 'pork eaters,' quarrelled about their rations, wished they were back in the Indian country again, &c., and when called to order by their officers and told to hold their tongues, one or more would reply, 'Ah, dear captain, let us off as quick as you can; some of us have not yet breakfasted, and it's upwards of an hour since I had a smoke.' If the officer was a North-Wester, he generally told them to have patience, and he would give them their *congé tout de suite*. In moments when danger ought to have produced a little steadiness, they completely set discipline at defiance, and the volatile volunteer broke out into all the unrestrained mirth and anti-military familiarity of the thoughtless *voyageur*. In vain the subaltern winked, in vain the captain threatened, in vain the colonel frowned; neither winks, threats, or frowns, could restrain the vivacious laugh, silence the noisy tongue, or compose the ever changing features into any thing like military seriousness.

"These repeated infractions of the *code militaire* subjected many of them to temporary confinement; but as night approached, if the sentinel was a *voyageur*, he told the prisoner to '*aller coucher avec sa femme, et retourner le lendemain de bonne heure.*' This friendly advice was immediately followed, and they had always the honour to return according to promise. They could not be got to wear stocks; and such as did not use cravats came on parade with naked necks, and very often with rough beards. In this condition they presented a curious contrast to the unchangeable countenances and well-drilled movements of the British soldiery, with whom they occasionally did duty. Notwithstanding these peculiarities the *voyageurs* were excellent partisans, and, from their superior knowledge of the country, were able to render material service during the war. They had great confidence in their officers, particularly their colonel, Mr. M'Gillivray, whose influence frequently saved them from the punishment to which their repeated breaches of discipline subjected them."

The first Canadian to lose his life in defence of his country was a voyageur, Pierre Rototte, of the Corps of Canadian Voyageurs, who fell at St. Regis, October 23,

1812.[11] Captain McDonell, one of his lieutenants, and thirty-five of his men were taken prisoners.[12] On November 5 of the same year voyageurs took part in the fight at Chrysler's Farm. On November 10 the Corps participated in the battle of La Colle. There may well have been other organizations of voyageurs within the British troops at this time. Dr. Bigsby refers to "three regiments of hardy *voyageurs*, of eight hundred or one thousand men each, which the Northwest Company sent into the field." [13]

The unique services of the voyageurs, however, were performed on the western front. The first engagement of the war was largely a voyageur victory. Michilimackinac was the great inland fur post, chiefly because of its strategic position on the trade route to the West and Northwest. The fur-traders as well as the Canadian Government were directly concerned in its fate. Should the Americans retain control, most of the fur trade of Canada would be intercepted and the western Indians would become the allies of the United States. Ruin faced Montreal merchants. Accordingly, on the outbreak of hostilities, steps were taken at once to secure British control of this fort. On July 15 Captain Charles Roberts, who commanded the nearest British post at St. Joseph's Island, received an order from his superior, Major-General Brock, authorizing an attack on Michilimackinac. On the following day Roberts and his "army" set out on their journey of fifty miles. His force consisted of some three hundred Indians, for whose presence Robert Dickson, a famous fur-trader of the Red River Valley, and his voyageurs were responsible; one hundred and eighty voyageurs; and forty-five men of the Tenth Royal Veterans. The Indians as effective soldiery can be discounted largely, for their influence was felt mainly in instilling in the Americans the fear of massacre. Two pieces of artillery were carried, which were unwieldy and caused the voyageurs much labor. "By the almost unparalleled exertions of the Canadians who manned the boats we arrived at the place of Rendezvous at 3 o'clock the following morning." [14] These are the words in which their commander, when reporting the affair, describes their services. The Americans, who numbered but fifty-nine effectives, saw the uselessness of an engagement and surrendered when they discovered a gun on an eminence commanding their garrison. This had been dragged thither with much difficulty "by the exertions of the Canadians." [15] Well had the voyageurs been trained for such herculean feats in the course of their canoe journeys. Incidentally one learns that of the fifty-nine in the American garrison, eighteen were voyageurs who after the capitulation of the post took the oath of allegiance to Great Britain and "after much solicitation, volunteered to serve for a limited period." [16]

It may be interesting to learn of further patriotic activities of voyageurs in this campaign. An eyewitness of events in this far corner, Toussaint Pothier, an agent of the Southwest Company, tells us that Captain Roberts consulted him on the deficiencies of men and provisions in his garrison as soon as he learned of the outbreak of war and that he, Pothier, sent an express canoe to Fort William, the great rendezvous of the Northwest Company's men, asking for assistance. "Those Gentlemen with great alacrity came down with a strong party to Cooperate; bringing to St Maries Several Carryage Guns and other arms. And altho the distance between St Josephs and Fort William is about 500 Miles they arrived at Michilimackinac the ninth day from the date of the Express." [17] And who but voyageurs made Captain William McKay's express canoe speed over the bosom of Lake Superior to Fort William with the request, and who if not voyageurs constituted the "strong party" that came down in the little schooner, *The Beaver?* Indeed, McKenzie at Fort William wrote: "Our agents ordered a general muster, which amounted to 1200, exclusive of several hundred of the natives. We are now equal in all to 1600 or 1700 strong . . . I have not the least doubt but our force will, in ten days hence, amount to at least five thousand effective men. Our young gentlemen and engagees offered most handsomely to march immediately for Michilimackinac." [18]

The fall of Michilimackinac had a direct effect on Hull's surrender of Detroit. In his trial the disgraced American officer referred to the four thousand *engagés* of the British traders as likely to be used against him and thus influencing him in his decision to yield the post.

Late in the war another victory in the West was due largely to voyageurs. This was the capture of Fort Shelby at Prairie du Chien. One corps, known locally as the Canadian Voyageurs, had already taken part in the campaign against Michilimackinac in 1812. Five other units took part, practically every man of which was either a trader or a voyageur. The official names of these units were: Michigan Fencibles, Mississippi Volunteers, Mississippi Volunteer Artillery, Dease's Mississippi Volunteers, and Green Bay Militia.[19]

Prairie du Chien was only less essential to the British fur-traders than Michilimackinac, for it controlled the entrance to the Sioux country where Robert Dickson, James Aird, John Lawe, and others had been building up an immense trade during the thirty years since the close of the Revolution. Montreal and London firms were deeply involved in this trade; hence, when the Americans under General Clark took Prairie du Chien in 1814 and proceeded to build a fort, the situation called for a drastic remedy. Accordingly Colonel McDouall, the British commander at Michilimackinac, sent forces under Captain William McKay to take possession. Among his officers one reads such names as Porlier, Rolette, Honoré, Grignon, Brisbois, Renville, Nolin, Lacroix, and Biron. In their scarlet uniforms they made a great showing when they arrived at the Prairie after a long journey by way of Green Bay and the portage between the Fox and Wisconsin rivers. The single gun, for which Wabasha and La Tête de Chien, chiefs of neighboring bands, had pleaded, was trained on the Americans' gunboat in the Mississippi and succeeded in hitting it. Its commander was obliged to cut the cable and get out of range, thus leaving the fort without assistance. Doubtless the red uniforms had their effect in persuading the little force that their opponents could more than equal them, and so the fort was surrendered. Prairie du Chien with its numerous voyageur residents thus became a British post and remained so till the end of the war. Many of the voyageurs who took part in this campaign also served during the next month, August, 1814, in the defence of Michilimackinac, when it was attacked by American forces. This again was a victory for the voyageurs. Among them were nearly a hundred armed and fitted out by John Johnston, the trader at Sault Ste. Marie.[20] We shall meet him again in the next chapter.

The voyageurs not only served with the land forces, but certain members of the craft very nearly had naval experience as well. In 1813 the *Isaac Todd*, on its way to Astoria, the new American post at the mouth of the Columbia River, was docked in Portsmouth, England. "We had on board half a dozen good Canadian *Voyageurs* . . . to make and man a canoe," writes John McDonald of Garth. "The Canadians [who] had been some time on board," asked and received shore leave. "Messrs. Ellice, McGillivray, McTavish and myself were dining at the principal hotel when the waiter came in and told us some men wished to see us. We knew immediately who they were . . . accordingly all made for the wharf, where they found a couple of the Canadians waiting. They had all made a little free with wine and women, and took a shore boat. They had not proceeded far when a press gang boarded them and were taking them all off to the hulk, an old 74, lying as a recruiting ship. Mr. McTavish made some resistance, . . . the midshipman took all except Mr. McTavish . . . and one of the clerks. We were still at table when McTavish came in all in a fury . . . blaming me for allowing the men to come ashore. Mr. Ellice winked at me and said: 'Never mind.' He was brother-in-law to

Earl Gray, and the Port Admiral was Earl Gray's brother. Next morning at breakfast, Mr. Ellice handed me an order from the Admiral for the release of our men, upon which I steered my course on board the hulk. The poor fellows had been put in close quarters all night for fear of escape. They were in a sad state of mind indeed, with the fear of being made sailors for the rest of their lives and of never seeing their fatherland again. . . . I returned with them to the Isaac Todd, all safe after what they believed a narrow escape."

Nor was this the last of their troubles. McDonald goes on with the narrative. "One evening while at Sancta Cruz, Tenerif, I had hardly gone to bed, when Mc-Tavish . . . came rushing into my cabin roaring out: 'McDonald, you allowed the Canadians to go ashore again! they have had a dust with the Spanish guard and half of them are taken prisoners and we will lose our men.' The fact was that the Spanish guard thought they were some of the French prisoners making their escape. . . . A scuffle ensued in which the *voyageurs* were wounded and locked up, but they were soon after released on their identity being made out." [21]

Something should be said, also, of the voyageurs in the party that founded Astoria, just at the outbreak of the war. On board the *Tonquin* were thirteen voyageurs. "An instance of the buoyant temperament and the professional pride of these people was furnished in the gay and braggart style in which they arrived at New York to join the enterprise. They were determined to regale and astonish the people of the 'States' with the sight of a Canadian boat and a Canadian crew. They accordingly fitted up a large but light bark canoe, such as is used in the fur trade; transported it in a wagon from the banks of the St. Lawrence to the shores of Lake Champlain; traversed the lake in it, from end to end; hoisted it again in a wagon and wheeled it off to Lansingburgh, and there launched it upon the waters of the Hudson. Down this river they plied their course merrily on a fine summer's day, making its banks resound for the first time with their old French boat songs; passing by the villages with whoop and halloo, so as to make the honest Dutch farmers mistake them for a crew of savages. In this way they swept, in full song, and with regular flourish of the paddle, round New York, in a still summer evening, to the wonder and admiration of its inhabitants, who had never before witnessed on their waters, a nautical apparition of the kind." [22]

They were told of the dangers that lay ahead of them in the storms of the Horn and the impressing ships of the British which might overtake them, but they replied that they were Nor'westers and that they could live hard, lie hard, sleep hard, eat dogs! Yet they were very lubberly on the *Tonquin* and excited the disgust of Captain Thorn. David Stuart, however, "had made various expeditions with voyageurs. He was accustomed, therefore, to the familiarity which prevails between that class and their superiors, and the gossipings which take place among them when seated round a fire at their encampments. Stuart was never so happy as when he could seat himself on the deck with a number of these men round him, in camping style, smoke together, passing the pipe from mouth to mouth, after the manner of the Indians, sing old Canadian boat-songs, and tell stories about their hardships and adventures."

The Astorians have been famous in American history for over a century. Ramsay Crooks, W. P. Hunt, Robert McLellan, Gabriel Franchere, and the two Stuarts, Robert and David—who does not know of their heroic adventures in crossing the great West and navigating around the Horn to found near the mouth of the Columbia an American trading post named in honor of the master spirit of the enterprise, John Jacob Astor? It is not generally recalled, however, that voyageurs were responsible to no inconsiderable extent for the success of the land expeditions. The canoes were propelled by them; by their sixth sense they detected rapids and falls in unfamiliar streams in time to avoid them; they knew the West from actual experience in many instances; and they were versed in wood lore and in making friendly contacts with Indians. Because they were inarticulate they should not be overlooked when history awards the glory for the planting of the American flag on the Pacific and for discovery of South Pass soon to be the gateway for an army of settlers on their way to Oregon and California.

VIII

THE VOYAGEUR AS SETTLER

VIII

OUR picture of the voyageur would be incomplete
without a representation of him in the rôle of a member
of a frontier community. Many a voyageur lost his life in
his hazardous calling; others remained about wilderness
posts till death overtook them; not a few returned to
spend the twilight of life in their native hamlets on the
great St. Lawrence; but a large proportion of them in the
later period of the fur-trade era became settlers on the
frontier. As the frontier moved inexorably westward, the
story of the voyageur as the first settler repeated itself at
Sault Ste. Marie, Chicago, Milwaukee, Green Bay,
Prairie du Chien, St. Paul, St. Louis, and Winnipeg, not
to mention fur-trading posts of lesser rank. First the
voyageurs lived at the trading forts of these regions; a
little later they took up land, on which they resided during the portion of the year when they were not employed
in paddling traders' canoes or absent on trading expeditions to the Indians. Finally the frontier reached their
little cabins and they became one with the new town
which sprang up almost overnight.

In certain localities, notably at Detroit, St. Louis, and
the French hamlets in the Illinois country, it is difficult
to distinguish in many cases between *habitants*, or actual
colonists, and voyageurs. Frequently the *habitant* engaged himself for a trading voyage or made his livelihood

as a small trapper. He is often referred to in the annals of the period as a "voyageur," a "Canadian," or a "Frenchman"—names by which the *engagé* of the fur trade, the true voyageur, is also mentioned. Thus it is difficult to distinguish the one from the other. Hence, it is necessary in studying the voyageurs to go to other frontier settlements where there were no *habitants* to be confused with them. The hamlets chosen for this study are Sault Ste. Marie, St. Peter's, and the Red River Settlement.

* * *

Sault Ste. Marie had been a mission station and fort during the French regime, but it came into its own after the fur trade was thrown open early in the British period. Thereafter for almost a hundred years it was known, alas too well, to voyageurs; for it was necessary to make a long and hard portage around the rapids that gave the place its name. In 1750 a plan had been afoot to establish a seigniory at "a place called the Sault Ste. Marie." [1] Settlements in that place "would be most useful, as voyageurs from the neighboring posts and those from the Western Sea would there find a safe retreat, and by . . . care and precaution . . . would destroy in those parts the trade of the Indians with the English." At least one Frenchman, probably a voyageur, settled there and began farming; but the struggle was soon on between France and Great Britain, and the voyageurs, instead of settling at frontier posts, accompanied Charles Langlade in his expedition against the British at Fort Duquesne. [2]

When the smoke of battle cleared away, Jean Baptiste Cadotte was found by Alexander Henry at the Sault, a

French Canadian there on sufferance by the new rulers.[3] Whether others of his compatriots remained, or whether there were accessions in the next ten years, is uncertain, but another traveler to that region in 1777, John Long, describes the place thus: "Here is a small picketted fort . . . and about ten log houses for the residence of English and French traders." [4]

In 1789 a still more famous traveler visited the Sault, Alexander Mackenzie. He writes: "Upon the South shore, there is a village . . . [of] about thirty families of the Algonquin Nation, who are one half the year starving and the other half intoxicated, and ten to twelve Canadians who have been in the Indian country from an early period of life and intermarried with the natives who have brought them families." [5]

Here, then, is a distinct allusion to a voyageur community. About 1800 a trading establishment of the Northwest Company which had grown up there, and possibly some of the voyageurs, moved to the north side of the strait to be on British soil. In May, 1800, Daniel W. Harmon, later a famous trader in the far West, found "on the opposite shore [the American side] . . . a few Americans, Scotch and Canadians, who carry on a small traffic with the natives and also till the ground a little." [6]

One of the most famous residents of the Sault was the Irishman, John Johnston, long a trader on Lake Superior. The romantic story of his protracted courtship of a chief's daughter, of their happy marriage and long residence at the Sault, of his royal hospitality to travelers passing that way, and of the marriage of his half-breed daughters to white men of respectability and even fame should be read by all Americans and Canadians.[7] He enters the story of the voyageurs because it was he who gathered them under the British flag in the War of 1812 and assisted in the capture of Michilimackinac. The fortunes of war were his, for while he was winning glory on the battlefield, the enemy reached Sault Ste. Marie and "plundered and destroyed" his property.[8]

At least one voyageur of Sault Ste. Marie emerges from obscurity in the attack on Mackinac. This was Augustin Nolin, who had retired before the war and built for himself a house at Sault Ste. Marie. It is said that at the siege he was of great assistance in restraining the Indians and thus prevented such a catastrophe as followed the surrender of Fort Dearborn not long after. It is likewise reported that in 1815 he warned the American officers at the Sault of an intended Indian attack. Later he sold his home at the Sault and removed to Pembina, on the Red River of the North.[9]

Franchere, the Astorian, tells in his narrative how over three hundred voyageurs and traders evaded the Americans who had just burned Sault Ste. Marie, and slipped by with an immensely valuable cargo of furs bound for Montreal:[10] "The value of the furs which they carried could not be estimated at less than a million of dollars: an important prize for the Americans, if they could have laid their hands upon it. We were three hundred and thirty-five men, all well armed; a large camp was formed, with a breast-work of fur-packs, and we kept watch all night." Since the forty-seven canoes that carried this valuable freight must have been propelled by voyageurs, we have here another instance of the manner in which these men served their country in time of need. What the loss of these furs would have meant to Canada at this time is partially revealed by the lengths to which the Northwest Company were willing to go to get them safely to Montreal. The course they proposed to take was none other than an appeal to their hated rivals, the Hudson's Bay Company, to allow their furs to go to England by way of Hudson Bay.

Franchere as he passed noted the appearance and character of the people living about the Sault. He mentions Charles Ermatinger, who was just finishing a grist mill. "He thought," says Franchere, "that . . . would lead the inhabitants to sow more grain than they did. These inhabitants are principally old Canadians, boatmen married to half-breed or Indian women. The fish afford them subsistence during the greater part of the year, and provided they secure potatoes enough to carry them through the remainder, they are content. It is to be regretted that these people are not more industrious, for the land is very fertile." [11]

In 1816 General McComb visited the Sault and expressed a desire to go up as far as the open lake. Accordingly John Johnston equipped him with a light canoe and nine of his most experienced voyageurs. When Point aux Pins was reached, a large camp of Indians came into view. Being drunk, they took offense at the American flag flying at the prow of the canoe and came rushing down to the river with war whoops and malicious intentions. One Indian aimed his gun at the General but fortunately missed his aim. Thereupon the leader of the *engagés*, Le Clair, rushed to the Indian, now priming his

181

gun for further action, wrested it from him, and "with
the butt end of it, laid him flat upon the ground." But
Le Clair was sufficiently well versed in Indian tactics to
warn against a further advance, and so the visit to Lake
Superior was abandoned.[12]

And now the second act in the drama of occupation
was about to begin. First always came the traders, who
picked out the best site for a principal fort. Here in the
course of time gathered, little by little, a hamlet of voyageurs. Then came the military. A post was erected, the
first evidence of the advance of the settler's frontier as
distinguished from that of the trader. In June, 1820,
Governor Cass of Michigan came to Sault Ste. Marie
accompanied by "ten Canadian *voyageurs* . . . to manage the canoes, ten United States soldiers to serve as an
escort, and ten Ottawa, Chippewa, and Shawnee Indians
to act as hunters," and others, the total numbering sixty-
four persons.[13] After a stormy session with the Indians,
who at first refused to grant land for a military post, the
Indian woman, Mrs. Johnston, and others succeeded in
bringing them to the point, and a treaty was finally
signed. By it the Chippewa ceded four square miles of
land, reserving a perpetual right to fish in the rapids. Fort
Brady was soon erected at the Sault.

Close on the heels of the military came the missionary.
Father Richard arrived in 1825 from his place of residence at Detroit. In his report of March 21, 1826, published in the *Annales de la Propagation de la Foi*, he
mentions the six hundred and more Canadian voyageurs
who were in the habit of assembling at Mackinac every
year between the first of May and the first of October.

He then goes on to enumerate the heads of families "originally from Canada" who lived at this time at numerous frontier hamlets. Sault Ste. Marie is credited with twenty families numbering 120 individuals. Other Catholic missionaries and some Protestant ministers served the inhabitants from time to time, notably the priests *en route* to or from Fort William and the Red River Settlement after 1818, including Fathers Tableau, Dumoulin, and Belcourt.[14] In 1836 Father Pierz began his labors at the Sault. Thereafter the French Canadians were not destitute of the consolations of their faith. In 1846 the Catholic mission was taken over by the Jesuits, and Father J. B. Menet was appointed the first active pastor. By this time the Catholic families are listed as 126, with such typical voyageur names as Benoît, Belanger, Brunette, Durocher, Des Jardins, Gauthier, La Roche, Nolin, and Rouleau.[15]

After 1834 a new industry was opened to the voyageurs of Sault Ste. Marie. This was the fishing industry inaugurated by the recently reorganized American Fur Company. From the first records penned by explorers down to the present day the rapids of Sault Ste. Marie have been famous for their white fish. The new president of the American Fur Company, Ramsay Crooks, believed that he could make the fish of the upper lakes redound to the profit of his firm. Moreover, he wished to dispense with sixty-five of his voyageurs (who were too numerous to be employed profitably as traders during the winter and spring) by building sailing vessels on Lake Superior. But sixty-five men, all conversant with the fur trade and more or less acquainted with the American Fur Company's policies, could be engaged by rivals to the great detriment of the Company. Therefore they were to be employed in catching fish.[16]

For almost a decade hooks, twine, salt, and other articles were supplied to agents at Mackinac, Sault Ste. Marie, and La Pointe. These men engaged voyageurs, Indians, and half-breeds to take the fish, pack them, and ship them in barrels to market.

No part of the story of early Sault Ste. Marie is more picturesque than accounts of the manner of taking fish in the rapids. The Canadians learned the difficult art from the Indians, whose canoes, bobbing about like eggshells on the boiling water, have been mentioned in nearly every visitor's narrative. Each canoe was manned by two men, each supplied with a push-pole, *pique de fond* in the voyageur's vocabulary. The man standing at the bow had by his side a scoop net with the opening four feet or so in diameter and with a handle some twelve or fourteen feet in length. With push-poles the canoe was forced against the stream while the eyes of the bowsman scanned the depths of the rushing waters until he saw his prey and brought the net into position. Then the canoe was allowed to drop suddenly down stream dragging the net with it. With a dextrous movement the bowsman brought the net out of the water, and the fish was flipped into the canoe.

Crooks' fisheries were eminently successful, and hundreds of barrels of fish were salted and sent to the Ohio Valley, down the Mississippi, and even to New York. But the crisis of 1837 and the bad times which followed for half a decade prevented them from reaching a satisfactory market, and so the plan was abandoned in the forties.

A description of a neighboring fishing hamlet of voyageurs has survived. It is representative of life at Sault Ste. Marie at this period no less than of La Pointe, about which it was written. Even after discounting some of the glamorous haze which the lapse of time enabled the author to throw about these inhabitants of Madeline Island, the reader will still see a village of charming, idyllic, grown-up children.[17]

"The town proper consisted of clusters of houses built on each side of a road-way running east and west, close to the lake shore, terminating on the west [at] Pointe De Fret, and on the east at Middle Fort, which was either an episcopalian or a presbyterian mission, but at which no missionary was stationed during my time. Still farther to the east was what was called Old Fort, consisting of a clearing on the eastern side of the island, from which all of the buildings had been removed, but which had grown up to grass and second growth timber.

"There were about three or four white families on the island; the people were mostly half-breeds, the descendants of intermarriage between the old voyageurs and the Indian woman, and nearly all the men of middle or beyond middle life were Canadian French and had been voyageurs or *coureurs des bois*, and had evidently settled upon the island to pass their old age there with their families. In addition to the groups of houses at La Pointe proper and Middle Fort, there was a settlement upon the western side of the island, at a distance of one or two miles.

"The people were a most innocent, affectionate and happy people. They made their own boats and nets, and the barrels, half-barrels and quarter-barrels in which they packed their fish. During the winter they were out trapping. They raised potatoes and other root crops, and one or two of the white men occasionally raised wheat and oats, but very little of it. There were only two or three horses in the entire settlement, and one or two cows. In winter nearly all the hauling was done with dog teams; nearly every family owning from three to four dogs. These animals were fed upon fish heads taken from the fish in the fall, filled frozen into barrels and kept during the winter for dog food. During the entire time of my residence on the island I never knew of a case of larceny but one, and that was committed by a negro who had been left there by some steamboat. I remember the thrill of horror that went through the entire community at the idea of such a crime being committed. Drunkenness was rare.

"The great events were the arrival of the first steamboat in the spring. Payment time in the fall, when everybody went to Bad River on the Reservation to attend the payment. Christmas day, when we had midnight Mass, and New Year's day, when visits were exchanged, and everybody who had a house kept it open.

"In the spring and fall great flights of migratory birds used to light upon the island and were killed for food; in June pigeons were particularly numerous. The berry season included strawberries, raspberries, and altogether the life, while perhaps monotonous, was of great simplicity and singular beauty.

186

"From the time navigation ceased until it opened, we were an isolated community. Provisions were stored and provided for in the fall, precisely as if one were going on a voyage, and the first boats used to bring small packages of meat and sausages in their ice-chests, which were sold to such of the inhabitants as could pay for them, and were considered rare delicacies.

"A more simple, hospitable, honest community could not exist anywhere, and there was an element of cheerfulness and good nature that permeated the entire community which I have never seen since.

"The old voyageurs were a singularly interesting class of men; uneducated, perhaps, but of a singular dignity of manner and speech and of the utmost morality: scrupulous in the performance of their duties both to God and man. On Sundays, in the little old church, the head of the family always sat with stately dignity on the outside of the pew, and while they indulged in chewing tobacco during the service to a very large extent, yet the habit was conducted in such a simple and dignified way that it ceased to surprise or annoy anybody. The choir in the church included four or five of these old men who sat within the chancel and sang the responses and all of the hymns. I can almost see them now, clad in their white surplices and red shirts, intoning with the utmost dignity all of the responses."

Copper mining began to attract immigration to the southern shore of Lake Superior in the middle forties; steamboats appeared on the lake; and Sault Ste. Marie soon ceased to be a voyageurs' hamlet. Yet even today one finds there names and faces reminiscent of the days

when red caps, plumes, sashes, and pipes were the fashion
at the Sault.

*   *   *

Just when voyageurs began to settle around "the
Entry," or "St. Peter's," that is, the mouth of the St.
Peter's, now the Minnesota, River, is somewhat uncertain. There is good reason to suppose that it was not till
the establishment of Fort St. Anthony, later Fort Snelling, in 1819 that a real hamlet existed in the neighborhood. From that year, however, until 1848 the region
became increasingly popular among this class of men.
For many years prior to 1834 Alexis Bailly was the principal trader. In 1817 he brought sixty voyageurs from
Montreal, eighty in 1818, and fifty-nine in 1827. Probably these figures are indicative of the average yearly
accession of new hands. His successor brought fifty in
1836 and thirty-three in 1837.[18] When Henry H. Sibley
came in the fall of 1834 to succeed Bailly, he found in
"the amphitheater where the hamlet was situated," to use
his own language, "only a group of log huts, the most
pretentious of which was the home of . . . Mr.
Bailly." [19] He further describes the hamlet as consisting
of "dwellings for the blacksmith, carpenter, and common
voyageurs in the vicinity of Mr. Bailly's quarters." This
was the beginning of Mendota, Minnesota.

Since the voyageur followed his own tradition in so
many phases of his existence, it should be stated here that
he had also his own peculiar method of building his
house. Perhaps the best description of it is by a missionary who himself was a skillful carpenter. In the following
extract from his letter of September 30, 1832, Sherman

188

Hall is describing the voyageurs' homes at Lac du Flambeau in western Wisconsin.[20]

"A few buildings are reared nearly in the old Yankee
manner of building log houses, that is, of round timbers
locked together at the ends. The most common method,
however, is to build with hewed timber. There is a great
abundance of good building timber almost everywhere in
this country. When a building is to be put up, the timber
of the sills, beams & posts is cut and squared into suitable sticks, usually with a common axe, for a hewing
broad axe is seldom seen here, and no body knows how to
use it. The sills & beams are generally locked, or halfed
together at the corners of the building, for few can frame
them together with tenant and mortice. A mortice is made
in the sill for a post wherever it is needed & an other in
the beam. A groove is made in each post from top to
bottom about 2 inches in width, and three or four inches
deep. Timbers are then hewed six or seven inches thick
and the ends cut till they are fitted to the groove in the
post, and of sufficient length to reach from one post to
another. They are then introduced one after another till
the walls of the building are completed. These timbers
answer every purpose answered by studs, braces, and
boarding in the English mode of building. Wherever a
window or a door is required, posts are erected, into
which the ends of the timbers are introduced, instead of
the main posts, and thus the required hole is made in the
wall. A post is placed at the centre of each end of the
building which is continued above the beam as high as
the top of the roof is intended to be. A stick of timber is
then laid on the top of these posts reaching from one end

189

of the building to the other, and forms the ridge pole. The roof is then formed by laying one end of timbers on this ridge pole and the other on the plate till the whole is covered. These timbers answer the purpose of boards on the roofs of English buildings. For shingling cedar barks are used. These barks are taken from the white cedar which is plenty in this part of the country, in the early part of summer. A single piece about 4 to 5 feet in length is pealed from each tree which is left standing. It is a smooth bark, not thick, rather stringy, and not brittle when dry. These barks are put upon the timbers of the roof in the manner of shingles, and are secured by narrow strips of boards which are laid across them and spiked to the timbers. A roof of this kind will last several years. The cracks between the timbers in the walls are plastered with a hard clay which abounds in this country and are then covered with cedar bark in the manner of the roof, if the building is intended for a house. We have now completed the body of our building without the use of boards. Windows are made of the same materials and in the same manner here as in N England, that is, a sash and glass makes a window, excep[t] occasionally a dried deer skin is used in the stead thereof.

"Sashes are made here; glass, nails, and all other foreign materials for building are imported as other foreign goods are. To this post they are brought more than 50 miles of the way *on men's backs*. We come now to the inside of our building where boards are at least convenient. These are all made by hand. The log is cut and hewed on two opposite sides to the thickness of 9 inches or a foot. It is then raised to the height of 6 or 7 feet from the ground and rests upon timbers. Lines are then struck as near to each other as the thickness of the board requires, which the saw is made to follow. One man stands upon the sticks to be sawed, and manages one end of a saw 5 or six feet in length . . . while a second . . . manages the other. The saw operates nearly in the same manner as that of a common saw mill. It is not however confined in a frame like [*manuscript torn*] The timber is cut only with the downward stroke which both the men contribute to produce. Two men will saw from a dozen to 20 of these boards per day, which are usually 10 or 12 feet in length. After our boards are made, floors, partitions, doors &c. can [be] made in this country as well as any other. For purposes of plastering, cementing, &c. clay is used instead of lime. . . . Chimneys are made of stones and clay, the art of brick making not having travelled so high up yet. The manner I cannot now describe. It is not howev[er] like the Yankee manner of building stone chimnies."

Unfortunately he nowhere in his letters describes just how these chimneys were constructed. A contemporary picture of such a chimney is in existence, however, and a reproduction of it incorporated in the wood-cut at the beginning of Chapter V will afford some idea of how it was made.[21]

In 1837 a rough census of the "white inhabitants" on the military reserve and about Fort Snelling was taken by Lieutenant E. K. Smith, who records a "total of 157 souls in no way connected with the military." [22] The fort itself was located in the angle between the Minnesota River (still the St. Peter's at this time) and the Mississippi, on the northern bank of the Minnesota. Just north of the fort, on the west bank of the Mississippi, was "Camp Coldwater," where the troops had been quartered for a time shortly after their arrival in 1819. Here and in its vicinity Smith found eighty-two persons. Across from the fort on the south bank of the Minnesota he found twenty-five residents about Sibley's trading post. Fifty others dwelt in the neighborhood, probably across the Mississippi on the Wisconsin side at "Le Clerc's."

The following year a famous English author, Captain Frederick Marryat, visited Fort Snelling. In the book he published later, *A Diary in America, with Remarks on Its Institutions*, he refers to the voyageur hamlet:[23] "The French Canadians, who are here employed by the Fur Company, are a strange set of people. There is no law here, or appeal to law; yet they submit to authority, and are managed with very little trouble. They bind themselves for three years, and during that time . . . they work diligently and faithfully; ready at all seasons and at all hours, and never complaining, although the work is often extremely hard. Occasionally they return to Canada with their earnings, but the major part have connected themselves with Indian women and have numerous families; for children in this fine climate are so numerous, that they almost appear to spring from the earth."

Who these early dwellers at St. Peter's were can be determined to a considerable extent by consulting the baptismal register in the cathedral at Dubuque, Iowa. In the year 1839 the good Bishop of Dubuque, Mathias Loras, was informed, probably by the great scientist Joseph N. Nicollet, who had been spending some years about the upper reaches of the Mississippi, that there were members of his flock at St. Peter's. Accordingly, early that summer he went up by steamboat to St. Peter's to make a visitation. Writing to his sister on July 26, he mentioned that "the Catholics of St. Peter's amounted to one hundred and eighty-five." [24] His list of baptisms, confirmations, and marriages reveals the fact that nearly every patronymic was French. Some of them were Brunelle, Prévot, Rèché, Dejarlat, Rondeau, Brissette, Papin, Le Claire, and Bouiderot. A study of these families shows that most of them were of voyageur origin. [25]

One of the best-known residents was Michel Le Claire, or Le Clere in the spelling of Americans with but a slender knowledge of French. To him is ascribed the honor of having been the first settler of the "Grand Marais," now within the limits of St. Paul, and probably thus the first settler on the site of the future capital of the state of Minnesota. When not employed as a voyageur, he was a carpenter, for it is recorded that he built a house for Alexander Faribault, a famous trader of the region, and that he made the doors and sashes for the home of another settler, Vetal Guerin.

Guerin was another voyageur, like his father before him. Born in Saint Rémi, Canada, in 1812, in 1832 he engaged himself to the American Fur Company for three years. After his term had expired, he settled near the trading post at St. Peter's and did odd jobs there and at Traverse des Sioux, another hamlet of voyageurs near the site of St. Peter, Minnesota, for three or four more years. Then he moved across the Mississippi and became one of the earliest residents of St. Paul.

Another early settler east of the Mississippi at the Entry was Joseph Turpin, a native of Montreal. His voyaging habits had taken him to Prairie du Chien, to the Red River Settlement for several years, and finally to Fort Snelling about 1831. With him on the long trek across the prairies had come in all probability another Canadian voyageur by the name of Chorette. Shortly after came another migration, among whom was Joseph Rondo or, probably, Rondeau. Rondeau's career had been that of the typical voyageur. He was born near Montreal in 1797. As a lad of seventeen or eighteen he had entered the fur trade as an employee of the Hudson's Bay Company, which in 1821 had coalesced with the great employer of voyageurs, the Northwest Company. Rondeau had paddled canoes across the breadth of the North American continent; had wintered on Fraser River, at Great Slave Lake, at Fort Edmonton, and elsewhere; and at last had settled at that favorite haven of voyageurs, the Red River Settlement. There he had married Josephine Boileau, a Kutenai half-breed, and had settled on a farm. Doubtless he would have continued there to the end of the story if plagues of mice, drought, grasshoppers, and floods, not to mention the onerous restrictions of the Hudson's Bay Company, had not beset the little colony and forced the numerous treks to St. Peter's and the "States." In 1835 he left, in company with many others, for St. Peter's. Some of the names of his companions are interesting—Gervais, Labissionère, Beaumette, and Dufeni. Rondeau, like others, settled under the walls of the fort and, like them, was ejected in the spring of 1840.

For tragedy found its way even to voyageur communities. Among the idyllic conditions at the Entry was one that brought disaster. The voyageurs had learned from their *bourgeois* how to traffic in fire water, and they were not long settled in their Eden, where land cost them nothing and where a benign government protected them with a stout fort, when they began to eke out their slender incomes by selling whiskey. It was not only to the great bands of Sioux and Chippewa that came often to visit the agent at the fort, but, alas, to the military also, that they offered their wares.

One of the worst offenders was a voyageur by the name of Pierre Parrant. Like the brethren of his profession, he had seen much of the continent, for he had been born in Canada and had lived at Sault Ste. Marie, at St. Louis, and at Prairie du Chien. From these points he had doubtless gone on extensive canoe trips. About 1832 he settled at the Entry, where he acquired among his fellows the sobriquet, *L'Œil de Cochon*, or "Pig's Eye," because of the ill-favored aspect of his single eye.

In 1837 the pressure of the frontier forced the United States Government to conclude treaties with the Sioux and Chippewa for the purchase of their lands east of the Mississippi as far north as the mouth of the Crow Wing River. In anticipation of these treaties, which would allow settlers to take up land, and because the authorities at the fort were obliging the settlers on the reserve to move, Parrant established himself across from the fort on the east bank of the Mississippi. Here, at Fountain Cave, within the present limits of the city of St. Paul, he built his cabin, close enough to the fort to attract its occupants, yet just outside the lines of the military reserve, as he believed. Indians and soldiers were not slow in finding him, and he and others became a great stench in the nostrils of the army officers at the fort. Accordingly the lines of the reserve were arbitrarily extended to take in the claims of Parrant and others who had settled near by, and in May, 1840, the poor settlers saw their cherished homes demolished by troops from the fort, when resistance was offered to the order to remove from the reserve. Parrant himself did not suffer with the others, for he had already lost his claim by another turn of Fortune's wheel. He had signed (with a cross) a note promising to pay Guillaume Beaumette ninety dollars. As security he had given his claim. The document itself is interesting:[26] "Know all men by these presents, that I, Pierre Parrant, residing near the entry of the Saint Peter's River, and in Wisconsin Territory, do hereby make over, transfer and quit-claim to Guillaume Beaumette, of said Saint Peter's, all my right, title, and interest in and to all that tract or portion of land which I, the said Parrant, now reside upon and occupy, at the cave, so-called, about four miles below Fort Snelling. . . ." Beaumette was also a voyageur who had migrated to the Red River about 1819. He was a stone mason and helped build the stone fort there.

Having lost his claim, Parrant moved down the river a little way and set up his grog shop once more, in the heart of the present business district of St. Paul. Still later he moved to the present Pig's Eye, then known as "Grand Marais." His notoriety may be judged from the fact that thereafter the place took his name. Here was quite a community of voyageurs: the Le Claire already mentioned; Amable Turpin, whose voyaging had taken him from Montreal to Mackinac, thence to Green Bay, and finally to St. Peter's before he settled near Fort Snelling and became the man who was always sent by the American Fur Company on its most difficult and hazardous trips; Charles Mousseau, born in Canada in 1807; Denis Cherrier, whose violin enlivened many an early dance in St. Paul; and a number of other voyageurs.

As a result of Bishop Loras' pastoral call of 1839, Father Lucian Galtier was sent to care for the little flock of voyageurs that had been so recently discovered by the Church. His residence was established at Mendota, but it was not long before he discovered the little settlements on the other side of the river. "I deemed it my duty," he wrote later, "to visit occasionally those families, and set to work to choose a suitable spot for a church. Three different points were offered, one called La Point Basse, or Point Le Claire . . . but I objected because that locality was the very extreme end of the new settlement, and in high water, was exposed to inundation. . . . Two miles and a half further up on his elevated claim, . . . Mr. Charles Mousseau offered me an acre of his ground, but the place did not suit my purpose. I was truly looking ahead, thinking of the future as well as of the present. Steamboats could not stop there; the bank was too steep, the place on the summit of the hill too restricted; communication difficult with the other parts of the settlement up and down the river. After mature deliberation, I resolved to put up the church at the nearest possible point to the cave. . . . I accepted the extreme eastern part of Mr. Vetal's claim, and the extreme west of Mr. Gervais'. . . . I had, previously to this time, fixed my residence at Saint Peter's and as the name of Paul is generally connected with that of Peter . . . I called it Saint Paul." [27] The church's name soon attached itself to the hamlet. When the land had been surveyed and opened to settlement in 1848, the hoards of incoming settlers took up land near or in the hamlet. Thus was a great city born. Thus, too, it was named, because of voyageurs and their need of religious instruction.

Sibley has left us some indication of the quaintness and fun-loving qualities of his voyageur neighbors. In his reminiscences he tells how they looked to him as the serfs of old England looked to their lords. He was consulted on all matters of importance. Thus in 1848, when the land upon which St. Paul has arisen was offered for sale by the United States Land Office, the squatters there realized that they must attend the sale at Stillwater if they were to keep possession of their lands. But who could accomplish such a weighty matter for them so well as Monsieur Sibley? Accordingly it was Sibley who did the bidding, surrounded by the squatters, each provided with a big stick with which to wreak vengeance on any speculator who should dare to bid higher than their chosen representative. After the sale was over, Sibley presented each man with a deed to his land. It was only after a long delay and much persuasion that he could induce them to take their deeds. Ignorant of American ways, they felt that their homes would be more secure in the hands of Monsieur Sibley than in their own.[28]

Sibley enjoyed contacts with these light-hearted, polite, vivacious French Canadians. In his reminiscences he devotes considerable space to them. The following extract will show something of his own fun-loving personality as well as that of the men whom he mentions: [29]

"Joseph Laframboise who died several years since, was a capital mimic, spoke with fluency four or five different languages and he was withal an inveterate practical joker. He and Alex. Faribault were wont to amuse themselves at the expense of Labathe, who was simple minded, honest sort of a man, and by no means a match for his tormentors.

"A standing jest at his cost, was his experience at a tea party at Fort Snelling. The trio mentioned was invited by Capt. G. of the army to take tea and spend the evening at his quarters, and the invitation was accepted. It was in the month of July, and the weather intensely warm. The party in due time were seated around the table, and the cups and saucers were of the generous proportions ignored in these modern and more fashionable days. It should be premised that Indian etiquette demands on all festive occasions, that the visitor shall leave nothing unconsumed of the meat or drink placed before him. The large cup filled with tea was handed to Labathe and the contents disposed of. The poor fellow at that time could speak nothing more of English than the imperfect sentence 'Tank you.' When his cup was empty, Mrs. G., who was at the head of the table, said in her suave and gentle manner, 'Mr. Labathe, please take some more tea.' Labathe responded, 'Tank you, madam,' which being interpreted by the waiter to mean an assent, he took the cup and handed it to the hostess, and Mr. Labathe was forthwith freshly supplied with the hot liquid. Labathe managed to swallow it, sweltering meanwhile with the fervent heat of the evening, and again he was requested to permit his cup to be replenished. 'Tank you, madam,' was the only reply the victim could give. Seven great vessels full of the boiling tea were thus successively poured down his throat, Laframboise and Faribault meantime almost choking with suppressed laughter. For the eighth time the waiter approached to seize the cup, when the aboriginal politeness which had enabled Labathe to bear up amid his sufferings gave way entirely, and rising from his seat to the amazement of the company, he exclaimed frantically, 'Laframboise, pour l'amour de bon Dieu, pourquoi ne dites vous pas a madame, que je n'en veut point davantage.' (Laframboise, for the love of God, why do you not tell madame that I do not wish for any more tea.) Labathe never heard the last of that scene while he lived.

"The old man Roque, mentioned as residing near Lake Pepin, afforded another instance of the inconvenience of not being able to speak English. He knew one compound word only, and that was roast beef, which he called 'Ros-bif.' He accompanied a Dakota delegation to Washington City on one occasion, and when asked at the public houses what he would be helped to, he could only say Ros-bif! So that the unhappy old gentleman, although longing for a chance at the many good things that he would have preferred, performed the round trip on 'Ros-bif.' "

* * *

The story of the Red River Settlement is not only the most unique chapter in the account of the voyageurs; it is also the explanation, in large measure, of their disappearance. It centers about that grim struggle between the Hudson's Bay Company and the Northwest Company which deluged the Northwest with blood, destroyed a peaceful community twice, and ended in the consolidation of the two great monopolies. The bitterness of that contest can hardly be imagined today.

From the days of Pierre Esprit Radisson and the founding of the Honourable Company of Adventurers of England Trading into Hudson's Bay until towards the close of the War of American Independence there had been little serious opposition to the Company's monopoly of the fur-trading areas about the frozen sea. Even after the founding of the Canadian concern, the Northwest Company, there was a period of some thirty years before it became obvious that the furs of the central portion of the continent were rapidly being depleted and that both companies must find new areas for exploitation. Then commenced the struggle. At first the advantage was all with the Montreal traders, despite their long line of unbelievably difficult transportation. Indeed, this very line of communication was a source of strength to the Northwest Company, for in order to maintain it they had developed a class of servants who proved the finest kind of weapon in the warfare with the "English," as their rivals were known locally. The latter had made use of Orkney men for the most part, but, excellent as they were, they were no match for French-Canadian voyageurs in withstanding the rigors of trade in the far North, especially in the wooded areas, and in establishing happy contacts with the natives.

When, therefore, the odds seemed going against the Honourable Company in its struggle to expand into the wooded valley of the Churchill River, hitherto regarded by the Northwesters as their sacred precinct, the members took stock in thorough, English fashion and reached certain revolutionary conclusions. One was that voyageurs should be pitted against voyageurs. This meant, however, more men and hence more provisions. Cheaper food and supplies than those hitherto brought by way of the Bay from England must be secured for these tried voyageurs from Montreal. Hence the conception of a colony near enough to the scene of warfare to be the source of supply.

Thus it came about that the noble Earl of Selkirk, the largest stockholder in the Hudson's Bay Company, was granted the District of Assiniboia in 1811 for another of his many philanthropic schemes. Probably philanthropic motives *were* mixed with other purposes in His Lordship's mind, but the correspondence of the Company at this time leaves no room to doubt what *its* aim was. One of the provisions of the grant is interesting in a study of the voyageur. Lord Selkirk was to set apart one-tenth of the district "to the use of such person or persons being or having been in the service or employ of the said Governor and Company for a term of not less than three years immediately preceding." Of this A. S. Morton says: "The first intention of this condition was that the settlement should be reinforced by such retiring servants as should choose to settle in it with their squaws and their dusky families. We may infer that as the company was contemplating employing French Canadians they thought of the Red River Settlement as becoming a retiring ground for them also and in the more distant future offering a reserve of the sort of servants that had contributed so much to the success of the rival traders from Montreal." [30] This long look into the future revealed halfbreed voyageurs from the colony in places which, but for this scheme, might have been occupied by their cousins from the little hamlets on the mighty St. Lawrence.

So it came to pass that the Hudson's Bay Company took to heart the lesson that canny John Jacob Astor, the president of the American Fur Company, had learned early in his struggle with the same rivals, the Northwest Company. Until the American Fur Company passed out of existence in the forties, Astor, and later his pupil and successor, Ramsay Crooks, recruited their canoemen and winterers from Montreal. It may not be amiss here to quote Crooks' convincing argument to his chief when the latter was getting Congress to legislate the Northwest Company out of the upper Mississippi Valley just after the War of 1812. Crooks, being then an agent at Mackinac and in close touch with the actual trade, perceived that Congress must make an exception in the case of voyageurs when passing a law excluding all foreigners from the American fur trade. He therefore wrote: "It will still be good policy to admit freely & without the least restraint the Canadian Boatmen. these people are indispensable to the successful prosecution of the trade, their places cannot be supplied by Americans, who are for the most part are [sic] too independent to submit quietly to a proper controul, and who can gain any where a subsistence much superior to a man of the interior and although the body of the Yankee can resist as much hardship as any man, tis only in the Canadian we find that temper of mind, to render him patient docile and perserving. in short they are a people harmless in themselves whose habits of submission fit them peculiarly for our business and if guided as it is my wish they should be, will never give just cause of alarm to the Government of the Union it is of course your object to exclude every foreigner except those for whom you obtain licenses." [31]

Crooks' advice was followed, and the American Fur Company employed Canadian voyageurs for twenty years and more after the coalition of the Northwest Company and the Hudson's Bay Company brought about the practical abandonment by English and Canadian traders of the long canoe route which was one of the chief *raisons d'être* of the voyageur. Then the failure of the American Fur Company, the advance of the frontier into Wisconsin, Minnesota, and neighboring regions, and the consequent abandonment by Americans of the old canoe route from Montreal in favor of steamboats and railroads sounded the final death knell of the voyageurs as a class. As a class they were gone by 1850. The Hudson's Bay Company still employed boatmen and canoemen, but they were Orkney men, half-breeds, and Iroquois now in the main, recruited largely from the Red River area.

To return to Selkirk's scheme and what came of it. His twofold plan of settling needy Europeans in his colony and making it the haven of refuge for the "great body of vagabond Canadians" he mentions in one of his letters was succeeding even at the time of his death in 1820.

One writer estimates the number of "supernumeraries" of the two companies there as fifteen hundred, "far exceeding all the settlers ever brought 'under the auspices of the Earl of Selkirk.'" [32]

In the years of famine, drought, floods, and pestilence that the little colony endured during the first two decades of its existence, many of the Europeans and some of the voyageurs migrated to St. Peter's and the "States." Yet it lived and eventually prospered. After one of the largest migrations, the Roman Catholic bishop wrote to his superior in Quebec that the loss had been more than offset by the providential arrival of a large body of voyageurs from the far Northwest. [33] It is not necessary here to go into the sordid warfare against the colony that was waged by the Northwest Company from 1811 till coalition. Twice the settlement was destroyed, in 1815 and 1816. In this warfare the companies relied to no slight degree on their voyageurs. Under the grim relentlessness of their *bourgeois* they did their hideous work thoroughly. *La Grenouillère* was the name by which they knew the famous battle of Seven Oaks, when Governor Semple and others were killed by them in 1816. Finally came peace with coalition. The expanded Company found itself embarrassed with servants, of both *bourgeois* and voyageur rank. Arrangements were made with both groups to settle in the colony. The voyageurs were given lands on the east bank of the Red River, and their expenses to the colony from the interior forts were defrayed. With them, of course, came their squaws and numerous half-breed children.

It is our good fortune that a contemporary noted and

wrote down how certain of these voyageurs made their way to their new home and the type of men they were. Alexander Ross, who likewise settled in the colony and became its historian, was on his way thither soon after the coalition.[34] At Norway House, one of the chief northern posts, he found a company of "infirm and superannuated servants of the Company," of whom a large percentage were destined for the same haven of refuge as himself. "Hearing that I was on my way thither," he writes, "rather than wait the Company's regular conveyance they applied for a passage with me, and promised to work their way." He surveyed them and found that "as far as appearances went they seemed to be worthless." But they assured him that they were experienced hands and, indeed, boasted of their ability in handling boats. He finally took six and started out. Of these six he has left a detailed picture:

"And as it may be interesting to the reader to know something of the character of these superannuated sons of the wilderness, we shall sketch them. In the first place, then, three of them were able to help themselves, if not others; but as for the other three, their day was gone by: all of them were poor, more or less mutilated, infirm, and clogged with large families. But they were, nevertheless, very talkative, and independent in their way—North-Westers to the backbone; they had long yarns to tell of their past lives, as all voyageurs have, and were full of life and spirits.

"Of this motley crew, we shall notice some striking peculiarities in the more aged and experienced of them: one was blind of an eye, and lame from having been frost-bitten; another was a cripple from the same cause; and a third had lost his thumb by accident. The last of this trio, the patriarchal head, had reached the wrong side of seventy years; and his wife, from infirmity, walked on crutches; but the froward old man, still active for his age, was as waggish and thoughtless as a youth of fifteen.

"One day, while in a jocular mood, the old man began to talk over his past life: it was full of adventure, and may appear amusing to others, as it did to us. I shall give it, as nearly as I can, in his own words.

" 'I have now,' said he, 'been forty-two years in this country. For twenty-four I was a light canoe-man; I required but little sleep, but sometimes got less than I required. No portage was too long for me; all portages were alike. My end of the canoe never touched the ground till I saw the end of it. Fifty songs a day were nothing to me. I could carry, paddle, walk, and sing with any man I ever saw. During that period, I saved the lives of ten Bourgeois, and was always the favourite, because when others stopped to carry at a bad step, and lost time, I pushed on—over rapids, over cascades, over chutes; all were the same to me. No water, no weather, ever stopped the paddle or the song. I had twelve wives in the country; and was once possessed of fifty horses, and six running dogs, trimmed in the first style. I was then like a Bourgeois, rich and happy: no Bourgeois had better-dressed wives than I; no Indian chief finer horses; no white man better-harnessed or swifter dogs. I beat all Indians at the race, and no white man ever passed me in the chase. I wanted for nothing; and I spent all my earnings in the enjoyment of pleasure. Five hundred pounds, twice told, have passed through my hands; although now I have not a spare shirt to my back, nor a penny to buy one. Yet, were I young again, I should glory in commencing the same career again, I would willing spend another half-century in the same fields of enjoyment. There is no life so happy as a voyageur's life; none so independent; no place where a man enjoys so much variety and freedom as in the Indian country. Huzza! Huzza! pour le pays sauvage!' " Clearly Baker in the opening quotation of this volume had this passage in mind.

Despite these voyageurs' protestations of expertness in handling a boat, the sequence of events proved them very awkward and incompetent. Indeed, says Ross, they were as awkward in managing a boat as they were adroit in handling a canoe. A storm arose on Lake Winnipeg which nearly ended the careers of all in the boat. "They lost all presence of mind, and in their confusion, let go the sail!" says Ross of his companions. "Those men who had but a short time before boasted so much of their skill and prowess among lakes, now abandoned their posts and began to count their beads and cross themselves: only one man stood at his duty; yet Providence favoured us, and we reached the island in safety." It took another storm, however, to teach the voyageurs that *traverses* made in boats in fine weather were one thing, and in foul weather quite another. Thereafter they were content to take the more tedious but safer route along the shore. In so doing they passed a small island on which "a fine tall pine, trimmed into a maypole, with its broom head, was conspicuous at a distance." One of the men pointed to it, remarking, "That's a lop-stick I trimmed eighteen years ago."

En route the men showed some of their characteristic traits. One of these was building air castles for the future. When it became obvious that they had been saved from a great peril, they became gay and voluble. The next evening at the encampment "they passed the evening cracking their jokes and forming new plans and projects for enjoying life in Red River. One observed, 'I will have my house built with double rooms'; another, 'I will have my rooms ceiled and painted.' It was really amusing to hear men without a shilling in the world enjoying life in their airy dreams, where nothing was real."

One of the stories told that evening related to a trip taken by the narrator from Fort Alexander to Jack River a few years before. A fearful storm arose, and it seemed almost impossible to reach the nearest shore. "Some baled out the water, while others kept a sharp look-out, which amounted to nothing; for except the lightning flashed, no one could see another in the boat, and we every moment fancied we heard the rush of waves dashing on the rocks ahead of us. Some said they saw the rocks, and called to prepare for the danger: death stared us in the face." Then an unusual phenomenon occurred. "In the midst of this confusion a . . . meteor of fire, resembling a lighted candle, settled on the left end of the yard-arm. Supposing it to have been fire communicated by the lightening, we secured our guns under the covering; this done, another light settled on the right end of the yard, and immediately afterwards another showed itself on the top of the mast. The lights were rather pale, and of a reddish hue. All the three continued bright and steady for more than half an hour, without shifting. . . . At length they dropped off and disappeared." Of course the voyageurs were terrified. Soon, however, they were aware of bushes and realized they were safe near some shore away from the fury of the storm. Then, in characteristic fashion, they set about linking the fires with their deliverance. "Some said it was two of the Apostles, Peter and Paul, guarding the Virgin Mary; others, that the appearance was ominous, and presaged that three of us would be drowned; while some said that only three out of the nine who were in the boat would survive the storm. We then knelt down, took our rosaries, and ran over our Ave-Marias and Pater-nosters; praying, some to one saint, some to another: I prayed to the Virgin Mary. This done, we made a solemn vow, that if we lived to see a priest we would have a grand mass offered up as a thanksgiving to the Virgin Mary for our miraculous deliverance." Ross goes on to remark that these vows, so often made by voyageurs in moments of peril, were always religiously observed.

For years the dusky families of the voyageurs, inhabitants of the posts, had been regarded as an ever-increasing menace to the Hudson's Bay and Northwest companies. Now they were collected at Red River and formed a nation no less picturesque than, though notably different from, their French-Canadian fathers. They were known as *gens libre* ("freemen"), as *métis*, and as *bois brulés*. From their ranks in future years the Hudson's Bay Company was to recruit its canoe- and boatmen, who

proved no less fitted for their work than their fathers be-
for them. Instead of being hired by the year, however,
the half-breeds were usually engaged for specific journeys
or to carry the freight to the distant posts by contract lot.
They were characterized by the same light-heartedness
and the same lack of responsibility that had endeared
their fathers to all who traveled with them. From their
mothers they inherited a love of the buffalo chase. Their
journeys onto the Dakota plains to hunt the buffalo have
been described many times.

Major Samuel Woods, who was sent by the Secretary
of War in 1849 to inspect the valley of the Red River
of the North preparatory to establishing a military post
there, found these half-breeds worthy of several pages
of his report on the expedition. "The greater part of
these people," he writes, "are descendants of the Canadian French. They speak the French language, are nearly
all Catholics, with mild and gentle manners, great vivacity, generous and honest in their transactions, and
disposed to be a civil and orderly community. They are
hale and hearty, robust men, evidently accustomed to
hardships and exposure, to which they submit cheerfully. . . . They now devote themselves entirely to fur
hunting and the chase. . . . They go to the plains in
the Spring and Fall, in parties of from 300 to 500
hunters. They appoint, before going out, a captain who
controls and directs their hunts, which assume rather
the character of an expedition than the unregulated ex-
cursions of Indians or whites when abroad with such
objects. Their families go with them, and each family
has from one to ten carts."

Accompanying his report is a letter from the Reverend Georges Antoine Belcourt, a French-Canadian priest who labored for years among the Red River *métis*. It describes in great detail the manner in which one of these chases was conducted. Belcourt accompanied the hunters and their families and watched how they formed their 213 carts into three long columns, one of ox-drawn vehicles, the other two of *charrettes* drawn by horses. These carts, a Red River product, were made entirely of wood and rent the air with the squeaks of their ungreased axles as they moved out onto the prairies. At night they were formed into a corral and served as protection against the Indians.

When scouts reported that herds had been sighted, cries of *"la vache, la vache!"* were heard through the encampment, and riders mounted and departed "beaming with the keenest joy," as Belcourt writes in French words that sparkle in remembrance of that lively scene. But no words can describe adequately the confusion and danger when the herd was charged by the hunters. These, on horses trained to respond to the slightest pressure or even to pursue the buffalo without guidance, came up with streaming sashes and mouths full of shot, and fired round after round from their awkward guns. No one but a *métis*, or perhaps an Indian, could have used these weapons with such speed and accuracy while charging at full tilt. Then came the work of cutting up the slaughtered animals, the selection of only the finer portions, and the transportation to the encampment. There the women took charge of the work of drying, pounding, and otherwise preparing the meat for future use. After weeks of this nomadic life the train wound its slow way back to Pembina laden with the remains of 1,776 *vaches*, that is to say, 228 *taureaux*, or leather bags of pemmican; 1,213 rolls of dried meat; 166 *boskoyas*, or bags of grease; and 556 bladders of marrow grease.[35]

Though at first entirely unlettered and pagan, these *métis* were soon supplied with schools and priests. As in the case of St. Peter's, voyageurs and their religious needs called the attention of the Church to this region far beyond her most distant outpost. On April 4, 1816, Lord Selkirk wrote the following in a letter to the Bishop of Quebec: [36]

"I have been informed by Mr. McDonell, late governor of the settlement on Red River that he had some Conversation with your Lordship last autumn, to recommend that a missionary should be sent into that country, to give spiritual aid to a great number of Canadians who have established themselves there, & who lead a wandering life in the manner of the savages, with whose women they have formed irregular connections. . . . I have been lately informed . . . that your Lordship has it in contemplation to send two ecclesiastics this summer to pay a visit to Lake Superior & Lake La Pluie [Rainy Lake] during the season when the voyageurs in the service of the North West Company resort there from the interior. As these people also are very much in want of wholesome advice, I am happy to hear of such a plan being in agitation . . . but on the other hand, a Missionary sent from Canada on a summer visit to these posts, would have no intercourse with the great body of the vagabond Canadians, to whom I have alluded, who are not in the service of the North West nor any other company, & who having renounced all idea of returning to their native places are more particularly in want of spiritual aid. . . . Mr. McDonell is to set out as soon as the ice will permit, in a light canoe, with which he expects to reach Red River about the end of May, or in the very beginning of June. He would be happy to have the company of the Missionary, who would thus have an opportunity of being for several weeks among the wandering Canadians of Red River before the period when any great number of the Northwest Company's voyageurs can be expected at Lake La Pluie or Lake Superior."

Some say that it was a voyageur, Jean Baptiste Lagimonière, who won the Earl's interest in sending missionaries to the settlement. This maternal grandfather of Louis Riel was born at Maskinongé. After some experience as a voyageur in the Northwest, he, unlike most of his fellows, returned to Canada for a bride. Their child, born in 1808 at Pembina, was probably the second (and the first legitimate) white child born on the banks of the Red River. In 1815, when the little colony was suffering from the horrors of warfare, a courier was needed to carry dispatches to Lord Selkirk, who had just arrived in the East on his first visit to his colony. An experienced and responsible man was needed, one who would make the trip in the shortest possible time and evade all efforts of the opposition to intercept his messages. For this hazardous undertaking Lagimonière was chosen.[37]

For years voyageurs had been used to carry the mail from the interior posts to Canada, and from one post to another. Probably Lagimonière had come to the attention of his superiors as expressman. Roderick Mackenzie tells us that "the first winter Express from the Interior for the Lake Superior, which was in 1798, left Fort Chipewean on the 1st Octr and arrived at the Sault St. Marie's on the 17th May following—229 days." Even more famous was the "Inland Packet."[38] These were perilous and lonely enterprises. Storms must be braved, nights must be spent in the open when spirit thermometers registered as low as sixty degrees below zero, hazardous rapids must be run, wild beasts must be warded off or killed, and Indians must be treated in just the way to ensure their friendship. Usually the messenger visited most of the posts, carrying mail to winterbound and lonesome *bourgeois* and *commis* and taking their replies, for which he waited. The importance of the dispatches must not be overlooked, for on them the chiefs of the trade based their calculations for the next year's operations. If great speed were necessary, the record of the first courier *could* be reduced by two-thirds. Thus in 1834, when Captain Back, the Arctic explorer who was searching for Captain Ross, wished to know the fate of his friend, a courier bearing news of Ross' safe arrival in England passed from Lake Superior to Fort Chipewyan in only seventy-four days.

Lagimonière's journey took him eighteen hundred miles from the colony in the dead of winter. Thirty-six days after his departure from Fort Douglas he handed over the precious dispatches to the Earl, having slipped by all the opposition's men. "The Scotch lord was so touched by this act of devotion that he could not help asking what favor he wished in return. 'Priests: give us priests,' said the humble Canadian. Then Selkirk asked Plessis." [39]

That summer Father Pierre Antoine Tabeau set forth. Though his instructions were to do as Lord Selkirk had suggested, he reached Rainy Lake just when the reports of the battle of Seven Oaks arrived and contented himself with a mission to the voyageurs there and at Fort William. His report of his summer's work did not favor the permanent mission at Red River that the bishop, as well as the Earl, wished to see established there. For his partiality to the known viewpoint of the Northwest Company, which saw a menace in anything permanent at Red River, he was soundly berated by his ordinary in a letter revealing much indignation.[40] In 1818 Father Joseph Norbert Provencher, accompanied by Father Sévère Dumoulin and a school teacher, William Edge, traveled the long canoe route with a body of voyageurs and arrived finally at Red River. On their journey they had ministered to the needs of several groups of voyageurs whom they had encountered.

The story of Father, later Bishop, Provencher and his several assistants at Red River is one of heroic self-sacrifice, discouragement, and final success. It was at "The Forks," as the junction of the Red and Assiniboine rivers was known locally, that Provencher worked, almost entirely with the Catholic voyageurs, their Indian or half-breed wives, and their children. Dumoulin and Edge and a number of their associates and successors labored at Pembina, a number of miles up the river and nearer the plains. This was a favorite gathering place for voyageurs and *métis* because of the nearness of the buffaloes. Among the Protestant colonists from Europe other clergymen worked, but they seldom attempted to interfere with the priests' work among the Canadians and half-breeds.

One of Bishop Provencher's hopes was to build a stone cathedral. Early in the thirties it became possible to erect this building. It is this church of which the poet Whittier sings in his well-known poem.

THE RED RIVER VOYAGEUR

Out and in the river is winding
    The links of its long, red chain,
Through belts of dusky pine-land
    And gusty leagues of plain.

Only, at times, a smoke-wreath
    With the drifting cloud-rack joins,—
The smoke of the hunting-lodges
    Of the wild Assiniboins!

Drearily blows the north-wind
    From the land of ice and snow;
The eyes that look are weary
    And heavy the hands that row.

And with one foot on the water,
    And one upon the shore,
The Angel of Shadow gives warning
    That day shall be no more.

Is it the clang of wild-geese?
    Is it the Indian's yell,
That lends to the voice of the north-wind
    The tones of a far-off bell?

The voyageur smiles as he listens
    To the sound that grows apace;
Well he knows the vesper ringing
    Of the bells of St. Boniface.

The bells of the Roman Mission,
That call from their turrets twain,
To the boatman on the river,
To the hunter on the plain!

For his mason, Provencher selected an erstwhile voyageur, Jean Baptiste Charbonneau. Since it is very seldom that a voyageur's life can be outlined throughout its entire course, for voyageurs were men without education or other means of leaving a record of their careers, it may be well to take this opportunity to tell the full life history of one member of the class whose record has been preserved.[41]

Charbonneau was born at Boucherville in the province of Quebec on December 25, 1795. His father, a simple farmer, was Joseph Charbonneau; his mother's maiden name was Marguerite Lamoureux. There were ten other children in the family. When Jean Baptiste was twelve years of age, he was apprenticed to a master mason in Montreal, and there he remained for four years. Then, the War of 1812 breaking out, he enlisted and fought in the engagement at Châteauguay. He also served on the River Raisin campaign and at Chambly. After the war he was discontented and dreamed of following in the footsteps of his grandfather, a voyageur. It was with Colin Robertson's famous brigade of voyageurs which left Montreal in the spring of 1815 to fight for the Hudson's Bay Company against their rivals that Jean Baptiste departed for the *pays d'en haut*. After the usual "march" he reached Lake Winnipeg, fifty days from Montreal. But he was not destined to remain with those whose business it was to resuscitate the colony and pro-

tect it from the Northwest Company. He was sent first
to Jack River. On this trip he was left on a peninsula
far from any post while his companions went on a day's
trip to another spot to trade with the Indians. He had
no firearms or other means of supplying himself with
food. After a little it became apparent that something
had happened to his comrades. Days passed. Famine and
its attendant calamities threatened what his fate might
be. Only by great good fortune did a canoe carrying
some *bourgeois* pass and discover him, almost dead with
hunger. He never learned the fate of his comrades. His
next assignment was to York Factory on Hudson Bay.
A month later he was sent to Isle-à-la-Crosse, in the heart
of the area so hotly contested at this time by the two companies. Most of the remainder of his service of many
years was spent at this post.

Since Charbonneau was not of the great stature and
force that were required for the battles fought between
the servants of the two companies, he was used as a
courier. This, however, was nearly as dangerous a service
as that of his comrades of more heroic proportions, for
it was to the advantage of the enemy to intercept messages and imprison and mistreat couriers of the opposition. Once he returned to his post to find it in the hands
of the enemy, who at once seized him and placed him
with the rest of the prisoners. But too much food and too
many guards were necessary to keep these prisoners, and
so they were removed to a desolate post, La Ronge, two
hundred miles distant. Here, on a large island in the lake,
the prisoners were left with only a few hatchets, fish-
hooks, and firearms. For them the outlook was not happy

when the little game and few hooks should be gone. Fortunately a truce was arranged between the two companies, and after two weeks canoes were sent to rescue them.

On one of his long journeys Charbonneau and his companion were visited in their encampment by an Indian who begged for powder. After a little had been given him, he opened his sack and proceeded to make a meal of the meat it contained. It did not take the two whites long to see that it was human flesh. Nor was the realization long in reaching them that with the powder they had given him they were more or less in his power. Next morning, after a sleepless night, they slipped away before he awakened. He followed them for three days, trying to ambush them, but in the end they escaped to a post.

Like most voyageurs, Charbonneau had his experiences in blizzards on the prairies. Safety lay in remaining encamped. Once he lay three days in a blizzard waiting for a respite, while his dogs became more and more ravenous and he himself was almost without food. At another time his dogs gave out on a long trip, and he and his companions were obliged to harness themselves to the sled and drag it for three weeks across the wilderness.

After fifteen years of this life he had a great desire to settle at Red River, especially since he had not seen a priest in all this time and many things lay sore on his conscience. He settled in the little village of St. Boniface and began to cultivate his land. But this was not the life for him, and so, in 1832, he became Provencher's mason for building the cathedral. Of a somewhat explosive and very proud nature, he resented the tall Bishop's efforts to aid his small mason. Once he lost his temper completely and offered to fight when the Bishop made some pleasantry on the subject.

Red River did not hold him long. Like so many of his fellows, he trekked to Minnesota. Here he lived as best he could and where he could, as hunter, fisher, and even as mail-carrier. When the great uprising of the Sioux occurred in 1862, it found him at the mouth of the Redwood River, on the upper waters of the Minnesota River. He and a companion were overtaken by the Sioux as they attempted to escape and were taken prisoners. He was thus a witness of the fiendish work of the savages in massacring the settlers. When General Henry H. Sibley's army arrived and effected the release of the prisoners, Charbonneau returned to St. Boniface to spend the evening of his life. In 1865 he became blind. He died in 1883 at the age of eighty-eight years.

It was characteristic of the voyageurs that they kept their respect for the Church and its ministers even when their work took them into regions where its priests were unknown and where they disobeyed nearly every rule of conduct inculcated by it. Sometimes it happened that a priest traveled part of the long canoe route with a brigade of canoes. In 1821 Father Tabeau, who has already been mentioned, accompanied the brigade that conveyed Dr. Bigsby, the physician and secretary to the British commissioners appointed under the convention of 1818 to survey the boundary between the United States and Canada from Grand Portage to Lake of the Woods. Dr. Bigsby relates how the good father, "a stout, rosy, happy-looking priest of middle age, of unaffected and even polished manners, fond of music, and reasonably so of good living," greeted each voyageur as the brigade started off, having a pleasant word for each.[42] "As soon as we were well settled down in our places, and the canoe began to feel the paddles, Mr. Tabeau, by way of asking a blessing on the voyage, pulled off his hat, and sounded forth a Latin invocation to the Deity, and to a long train of male and female saints, in a loud and full voice, while all the men, at the end of each versicle, made response, 'Qu'il me bénisse.' "

Of course, the priest held a service on Sundays. The description Dr. Bigsby gives of one such gathering affords no little insight into the fundamentals of the voyageur's character. "It being Sunday, Mr. Tabeau had the tent set up; and he dressed an altar within it with crucifix and candles, little pictures, and clean linen cloth. With his singing-boy and bell he performed a religious service, all the *voyageurs* kneeling round the tent door with great seriousness." With this seriousness was mixed a half-superstitious awe. This explains the voyageurs' respect for Latin, "it being the only language the Devil does not understand and cannot learn," according to David Thompson, a renowned trader, geographer, and explorer of the region west of Hudson Bay and Lake Superior.

*   *   *

In all these voyageur hamlets a charming, Arcadian simplicity prevailed. There was time for friendliness, politeness, the trinket or ribbon that added a note of picturesqueness to the attire, a simple faith, and a childlike objectivity. The background of this Norman stock had not prepared them for more endeavor than the immediate

present demanded. Hence they kept the friendship of the
Indians by taking only the land needed for poorly-kept
gardens which American settlers derided. They accepted
the Indian at his own valuation, which was not low,
whereas the American frontiersman could scarcely find
words for his contempt of what he considered a thieving,
shiftless, dirty race. They had no social ambitions and
accepted as a matter of course the superior standing of
their traders. Their magistrates and their priests were
all worthy of respect and homage in their eyes. It sometimes happened that their traders were scoundrels and
their magistrates ignorant, but who were simple voyageurs to judge of men of such quality?

Many stories are told of one French-Canadian justice
at Green Bay, Charles Reaume.[43] In this voyageur community he held an enviable position, though he could
read and write but little. Acting under the laws of the
territory of Indiana, he nevertheless administered the
coutume de Paris, as a good descendant of Norman for-
bears should. Many a voyageur was told peremptorily
by this arbitrary lawmaker to obey his *bourgeois* in all
cases whatsoever. Before him came one day Boisvert and
Crely. Reaume listened to the plaintiff and to the de-
fendant, then rose in all the majesty of the law to pro-
nounce judgement: "You are both wrong. You, Boisvert,
you bring me one load of hay, and you, Crely, you bring
me one load of wood; and now the matter is settled."
Where but among voyageurs could such a justice long be
held in awe?

Reaume, like other justices in the fur country, found
himself faced again and again with the problem of fron-

tier marriage and divorce. Since priests were seldom if ever seen in these early settlements, men and women lived together without formal marriage. When married under the provisions of the *coutume de Paris*, they were often divorced. Of course, the enormity of their sins was brought forcibly to their attention when a priest *did* come. Thus in 1817 a Catholic priest from St. Louis appeared at the voyageur hamlet of Prairie du Chien and disturbed many domestic arrangements. He found several women living with men other than their husbands, and these he required to return to their former mates. Likewise at the Red River Settlement, Provencher, Dumoulin, and others of the earliest priests were scandalized at the matrimonial arrangements in vogue among the voyageurs. But respect for the orders of the Church was ingrained in the voyageur, and accordingly resident priests seldom had to reprove their flock on this score. As long as a guide in morals was at hand, all went well; it was in his prolonged absence that the voyageur lapsed from grace.

Much more might be written of these three typical voyageur settlements, but it would be mainly but an elaboration of what has already been given. Stress has been laid on this colonizing aspect of the voyageurs because many western towns, even Sault Ste. Marie, St. Paul, and Winnipeg, do not appear to appreciate the rôle played by the voyageurs in locating and beginning them.

IX

THE VOYAGEUR AS EXPLORER

IX

PROBABLY the greatest contribution of the voyageur to the development of the continent was the knowledge of the wilderness and its ways that he put freely and with no hope of recognition at the disposal of the great explorers of the West and North. It may be said without fear of gainsay that practically every exploring trip in western Canada after the British conquest made use of voyageurs. The exact proportion of the success of those ventures that was due to them cannot be gauged, but it was great.

Voyageurs were useful in exploration even during the French period. Mention has been made of Radisson's recognition of them. La Vérendrye, Lahontan, Le Sueur, Du Lhut, St. Pierre, Perrot, La Salle, Nicolet, and others must have found them indispensable, since they are mentioned so freely in contemporary documents.

The first explorer of note after the conquest was Alexander Henry. His narrow escape from the general massacre at Mackinac during Pontiac's uprising, his captivity and trading adventures during the next years on Lake Superior, and finally his advance into western Canada by the well-marked route *via* Grand Portage are all described in his book of travels. Now and then he mentions his voyageurs, who must have been his guides, since this was *terra incognita* to him; but his remarks are not sufficient to enable us to gain any real knowledge of their services to him. In one brief passage he pauses in his narrative long enough to pay tribute to his subordinates: "And often, notwithstanding every exertion, the men went supperless to bed. In a situation like this the Canadians are the best men in the world; they rarely murmur at their lot, and their obedience is yielded cheerfully." [1]

Another early explorer was the Massachusetts Yankee, Jonathan Carver. Long maligned, because his plagiarisms ended in casting doubts on the authenticity of any part of his *Narrative,* he has come into his own since the discovery of his diary and the narrative based on it. These are now in the British Museum. We know from them and other documents that he was advance agent and draftsman of a party attempting to find the "Ouragan" River and a waterway to the Pacific in 1766 and 1767. Though his writings mention voyageurs, especially one who accompanied him from Prairie du Chien to the St. Peter's River, again the evidence is too slight to form any estimate of the servant's contribution to the success of his master's journey.

More unique and of more significance because of his explorations was another Yankee, Peter Pond. His description of voyageurs' customs has been given in part in an earlier chapter. His map of the Athabasca region and its environs, prepared, it is said, for the Empress of Russia, was admittedly drawn in part from the accounts of voyageurs. Since this map and Pond's accounts influenced Alexander Mackenzie to his two great exploring trips in the Northwest, the region especially mapped from the voyageurs' accounts, and because of the reputed use of this map by Benjamin Franklin and others in making the treaty of 1783, it is obvious that North America owes much to a number of unknown voyageurs.

Sir Alexander Mackenzie devotes a good deal of space to his voyageurs in the narrative of his explorations of 1789 and 1793. The naming of a mighty stream for him and a baronetcy were his rewards for these arduous adventures, but probably not one reader in a hundred remembers even the names of his voyageurs.

His first trip, down the Mackenzie River, did not require so much of his voyageurs as the second. The perils and the labor of that voyage of exploration are almost unbelievable. Mackenzie himself refers in one of his journal entries to the "inexpressible toil these people had endured, as well as the dangers they had encountered." [2] It must be added that on several occasions only the leader's grim determination to go on held his people to their tasks.

After a winter spent in the mountains on Peace River, Mackenzie with his six voyageurs, Alexander Mackay, and two Indians started on May 9, 1793, in a small birch canoe, twenty-five feet long and so light that "two men could carry her on a good road three or four miles without resting." [3] Two of his men, Joseph Landry and Charles Ducette, had accompanied him on his earlier voyage. His steersman had been with him for five years in that capacity. The pride that he had in his men comes out in the statement: "I had imagined that the Canadians who accompanied me were the most expert canoe-men in the world." [4]

Up the Peace River and over the divide into a small

stream, a branch of the Fraser River, running toward the
Pacific, they journeyed. From the time they approached
the Fraser, hazards, hostility of Indians, toil beyond
words, discontent, desertions, and other embarrassments
faced the little party. On the small stream already mentioned an unusual accident occurred: [5]

"At an early hour of this morning the men began to
cut a road, in order to carry the canoe and lading beyond
the rapid; and by seven they were ready. That business
was soon effected, and the canoe reladen, to proceed with
the current which ran with great rapidity. In order to
lighten her, it was my intention to walk with some of
the people; but those in the boat with great earnestness
requested me to embark, declaring, at the same time,
that, if they perished, I should perish with them. I did
not then imagine in how short a period their apprehen-
sion would be justified. We accordingly pushed off, and
had proceeded but a very short way when the canoe
struck, and notwithstanding all our exertions, the violence of the current was so great as to drive her sideways
down the river, and break her by the first bar, when I
instantly jumped into the water, and the men followed
my example; but before we could set her straight, or stop
her, we came to deeper water, so that we were obliged to
re-embark with the utmost precipitation. One of the men
who was not sufficiently active, was left to get on shore
in the best manner in his power. We had hardly regained
our situations when we drove against a rock which shattered the stern of the canoe in such a manner, that it held
only by the gunwales, so that the steersman could no
longer keep his place. The violence of this stroke drove

us to the opposite side of the river, which is but narrow, when the bow met with the same fate as the stern. At this moment the foreman seized on some branches of a small tree in the hope of bringing up the canoe, but such was their elasticity that, in a manner not easily described, he was jerked on shore in an instant, and with a degree of violence that threatened his destruction. But we had no time to turn from our own situation to enquire what had befallen him; for, in a few moments, we came across a cascade which broke several large holes in the bottom of the canoe, and started all the bars, except one behind the scooping seat. If this accident, however, had not happened, the vessel must have been irretrievably over-set. The wreck becoming flat on the water, we all jumped out, while the steersman, who had been compelled to abandon his place, and had not recovered from his fright, called out to his companions to save themselves. My peremptory commands superseded the effects of his fear, and they all held fast to the wreck; to which fortunate resolution we owed our safety, as we should otherwise have been dashed against the rocks by the force of the water, or driven over the cascades. In this condition we were forced several hundred yards, and every yard on the verge of destruction; but, at length, we most fortunately arrived in shallow water and a small eddy, where we were enabled to make a stand, from the weight of the canoe resting on the stones, rather than from any exertions of our exhausted strength. For though our efforts were short, they were pushed to the utmost, as life or death depended on them.

"This alarming scene, with all its terrors and dangers,

occupied only a few minutes; and in the present suspension of it, we called to the people on shore to come to our assistance, and they immediately obeyed the summons. The foreman, however, was the first with us; he had escaped unhurt from the extraordinary jerk with which he was thrown out of the boat, and just as we were beginning to take our effects out of the water, he appeared to give us his assistance."

This accident had such a dampening effect on Mackenzie's men that he was obliged to remind them of their engagement to go with him to the end of his journey: [6] "I also urged the honour of conquering disasters, and the disgrace that would attend them on their return home, without having attained the object of the expedition. Nor did I fail to mention the courage and resolution which was the peculiar boast of the North men; and that I depended on them, at that moment, for the maintenance of their character." Appeals of this sort were seldom made in vain to Northmen, and Mackenzie soon had the satisfaction of promises to go wherever he might lead. Appeals to them were always more effective than threats.

The canoe, repaired again and again, and only passably with the substances at hand, became more and more crazy as the journey progressed. Portages became a serious matter,[7] "for the canoe was now become so heavy, from the additional quantity of bark and gum necessary to patch her up, that two men could not carry her more than an hundred yards, without being relieved; and as their way lay through deep mud, was rendered more difficult by the roots and prostrate trunks of trees, they were every moment in danger of falling; and beneath

such a weight, one false step might have been attended
with fatal consequences."

Indians were encountered here and there, most of
whom had never before seen a white man. Cajolery,
threats, medicine, and apparent magic were expedients to
which Mackenzie had to have recourse at times with these
simple people. His men seem to have established amica-
ble relations in a more effective fashion and one which
was common with them throughout the Indian country:[8]
"When the dawn appeared I had already quitted my bed,
and was waiting with impatience for another conference
with the natives. The sun, however, had risen before
they left their leafy bowers, whither they had retired
with their children, having most hospitably resigned their
beds, and the partners of them, to the solicitations of my
young men."

The large river on the west of the mountain ridge was
entered with "inexpressible satisfaction." On the second
day on this stream rapids were encountered which were
deemed too boisterous for the canoe. Accordingly a portage had to be made. Of this task the leader writes: "The
labour and fatigue of this undertaking, from eight till
twelve, beggars all description . . . we at length conquered this afflicting passage, of about half a mile, over
a rocky and most rugged hill." [9]

The next rapids were also dangerous, and Mackenzie
ordered a portage, "but she was now become so heavy
that the men preferred running the rapid to the carrying
her overland. . . . Four of them undertook this hazardous expedition, and I hastened to the foot of the rapid
with great anxiety, to wait the event, which turned out

as I expected." [10] In other words, the canoe was wrecked, and the men "in an half-drowned condition arrived safe on shore." Three hours were required to mend the canoe and add even more to its already great weight. Indians were now encountered who were very hostile and suspicious at first and who later gave most discouraging accounts of the navigation and other Indians lower down. Such reports, acting on the lively imaginations of the voyageurs, filled them with dismay, and they began to evidence extreme discontent. Their leader, convinced now that he was not on a river which emptied "into the ocean to the North of what is called the river of the West," and realizing that though he might overcome the tremendous difficulties of navigation on the downward trip he would still have to return *against* them and the mighty current, resolved to go overland: "I now called those of my people about me, who had not been present at my consultation with the natives; and after passing a warm eulogium on their fortitude, patience, and perseverance, I stated the difficulties that threatened our continuing to navigate the river, the length of time it would require, and the scanty provision we had for such a voyage: I then proceeded for the foregoing reasons to propose a shorter route, by trying the overland road to the sea. . . . This proposition met with the most zealous return, and they unanimously assured me, that they were as willing now as they had ever been, to abide by my resolutions, whatever they might be, and to follow me wherever I should go." [11]

The retrograde movement that was necessary to take them to the beginning of the overland route, however, excited the fears of the Indians, and considerable trouble was experienced. "This alarm among the natives was a very unexpected as well as perilous event, and my powers of conjecture were exhausted in searching for the cause of it. A general panic seized all around me, and any further prosecution of the voyage was now considered by them as altogether hopeless and impracticable." [12] Mackenzie, however, held them to their course. "Throughout the whole of this day the men had been in a state of extreme ill-humour, and as they did not choose openly to vent it upon me, they disputed and quarreled among themselves. About sun-set the canoe struck upon the stump of a tree, which broke a large hole in her bottom; a circumstance that gave them an opportunity to let loose their discontents without reserve." [13] Next day it was evident that a new canoe must be constructed, and a halt was made at an appropriate place. Parties were sent out, some to get wood, some *wattape*, and others gum. Bark had been obtained a number of days earlier. There in the wilderness, thousands of miles from white habitations, this little band of voyageurs constructed a totally new craft. What other vehicle could have been so constructed, without nails or other substances than what the forests afforded? Four days later all was ready. "She proved a stronger and better boat than the old one, though had it not been for the gum obtained from the latter, it would have been a matter of great difficulty to have procured a sufficiency of that article to have prevented her from leaking." [14]

Soon the bad rapid where misfortune had met the party on its way down was reached. This time a curious and very hazardous manner of getting by the obstruction was devised. "Two of the men . . . [took] the line, which was seventy fathoms in length, with a small roll of bark, and . . . [climbed] up the rocks, from whence they . . . [descended] on the other side of that which opposed our progress; they then . . . [fastened] the end of the line to the roll of bark, which the current . . . [brought] to us; this being effected, they . . . [drew] us up . . . though to get to the water's edge above, the men were obliged to let themselves down with the line, run round a tree, from the summit of the rock." [15]

Now the party struck westward, up a smaller stream. Soon they had to leave their canoe, cache their goods, and go forward on foot, each man carrying about ninety pounds besides his gun and some ammunition. For several days they traveled, meeting Indians, sleeping in their encampments, climbing mountains, and descending into valleys. Finally, "before us appeared a stupendous mountain, whose snow-clad summit was lost in the clouds; between it and our immediate course, flowed the river to which we were going." [16]

Here two canoes and seven natives took them down the river. In a few days the mouth of the stream and the sea came into sight. The great feat had been accomplished: North America had been crossed in northern latitudes from coast to coast for the first time.

On the return trip more Indian hostility was encountered, and part of the voyageurs refused to go on by water. So the party divided for a time, some going by land and the remainder in a canoe. The land party had its misfortunes, too, for one of the men was attacked by a female bear with two cubs. The opportune arrival of one of his mates, who shot the old bear, saved him, however. After great labor and many frights the divide was surmounted, and the cached provisions and the canoe were found intact. "We now pitched our tent, and made a blazing fire, and I treated myself, as well as the people, with a dram; but we had been so long without tasting any spirituous liquor, that we had lost all relish for it." [17] On August 17 they "began to glide along with the current of Peace River," and at four o'clock in the afternoon of August 24, they arrived at the Fort they had left on the ninth of May. "The men were in such spirits, and made such an active use of their paddles, that we arrived before the two men whom we left here in the spring, could recover their senses to answer us," is the entry in the leader's diary for a day long to be remembered by all of the group.[18]

*   *   *

Other thrilling adventures of an explorer of the first rank were those of Simon Fraser. His name still attaches to the river he explored in 1808 at the greatest hazard to himself, his nineteen voyageurs, and four other companions. For three or four years prior to this exploit he had been making reconnaissances in the far Northwest for his partners of the Northwest Company. This was practically an unknown country, and to Fraser goes the credit of having opened it to trade. In the autumn of 1807, Fraser, at Fort New Caledonia, about 55 degrees north latitude, received instructions from his company to descend the *"Grande Rivière"* then known by its Indian name, *Tacoutché Tesse*, and believed to be the Columbia

River. Lewis and Clarke's expedition had roused the Northwest Company to a sense of its danger from American competition in a region whose ownership was contested. Hence Fraser's mission was to explore and hold it for the British Crown.

In May, 1808, Fraser, accompanied by John Stuart, Jules-Maurice Quesnel, nineteen voyageurs, and two Indians, embarked in four canoes on a trip whose dangers could not have been foreseen at the start.[19] The upper stretches of the river, where Mackenzie had already explored, were passed without trouble. On June 1, however, the voyageurs had a foretaste of the experiences that were to be theirs almost continuously for many days. A narrow channel between high rocks forced the water through at terrific speed and with deafening noise. "Nevertheless, since it was considered as next to impossible to carry the canoes across the land on account of the height and steepness of the hills, it was resolved to venture them down this dangerous pass." As a test, one canoe manned by "the five best men out of the crews" was sent down. "Flying from one danger to another until the last cascade but one" was reached, the canoe at that point was wrecked on a low, projecting rock. Happily the men were able to save both themselves and their freight but found themselves stranded in a deep gorge. There was but one recourse. Steps were cut in the steep bank, and a line was fastened to the end of the canoe. Some of the voyageurs ascended with the line while others remained to push the canoe. Inch by inch the precious craft was lifted. "Our situation was most precarious; our lives hung, as it were, upon a thread, as the failure of the line or a false step of one of the men might have hurled the whole of us into Eternity." Before dark that night the top was reached.

Three days later another rapid nearly cost the lives of the party. "The nature of our situation . . . left us no choice, we were under the necessity, either of running down the canoes, or of abandoning them; we therefore unloaded and provided each of them with five men." It was a desperate undertaking. Between their efforts to keep away from the whirlpools on one hand and the rocks on the other the men nearly exhausted their strength. But again they were victorious. When bringing the baggage by land around this rapid, one of these men found himself in a perilous predicament. The voyageurs, carrying their heavy burdens, were "obliged to pass on a declivity which formed the border of a huge precipice, on loose stones and gravel which constantly gave way under their feet." One of them lost his way and with a large package on his back "got so engaged among the rocks that he could neither move forward nor backward, nor yet unload himself, without imminent danger." Finally the leader of the party himself crawled to the poor wretch's assistance and by cutting the load loose and allowing it to be lost over the precipice saved his canoeman's life.

Other challenges to the strength and coolness of the men followed now in quick succession till navigation finally had to be given up in favor of overland journeying. The leader of the expedition describes the worst of these dangers, the famous *rapide couvert*, where the channel of the great river contracts to about forty yards and is nearly enclosed by overhanging walls of stone: [20]

"Once engaged, the die was cast, our great difficulty consisted in keeping the canoes within the medium, or *fil
d'eau*, that is, clear of the precipice on one side and from
the gulfs formed by the waves on the other. Thus skim-
ming along as fast as lightning, the crews, cool and determined, followed each other in awful silence, and when
we arrived at the end, we stood gazing at each other in
silent congratulation at our narrow escape from total
destruction."

The Indians for most of the way were friendly, though
very curious. Since most of them had never encountered
white men before and were totally unacquainted with
firearms, they were probably more overawed than genu-
inely friendly. Once, when a curious Indian took the
interpreter's gun, one of the voyageurs saved the situation
by knocking up the muzzle, which was aimed directly at
some of the Indians, when the would-be investigator
pulled the trigger. To have killed a native, however acci-
dentally, would have brought down on the little party the
wrath of all the Indians. The men had to be eternally
vigilant, standing guard at night, keeping the natives
from the luggage, and yet convincing them of the friendliness of the whites.

After the canoes had been abandoned, Indian trails
were followed over the precipices. Native guides were
employed who, monkey-fashion, climbed easily the twig
ladders that formed the way up the faces of precipices
and over yawning chasms. Trained as they were to face
danger, the voyageurs had all they could do to follow
their guides over these swaying bridges and up swinging
ladders. On the return trip they were obliged at times to

put their burdens on the shoulders of the Indians when descending by means of these ladders. When a voyageur yielded his gun to an Indian, it was indeed a hazardous trail.

The Indians on the lower river were not friendly, and the expedition started on their return trip without having actually been to the mouth. It was truly mortifying to the leader to be obliged to conclude that he had descended another stream than the Columbia. Yet his astronomical instruments showed him that he was nearly three degrees north of the mouth of that river and so had not accomplished what his company had desired. He did not realize, of course, that he had performed a more remarkable feat.

On the return trip the lower Indians became so menacing that the voyageurs refused to penetrate farther into their midst. Preferring even blistered feet and rocks that wore out a pair of moccasins a day, they showed how much their morale had been shattered by insisting upon abandoning the water route. Ordinarily a voyageur would face Death itself if thereby he saved himself a trip by land. Fraser and his friends had to remonstrate, cajole, and threaten. "After much debate on both sides, they yielded and we all shook hands, resolved not to separate during the voyage, which resolution was immediately confirmed by the following oath taken on the spot by each of the party. 'I solemnly swear before Almighty God that I shall sooner perish than forsake in distress any of our crew during the present voyage.'" Thereupon "all hands dressed in their best apparel and . . . decamped full of spirits, singing and making a great noise." [21] The Indians lost heart at so much confi-

241

dence and eventually dropped back, allowing the whites to proceed unmolested. In due time they arrived at the point whence they had started. The river is known by the name of the leader, but not all the credit should go to him. Without his voyageurs the trip was unthinkable.

*   *   *

Another famous explorer of the Northwest who has left an account of the services rendered by his voyageurs was Sir John Franklin, whose story is entitled, *Narrative of a Journey to the Shores of the Polar Sea in the Years 1819-20-21-22.* Leaving Fort Chipewyan on Lake Athabasca, he started for the mouth of the Coppermine River assisted by fifteen Canadian voyageurs, an Italian canoeman, an Englishman, a Norwegian trader, two interpreters, an Iroquois Indian, and an Indian woman. The start was not auspicious, because of shortage of food and ammunition. Nevertheless, it lacked none of that picturesqueness with which voyageurs always enveloped their departures and arrivals. "It was gratifying . . . to perceive," writes the leader, "that this scarcity of food did not depress the spirits of our Canadian companions, who cheerfully loaded their canoes, and embarked in high glee after they had received the customary dram. . . . The crews commenced a lively paddling song on quitting the shore, which was continued until we had lost sight of the houses." [22]

Franklin was interested in the voyageur class and studied them. In his *Narrative* he tells of attending their New Year's dance, so much in favor among the squaws, who were the men's partners; of their marriages and morals, or perhaps more accurately, their lack of morals;

of the terrible Methye Portage, which was twelve miles in length and much of it so steep that it was descended by sliding, the voyageurs guiding their sledges as best they could at amazing speed; of their cruelty to their dogs, whom they beat incessantly and on whom they vented "the most dreadful and disgusting imprecations"; and of nightly encampments, where the men "stretch out before the fire and pass the evening recounting their former feats in traveling."

It had been a task of some magnitude to assemble a sufficient number of voyageurs for this trip, for in the Northwest encounters with the Esquimaux had made the men very fearful of further intercourse. These were, therefore, picked men, and accordingly they demanded unusually high wages. Their names are typical: Joseph Peltier, Matthew Pelonquin (*alias* Crédit), Solomon Belanger, Joseph Benoit, Joseph Gagné, Pierre Dumas, Joseph Forcier, Ignace Perrault, François Samandré, Gabriel Beauparlant, Registe Vaillant, Jean Baptiste Parent, Jean Baptiste Belanger, Jean Baptiste Belleau, and Emanuel Cournoyée. There is the usual proportion of Jean Baptistes. One wonders at times how many Jean Baptistes were scattered over the Canadian and American West at any given time during the eighteenth and early nineteenth centuries.

The journey had not progressed far before the leader realized what some of his trials were to be. The meagerness of the diet made the Canadians, "who had been for some days past murmuring . . . and striving to get the whole of our little provision to consume at once," break out into open rebellion.[23] Franklin was obliged to "address them in the strongest manner on the danger of in-subordination," and to threaten with "the heaviest punishment . . . any that should persist in their re-fusal to go on, or in any other way attempt to retard the Expedition." He then explains his course to the reader: "I considered this decisive step necessary, having learned from the gentlemen, most intimately acquainted with the character of the Canadian voyageurs, that they in-variably try how far they can impose upon every new master, and that they will continue to be disobedient and intractable if they gain any ascendancy over him." But the Englishman's sense of justice required him to add: "I must admit, however, that the present hardships of our companions were of a kind which few could support without murmuring, and no one could witness without a sincere pity for their sufferings." That night, to show how far these men were creatures of the moment, a little food was secured; it "instantly revived the spirits of our com-panions, and they immediately forgot all their cares."

A halt was made for the winter, and a house, Fort Enterprise, was erected by the voyageurs under W. F. Wentzel's direction. "It was merely a log-building, fifty feet long, and twenty-four wide, divided into a hall, three bed rooms and a kitchen. The walls and roof were plastered with clay, the floors laid with planks rudely squared with the hatchet, and the windows closed with parchment of deer-skin. . . . Having filled our capa-cious clay-built chimney with fagots, we spent a cheerful evening before the invigorating blaze." At first every-one lived on the floor, but the voyageurs soon proved their versatility. "Our working party, who had shown such skill as house carpenters, soon proved themselves to be, with the same tools (the hatchet and crooked knife), excellent cabinet makers, and daily added a table, chair, or bedstead, to the comforts of our establishment. The crooked knife generally made of an old file, bent and tempered by heat, serves an Indian or Canadian voyager for plane, chisel, and auger. With it the snow-shoe and canoe-timbers are fashioned, the deals of their sledges reduced to the requisite thinness and polish, and their wooden bowls and spoons hollowed out." [24] Besides this home for the officers the voyageurs built a storehouse and a house for themselves.

An expedition of voyageurs had to be sent back to Fort Providence in the dead of winter for supplies. When they returned, they were greeted with great joy. "They had been twenty-one days on their march from Slave Lake, and the labour they underwent was sufficiently evidenced by their sledge-collars having worn out the shoulders of their coats." [25] They carried about 180 pounds apiece when they started. But alas, they were typical voyageurs. Much of the provisions and liquor had disappeared down their voracious gullets. "As they were pretty well aware that such a circumstance could not long be concealed from us," writes Franklin, "one of them came the next morning with an artful apology for their conduct. He stated, that as they knew it was my intention to treat them with a dram on the commencement of the new year, they had helped themselves to a small[!] quantity on that day, trusting to my goodness for forgiveness." [26]

From this hospitable winter home one of the officers,

George Back, set out on one of the most extraordinary trips on record for this northwest country. He went on snowshoes and was accompanied as far as Great Slave Lake by Mr. Wentzel, two Canadians, and two Indians and their wives. Just before reaching Fort Providence they came to a river which was not frozen even at the edges. So the voyageurs had to make a raft. On this all the party crossed, ankle deep in water, each with a pine branch for a paddle. At the fort, supplies could not be obtained, and the party determined to go on, being now composed of Back, Wentzel, Beauparlant, and two other Canadians. Now they had dogs and sledges. At Moose-Deer Island Fort it was determined, because of inadequate supplies, to go on to Fort Chipewyan. This time Back, his faithful Beauparlant, a half-breed, and dog-sleds composed the party. The traveling was hazardous and fatiguing. Along the rapids of one of the rivers, Beauparlant, though an old Nor'wester, complained bitterly of the cold, from which even he received frost-bites. But no sooner had he reached the upper part of the river than he found the change of the temperature so great that he vented his indignation against the heat. "*Mais c'est terrible*," said he, to be frozen and sunburnt in the same day. "The poor fellow," explains Franklin, "who had been a long time in the country, regarded it as the most severe punishment that could have been inflicted on him, and would willingly have given a part of his wages rather than this disgrace had happened; for there is a pride amongst 'Old Voyagers,' which makes them consider the state of being frost-bitten as effeminate, and only excusable in a 'Pork-eater.' " [27]

The astonishment of the men at Fort Chipewyan was great when this little party arrived from the great frozen North. After about five weeks at the fort they set out again with five sledges, four of which carried goods for Franklin's expedition. The outward route was followed substantially on the return, and on March 17, after nearly five months, Back and his party were back at Fort Enterprise after a walk of 1,104 miles on snowshoes, with "no other covering at night, in the woods, than a blanket and deer-skin, with the thermometer frequently at —40°, and once at —57°; and sometimes passing two or three days without tasting food." [28]

At Fort Enterprise the whole company, officers, voyageurs, and Indians, were amusing themselves sliding down the steep banks of the river and far out on the ice. It was uproarious fun and was encouraged by the officers to keep the men's minds off their scanty provisions. Games were also played, such as prison bars, of the sort with which the Canadians were wont to amuse themselves.

Then came the summer's rush to the shore of the frozen sea. Nothing more harrowing can be found in travel literature than the simple, restrained tale told by the officers of the end of this expedition. Food gave out, starvation and freezing took one after another, and insanity and murder finished the terrible work. Finally, when the outposts of civilization were reached, it was found that Hood, Beauparlant, Samandré, Peltier, J. B. Belanger, Perrault, Vaillant, and Crédit were dead, besides Michel, the Iroquois, and Fontano, the Italian canoeman. Possibly others were gone, for Cournoyée and Belleau are not mentioned among the survivors. As with most childlike natures, the harrowing circumstances in which they found themselves brought out the worst in the voyageurs. Thieving, lying, and shirking duties were recorded against them. Yet it is interesting to note that the only one to become so demoralized as to eat human flesh was the Indian, Michel.[29]

Most of these men become personalities to us as we read of them again and again in Franklin's account: Beauparlant, who had a horror of being thought a tenderfoot; Perrault, who saved his little store of food and distributed it when the others were starving; Solomon Belanger, considered the most trustworthy and conscientious of the lot, but who, under stress of starvation, proved otherwise, at least temporarily; and J. B. Belanger, who risked his life to hold a canoe in midstream in almost freezing water. These are a few of the men of the famous Franklin expedition.

*   *   *

Of quite another kind was a journey taken in 1828 by that famous traveler Sir George Simpson. As Governor of the Hudson's Bay Company from 1821 to 1860, he was accustomed to annual visitations of the corporation's far-flung domain. Before the days of railroads, automobiles, or airplanes he covered every year an area which would be considered great even for travelers of this day of easy and quick transportation. His canoes, his voyageurs, his dogs, his guides, and his horses were all of the best, and he was such an adept in the art of traveling that he literally sped from post to post with what seems, even today, incredible swiftness. George Bryce tells of hearing a story, current in the Red River country, of a stalwart voyageur in Simpson's canoe. Frenzied by the Governor's urging more speed, he seized his tormentor, who was small in stature, and dipped him in the lake to the accompaniment of an expressive French oath.[30]

Two light canoes carrying eighteen men, the Governor, a doctor, and Chief Factor Archibald McDonald, who kept a diary, composed the party of 1828. They left York Factory on Hudson Bay on July 12 with three cheers and a salute of seven guns from the fort and a paddling song from the voyageurs. The Governor's Scotch piper played a few strathspeys on the bagpipes as they advanced "on the line" up the river, low water necessitating this mode of travel. The diarist evidently found the Scotch music less appropriate for this labor than the men's paddling songs, for he remarked that it "as yet makes but a poor accordance with either the pole or the paddle." [31]

The crews of the two canoes soon began their usual rivalry, and the Governor's shot far ahead of the other and smaller craft. The crew of the latter argued that the vessel caused the difference. An exchange was thereupon effected, when, to the chagrin of the others, "the Governor's men with much ado, pushed the small canoe ahead." [32] Nevertheless, the winners conceded the superiority of the larger canoe, and the next day the Governor took two of the inferior crew and put two of his good hands in the smaller vessel.

A week's paddling and tracking brought them to the newly established Norway House. To make the impressive appearance that Simpson, not less than his voyageurs, loved, every man changed his clothes just before the fort was sighted, and the paddlers mounted new feathers. "As we wafted along under easy sail, . . . the Highland bagpipes in the Governor's canoe, was echoed by the bugle in mine!" writes McDonald. "Then these were laid aside, on nearer approach to port, to give free scope to the vocal organs of about eighteen Canadians (French) to chant one of those voyageur airs peculiar to them, and always so perfectly rendered. Our entry . . . was certainly more imposing than anything hitherto seen in this part of the Indian country." [33]

A boy who saw this impressive sight wrote his recollections of it in his old age. Standing by his Scotch trader father, who had just finished building the fine new Norway House, the boy noted the flag flying from "a tall Norway Pine shaft" on the "signal hill of rock," the skirl of the pipes with their "Campbell's are coming, hourray! hourray!" or some such "music of our mountain land," and then, "as a *cadenza* of soothing, gladdening, exquisite charm—the deep and soft and so joyously toned voices of those full throated *voyageurs*, timed with a stroke—so quick—of glittering paddle blade, singing with such heart their *'La Claire Fontaine'* or some such loved air of *their* native land." Then he saw "the Governor's canoe, with its grand high prow, rounded, and brightly painted," coming into view. "Never; never, had anything so grand and splendid, and delightful withal, been seen in those primitive wilds." [34]

Only one evening and part of the next morning could be spared for business and rest, and then the Lake Winnipeg journey was begun. The next day but one brought the party to the mouth of the Saskatchewan. Up this stream now they labored, and on to Cumberland House, which they reached on the 27th. Here more provisions were taken on board, and after a very brief stop they were off once more "with fair weather, and a touch up of a favorite song chorused by both canoes." [35] On August 4 they were at the fort of Isle à la Crosse, where they met two important traders who brought the returns of the Mackenzie River District of the Company. On the 7th they were on the dreaded Methye Portage, the great watershed of this region. Twelve miles of the hardest kind of physical labor were accomplished, with the aid of ten Indians who met them there, in a single day. By seven in the evening they had gone on their way to still another portage. It is consoling to read that the men were rewarded for their toil of that strenuous day with "two or three extra glasses of spirits" at the night's encampment and two hours' extra sleep in the morning.

On August 11 they reached one of the most important posts, Fort Chipewyan, just a month from Hudson Bay. Here the Governor conducted a great amount of business and had an audience with a large number of Indians. On the 14th they were under way again with as imposing a departure "as the firing of guns, heavy cheers from master and men on the rocks, and the waving of flags, and songs in abundance on our part could make it." The next day they entered Peace River, and on the 20th Fort Vermilion was reached. The preceding day's entry in the diary contains the following sentence which says much of what was happening among the canoemen: "In the course of the day the foreman of the second canoe was called to account for not keeping up with the other, which seems to have had the effect of spurring them on the remainder of the day." On the 27th another land-mark was reached, Fort Dunvegan, where the men were given a well-deserved rest. On September 2 the Rocky Mountains were reached—and a portage "about a mile of the worst road in Christendom." On the 5th they were all at the "upper end" of the portage, where the men repaired the canoes, washed and mended their shirts and trousers, and got almost an entire day for rest. On the 13th they left McLeod's Fort and their canoes, for the mountain divide made them useless, and continued over-land, pack on back. On the 17th, as they neared Fort St. James, they changed their clothes, "and every arrange-ment was made to arrive . . . in the most imposing manner . . . for the sake of the Indians. . . . Accord-ingly, when within about a thousand yards of the estab-lishment, descending a gentle hill, a gun was fired, the bugle sounded, and soon after, the piper commenced the celebrated march of the clans—'Si coma leum cogadh na shea.' . . . The guide, with the British ensign, led the van, followed by the band; then the Governor, on horse-back, supported behind by Doctor Hamlyn and myself on our chargers, two deep; twenty men, with their bur-dens, next formed the line; then one loaded horse, and lastly, Mr. McGillivray closed the rear." Here they took to canoes again on the 24th, and now their way lay down a branch of that Fraser River which an intrepid trader and his voyageurs had opened to the fur-traders just twenty years earlier. On the 27th the party was at Fort Alexandria. On the 4th of October, after a trip partly by canoe, partly by horse, Kamloops Fort was reached in the usual impressive manner. Here a boat took most of the group, and on October 8 a meeting with another contingent of the party was successfully made. "This meeting is rendered still more interesting, from the circumstance of both parties descending rivers that were never ran before and that were always considered next to impossible."

The most thrilling part of the trip is told very unemotionally in the entry for October 10. It was the leaping of Simpson's Falls, under overhanging cliffs in the narrowest gorge of Fraser River Canyon. First went the guide in his bark canoe. When he had whizzed down the current past rocks and eddies to safety, the boat followed, and, finally, the second canoe. On that same day at eight in the evening, Fort Langley, the end of the diarist's trip, was reached. Of the remainder of the Governor's trip, to the Columbia and back to York Factory, we do not have the same detailed account. He and his men had crossed the continent from Hudson Bay to the Pacific in almost exactly three months.

* * *

Another Arctic expedition made use of Canadian voyageurs, but not to the extent that Franklin's had done. This was the undertaking of Chief Factor Peter Warren Dease and Thomas Simpson in the years from 1836 to 1839. Simpson, the leading spirit of this enterprise, was a relative of the famous Governor of the Hudson's Bay Company, which sponsored this expedition. His account of the discoveries that his party made west and east of the farthest limits of Franklin's travels, which appeared posthumously in 1843, furnished information which enabled cartographers to map thereafter most of the outline of the northern shores of North America from Point Barrow in the west to Hudson Bay. Of the twelve men who left Fort Norman on the Mackenzie River in July, 1837, two were Canadians, one of whom, François Felix, had accompanied Franklin in 1826. To him Simpson, not given to admiration of his race, pays a tribute in the latter part of his work:[36] "Our excellent assistant Ritch was left this summer, as usual, in charge of Fort Confidence, assisted by Felix and Morrison, two men specially selected for this important duty, on account of their steady, industrious habits."

Apparently, too, Ritch's assistants in building winter quarters on Great Bear Lake (Fort Confidence) were mainly Canadians, if one may judge by their names—John Norquay, Laurent Cartier, and François Framond. "This most important duty" of erecting buildings and providing stores of fish and other provisions with which to supply the entire party when it should be reunited after the first summer's expeditions was of outstanding significance for the success of the enterprise. It is interesting, also, to note that in the crew picked for the dangerous descent of the Coppermine River the bowsman was Laurent Cartier.

Simpson does not have much to say of any of his subordinates, in contrast to the full-length pictures that Franklin has left of his men. Occasionally, however, we catch a glimpse of them, as, for instance, when some native vehicles were found of a craftmanship which surprised the party. The large sledge with side rails was pro-

nounced made "comme à Montreal" by "our Canadians."
This remark led Simpson to an enlightening comment on
voyageur personality: [37] "French vanity has lost nothing
of its point in the New World. The largest sort of ducks
in the interior are called 'Canards de France'; English
tan-leather shoes, 'Souliers François'; the whites in general, 'les François'; as all Europeans of old were Franks:
and one old guide, talking of the place whence the Company's merchandise came, took it for granted that it was
from 'la vieille France de Londres!' "

The author also pays his tribute to voyageur appetites,
which he thought unreasonable, for their work was
"physically less severe than the compulsory tracking on
the rivers of Russia and China." He describes the daily
ration of twelve pounds of venison or four or five whitefish allotted to each person at Fort Confidence. "Yet,"
says he, "there was one of them who complained he had
not enough, and did not scruple to help himself to an
additional supply whenever the opportunity offered: it
would have taken twenty pounds of animal food daily to
satisfy him. This man, Framond, being in other respects
a very indifferent servant, was discharged the following
year." [38]

The voyageurs were admittedly a witty race, yet few
of their witticisms have come down to us. We are
obliged to take the word of traders and explorers, as in
poor novels we have to accept on faith the same quality
in heroes and heroines. It is pleasant, therefore, to find a
concrete illustration of voyageur humor in Simpson's
Narrative. To understand it, however, we must have in
mind that most of these men came originally from the

vicinity of Montreal, which is situated on an island of the same name, and that the French word *taureau* ordinarily means "bull." With this explanation it is easy to understand how delighted Simpson was when the discovery of a *cache* of Sir George Back's supplies on Montreal Island in the far north enabled him to record the following incident: "The pemican, or 'taureau,' as the voyageurs call it, was literally *alive;* and it was wittily remarked, 'L'isle de Montreal sera bientôt peuplée de jeunes *taureaux'* " [39] ("Montreal Island will soon be stocked with young bulls").

Unlike Franklin's expedition, Simpson's travels were attended with only one casualty, and that a natural death. The leader himself was one of the most energetic of travelers and explorers and outdid all the others in mileage covered. When he took his long trips across the plains with his dog trains, did he realize, we wonder, his indebtedness to the men he understood so little and affected to condemn on so many scores? Did he ever think that the trails had been marked out, the ways learned, the dogs trained, the places named, and the best manner of withstanding winter's cold discovered by these selfsame humble voyageurs, despite their gluttony, their laziness, their boastfulness, and their filth? Probably not, for Simpson was still in the full flush of youth's judgment by appearances. Perhaps it was this very blindness and intolerance of other ways of living that caused his death at thirty-two at the hands of sons of this very class of men. The story of his mysterious death is as follows. He left the Red River Settlement for Fort Snelling in June, 1840, accompanied by quite a large party, mostly half-breeds. Finding the main body traveling too slowly to suit him, he and four men started ahead. On the 14th of June, so the survivors reported, he shot two of his men. Later he himself was found shot. No one seemed able or willing to tell what really happened. Some at the time believed he met his death at the hands of the half-breeds in retaliation for a severe chastisement he had given a half-breed at the Settlement a few years earlier.

*   *   *

It is impossible within the limits of a work of this scope to describe all the exploring trips and other important expeditions in Canada and western United States that made use of the services of voyageurs. The leaders of several of them have already been quoted in other chapters, as, for example, one of the boundary commissioners provided by the convention of 1818 between the United States and Great Britain, Long, Garry, McKenney, Kane, Kennicott, and Franklin. Among the others may be mentioned the overland Astorians like Robert Stuart, whose diary is soon to be published, and Ramsay Crooks; Lewis Cass, whose trip up the Great Lakes to the headwaters of the Mississippi in 1820 resulted in naming an important lake in Minnesota for him; Henry R. Schoolcraft, who in 1832 did what Cass had hoped to do, discover the source of the Mississippi; Joseph N. Nicollet, a French scientist, who with John C. Frémont explored the region between the Mississippi and the Missouri in the thirties and then published the first scientific map of that area; George Catlin, whose pictures of the Indian life of much of that same territory are so coveted today; Major John Pope, who explored the valley of the Red River of the North in 1849 whilst it was still a wild, unsettled territory; and scores of others like the bishops of Juliopolis and Montreal, the priests and other missionaries that went in numbers to the Indians after Calhoun proclaimed a new Indian policy for the United States in 1817, Lord Selkirk, great traders like Daniel Harmon and David Thompson, British sportsmen like Lord Milton and the Earl of Southesk, artists like Manton Marble and Frank B. Mayer, railroad promoters like James J. Hill and Lord Mount Royal, scientists like Captain J. H. Lefroy and Captain John Palliser, and even women sightseers like Mrs. Jameson. In short, everyone who traveled in the Northwest before the days of the railroad sooner or later used French-Canadian voyageurs or their half-breed descendants to paddle their canoes, drive their dogs, lead their packhorses, choose their routes, or guide their York boats. Their services in opening up the West are incalculable.

Besides aiding travelers by conducting them through the fur country, the voyageurs rendered the very useful service of naming nearly every topographical feature, bird, animal, insect, fish, and reptile that the eye of the wayfarer encountered. At first glance this service may not seem to be extraordinarily valuable, because, one may say, the traveler could easily have supplied his own terminology. A traveler, Radisson, who explored the West before voyageurs had labeled all objects that came within his ken obviously must have thought otherwise. Read his account of travels in the country around Lake Superior about the year 1660. Had we some way of identifying "ye great river that divides itself in 2," or "the first landing Isle," or a certain "little lake," south of Lake Superior, how joyfully we should welcome it! As it is, we must forever wonder just where his route took him.

It is enlightening and amusing to note the geographic names supplied by the voyageurs. To be sure, they merely translated many of them from the Indian names, but who among the white men knew enough of the natives' speech to translate them? Few traders could deal with the Indians except through an interpreter, usually a voyageur or half-breed. As a sample of voyageur nomenclature, let us follow a part of Sir John Richardson's route from Lachine to Lake Winnipeg and on to the Arctic Ocean in 1848. The following names of places, flora, and fauna are supplied in both French and English quite as a matter of course, as though it was to be expected that both should be known: [40]

Sturgeon River	*La Rivière Maligne*
(Actaea alba)	*la racine d'ours*
Birch lightening-place	*Demi-charge du bouleau*
Pine Portage	*Portage des Epinettes*
Half-Moon Lake	*Lac Mi-rond*
Pelican lightening-place	*Demi-charge de chetauque*
Frog Portage	*Portage de Traite*
(root of the Sium lineare)	*Queue de rat*
(non-edible " ")	*carotte de moreau*
Steep Bank Portage	*Portage des Ecores*
Thicket Portage	*Portage des Haliers*
Angle Rapid	*Rapide de l'Equerre*
Noisy Rapid	*Rapide Sonnant*
Deep River	*Rivière Creuse*
Rapid of the Tomb	*Le Cimetière*
Methy River	*La Loche*
mink	*foutreau* or *foutereau*

(pinus banksiana)	*cyprès*
Nurse Portage	*Portage de Bonne*
dogbane	*herbe à la puce*
Rocky Islands	*Isles des Pierres*
Great Balsam Fir Island	*La Grande Isle des Epinettes*
Portage of the Drowned	*Portage des Noyés*

Besides these he mentions many French terms for which there were, apparently, no English equivalents.

Many of the place names of the voyageurs have remained, either in their original form or corrupted, sometimes beyond recognition. Consider as examples the following place names in the state of Minnesota: Grand Portage, Grand Marais, Fond du Lac, St. Croix River, Mille Lacs Lake, Lac Qui Parle, Lake Traverse, Zumbrota River (a corruption of Rivière aux Embarras), and Cannon River (a corruption of Canot, or Canoe River). Or take these in Wisconsin: Prairie du Chien, Eau Claire, La Crosse, Racine, Trempealeau, and Little Chute. Or the following in Michigan: Presque Isle, Au Sable County, Traverse City, Detroit, Bois Blanc Island, Point Seul, Isle Royal, Isle Chapeau, Grossepoint, Grosse Isle, Au Train Bay, Bete Grise Bay, Grand Sable Lake, Parisienne Island, and Point aux Barques. Almost without exception these places owe their names to voyageurs. Behind most of these place names is a story, more frequently a distressing tale than a humorous one. It was the difficulty of voyaging that accounts for the frequency of *Traverse*, *Portage*, and *Embarras* on our maps today. Sometimes the memory of the naming of a spot has triumphed over time. Thus, Miette's Rock in western Canada was named for a calm-nerved voyageur who mounted to its summit, fifteen hundred feet above a yawning abyss, and sat there, his legs hanging over the edge, while he contemplated the scenery and smoked his pipe. Such daring always struck a responsive chord in the innermost being of other voyageurs. The matter of geographic names in the United States deserves more study than has ever been accorded it. For example, when shall we have a map of the voyageur's habitat, showing the French names for topographical features?

*　　*　　*

The passing of the voyageur was so gradual that no one noticed, much less lamented, his loss. A few writers like Taché and Dugas realized his significance for the history of North America. Most historians have not even comprehended the meaning of the term *voyageur.* If this book has succeeded in giving him his proper place in history, its purpose has been fulfilled. One poet of modern times has honored him with a poem which catches not a little of his jauntiness, *naïveté*, and young-heartedness: [41]

The Voyageur

Dere's somet'ing stirrin' ma blood tonight,
　On de night of de young new year,
W'ile de camp is warm an' de fire is bright,
　An' de bottle is close at han'—
Out on de reever de nort' win' blow,
　Down on de valley is pile de snow,
But w'at do we care so long we know
　We're safe on de log cabane?

Drink to de healt' of your wife an' girl,
　Anoder wan for your frien'
Den geev' me a chance, for on all de worl'
　I've not many frien' to spare—

261

THE VOYAGEUR

I'm born, w'ere de mountain scrape de sky,
An' bone of ma fader an' moder lie,
　So I fill de glass an' I raise it high
An' drink to de Voyageur.

For dis is de night of de jour de l'an,
　W'en de man of de Grand Nor' Wes'
T'ink of hees home on de St. Laurent,
　An' frien' he may never see—
Gone he is now, an' de beeg canoe
　No more you'll see wit' de red-shirt crew,
But long as he leev' he was alway true,
　So we'll drink to hees memory.

Ax' heem de nort' win' w'at he see
　Of de Voyageur long ago,
An' he'll say to you w'at he say to me,
　So lissen hees story well—
"I see de track of hees botte sau-vage
　On many a hill an' long portage
Far far away from hees own vill-age
　An' soun' of de parish bell—

"I never can play on de Hudson Bay
　Or mountain dat lie between
But I meet heem singin' hees lonely way
　De happies' man I know—
I cool hees face as he's sleepin' dere
　Under de star of de Red Rivière,
An' off on de home of de great w'ite bear,
　I'm seein' hees dog traineau.

"De woman an' chil'ren's runnin' out
　Of de wigwam of de Cree—
De leetle papoose dey laugh an' shout
　W'en de soun of hees voice dey hear—
De oldes' warrior of de Sioux
　Kill hese'f dancin' de w'ole night t'roo,
An de Blackfoot girl remember too
　De ole tam Voyageur.

262

"De blaze of hees camp on de snow I see,
  An' I lissen hees 'En Roulant'
On de lan' w'ere de reindeer travel free,
  Ringin' out strong an' clear—
Offen de grey wolf sit before
  De light is come from hees open door,
An' caribou foller along de shore
  De song of de Voyageur.

"If he only kip goin', de red ceinture,
  I'd see it upon de Pole
Some mornin' I'm startin' upon de tour
  For blowin' de worl' aroun'—
But w'erever he sail an' w'erever he ride,
  De trail is long an' de trail is wide,
An' city an' town on ev'ry side
  Can tell of hees campin' groun'."

So dat's de reason I drink tonight
  To de man of de Grand Nor' Wes',
For hees heart was young, an' hees heart was light
  So long as he's leevin' dere—
I'm proud of de sam' blood in my vein
  I'm a son of de Nort' Win wance again—
So we'll fill her up till de bottle's drain
  An' drink to de Voyageur.

WILLIAM HENRY DRUMMOND *

* From *The Voyageur and Other Poems,* by permission of the publishers, G. P. Putnam's Sons.

NOTES

vi. The quotation is from James H. Baker, "Lake Superior," *Minnesota Historical Collections*, 3:342.

I

FURS AND FUR-TRADERS

1. Abstracts of these licenses have been made and indexed for the period from 1768 to 1776. Consolidated returns of licenses cover the years from 1777 to 1790. These also have been indexed. A copy of the abstracts and index is filed with the Minnesota Historical Society, and other copies may be found in several libraries in Canada and the United States. For those interested in the licenses for the French period the following references will prove useful: E. Z. Massicotte, "Répertoire des Engagements pour l'Ouest Conservés dans les Archives Judiciaires de Montréal" in *Rapport de l'Archiviste de la Province de Québec, 1929-1930*, pp. 191-466; "Congés et Permis Déposés ou Enrégistrés à Montréal sous le Régime Français," in *Rapport de l'Archiviste de la Province de Québec, 1921-1922;* and "Les Congés de Traite sous le Régime Français au Canada," in *ibid.*, 1922-1923.

2. Since this paragraph was written, Harold A. Innis' *The Fur Trade in Canada* (New Haven, 1930) has appeared. It emphasizes a number of the points mentioned.

3. For further data on these companies see Gordon C. Davidson, *The Northwest Company*, which is Volume 7 of the *University of California Publications in History* (Berkeley, 1918); George Bryce, *Remarkable History of the Hudson's Bay Company*, 3d ed. (New York, 1910); Hiram M. Chittenden, *The American Fur Trade of the Far West*, three volumes (New York, 1902); and Grace Lee Nute, "The Papers of the American Fur Company," in *American Historical Review*, April, 1927.

4. See Grace Lee Nute, "Posts in the Minnesota Fur-trading Area, 1660-1855," in *Minnesota History*, 11:353-85.

NOTES

II

PORTRAIT OF THE VOYAGEUR

1. Sherman Hall's diary in the archives of the American Board of Commissioners for Foreign Missions in Boston, Volume 74, Number 44, entry for September 18, 1832.
2. Thomas L. McKenney, *Sketches of a Tour to the Lakes, of the Character and Customs of the Chippeway Indians and of Incidents Connected with the Treaty of Fond Du Lac*, 417, 418 (Baltimore, 1827).
3. John J. Bigsby, *The Shoe and Canoe or Pictures of Travel in the Canadas*, 1:132, 133 (London, 1850).
4. "Diary of Nicholas Garry," in *Proceedings and Transactions of the Royal Society of Canada*, 113 (Second Series, Volume 6, Section 2, 1900).
5. William H. Keating, *Narrative of an Expedition to the Source of St. Peter's River, Lake Winnepeek, Lake of the Woods, &c. Performed in the Year 1823*, 2:85 (London, 1825).
6. McKenney, *Tour to the Lakes*, 350, 351.
7. *Ibid.*, 199.
8. "Robert Kennicott," in *Transactions of the Chicago Academy of Sciences*, 1869. The references are to page 160 of Volume 1, Part 2.
9. *Ibid.*, 151, 152.
10. McKenney, *Tour to the Lakes*, 228.
11. "Robert Kennicott," 187.
12. *Ibid.*, 192, 194, 195.

III

THE VOYAGEUR'S CANOE

1. Merchants of Montreal to Simcoe, April 23, 1792, in *The Correspondence of Lieut. Governor John Graves Simcoe, with Allied Documents Relating to His Administration of the Government of Upper Canada*, ed. E. A. Cruikshank, 1:135, 136 (Toronto, 1923).
2. For canoes and their equipment consult the following: McKenney, *Tour to the Lakes*, 199, 200; "Robert Kennicott," 146, 148; Daniel W. Harmon, *A Journal of Voyages and Travels in the Interior of North America*, 1, 2 (Toronto, 1911); John McDonell's manuscript diary in the library of McGill University, Montreal, entry for May 25, 1793; and Innis, *Fur Trade in Canada*, 192-265.
3. McKenney, *Tour to the Lakes*, 382, 383.
4. "Robert Kennicott," 147.
5. McKenney, *Tour to the Lakes*, 211.

NOTES

6. From E. Z. Massicotte and C. M. Barbeau, "Chants populaires du Canada," in *Journal of American Folk-Lore*, 32:78, 79 (January-March, 1919). The air accompanies the words.
7. Mrs. William Lewis to James R. Wright, May 29, 1844, in the possession of the Minnesota Historical Society.

IV

VOYAGING

1. See *ante*, p. 6.
2. Wages and equipment varied greatly in different periods and departments. A good summary of the details of engagements, wages, costs of transportation, and equipments may be found in Innis, *Fur Trade in Canada*, 242-245. This author also mentions a sort of insurance that was provided for disabled voyageurs by the deduction of one per cent of the wages of all the *engagés*. See p. 242.
3. Ramsay Crooks to John Jacob Astor, May 3, 1817, in a letterbook of the American Fur Company at Mackinac. Photostatic copies of this volume have been made by the State Historical Society of Wisconsin and the Minnesota Historical Society.
4. The remnant of Peter Pond's diary is reprinted in *Wisconsin Historical Collections*, 18:326 (Madison, 1908).
5. Harmon, *Journal*, 10.
6. The account of this custom is drawn from J. C. Taché, *Forestiers et Voyageurs*, 158-164 (Montreal, 1884). A different version is given *post*, p. 151.
7. Keating, *Narrative of an Expedition to the Source of St. Peter's River*, 2:85, 86.
8. The diary of Sherman Hall describes the forty-five mile portage to Lac du Flambeau from Lake Superior. See entries for September 11 and 18, 1832.
9. Manuscript diary of Boutwell, a copy made by J. Fletcher Williams from the original, in the possession of the Minnesota Historical Society. The entry was for September 18, 1833.
10. Hall's diary, entry for September 18, 1832.
11. Boutwell's diary, entry for September 12, 1833.
12. *The Journal of Duncan M'Gillivray of the North West Company at Fort George on the Saskatchewan, 1794-5, with Introduction, Notes and Appendix* by Arthur S. Morton, entry for August 3, p. 6 (Toronto, 1929).
13. See *post*, pp. 232, 234, 235, 241, 243.
14. Ross Cox, *The Columbia River*, 2:253 (London, 1832).
15. Garry specifies that Indian corn was used. See his diary, p. 122.
16. "Personal Narrative of Capt. Thomas G. Anderson," in *Wisconsin Historical Collections*, 9:140, 141 (Madison, 1882).
17. McKenney, *Tour to the Lakes*, 201.

18. Boutwell's diary, entry for June 12, 1832.
19. *Ibid.*, entry for June 27, 1832.
20. "Robert Kennicott," 154, 161, 162.
21. *Ibid.*, 177.
22. *Journal of the Reverend Peter Jacobs, Indian Wesleyan Missionary,* 72, 73 (New York, 1857).
23. McKenney, *Tour to the Lakes,* 351.
24. Bigsby, *Shoe and Canoe,* 2:92-94.
25. "Diary of Nicholas Garry," 130, 131.
26. Paul Kane, *Wanderings of an Artist among the Indians of North America* in *Master-Works of Canadian Authors,* ed. John W. Garvin, 114 (Toronto, 1925).
27. See a manuscript account of fur-trade methods by an erstwhile voyageur, Paul Beaulieu, in the possession of the Minnesota Historical Society; and Sir John Richardson, *Arctic Searching Expedition: A Journal of a Boat-Voyage Through Rupert's Land and the Arctic Sea in Search of the Discovery Ships Under Command of Sir John Franklin,* 1:92 (London, 1851).
28. "Voyages of Peter Esprit Radisson," ed. Gideon D. Scull, in *Prince Society Publications,* 192 (Boston, 1885).
29. Washington Irving, *Astoria,* 23, 24 (N. Y. and London, 1849).
30. Kane, *Wanderings of an Artist,* 235, 236.
31. *Journal of Duncan M'Gillivray,* 11, 12.
32. Diary of John McDonell, entry for August 11, 1793.
33. "Robert Kennicott," 155, 159; John Franklin, *Narrative of a Journey to the Shores of the Polar Sea, in the Years 1819-20-21-22,* 61 (London, 1824); Kane, *Wanderings of an Artist,* 236.
34. "Robert Kennicott," 155-159.
35. "Diary of Nicholas Garry," 129, 133.
36. *Ibid.*, 98.
37. *Ibid.*, 149.
38. *Ibid.*, 149, 150.
39. *Ibid.*, 150, 151.
40. *Ibid.*, 122; diary of John McDonell, entry for August 5, 1793.
41. Gabriel Franchere's letter to Valée, Boyer and Company, quoted in Otto Fowle, *Sault Ste. Marie and Its Great Waterway,* 387, 388 (New York, 1925).
42. Bigsby, *Shoe and Canoe,* 1:141, 143, 147, 151, 154.

V

FORT LIFE

1. See *post,* p. 189.
2. The diary is anonymous, but references in contemporary lists of traders seem to indicate that Thomas Connor was in charge of the Snake River post to which allusion is made. It is in the possession of the Canadian Archives, Ottawa.
3. Connor's diary, entry for October 10, 1804.

NOTES

4. The diary of Archibald Norman McLeod, 1800-1801, is preserved in the library of McGill University. The entries to which reference is made are for March 3 and 4, 1801.
5. Connor's diary, entries for February 18 and 20, March 1 and 3, 1805.
6. Harmon, *Journal*, 60, 77; McLeod's diary, entry for December 7, 1800.
7. Harmon, *Journal*, 86.
8. Grace Lee Nute, "A Description of Northern Minnesota by a Fur-Trader in 1807," in *Minnesota History Bulletin*, 5: 36, 38, and notes 20 and 26; Joseph N. Provencher, "Notice sur la Rivière Rouge," in *Les cloches de Saint-Boniface*, 26: 90.
9. Issue of February 9, 1860.
10. Harmon, *Journal*, 94.
11. *Ibid.*, 73.
12. "Robert Kennicott," 195.
13. Franklin, *Journey to the Shores of the Polar Sea*, 1: 84.
14. Robert Michael Ballantyne, *Hudson's Bay: Or Every-Day Life in the Wilds of North America*, 167 (London, 1859).
15. "Mr. James McKenzie: Extracts from His Journal, 1799-1800," in L. R. Masson, *Les bourgeois de la compagnie de nord-ouest*, 2: 377, 378 (Quebec, 1890).
16. McLeod's diary, entry for November 30, 1800.
17. Harmon, *Journal*, 23, 57, 58.
18. "Diary of Nicholas Garry," 92, 93.
19. Kane, *Wanderings of an Artist*, 260, 261.
20. Ross Cox, *The Columbia River*, 2: 294.
21. Various manuscripts or copies of documents in the possession of the Minnesota Historical Society, such as Boutwell's diary, the reports of missionaries of the American Board of Commissioners for Foreign Missions, and notes on F. A. Larocque's diary, give information on the careers of these men. See also Harmon, *Journal*, 126, 130.
22. The diaries of McLeod, Harmon, and McDonell have already been cited. François Victoire Malhiot's "Journal du Fort Kamanaitiquoya à la Rivière Montréal" is published in Masson, *Les bourgeois*, 1: 228-263, and is especially valuable for preserving the everyday language of the voyageurs.
23. Connor's diary, entry of April 25, 1805.
24. "Diary of Nicholas Garry," 135, 136.
25. Kane, *Wanderings of an Artist*, 260.
26. David Thompson's *Narrative*, in *Publications of the Champlain Society*, XII, 216.
27. An anonymous diary, perhaps written by Hugh Faries, in the possession of the Canadian Archives.
28. Egerton R. Young, *The Apostle of the North, Rev. James Evans*, 166 (New York, 1899).
29. "Robert Kennicott," 188.

NOTES

30. Frederick Ayer to students at Oberlin College, February 24, 1843, in the *Oberlin Evangelist*, May 10, 1843.
31. Kane, *Wanderings of an Artist*, 108, 109.
32. Harmon, *Journal*, 61.

VI

VOYAGEUR SONGS

1. "Robert Kennicott," 193. The words and music of practically all the songs given in this chapter can be found in Ernest Gagnon's work cited below.
2. James Lanman, "The American Fur Trade," in *Hunt's Merchants' Magazine*, 3: 189 (September, 1840).
3. Ernest Gagnon, *Chansons populaires du Canada*, 178, 179 (Quebec, 1894).
4. Lanman's version may be found in "The American Fur Trade," 189.

> *Tous les printemps,*
> *Tant de nouvelle,*
> *Tous les amants*
> *Changent de maîtresses;*
> *Le bon vin m'endort,*
> *L'amour me réveille.*
>
> *Tous les amants*
> *Changent de maîtresses.*
> *Qu'ils changent qui voudront,*
> *Pour moi je garde la mienne;*
> *Le bon vin m'endort,*
> *L'amour me réveille.*

5. Bela Hubbard, *Memorials of a Half-Century*, 153 (New York, 1887).
6. Hubbard's version makes the girl resist as she remembers another jealous lover.

> *La jeune Sophie*
> *Chantait l'autre jour,*
> *Son echo lui repete,*
> *Que non pas d'amour*
> *N'est pas de bon jour.*
>
> *Je suis jeune et belle,*
> *Je vieux mé engagé*
> *Un amant fidele,*
> *Je suis jeune, etc.*

Mais ce vous etre belle,
Ce n'est pas de jour;
Ce n'est que vos yeaux
Qui bris à la chandelle.
Mais ce vous, etc.

Unisons ensemble,—
Son cour et le mein,—
Pourquoi tant le defendre,
Puis qu'il s'amaient bien?
Unisons, etc.

Point temps de badinage,
Envers mon amant,
Car il est jaloux:
Tout lui port embrage.
Point temps, etc.

7. Bigsby, *Shoe and Canoe*, 2:81.
8. Gagnon, *Chansons populaires*, 82-86.
9. McKenney, *Tour to the Lakes*, 210.
10. Ballantyne, *Hudson's Bay*, 222.
11. Gagnon, *Chansons populaires*, 87-89.
12. "Diary of Nicholas Garry," 159, 160. The following is Garry's version:

Cueillons la, la belle Rose
Cueillons la, la belle Rose
Cueillons la, car il est tard, la belle Rose
Cueillons la, car il est tard.
  La belle Rose du Rosier blanc.
Cueillons la feuille et par feuille
Cueillons la feuille et par feuille
Mise dans mon tableau [sic] blanc
  La belle Rose du Rosier blanc.
Je l'ai portée chez mon Père
Je l'ai portée chez mon Père
Entre Paris et Rouen
Entre Paris et Rouen
  La belle Rose du Rosier blanc.

Dans mon Chemin je récontrai [sic]
Dans mon Chemin je récontrai
Un Rossignol chantant la belle Rose
Un Rossignol chantant la belle Rose
  La belle Rose du Rosier blanc.
Qui m'a dit dans son Langage
Qui m'a dit dans son Langage

Mariez-toi—car il est temps, la belle Rose
Mariez-toi—car il est temps, la belle Rose
La belle Rose du Rosier blanc.

Eh! Comment me marierai je
Eh! Comment me marierai je?
Mon Père n'est pas content
Mon Père n'est pas content
Ni mon Père, ni ma Mère
Ni mon Père, ni ma Mère
Ni aucune de mes Parents
Ni aucune de mes Parents
Je m'en irai au Service
Je m'en irai au Service;
En Service pour un An
Et la belle Rose du Rosier blanc
En Service pour un An
Et la belle Rose du Rosier blanc.

Combien gagnez vous, la belle
Combien gagnez vous, la belle
Combien gagnez vous par An
Combien gagnez vous par An
Je ne gagne que cinq cent Livres
Je ne gagne que cinq cent Livres
Cinq cents Livres en Argent blanc
Cinq cents Livres en Argent blanc
La belle Rose du Rosier blanc.

13. Garry's version, given below, may be found in "Diary of Nicholas Garry," 160-161.

Quand j'étais chez mon Père,
Petite Janeton,
Il m'envoyait à la fontaine
Pour pêcher du poisson.
La Violette Dandon, oh! la Violette dondé.

Il m'envoyait à la fontaine
Pour pêcher du poisson.
La fontaine est profonde
Je suis coulée au fond.
La Violette, etc.

Il m'envoyait à la fontaine
Pour pêcher du poisson.
Par-ici ils passèrent trois
Trois Cavaliers barons.
La Violette, etc.

NOTES

Par-ici ils passèrent trois
Trois Cavaliers barons.
"Que donneriez vous, ma belle,
Qui vous tireront du fond?"
La Violette, etc.

"Que donneriez vous, ma belle,
Qui vous tireront du fond?"
"Tirez, tirez," dit elle;
"Après ça, nous verrons."
La Violette, etc.

"Tirez, tirez," dit elle;
"Après ça, nous verrons."
Quand la belle fût tirée
Elle va à sa Maison.
La Violette, etc.

Quand la belle fût tirée
Elle va à sa Maison.
S'asseyant sur un fenêtre
Elle composait un Chanson.
La Violette, etc.

S'asseyant sur un fenêtre
Elle composait un Chanson.
"Ce n'est pas ce, ma belle,
Ce que nous demandons."
La Violette, etc.

"Ce n'est pas ce, ma belle,
Ce que nous demandons.
Votre petit Cœur en gage
Sçavoir si nous l'aurons."
La Violette Dandon, oh! la Violette dondé.

14. Marius Barbeau and Edward Sapir, *Folk Songs of French Canada*, 83, 84 (New Haven, 1925).
15. "Diary of Nicholas Garry," 194; Gagnon, *Chansons populaires*, 12-15.
16. Gagnon, *Chansons populaires*, 189, 190.
17. Mrs. Jameson, *Sketches in Canada, and Rambles Among the Red Men*, 299 (London, 1852).
18. Gagnon, *Chansons populaires*, 129, 130.
19. Mrs. Jameson, *Sketches in Canada*, 299.
20. F. A. H. La Rue, "Les chansons populaires et historiques du Canada," in *Le foyer canadien*, 1: 360; Gagnon, *Chansons populaires*, 8, 9.
21. Gagnon, *Chansons populaires*, 68; La Rue, "Les chansons populaires," 365.

NOTES

22. La Rue, "Les chansons populaires," 365.
23. *Ibid.*, 365, 366.
24. *Ibid.*, 367. It is only fair to remark that the word *voyageur* here probably was used in the sense of traveler, though doubtless the canoemen believed it had reference to themselves. The French of the Barbeau and Sapir version of this song is as follows:

> *Quand le soldat arrive en ville* (bis)
> *Bien mal chaussé, bien mal vêtu:*
> *"Pauvre soldat, d'où reviens-tu?"*

> *S'en fut loger dans une auberge:*
> *"Hôtesse, avez-vous du vin blanc?"*
> *—"Voyageur, a'-vous de l'argent?"*

> *—"Pour de l'argent, je n'en ai guère;*
> *J'engagerai mon vieux chapeau,*
> *Ma ceinture, aussi mon manteau."*

> *Quand le voyageur fut à table,*
> *Il se mit à boire, à chanter;*
> *L'hôtess' ne fit plus que pleurer.*

> *"Oh! qu'avez-vous, petite hôtesse?*
> *Regrettez-vous votre vin blanc*
> *Qu'un voyageur boit sans argent?"*

> *—"N'est pas mon vin que je regrette;*
> *C'est la chanson que vous chantez:*
> *Mon défunt mari la savait.*

> *"J'ai un mari dans les voyages;*
> *Voilà sept ans qu'il est parti,*
> *Je crois bien que vous êtes lui."*

> *—"Ah! taisez-vous, méchante femme.*
> *Je vous ai laissé deux enfants,*
> *En voilà quatre ici présents!"*

> *—"J'ai tant reçu de fausses lettres,*
> *Que vous étiez mort, enterré.*
> *Et moi, je me suis marié'."*

> *—"Dedans Paris, il y-a grand guerre,*
> *Grand guerre rempli' de tourments.*
> *Adieu, ma femme et mes enfants!"*

25. La Rue, "Les chansons populaires," 371, 372; Gagnon, *Chansons populaires*, 200-208. La Rue's version is as follows:

Petits oiseaux, dedans vos charmants nids,
Vous qui chantez pendant que je gémis,
Si j'avais des ailes comme vous,
Je vivrais content avant qu'il fut jour.

Rossignolet, va dire à ma maitresse,
Que de mon cœur engagé je la laisse,
Que de mon cœur engagé, je la laisse;
Que désormais elle ne pense plus à moi.

Par un beau jour m'en allant à la chasse,
Pensant toujours à mes chers camarades,
Je me suis dit, hélas! sont'ils noyés,
Ou les Iroquois les ont-ils tués.

Un autre jour, revenant de la chasse,
J'ai aperçu une petite boucane;
Je me suis dit: ah! Grand Dieu! qu'est-ce que ceci,
Les Iroquois ont-ils pris mon logis?

Tout aussitôt je fus en embuscade,
Pour reconnaître ces visages;
Je crus connaître trois visages français,
Qui me causa une très-grande joie.

Un loup hurlant tout près de ma cabane:
Il me disait: je sens ton corps qui est malade;
Je lui ai dit: retire-toi d'ici,
Car sur ma foi, je percerai ton habit.

Va-t-en là-haut, là-bas sur ces montagnes,
Tu trouveras des tripes, aussi des os,
Tu trouveras des tripes, aussi des os;
Mange ton saoul, et laisse-moi en repos.

Tous ces corbeaux qui vont à l'aventure,
Toujours cherchant une herbe de nature,
Je leur ai dit: mangeurs de chair humaine,
Allez ailleurs chercher un autre corps que le mien.

C'est aujourd'hui que le monde j'abandonne,
Je n'ai recours qu'à vous, Sauveur des hommes;
Ah! Sainte-Vierge, ne m'abandonnez pas,
Permettez-moi que je me rende entre vos bras.

NOTES

26. La Rue, "Les chansons populaires," 372, 373.
27. Keating, *Narrative of an Expedition to the Source of St. Peter's River*, 2:92.
28. Bigsby, *Shoe and Canoe*, 1:119.
29. *Ibid.*, 1:134.
30. "Mr. W. F. Wentzel, Letters to the Hon. Roderic McKenzie, 1807-1824," in Masson, *Les bourgeois*, 1:71.

VII

THE VOYAGEUR AS SOLDIER

1. Louise P. Kellogg, *Frontier Advance on the Upper Ohio, 1778-1779*, 14, in *Wisconsin Historical Collections*, 23 (Madison, 1916).
2. *Ibid.*, 83, 92, 114, 115, 119.
3. *Wisconsin Historical Collections*, 18:161.
4. *Ibid.*, 18:375.
5. A. P. Nasatir, "The Anglo-Spanish Frontier in the Illinois Country during the American Revolution, 1779-1783," in the Illinois Historical Society *Journal*, 21:353 (October, 1928).
6. *Wisconsin Historical Collections*, 18:396, 397.
7. Lord Selkirk, the sworn enemy of the Northwest Company, tarnished the glory of their act by declaring that they had an eye to business in securing voyageurs, who would thus be ready for signing trade engagements in the spring without the usual difficulties incident to rounding up crews. See Thomas, Earl of Selkirk, *A Sketch of the British Fur Trade in North America*, 30-36 (London, 1816); and [John Halkett] *Statement Respecting the Earl of Selkirk's Settlement upon the Red River in North America*, 13-15, vi (London, 1817). In this work, the date of the discharge of the corps is given as March 12, 1813.
8. Selkirk, *Sketch of the British Fur Trade in North America*, 33, 34.
9. Halkett, *Statement Respecting the Earl of Selkirk's Settlement*, 13; L. Homfray Irving, *Officers of the British Forces in Canada during the War of 1812-15*, 103, 114 (Welland, 1908).
10. Ross Cox, *The Columbia River*, 2:294-297.
11. William Wood, *Select British Documents of the Canadian War of 1812*, in *Publications of the Champlain Society*, No. XIII, 1:669, 676 (Toronto, 1920).
12. A. G. Morice, *Histoire de l'église catholique dans l'ouest canadien du Lac Supérieur au Pacifique (1659-1915)*, 1:390 (Winnipeg, 1928).
13. Bigsby, *Shoe and Canoe*, 1:124.
14. Wood, *Select British Documents*, 1:24.
15. *Ibid.*, 1:432.
16. *Ibid.*, 1:438.

NOTES

17. Wood, *Select British Documents*, 1:448-452.
18. *Ibid.*, 1:437.
19. Irving, *Officers of the British Forces in Canada*, 96-99.
20. James H. Lockwood, "Early Times and Events in Wisconsin," in *Wisconsin Historical Collections*, 2:124.
21. "John McDonald of Garth Autobiographical Notes," in Masson, *Les bourgeois*, 2:44, 45.
22. Irving, *Astoria*, 49, 50.

VIII

THE VOYAGUER AS SETTLER

1. See D. L. Crossman, "How the Last French Claim to a Michigan Farm was Extinguished," in *Michigan Pioneer and Historical Collections*, 14:644 (Lansing, ——) quoting a report of La Jonquière and Bigot, governor and intendant of New France, respectively, in a document dated October 18, 1750. The translator has used "travelers" for the French word *voyageurs*, without a doubt the word used in the original.
2. See La Jonquière to the Minister of Colonies, October 5, 1751, quoted in William W. Warren, *History of the Ojibway Nation*, 433-436 (*Minnesota Historical Collections*, Volume 5, St. Paul, 1885).
3. Henry, *Travels*, 60.
4. John Long, *Voyages and Travels of an Indian Interpreter and Trader*, ed. Reuben Gold Thwaites, 2:79 (Cleveland, 1904).
5. Alexander Mackenzie, *Voyages from Montreal through the Continent of North America to the Frozen and Pacific Oceans in 1789 and 1793*, ed. W. L. Grant, 47 (Toronto, 1911).
6. Harmon, *Journal*, entry for May 30, 1800.
7. See a brief biographical account of Johnston in Masson, *Les bourgeois*, 2:137-142, as an introduction to Johnston's "An Account of Lake Superior, 1792-1807."
8. "Memoir of John Johnston," in *Michigan Pioneer and Historical Collections*, 25:663 (Lansing, 1894).
9. "The Fur-Trade in Wisconsin, 1812-15," in *Wisconsin Historical Collections*, 20:155, note 18 (Madison, 1911).
10. Gabriel Franchere, *Narrative of a Voyage to the Northwest Coast of America*, 354 (New York, 1854).
11. *Ibid.*, 352.
12. George Johnstone's "Reminiscences of Sault Ste. Marie, 1815," in *Michigan Pioneer and Historical Collections*, 12:607, 608 (Lansing, 1888).
13. Henry R. Schoolcraft, *Summary Narrative of an Exploring Expedition to the Sources of the Mississippi River in 1820*, 48 (Philadelphia, 1855).

277

14. Reports of these priests may be found among the archiepiscopal archives of Quebec.
15. Franz Pierz, *Die Indianer in Nord-Amerika*, 68-70 (St. Louis, 1855); *Annales de la propagation de la foi*, 3:326-328; Antoine Ivan Rezek, *History of the Diocese of Sault Ste. Marie*, 2:44-48 (Houghton, Michigan, 1907).
16. Grace Lee Nute, "The American Fur Company's Fishing Enterprises on Lake Superior," in the *Mississippi Valley Historical Review*, 12:483-503 (March, 1926).
17. A quotation from C. D. O'Brien in P. Chrysostomus Verwyst, *Life and Labors of Rt. Rev. Frederic Baraga*, 291-293 (Milwaukee, 1900).
18. A master's thesis by Rollo Keithahn entitled "The American Fur Company in the Upper Mississippi Valley," University of Minnesota, p. 57.
19. "The Unfinished Autobiography of Henry Hastings Sibley," in *Minnesota History*, 8:353, 354.
20. This letter is addressed to Aaron Hall, Jr.; a copy is in the possession of the Minnesota Historical Society.
21. The pencil sketch is to be found among the Frank B. Mayer papers in the possession of the Edward E. Ayer collection of the Newberry Library, Chicago, Volume 42, 64-65. Faintly discernible above the mantel is the word "mud," indicating the main substance of which the chimney was made.
22. E. K. Smith to Major J. Plympton, October 19, 1837, in *Sale of Fort Snelling Reservation*, 16 (40th Congress, 3rd session, *House Executive Documents*, No. 9—Serial 1372); M. M. Hoffmann, "New Light on Old St. Peter's and Early St. Paul," in *Minnesota History*, 8:38.
23. Volume 2, p. 98 (London, 1839).
24. *Annals of the Propagation of the Faith* (Dublin), 3:339 (September, 1840).
25. Information on the ensuing individuals may be found in Hoffmann, "New Light"; and in J. Fletcher Williams, *A History of the City of Saint Paul, and of the County of Ramsey* (*Minnesota Historical Collections*, Volume 4). For the "atmosphere" of life at the Entry about 1840, read Maud Hart Lovelace, *Early Candlelight, A Novel* (New York, 1929), in which many voyageurs appear under their own names.
26. Williams, *Saint Paul*, 75.
27. *Ibid.*, 111, 112.
28. *Ibid.*, 184, 185.
29. Henry H. Sibley, "Reminiscences of the Early Days of Minnesota," in *Minnesota Historical Collections*, 3:248, 249.
30. A. S. Morton, "The Place of the Red River Settlement in the Plans of the Hudson's Bay Co., 1812-1825," in the Canadian Historical Association, *Report of the Annual Meeting held at Ottawa . . . 1929*, 106.

NOTES

31. Ramsay Crooks to John Jacob Astor, about April, 1817 [the first portion of the letter is missing], in a letterbook of the American Fur Company preserved at Mackinac, p. 12. Crooks knew the voyageur thoroughly and comprehended his needs and modest requirements with a genuine concern for his wellbeing that is a credit to one of the busiest and acutest business men of his age. Thus in this same letter he writes: "The necessity of an Agent at this place [*Montreal*] is obvious . . . [a portion is missing relating to the payment of voyageurs at Montreal on their return from the interior] to pay punctually for duties faithfully performed is one of the strongest pillars of commerce, and in this trade perhaps of more moment than in any other, for the family of the *Voyageur* in his absence not unfrequently subsists in part on the credit of the voyage he is then performing. Independent of every other consideration it is only necessary to recollect that [a] servant once disappointed in his just expectations will not be very likely to put himself again into the power of his deceiver. I would therefore recommend that a person be appointed Agent here for the above purposes. And that funds be always placed in time at his disposal, to meet every engagement on the day appointed."

32. E. H. Oliver, *The Canadian Northwest*, 632, "Introductory Remarks upon the Minutes of the Council of the Northern Department of Rupert's Land, 1830 to 1843, supplementary to those of Professor Oliver, by Isaac Cowie, formerly a Commissioned Official of the Hudson's Bay Company." In this paragraph Cowie refers to "the old plan of the North Westers to form a settlement on the Rainy River for their retired servants." He suggests that this may have given the Earl his idea of such a colony.

33. J. N. Provencher to Bishop Plessis, July 19, 1824, in Quebec archiepiscopal archives; printed in "Lettres de Monse..gneur Joseph-Norrert Provencher, premier evêque de Saint-Boniface," in *Bulletin de la société historique de Saint-Boniface,* Volume 3, p. 100 (St. Boniface, 1913).

34. The ensuing quotations are from Alexander Ross, *The Fur Hunters of the Far West,* 2:234-247 *passim* (London, 1855).

35. *Report of Major Wood, relative to his expedition to Pembina Settlement, and the condition of affairs on the North-Western frontier of the Territory of Minnesota,* in 31st Congress, 1st session, *House Executive Documents,* No. 51—Serial 577.

36. Lord Selkirk to Bishop Plessis, Quebec archiepiscopal archives.

37. Morice, *Histoire de l'église catholique,* 1:137, note 13. See also the testimony of William M'Gillivray in A. Amos, *Report of Trials in the Courts of Canada Relating to the Destruction of the Earl of Selkirk's Settlement,* 275, 303 (London, 1820). On the return trip Lagimonière was captured, beat "in a shocking manner, and plundered . . . of his dispatches, his canoe, and everything it contained." See Halkett, *Statement Respecting the Earl of Selkirk's Settlement,* 41, 42, note.

NOTES

38. A manuscript history of the Northwest Company by Roderic Mackenzie in Canadian Archives, p. 165.
39. Morice, *Histoire de l'église catholique*, 1:137.
40. Bishop Plessis to Tabeau, March 8, 1818.
41. The details of Charbonneau's life are based on G. Dugas, *Un voyageur des pays d'en haut* (Montreal, 1912).
42. Bigsby, *Shoe and Canoe*, 1:130, 134, 148.
43. James H. Lockwood, "Early Times and Events in Wisconsin," in *Wisconsin Historical Collections*, 2:105, 107, 121, 122.

IX

THE VOYAGEUR AS EXPLORER

1. *Alexander Henry's Travels and Adventures in the Years 1760-1776*, 306 (Chicago, 1921).
2. Mackenzie, *Voyages*, 2:73, 74.
3. *Ibid.*, 2:29.
4. *Ibid.*, 2:251.
5. *Ibid.*, 2:112-115.
6. *Ibid.*, 2:116.
7. *Ibid.*, 2:123.
8. *Ibid.*, 2:94, 95.
9. *Ibid.*, 2:133, 134.
10. *Ibid.*, 2:142.
11. *Ibid.*, 2:167, 168.
12. *Ibid.*, 2:173.
13. *Ibid.*, 2:184, 185.
14. *Ibid.*, 2:192.
15. *Ibid.*, 2:194, 195.
16. *Ibid.*, 2:240.
17. *Ibid.*, 2:319, 320.
18. *Ibid.*, 2:340.
19. The ensuing quotations are taken from "Mr. Simon Fraser, Journal of a Voyage from the Rocky Mountains to the Pacific Coast 1808," in Masson, *Les bourgeois*, 1:157-221. Page numbers are not given if the date is indicated.
20. *Ibid.*, 170, 171.
21. *Ibid.*, 207, 208.
22. John Franklin, *Narrative of a Journey to the Shores of the Polar Sea, in the Years 1819-20-21-22*, 1:301, 302 (London, 1824).
23. *Ibid.*, 1:339, 340.
24. *Ibid.*, 2:3, 4.
25. *Ibid.*, 2:36.
26. *Ibid.*, 2:37.
27. *Ibid.*, 2:69.
28. *Ibid.*, 2:75.

NOTES

29. Wentzel insinuates very broadly that some of the voyageurs were eaten by the officers. He also takes occasion to score the printed accounts for injustice to the voyageurs. See his letters to [Roderic] Mackenzie, especially that of March 1, 1824, in Masson, *Les bourgeois,* 1: 149.

30. George Bryce, *The Remarkable History of the Hudson's Bay Company,* 272, 273 (New York, 1910).

31. Archibald McDonald, *Journal of Canoe Voyage from Hudson's Bay to the Pacific. By the Late Sir George Simpson, Governor of the Honorable Hudson's Bay Company,* 2 (Ottawa, 1872).

32. *Ibid.,* 3.

33. *Ibid.,* 4.

34. *Ibid.,* 52.

35. *Ibid.,* 6.

36. Thomas Simpson, *Narrative of the Discoveries on the North Coast of America,* 342 (London, 1843).

37. *Ibid.,* 112.

38. *Ibid.,* 218, 219.

39. *Ibid.,* 370.

40. Sir John Richardson, *Arctic Searching Expedition: A Journal of a Boat-Voyage Through Rupert's Land and the Arctic Sea* (London, 1851).

41. William Henry Drummond, M.D., *The Voyageur and Other Poems* (New York, 1905).

INDEX

283

INDEX

INDEX

286

INDEX

INDEX

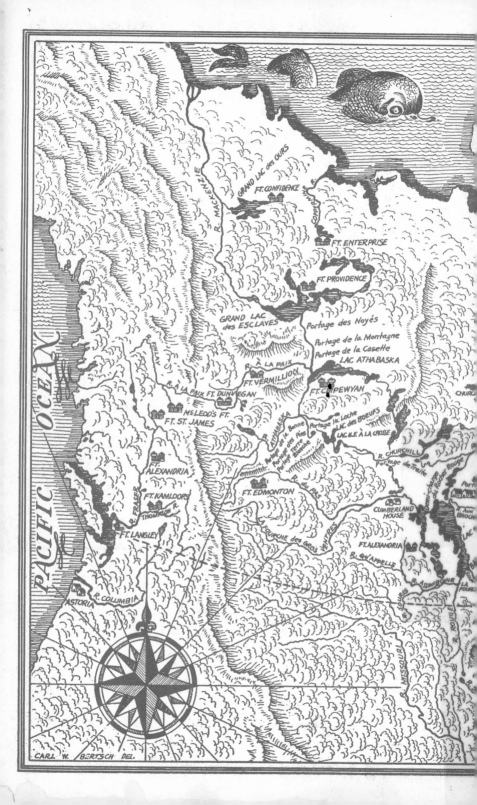